BATMAN
DEATH MASK

YOSHINORI NATSUME

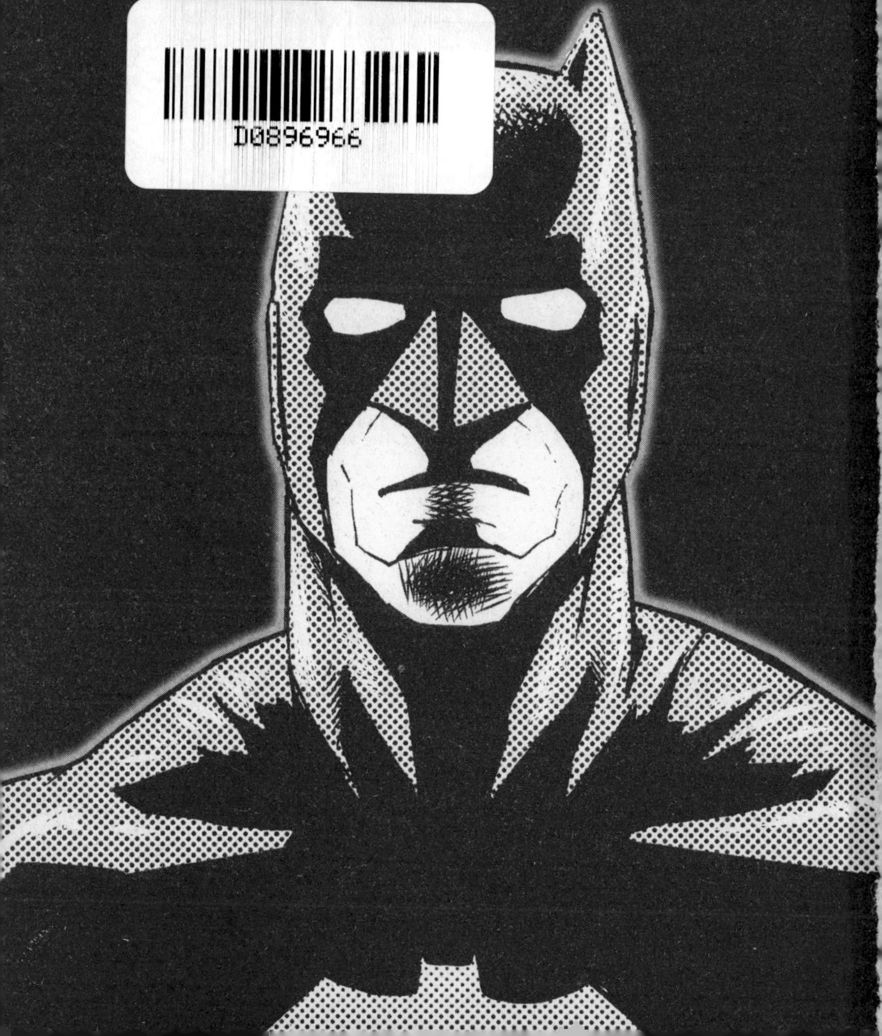

Story and art by **Yoshinori Natsume**

Cover color by **Jonny Rench**   Letters by **Rob Leigh**

Translation: **Sheldon Drzka**   BATMAN created by Bob Kane

BATMAN: DEATH MASK published by DC Comics, 1700 Broadway, New York, NY 10019. Cover, illustration, interview and compilation Copyright © 2008 DC Comics. All Rights Reserved. BATMAN, all characters, the distinctive likenesses thereof and all related elements are trademarks of DC Comics. CMX is a trademark of DC Comics. Originally published in magazine form as BATMAN: DEATH MASK #1-4 © 2008. The stories, characters, and incidents mentioned in this magazine are entirely fictional. DC Comics does not read or accept unsolicited submissions of ideas, stories or artwork. Printed in Canada.

DC Comics, a Warner Bros. Entertainment Company.

ISBN: 978-1-4012-1924-6

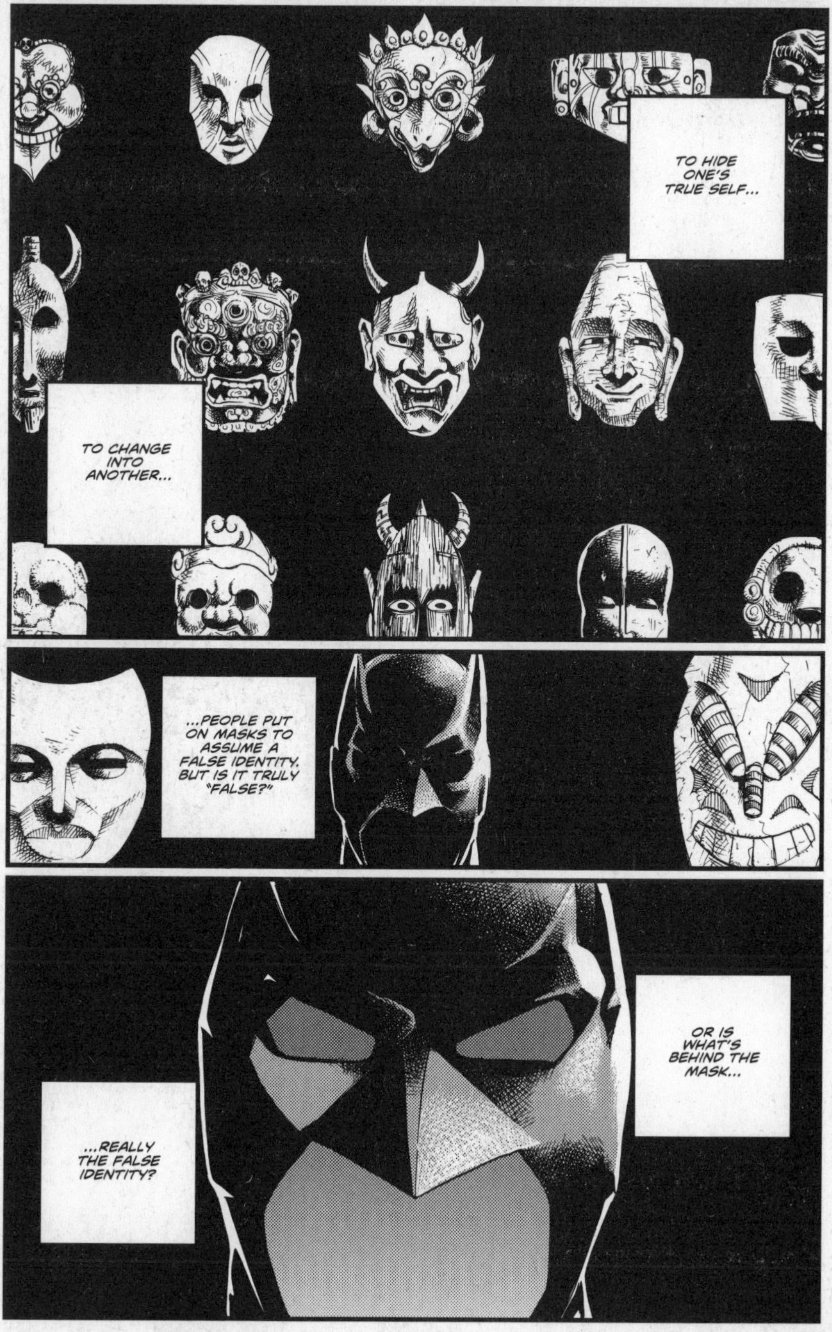
TO HIDE ONE'S TRUE SELF...
TO CHANGE INTO ANOTHER...
...PEOPLE PUT ON MASKS TO ASSUME A FALSE IDENTITY. BUT IS IT TRULY "FALSE?"
OR IS WHAT'S BEHIND THE MASK...
...REALLY THE FALSE IDENTITY?

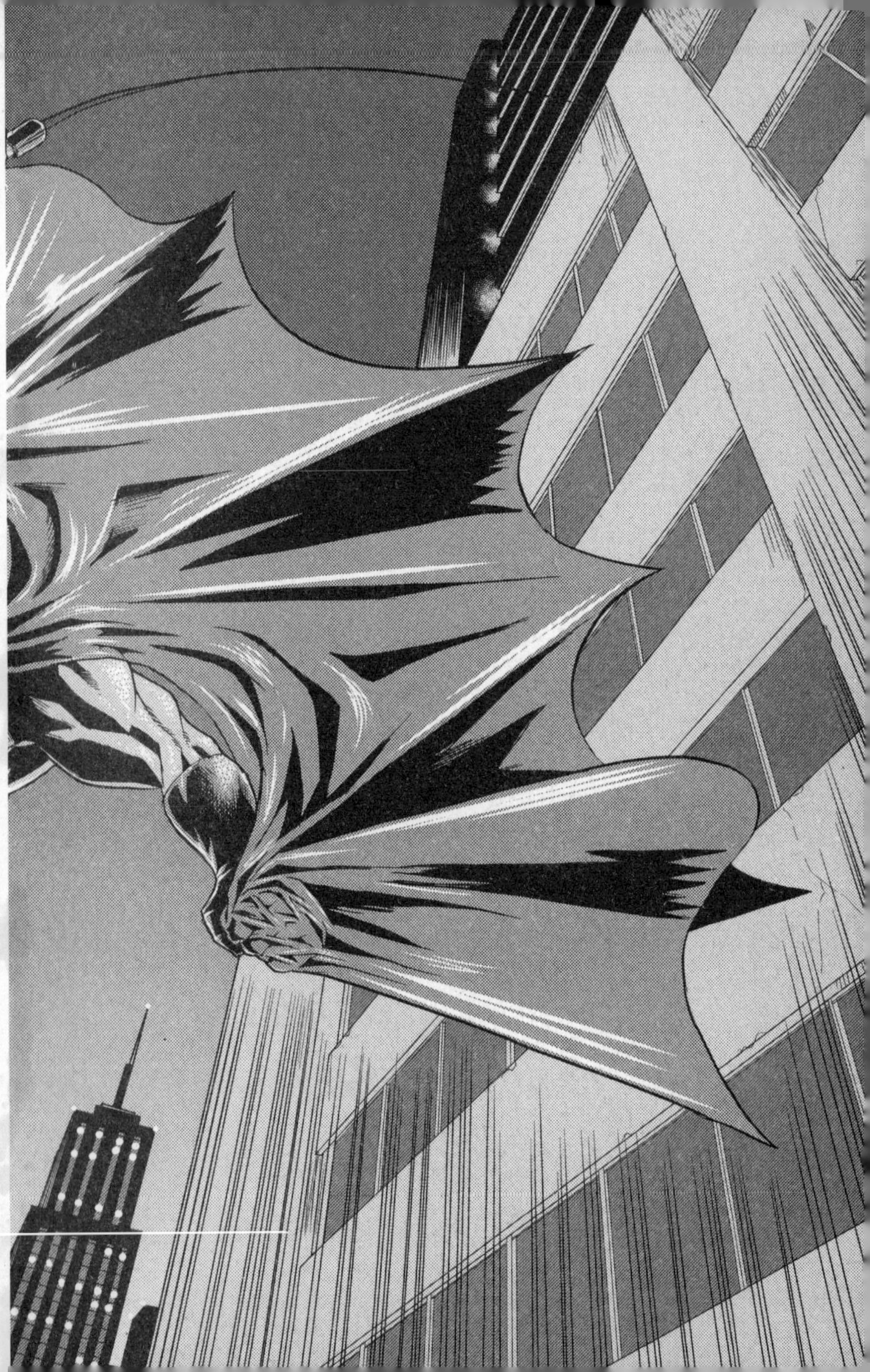

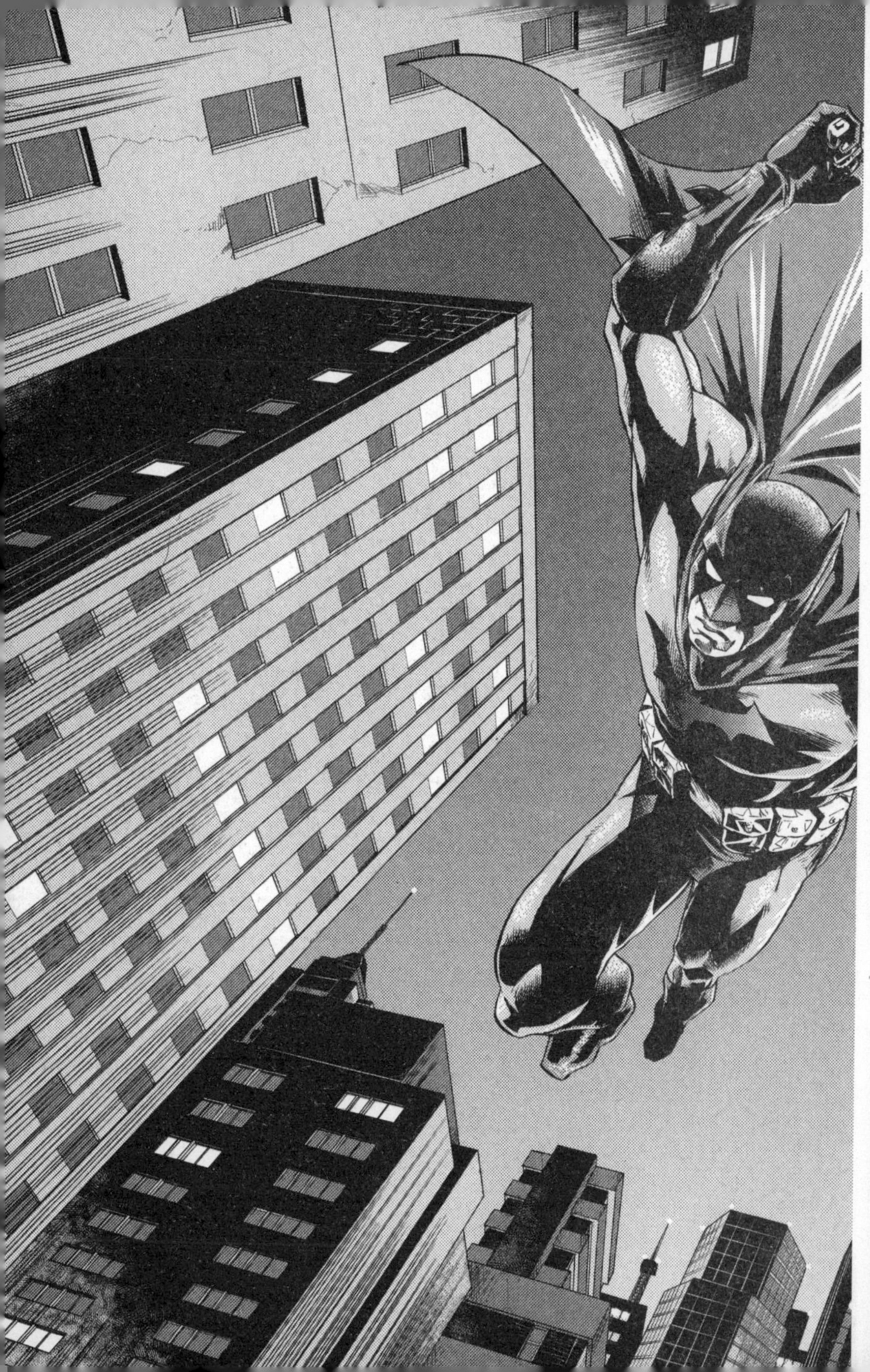

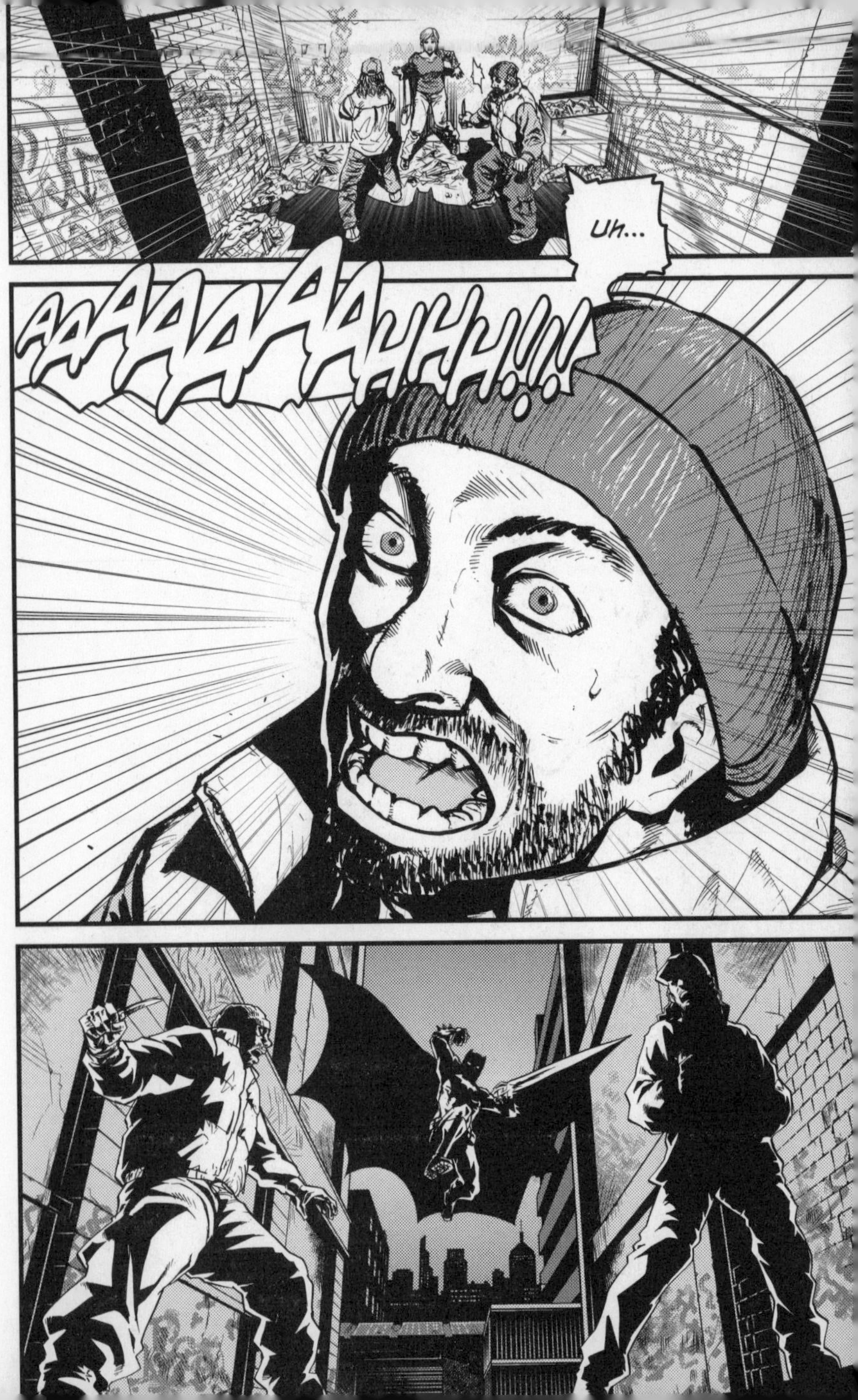
Uh...
AAAAAAAAHHH!!!!

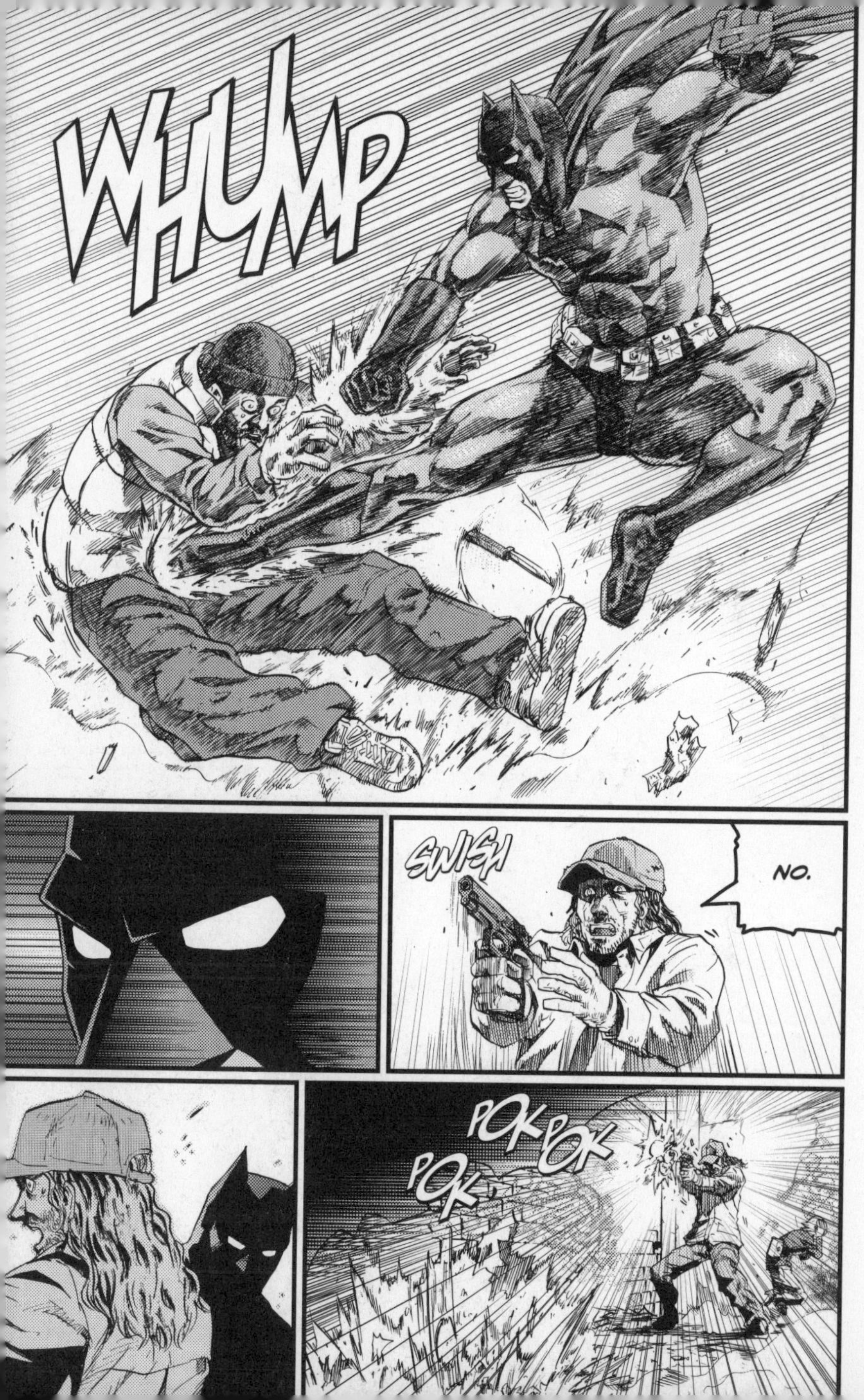
WHUMP
SWISH
NO.
POK POK
POK

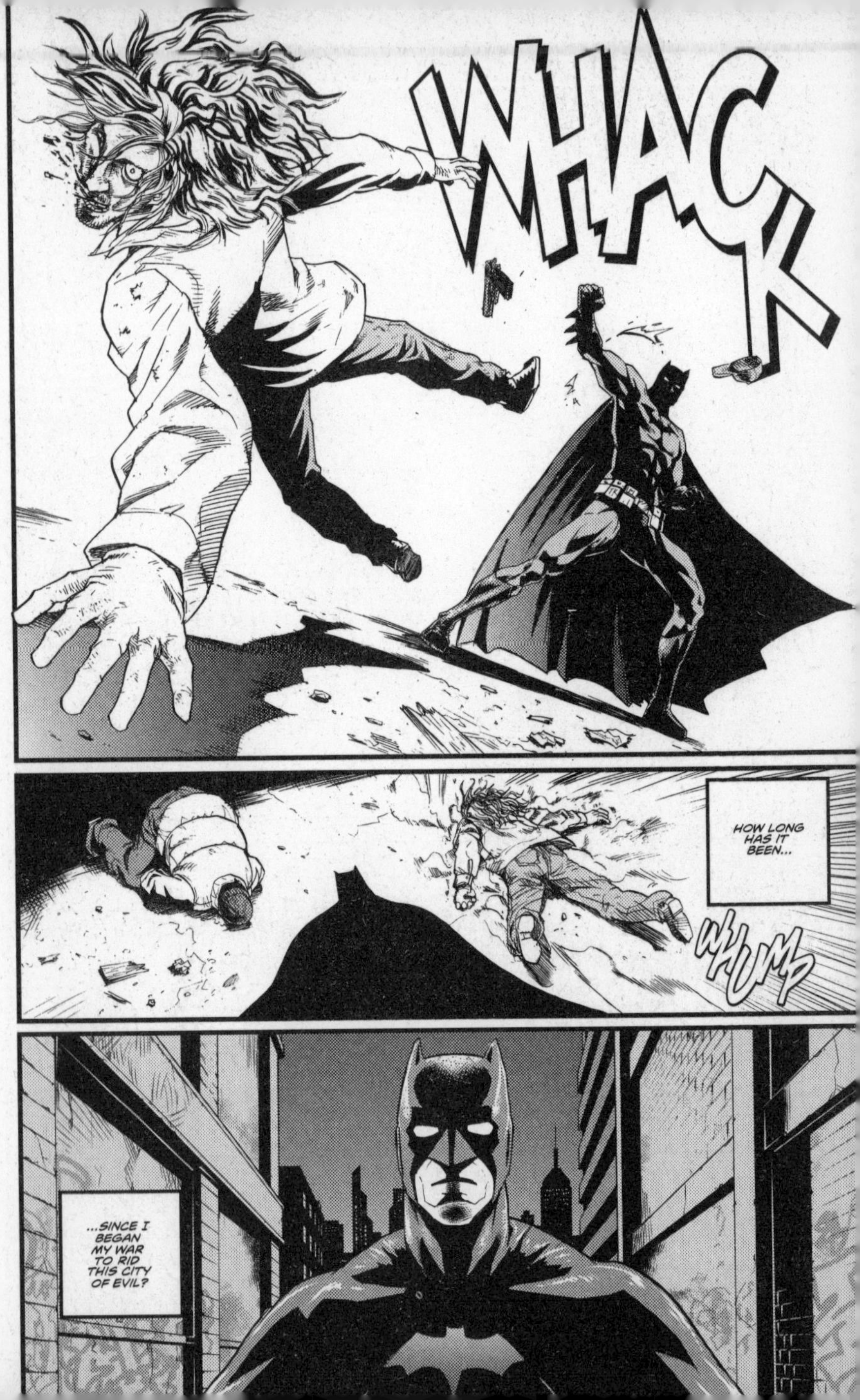
WHACK
HOW LONG HAS IT BEEN...
WHUMP
...SINCE I BEGAN MY WAR TO RID THIS CITY OF EVIL?

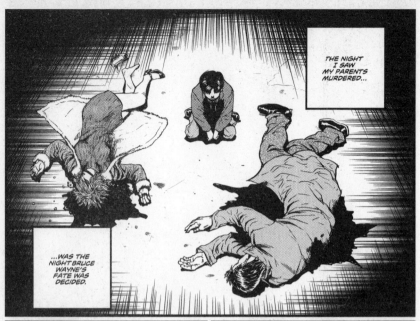

THE NIGHT I SAW MY PARENTS MURDERED...

...WAS THE NIGHT BRUCE WAYNE'S FATE WAS DECIDED.

I'VE TRAVELED ALL OVER THE WORLD TO MASTER EVERY POSSIBLE FORM OF MARTIAL ARTS.

SINCE THEN, I'VE DEVOTED MY LIFE TO THE SCIENCE OF CRIMINAL INVESTIGATION.

AND I BECAME THE PROTECTOR OF GOTHAM, A KNIGHT IN THE DARKNESS...

I BECAME THE BATMAN.

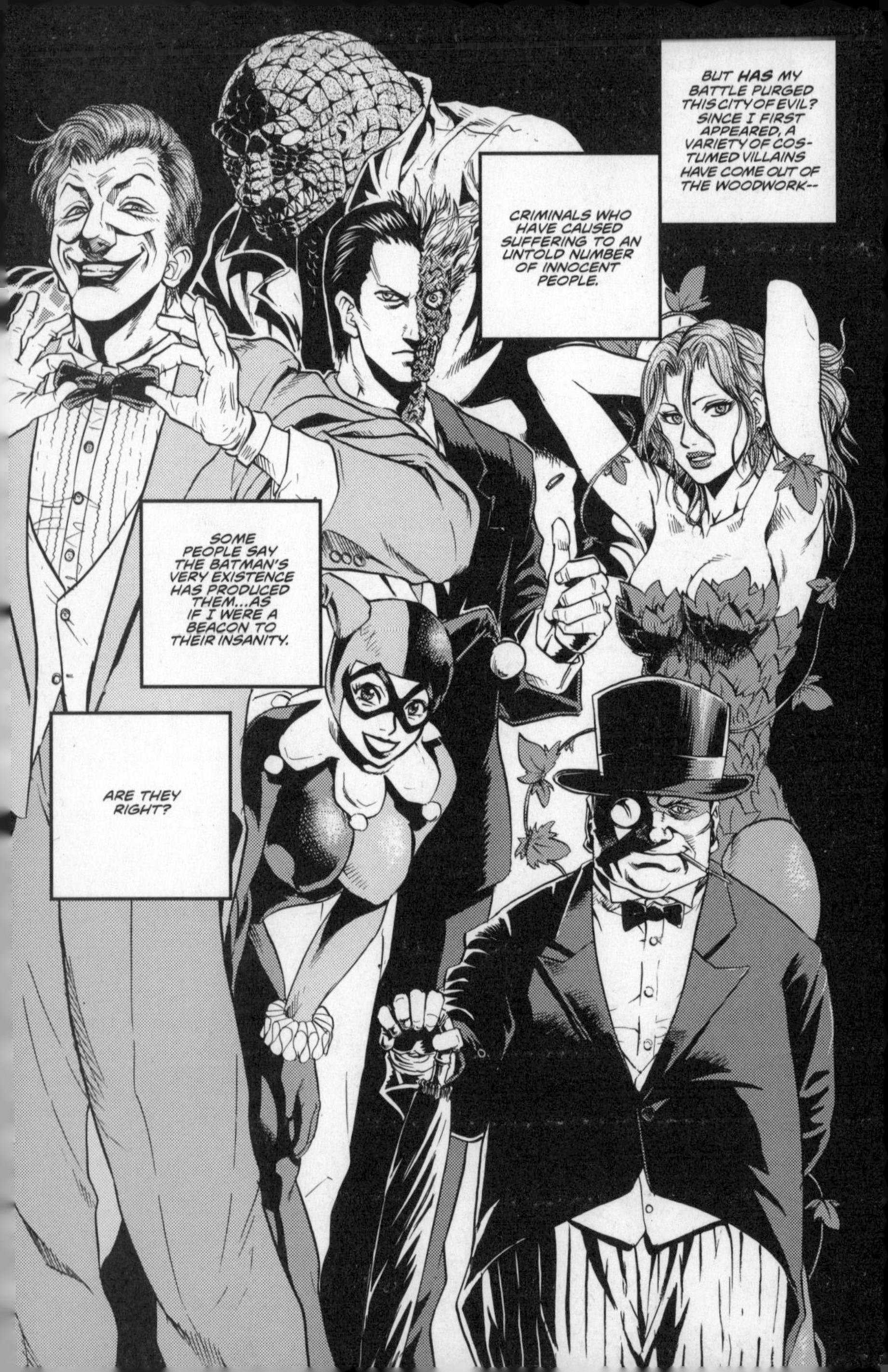
BUT HAS MY BATTLE PURGED THIS CITY OF EVIL? SINCE I FIRST APPEARED, A VARIETY OF COS-TUMED VILLAINS HAVE COME OUT OF THE WOODWORK--
CRIMINALS WHO HAVE CAUSED SUFFERING TO AN UNTOLD NUMBER OF INNOCENT PEOPLE.
SOME PEOPLE SAY THE BATMAN'S VERY EXISTENCE HAS PRODUCED THEM...AS IF I WERE A BEACON TO THEIR INSANITY.
ARE THEY RIGHT?

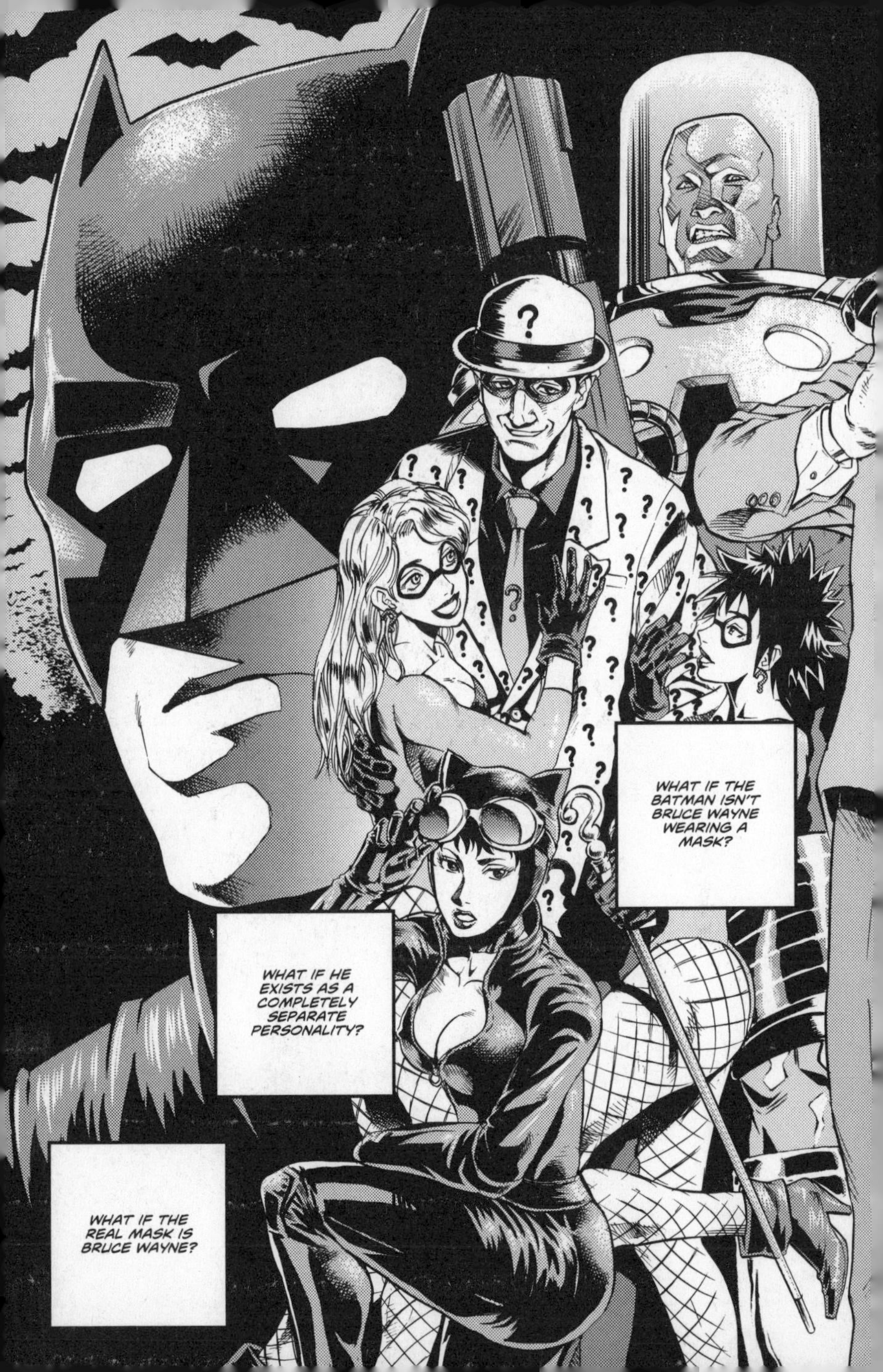
WHAT IF THE BATMAN ISN'T BRUCE WAYNE WEARING A MASK?
WHAT IF HE EXISTS AS A COMPLETELY SEPARATE PERSONALITY?
WHAT IF THE REAL MASK IS BRUCE WAYNE?

...WHERE AM I?

IN A CAGE?

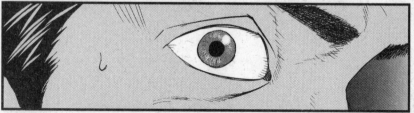

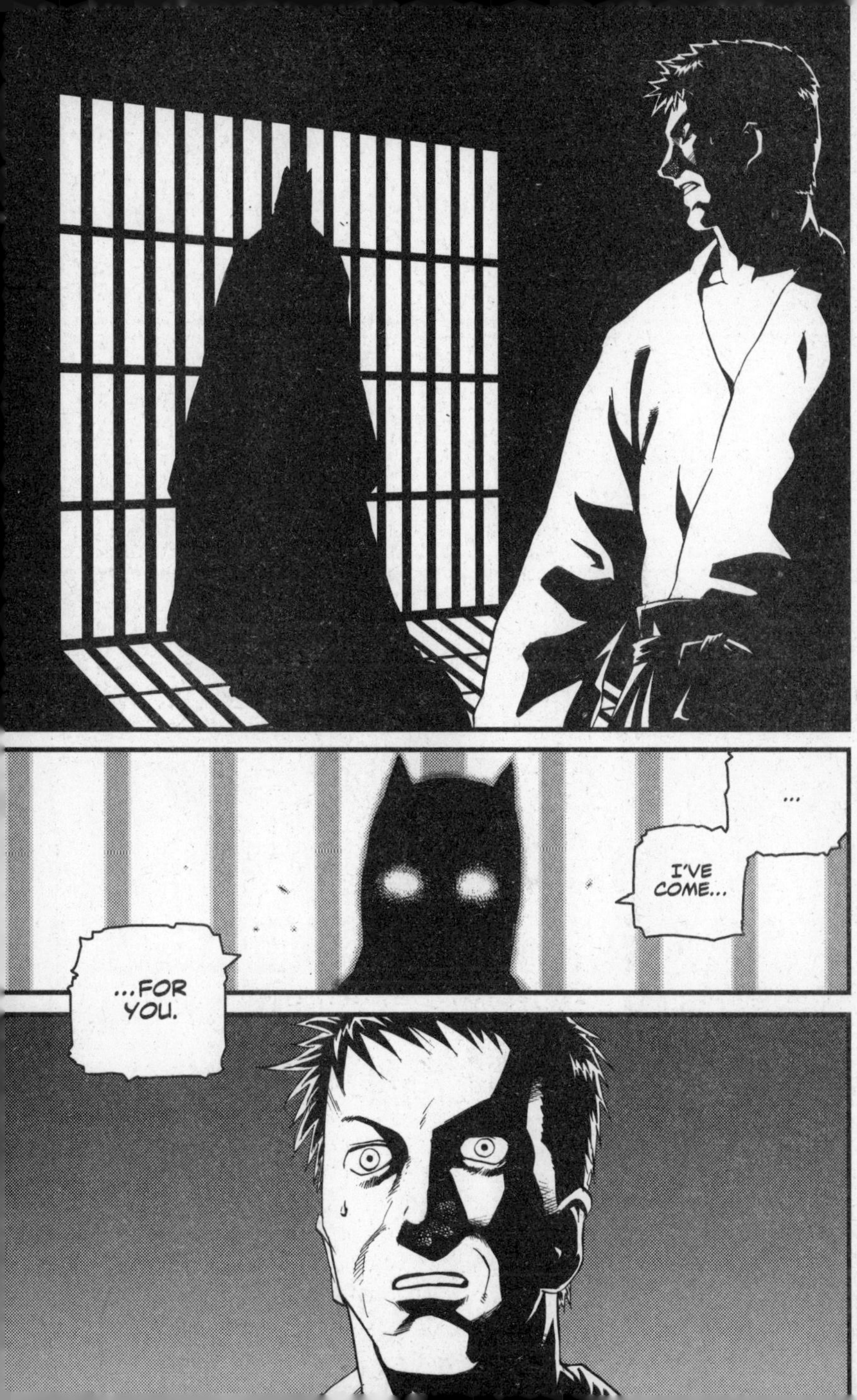
...
I'VE COME...
...FOR YOU.

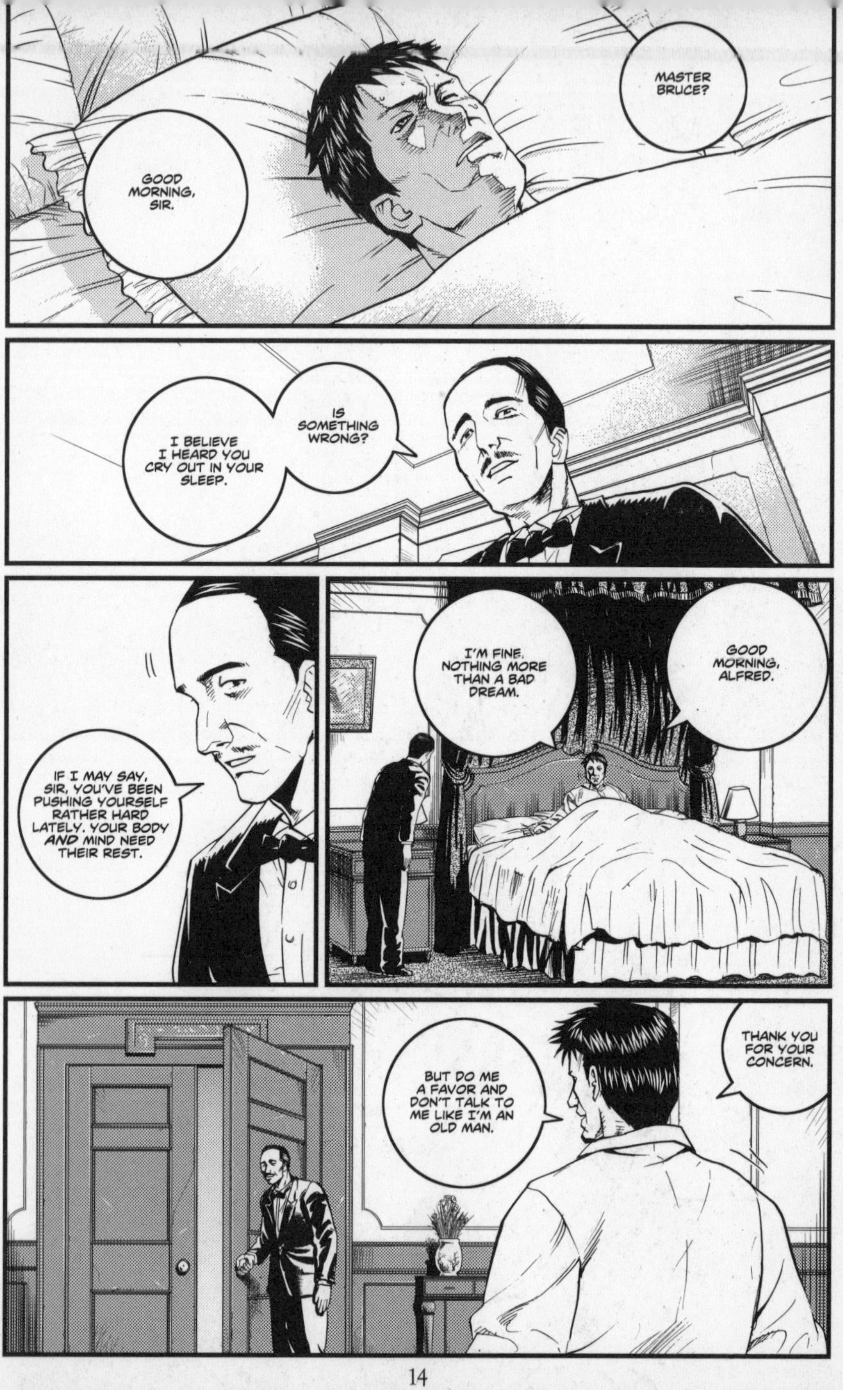
MASTER BRUCE?
GOOD MORNING, SIR.
IS SOMETHING WRONG?
I BELIEVE I HEARD YOU CRY OUT IN YOUR SLEEP.
GOOD MORNING, ALFRED.
I'M FINE. NOTHING MORE THAN A BAD DREAM.
IF I MAY SAY, SIR, YOU'VE BEEN PUSHING YOURSELF RATHER HARD LATELY. YOUR BODY AND MIND NEED THEIR REST.
THANK YOU FOR YOUR CONCERN.
BUT DO ME A FAVOR AND DON'T TALK TO ME LIKE I'M AN OLD MAN.

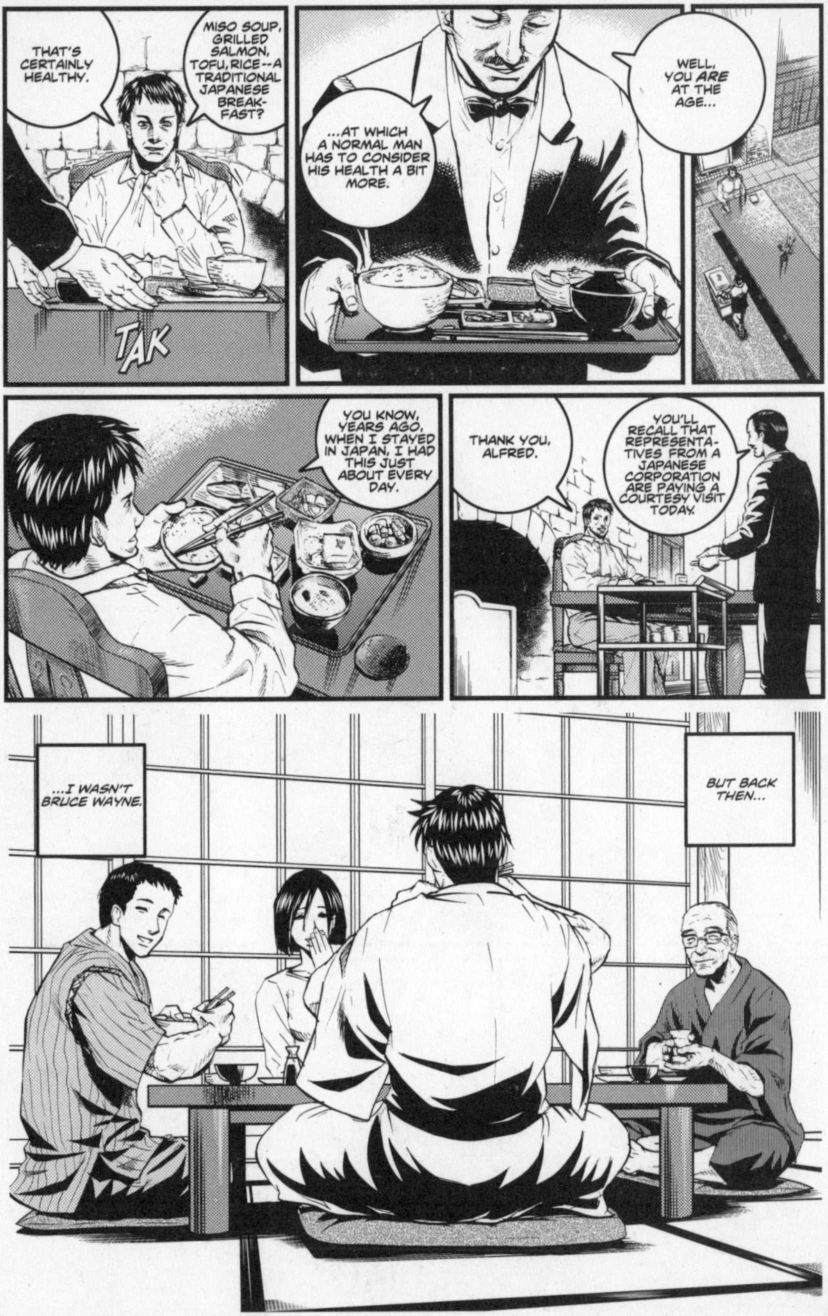
THAT'S CERTAINLY HEALTHY.
MISO SOUP, GRILLED SALMON, TOFU, RICE--A TRADITIONAL JAPANESE BREAK-FAST?
TAK
...AT WHICH A NORMAL MAN HAS TO CONSIDER HIS HEALTH A BIT MORE.
WELL, YOU ARE AT THE AGE...
YOU KNOW, YEARS AGO, WHEN I STAYED IN JAPAN, I HAD THIS JUST ABOUT EVERY DAY.
THANK YOU, ALFRED.
YOU'LL RECALL THAT REPRESENTA-TIVES FROM A JAPANESE CORPORATION ARE PAYING A COURTESY VISIT TODAY.
BUT BACK THEN...
...I WASN'T BRUCE WAYNE.

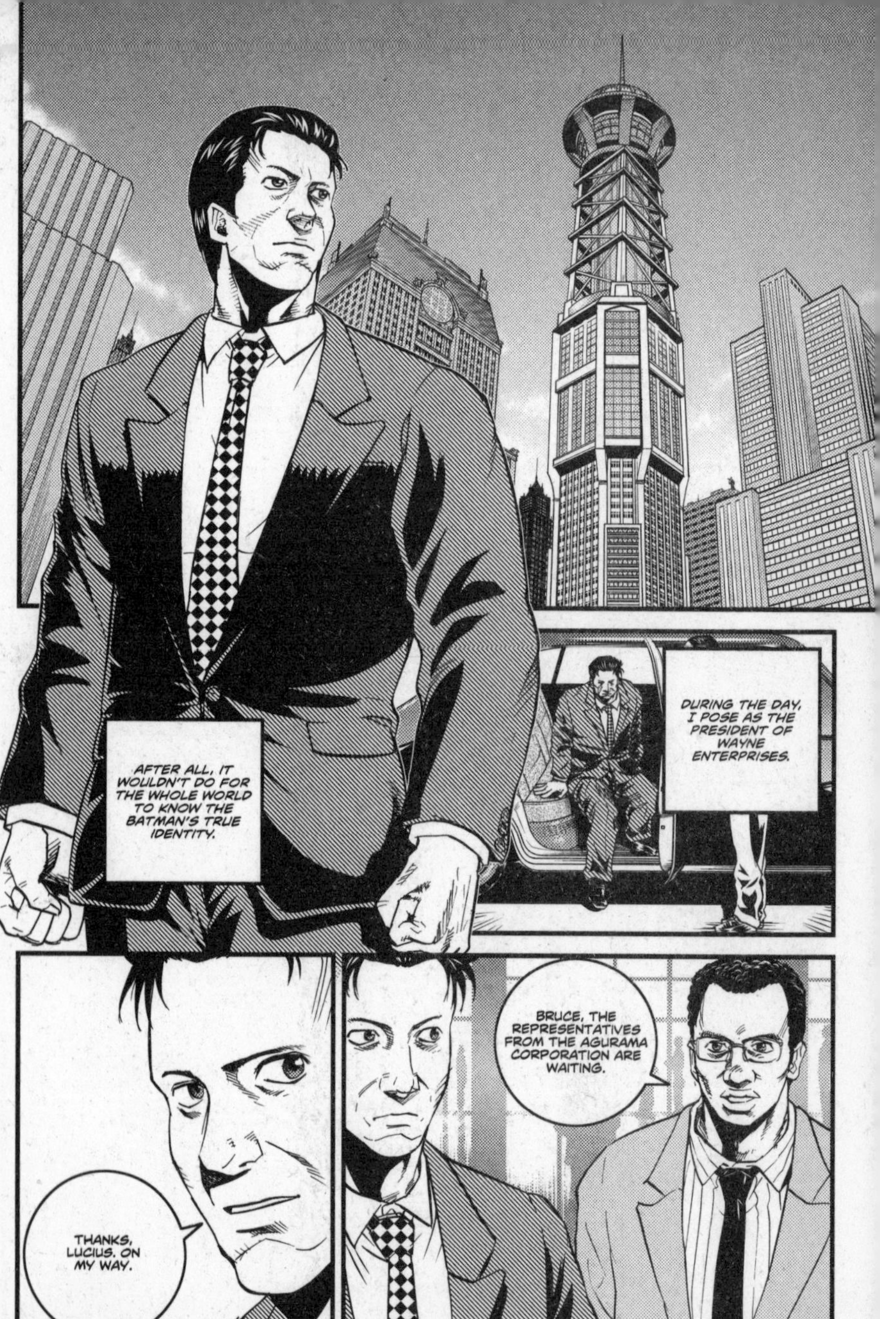
AFTER ALL, IT WOULDN'T DO FOR THE WHOLE WORLD TO KNOW THE BATMAN'S TRUE IDENTITY.
DURING THE DAY, I POSE AS THE PRESIDENT OF WAYNE ENTERPRISES.
BRUCE, THE REPRESENTATIVES FROM THE AGURAMA CORPORATION ARE WAITING.
THANKS, LUCIUS. ON MY WAY.

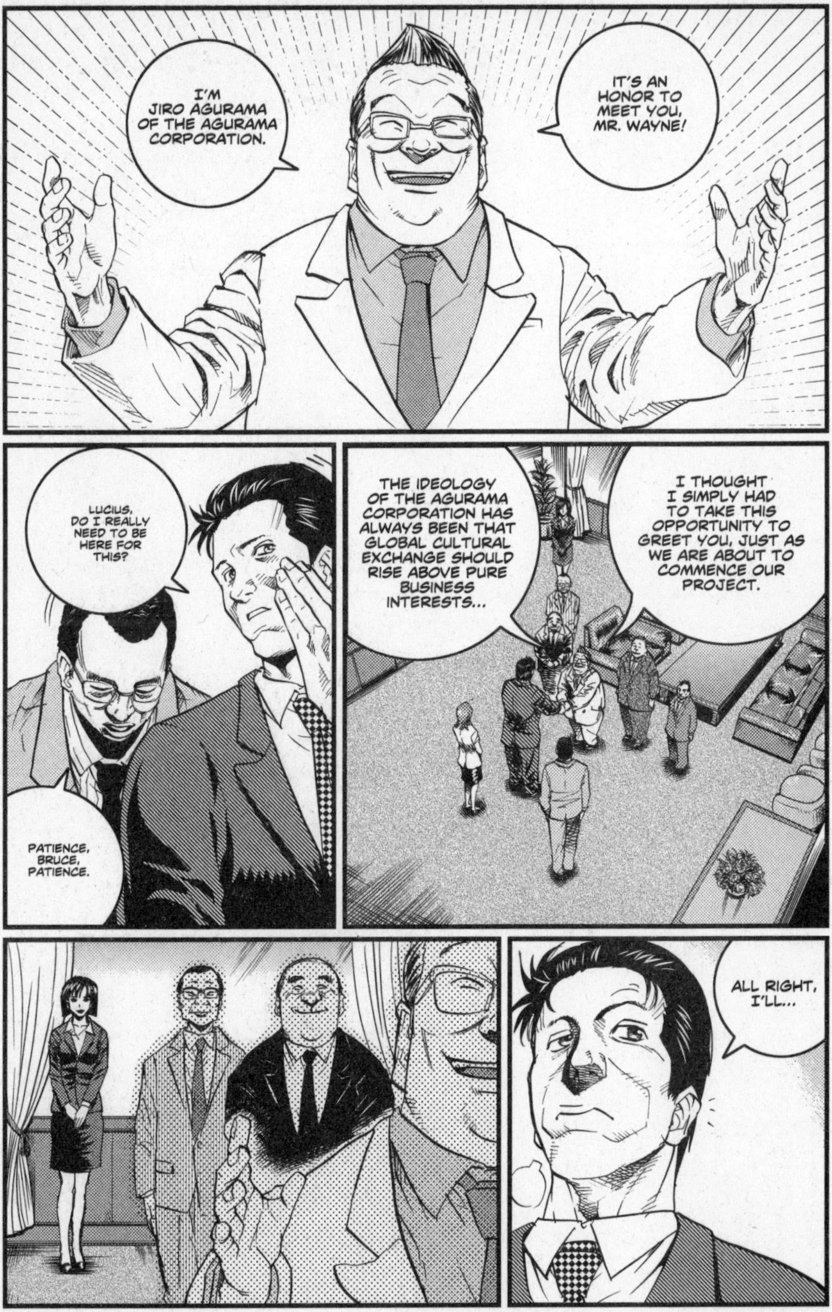
I'M JIRO AGURAMA OF THE AGURAMA CORPORATION.
IT'S AN HONOR TO MEET YOU, MR. WAYNE!
LUCIUS, DO I REALLY NEED TO BE HERE FOR THIS?
PATIENCE, BRUCE, PATIENCE.
THE IDEOLOGY OF THE AGURAMA CORPORATION HAS ALWAYS BEEN THAT GLOBAL CULTURAL EXCHANGE SHOULD RISE ABOVE PURE BUSINESS INTERESTS...
I THOUGHT I SIMPLY HAD TO TAKE THIS OPPORTUNITY TO GREET YOU, JUST AS WE ARE ABOUT TO COMMENCE OUR PROJECT.
ALL RIGHT, I'LL...

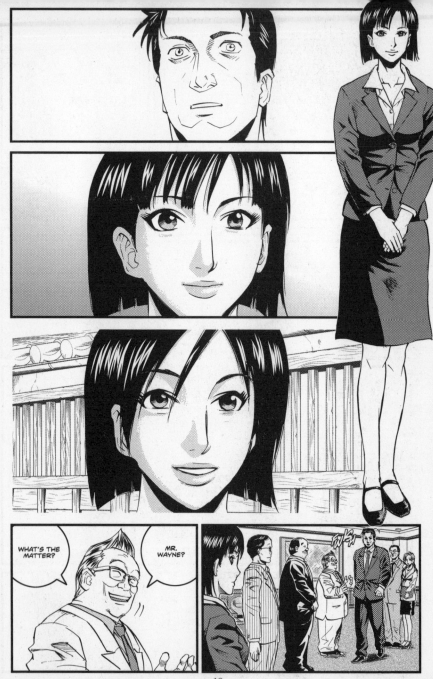

WHAT'S THE MATTER?

MR. WAYNE?

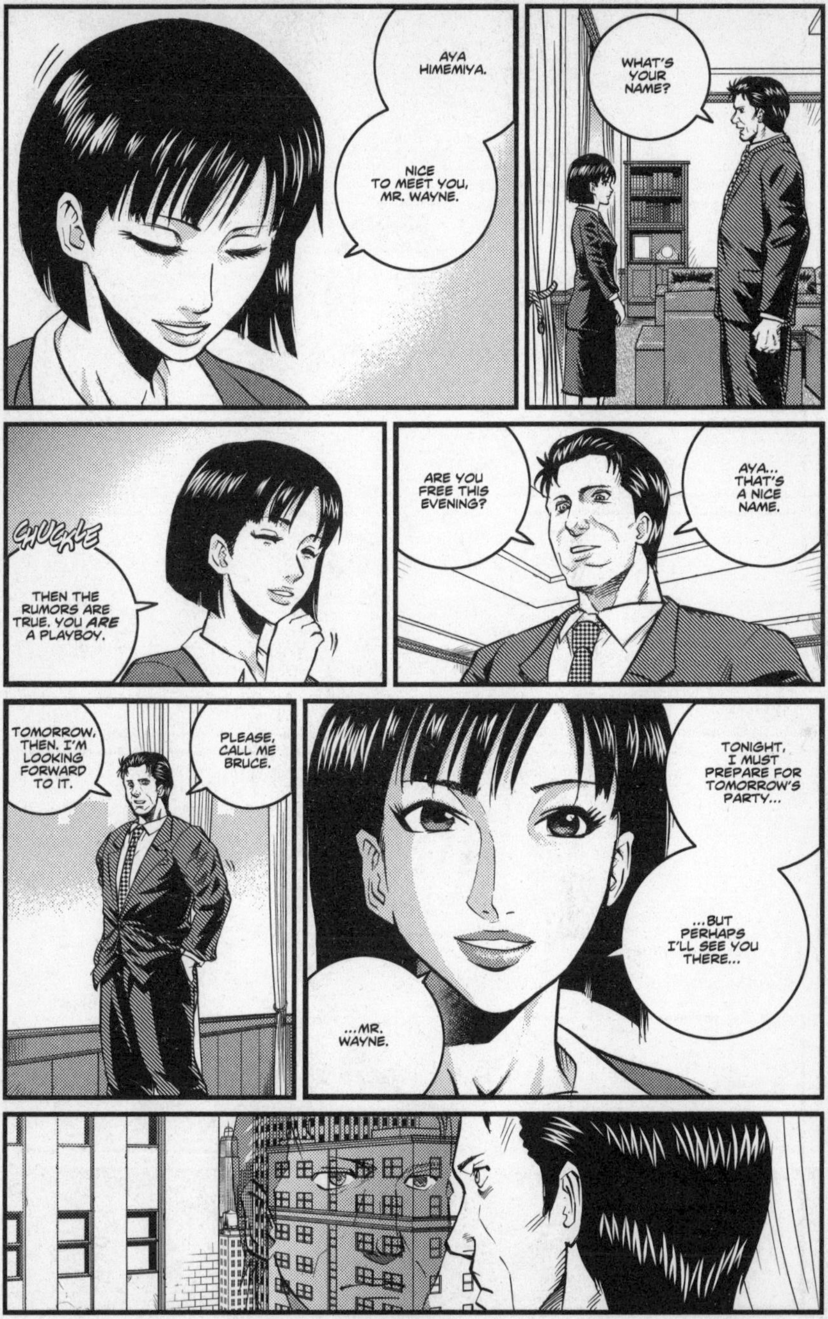
WHAT'S YOUR NAME?
AYA HIMEMIYA.
NICE TO MEET YOU, MR. WAYNE.
AYA... THAT'S A NICE NAME.
ARE YOU FREE THIS EVENING?
CHUCKLE
THEN THE RUMORS ARE TRUE. YOU *ARE* A PLAYBOY.
TONIGHT, I MUST PREPARE FOR TOMORROW'S PARTY...
...BUT PERHAPS I'LL SEE YOU THERE...
...MR. WAYNE.
PLEASE, CALL ME BRUCE.
TOMORROW, THEN. I'M LOOKING FORWARD TO IT.

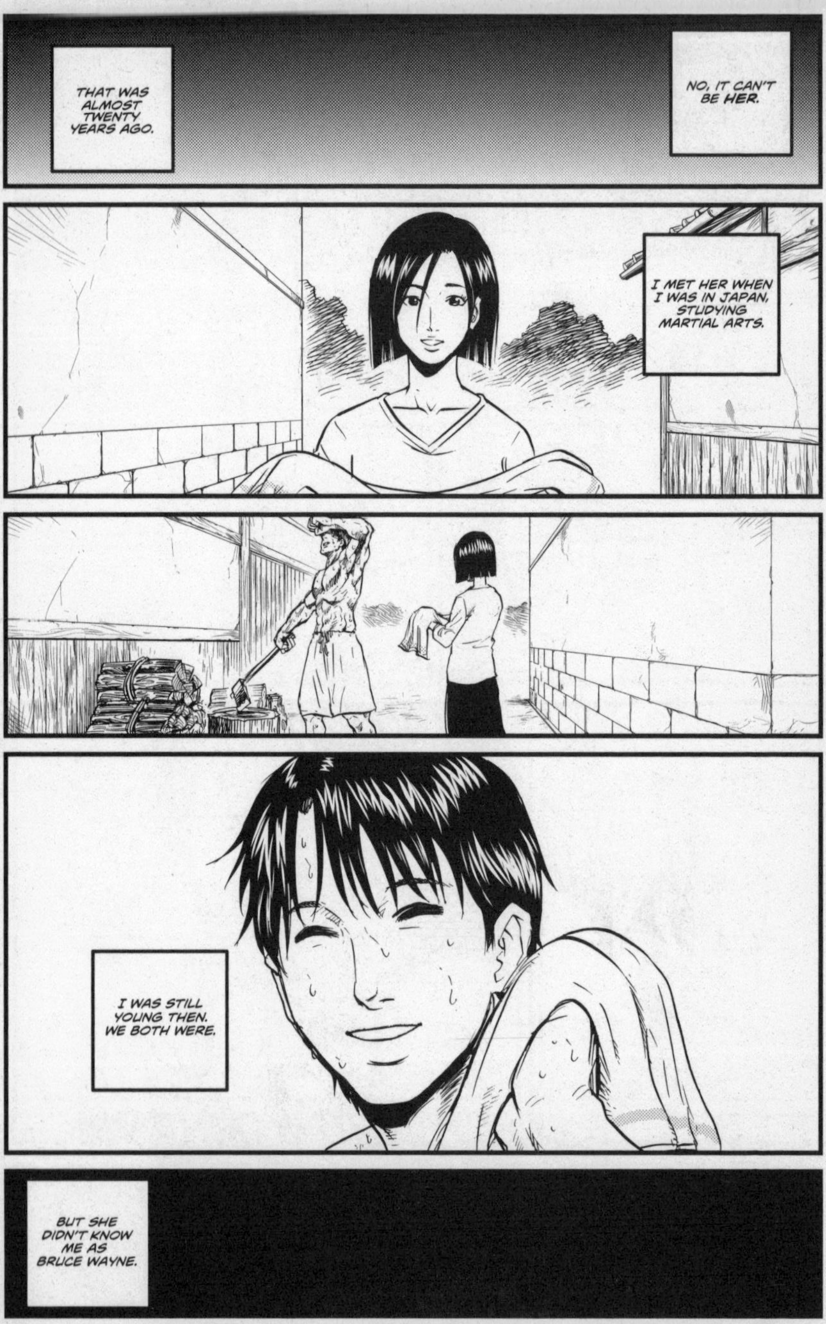
THAT WAS ALMOST TWENTY YEARS AGO.
NO, IT CAN'T BE HER.
I MET HER WHEN I WAS IN JAPAN, STUDYING MARTIAL ARTS.
I WAS STILL YOUNG THEN. WE BOTH WERE.
BUT SHE DIDN'T KNOW ME AS BRUCE WAYNE.

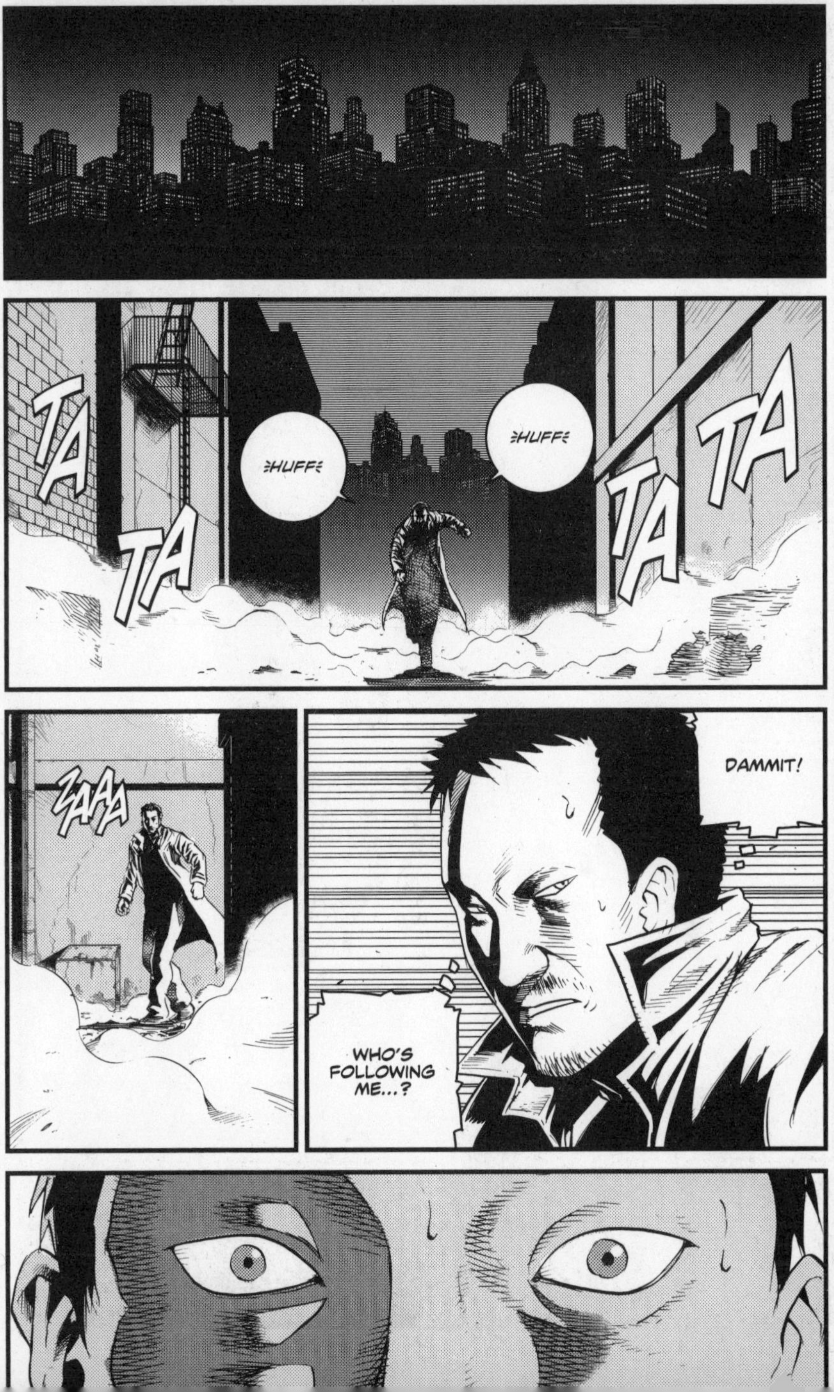
TA
TA
HUFF
HUFF
TA
TA
ZAAA
DAMMIT!
WHO'S FOLLOWING ME...?

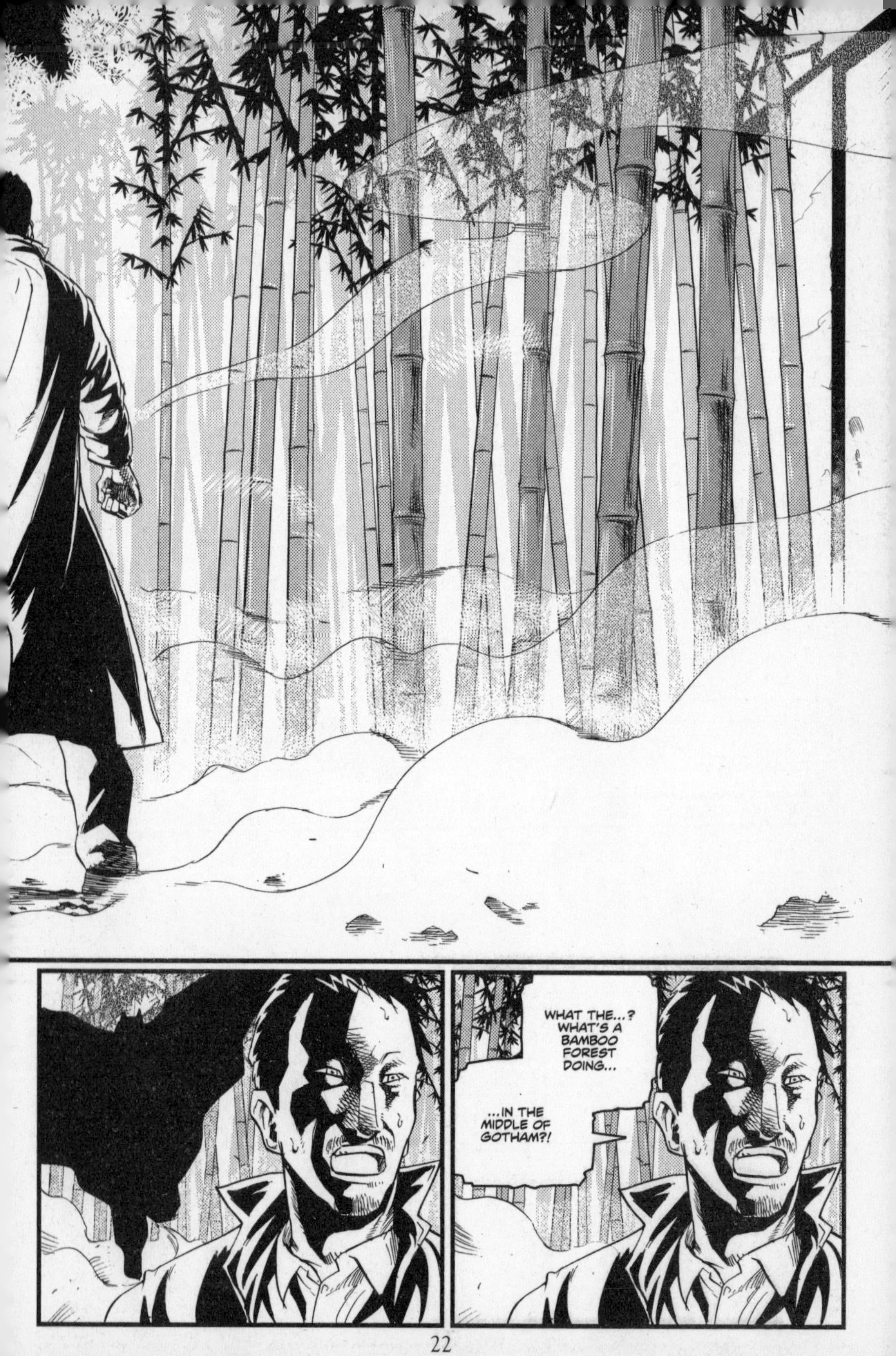
WHAT THE...? WHAT'S A BAMBOO FOREST DOING...
...IN THE MIDDLE OF GOTHAM?!

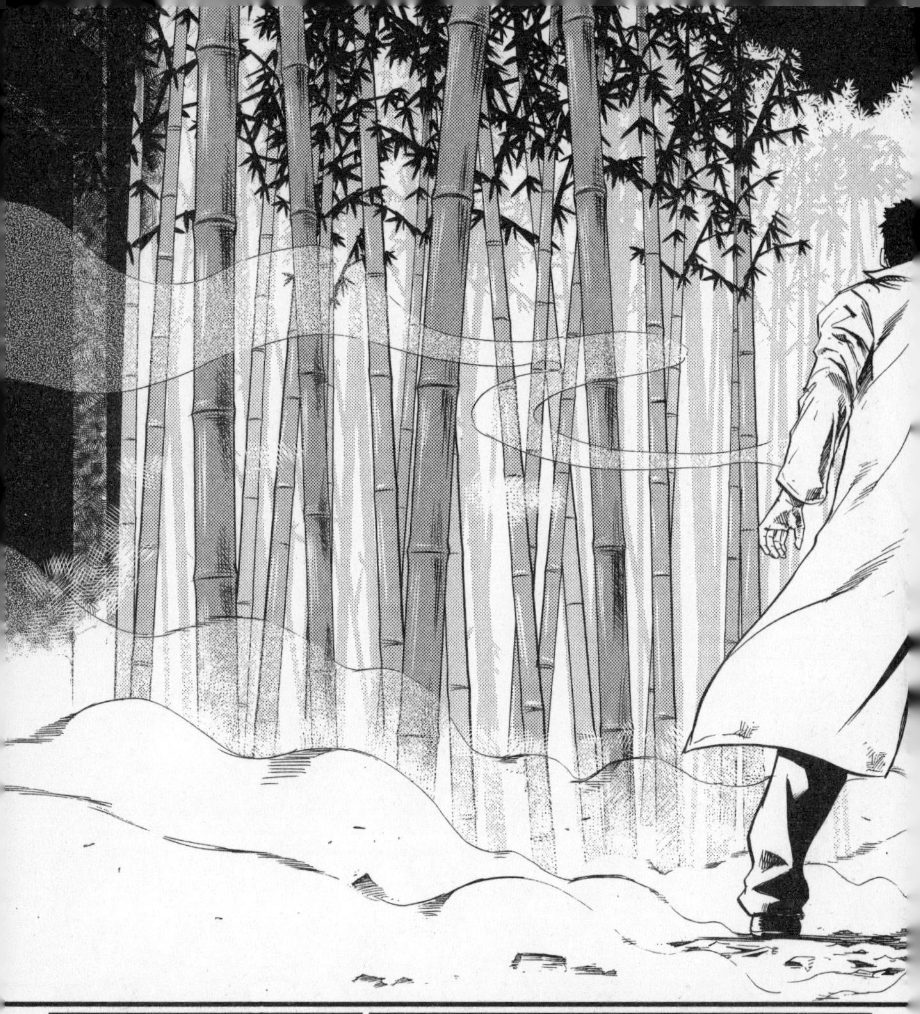

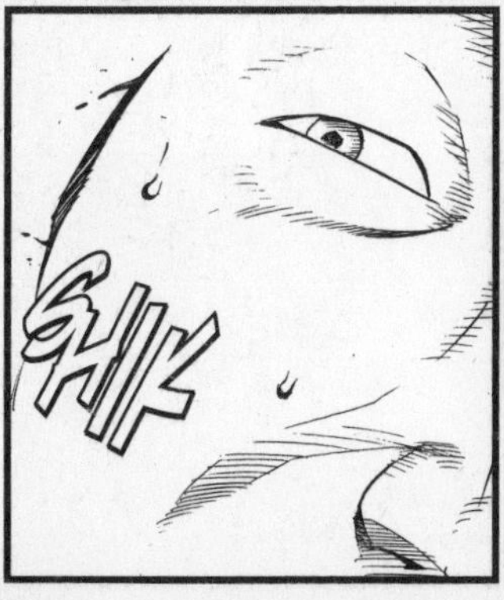
SHIK

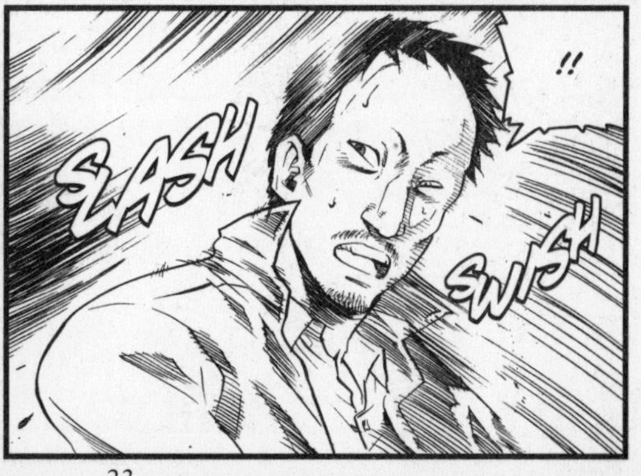
!!
SLASH
SWISH

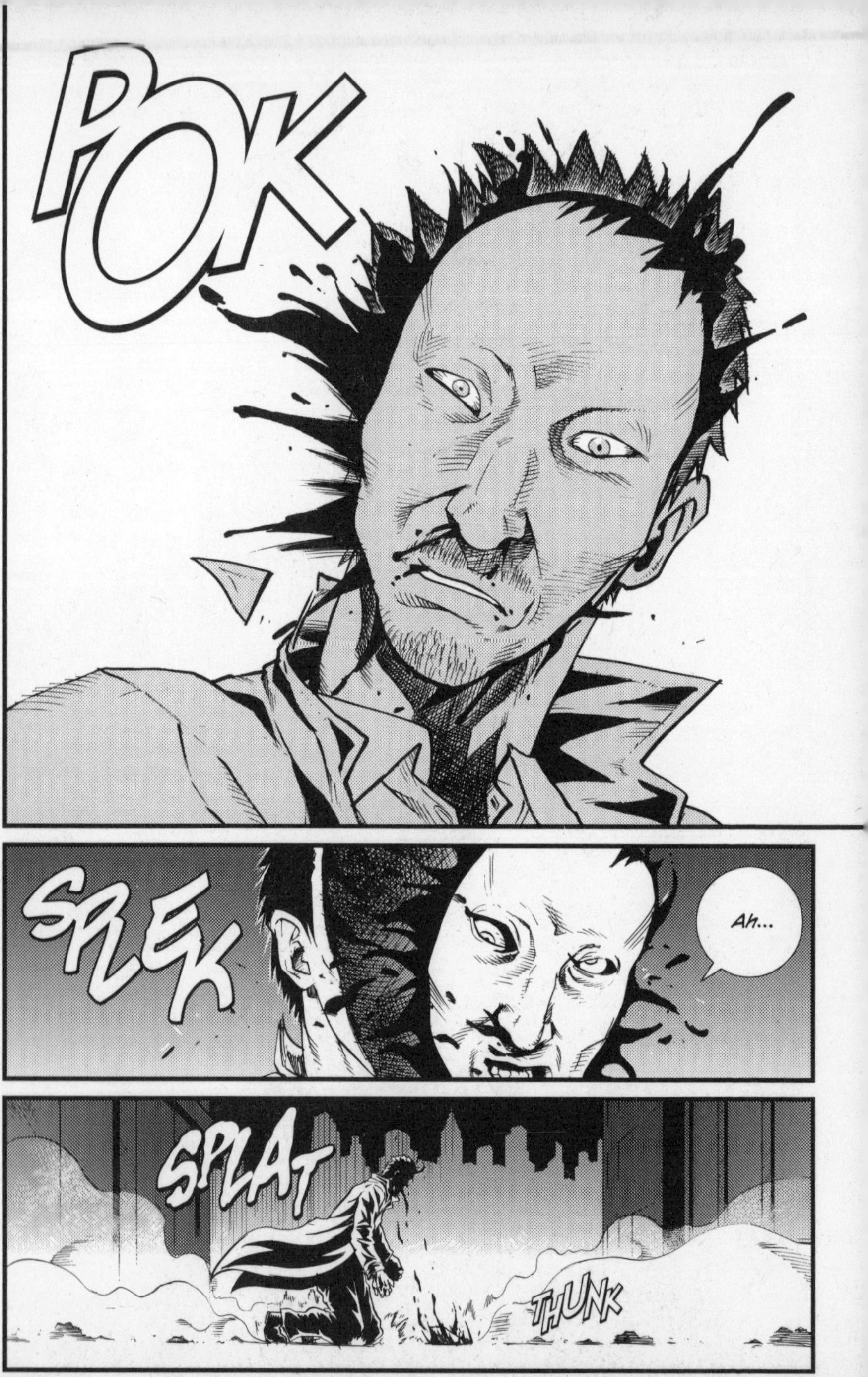
POK
SPLEK
Ah...
SPLAT
THUNK

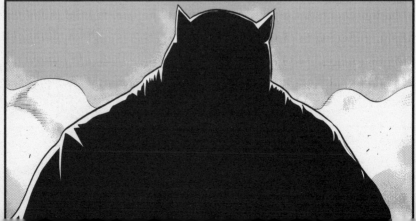

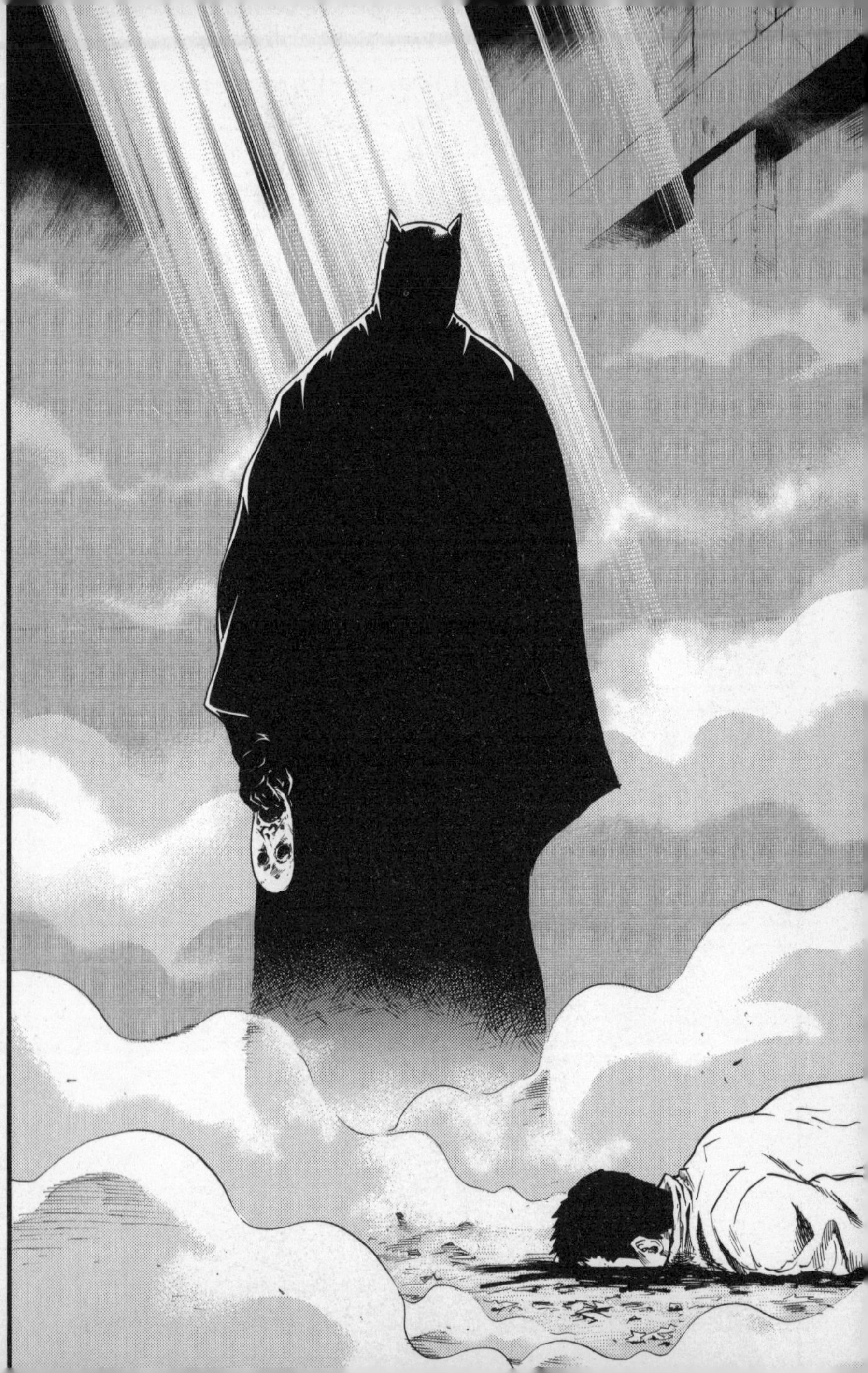

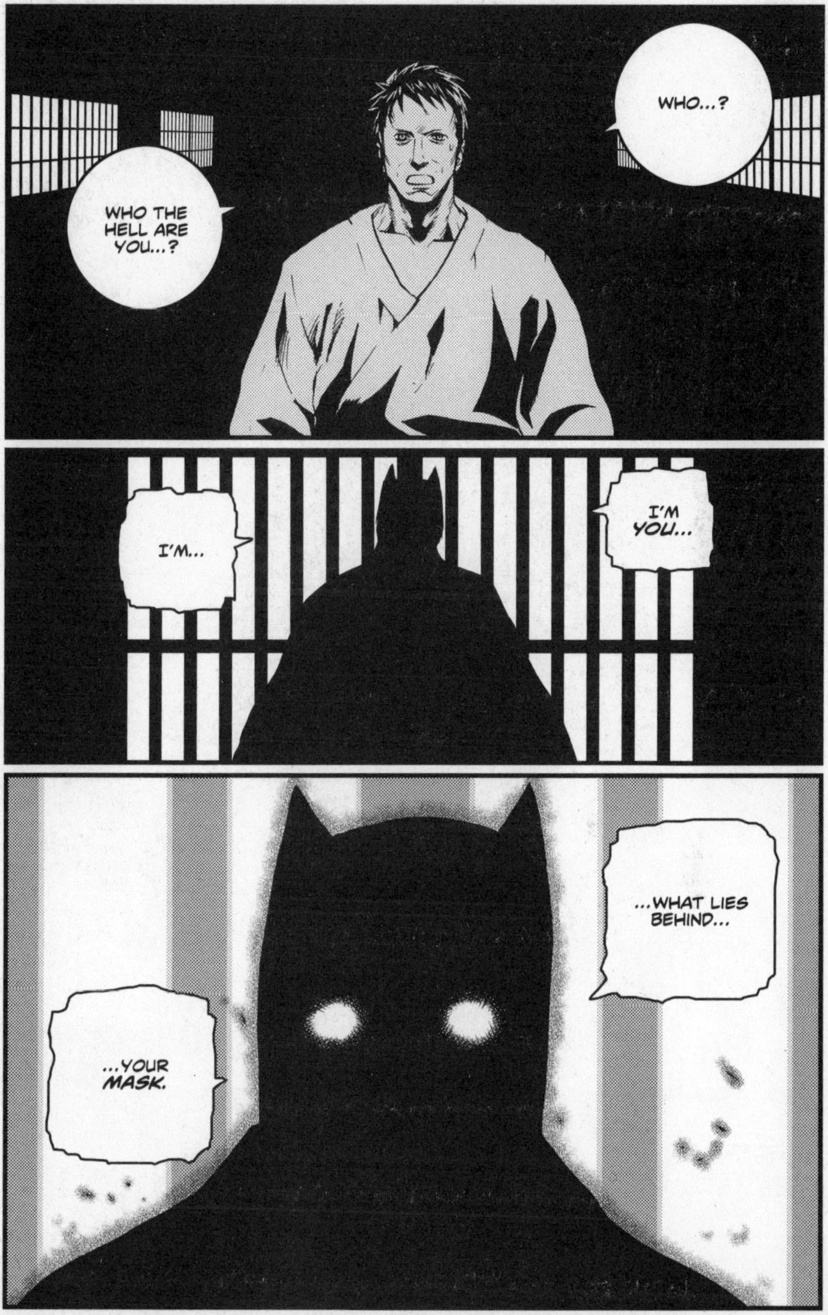
WHO...?
WHO THE HELL ARE YOU...?
I'M...
I'M YOU...
...WHAT LIES BEHIND...
...YOUR MASK.

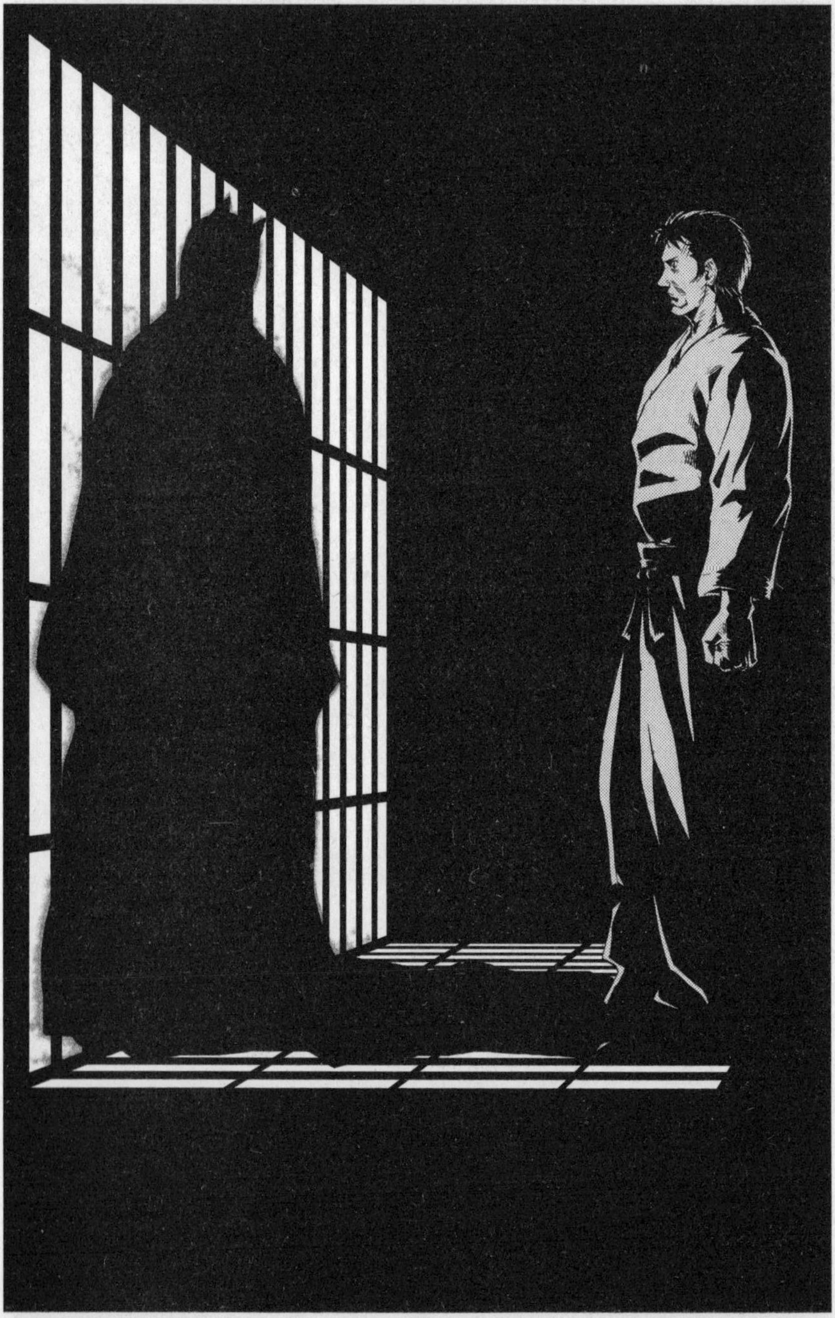

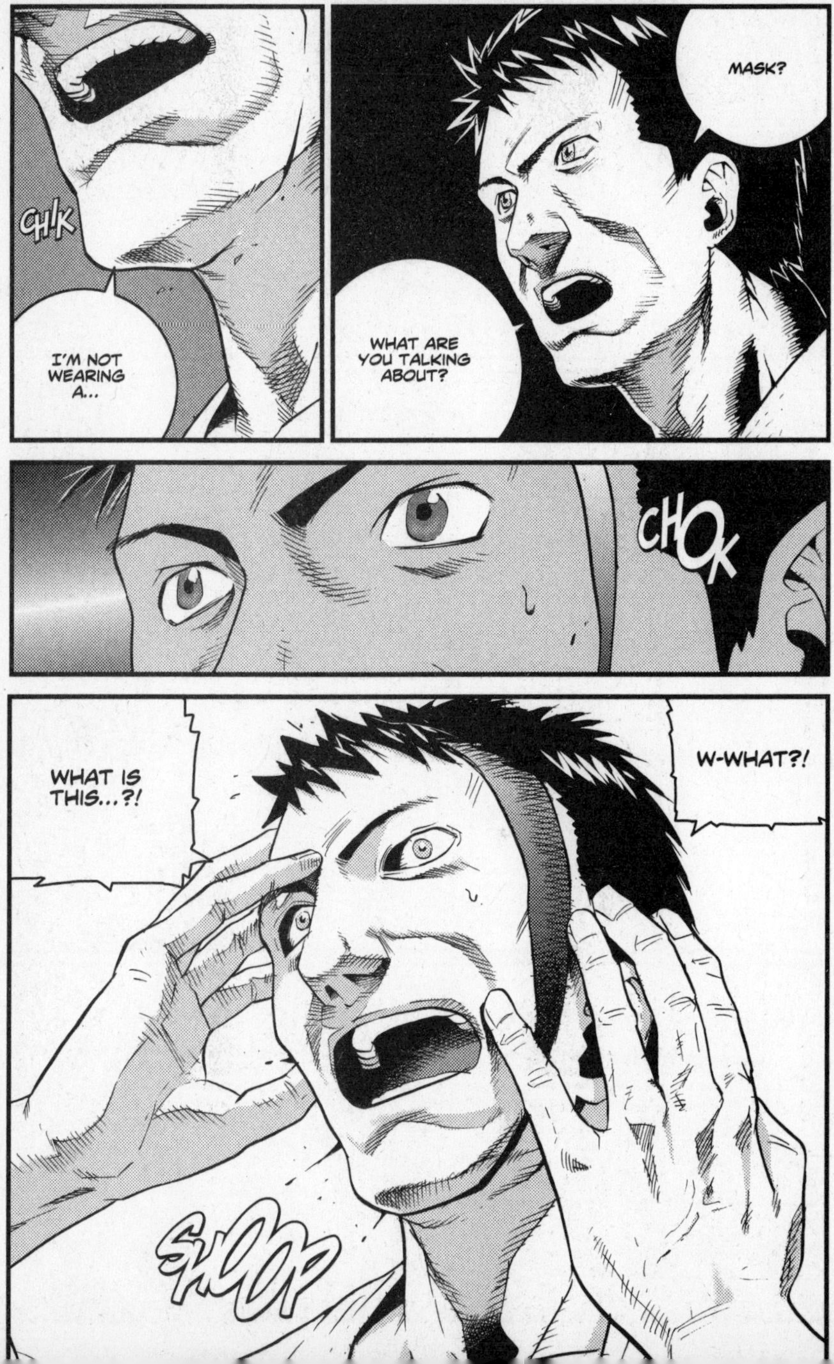
CHIK
I'M NOT WEARING A...
MASK?
WHAT ARE YOU TALKING ABOUT?
CHOK
W-WHAT?!
WHAT IS THIS...?!
SHOOP

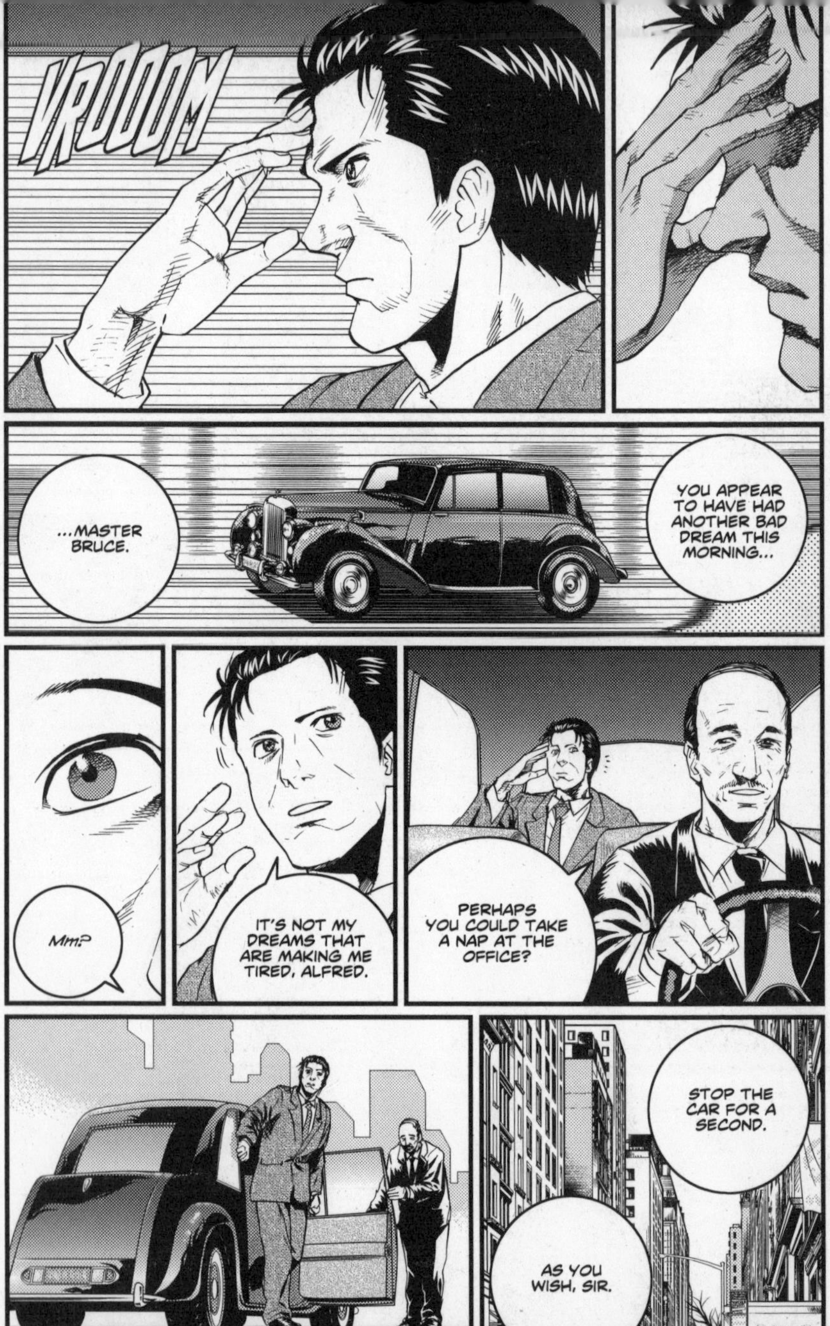
VROOOM
...MASTER BRUCE.
YOU APPEAR TO HAVE HAD ANOTHER BAD DREAM THIS MORNING...
Mm?
IT'S NOT MY DREAMS THAT ARE MAKING ME TIRED, ALFRED.
PERHAPS YOU COULD TAKE A NAP AT THE OFFICE?
STOP THE CAR FOR A SECOND.
AS YOU WISH, SIR.

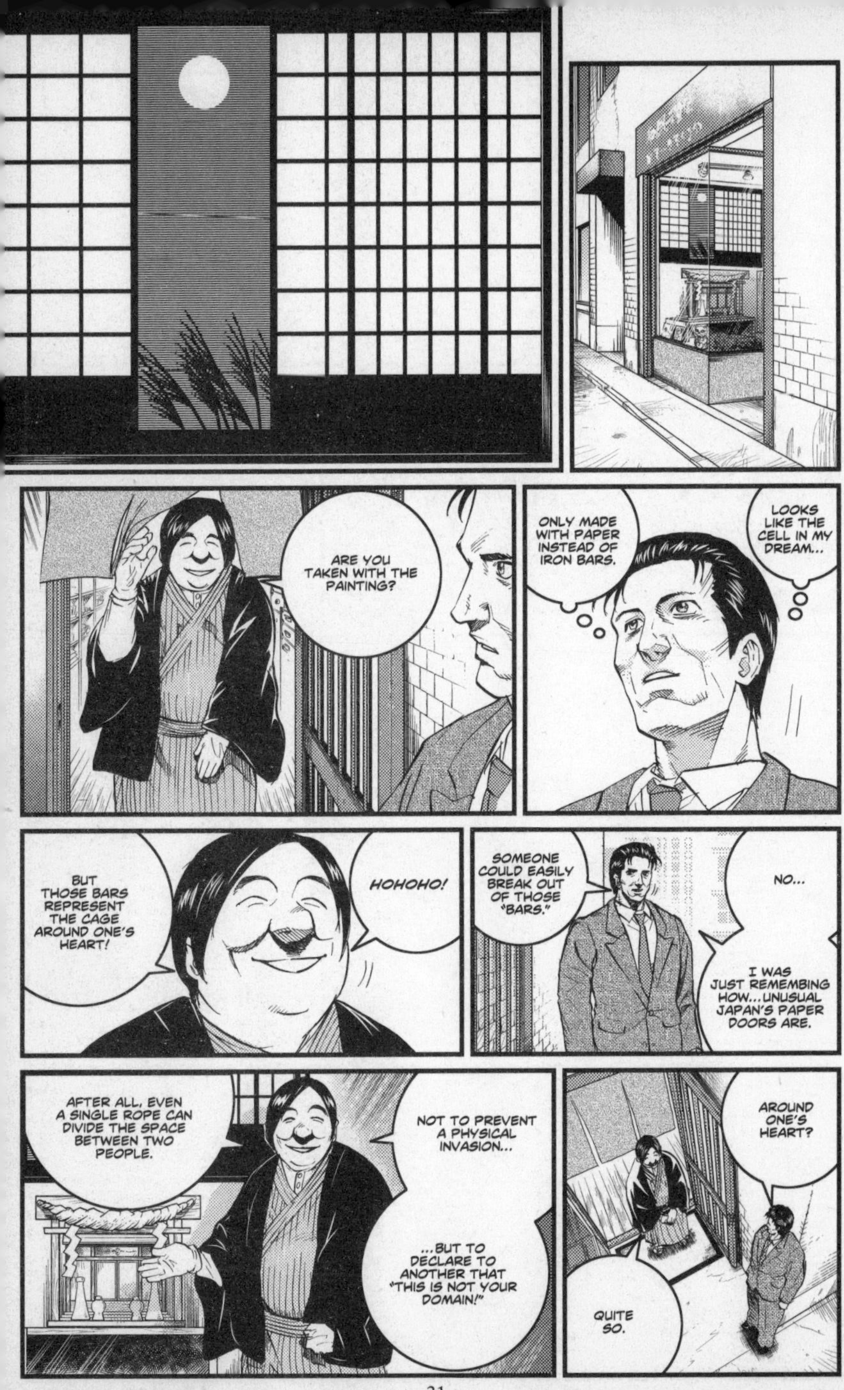

ARE YOU TAKEN WITH THE PAINTING?
LOOKS LIKE THE CELL IN MY DREAM...
ONLY MADE WITH PAPER INSTEAD OF IRON BARS.
NO...
I WAS JUST REMEMBING HOW...UNUSUAL JAPAN'S PAPER DOORS ARE.
SOMEONE COULD EASILY BREAK OUT OF THOSE "BARS."
HOHOHO!
BUT THOSE BARS REPRESENT THE CAGE AROUND ONE'S HEART!
AROUND ONE'S HEART?
QUITE SO.
AFTER ALL, EVEN A SINGLE ROPE CAN DIVIDE THE SPACE BETWEEN TWO PEOPLE.
NOT TO PREVENT A PHYSICAL INVASION...
...BUT TO DECLARE TO ANOTHER THAT "THIS IS NOT YOUR DOMAIN!"

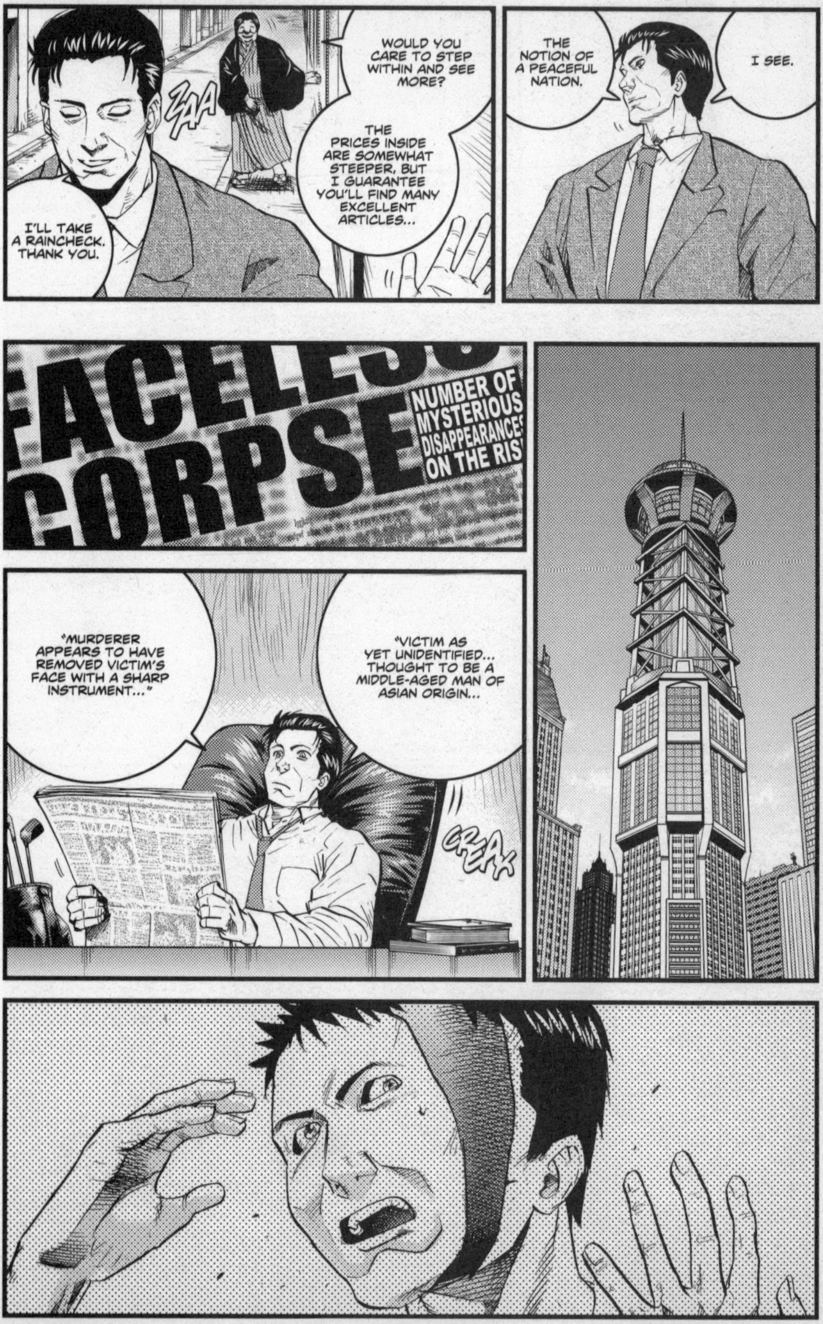
WOULD YOU CARE TO STEP WITHIN AND SEE MORE?
THE PRICES INSIDE ARE SOMEWHAT STEEPER, BUT I GUARANTEE YOU'LL FIND MANY EXCELLENT ARTICLES...
ZAA
I'LL TAKE A RAINCHECK. THANK YOU.
THE NOTION OF A PEACEFUL NATION.
I SEE.
FACELESS CORPSE
NUMBER OF MYSTERIOUS DISAPPEARANCES ON THE RIS
"MURDERER APPEARS TO HAVE REMOVED VICTIM'S FACE WITH A SHARP INSTRUMENT..."
"VICTIM AS YET UNIDENTIFIED... THOUGHT TO BE A MIDDLE-AGED MAN OF ASIAN ORIGIN...
CREAK

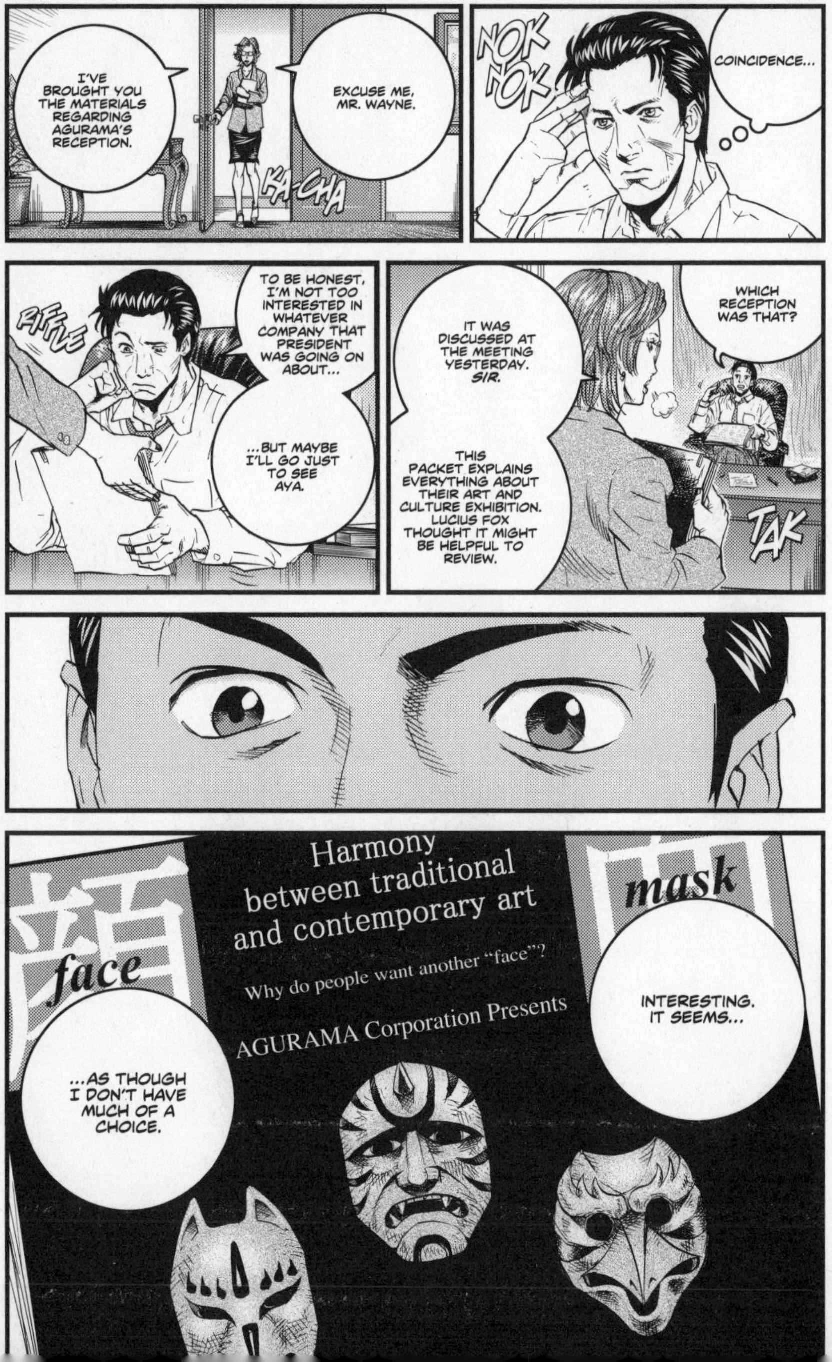
EXCUSE ME, MR. WAYNE.
I'VE BROUGHT YOU THE MATERIALS REGARDING AGURAMA'S RECEPTION.
KA-CHA
NOK NOK
COINCIDENCE...
RIFFLE
TO BE HONEST, I'M NOT TOO INTERESTED IN WHATEVER COMPANY THAT PRESIDENT WAS GOING ON ABOUT...
...BUT MAYBE I'LL GO JUST TO SEE AYA.
WHICH RECEPTION WAS THAT?
IT WAS DISCUSSED AT THE MEETING YESTERDAY. SIR.
THIS PACKET EXPLAINS EVERYTHING ABOUT THEIR ART AND CULTURE EXHIBITION. LUCIUS FOX THOUGHT IT MIGHT BE HELPFUL TO REVIEW.
TAK
Harmony between traditional and contemporary art
Why do people want another "face"?
AGURAMA Corporation Presents
face
mask
INTERESTING. IT SEEMS...
...AS THOUGH I DON'T HAVE MUCH OF A CHOICE.

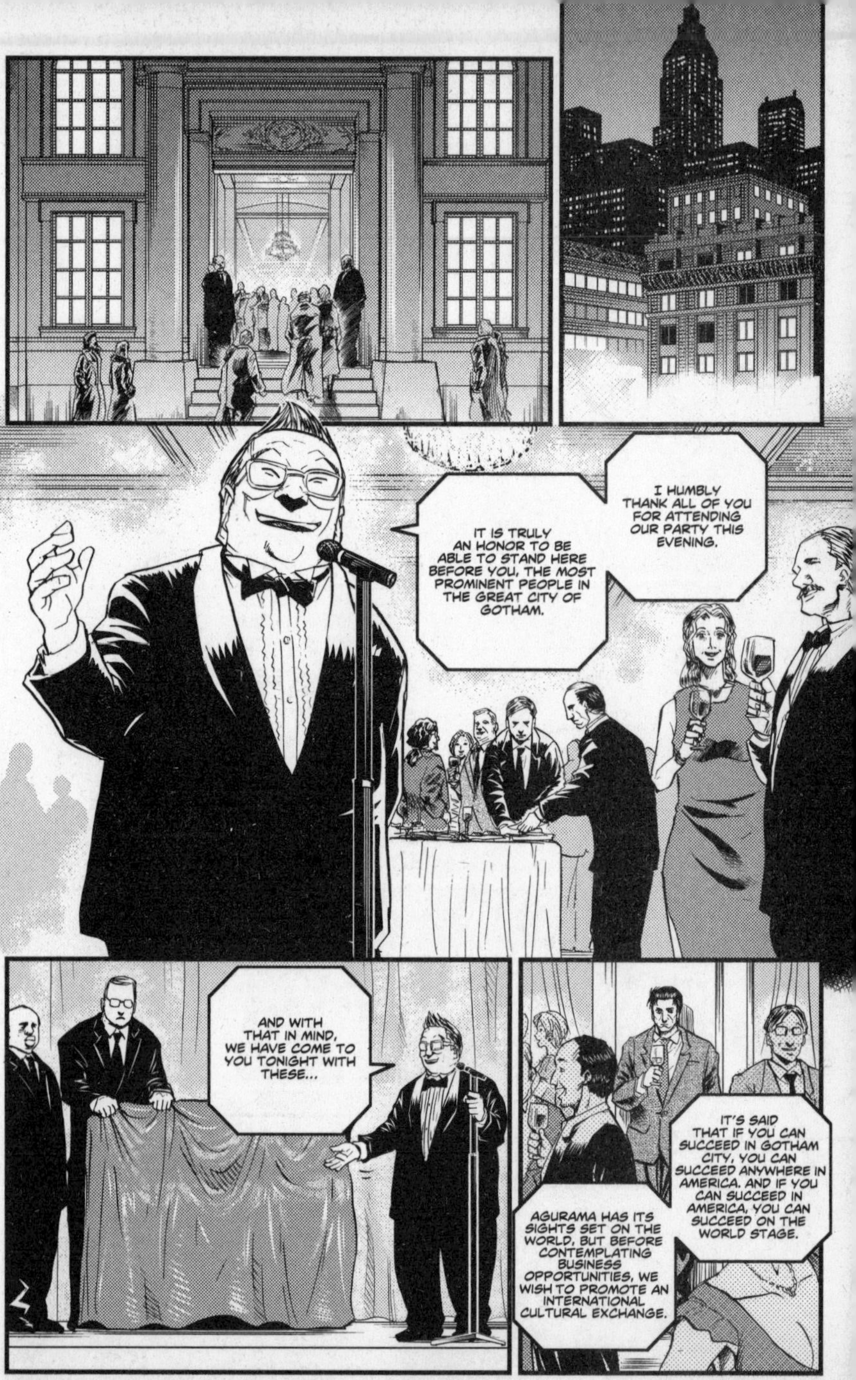

I HUMBLY THANK ALL OF YOU FOR ATTENDING OUR PARTY THIS EVENING.
IT IS TRULY AN HONOR TO BE ABLE TO STAND HERE BEFORE YOU, THE MOST PROMINENT PEOPLE IN THE GREAT CITY OF GOTHAM.
IT'S SAID THAT IF YOU CAN SUCCEED IN GOTHAM CITY, YOU CAN SUCCEED ANYWHERE IN AMERICA. AND IF YOU CAN SUCCEED IN AMERICA, YOU CAN SUCCEED ON THE WORLD STAGE.
AGURAMA HAS ITS SIGHTS SET ON THE WORLD, BUT BEFORE CONTEMPLATING BUSINESS OPPORTUNITIES, WE WISH TO PROMOTE AN INTERNATIONAL CULTURAL EXCHANGE.
AND WITH THAT IN MIND, WE HAVE COME TO YOU TONIGHT WITH THESE...

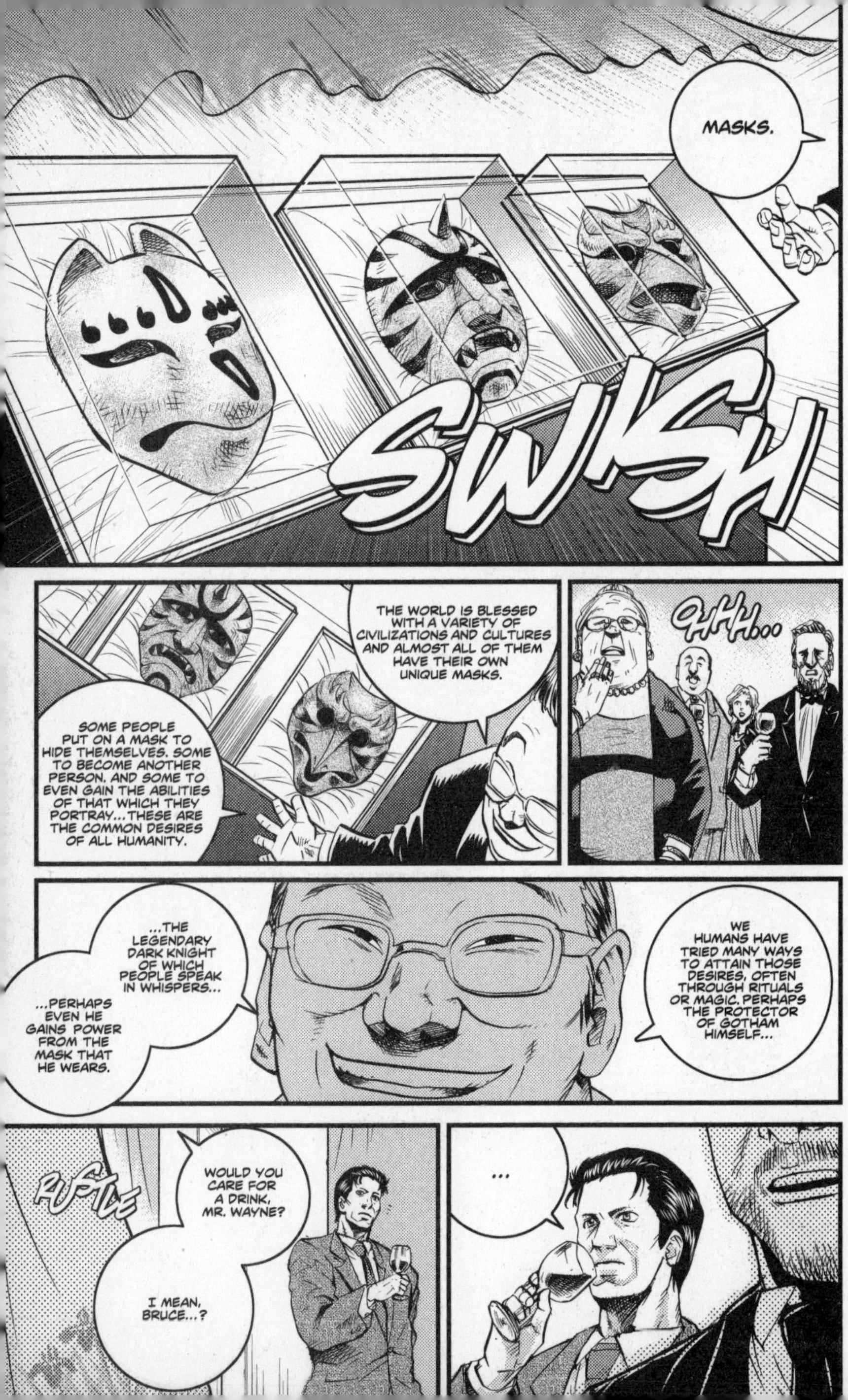
MASKS.
SWISH
THE WORLD IS BLESSED WITH A VARIETY OF CIVILIZATIONS AND CULTURES AND ALMOST ALL OF THEM HAVE THEIR OWN UNIQUE MASKS.
SOME PEOPLE PUT ON A MASK TO HIDE THEMSELVES. SOME TO BECOME ANOTHER PERSON. AND SOME TO EVEN GAIN THE ABILITIES OF THAT WHICH THEY PORTRAY... THESE ARE THE COMMON DESIRES OF ALL HUMANITY.
WE HUMANS HAVE TRIED MANY WAYS TO ATTAIN THOSE DESIRES, OFTEN THROUGH RITUALS OR MAGIC. PERHAPS THE PROTECTOR OF GOTHAM HIMSELF...
...THE LEGENDARY DARK KNIGHT OF WHICH PEOPLE SPEAK IN WHISPERS...
...PERHAPS EVEN HE GAINS POWER FROM THE MASK THAT HE WEARS.
RUSTLE
WOULD YOU CARE FOR A DRINK, MR. WAYNE?
I MEAN, BRUCE...?
...

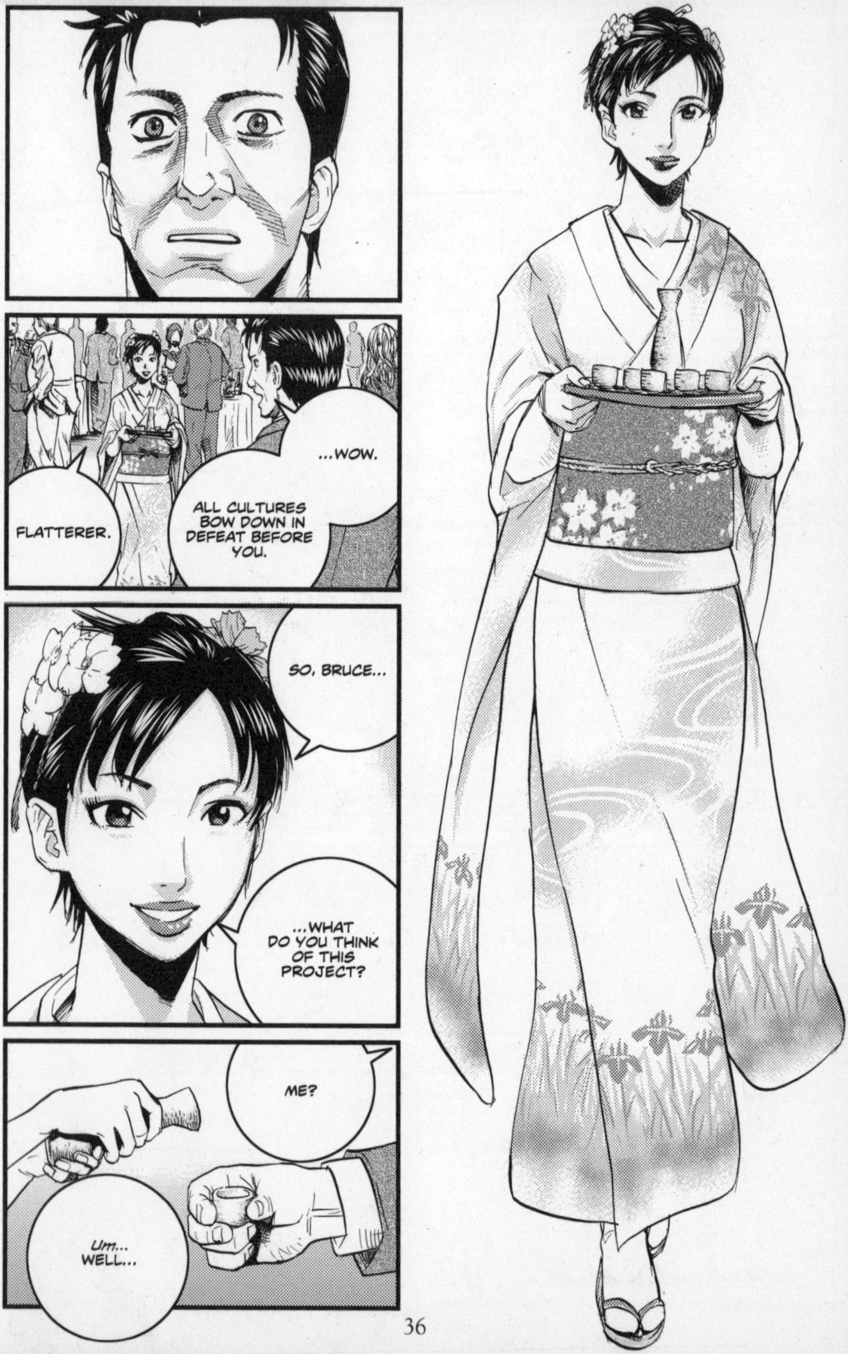
...WOW.
ALL CULTURES BOW DOWN IN DEFEAT BEFORE YOU.
FLATTERER.
SO, BRUCE...
...WHAT DO YOU THINK OF THIS PROJECT?
ME?
Um... WELL...

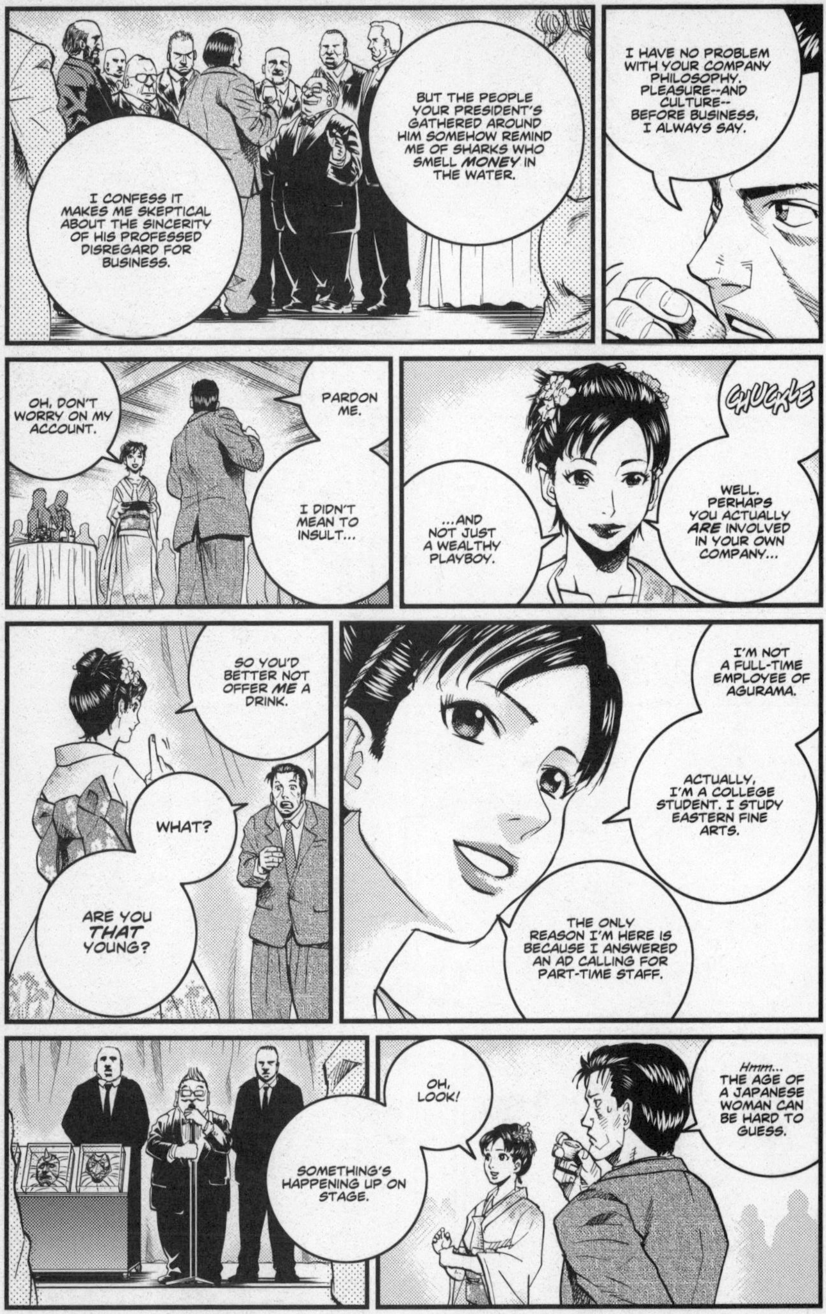
I HAVE NO PROBLEM WITH YOUR COMPANY PHILOSOPHY. PLEASURE--AND CULTURE--BEFORE BUSINESS, I ALWAYS SAY.
BUT THE PEOPLE YOUR PRESIDENT'S GATHERED AROUND HIM SOMEHOW REMIND ME OF SHARKS WHO SMELL MONEY IN THE WATER.
I CONFESS IT MAKES ME SKEPTICAL ABOUT THE SINCERITY OF HIS PROFESSED DISREGARD FOR BUSINESS.
PARDON ME.
I DIDN'T MEAN TO INSULT...
OH, DON'T WORRY ON MY ACCOUNT.
CHUCKLE
WELL. PERHAPS YOU ACTUALLY ARE INVOLVED IN YOUR OWN COMPANY...
...AND NOT JUST A WEALTHY PLAYBOY.
I'M NOT A FULL-TIME EMPLOYEE OF AGURAMA.
ACTUALLY, I'M A COLLEGE STUDENT. I STUDY EASTERN FINE ARTS.
THE ONLY REASON I'M HERE IS BECAUSE I ANSWERED AN AD CALLING FOR PART-TIME STAFF.
SO YOU'D BETTER NOT OFFER ME A DRINK.
WHAT?
ARE YOU THAT YOUNG?
Hmm... THE AGE OF A JAPANESE WOMAN CAN BE HARD TO GUESS.
OH, LOOK!
SOMETHING'S HAPPENING UP ON STAGE.

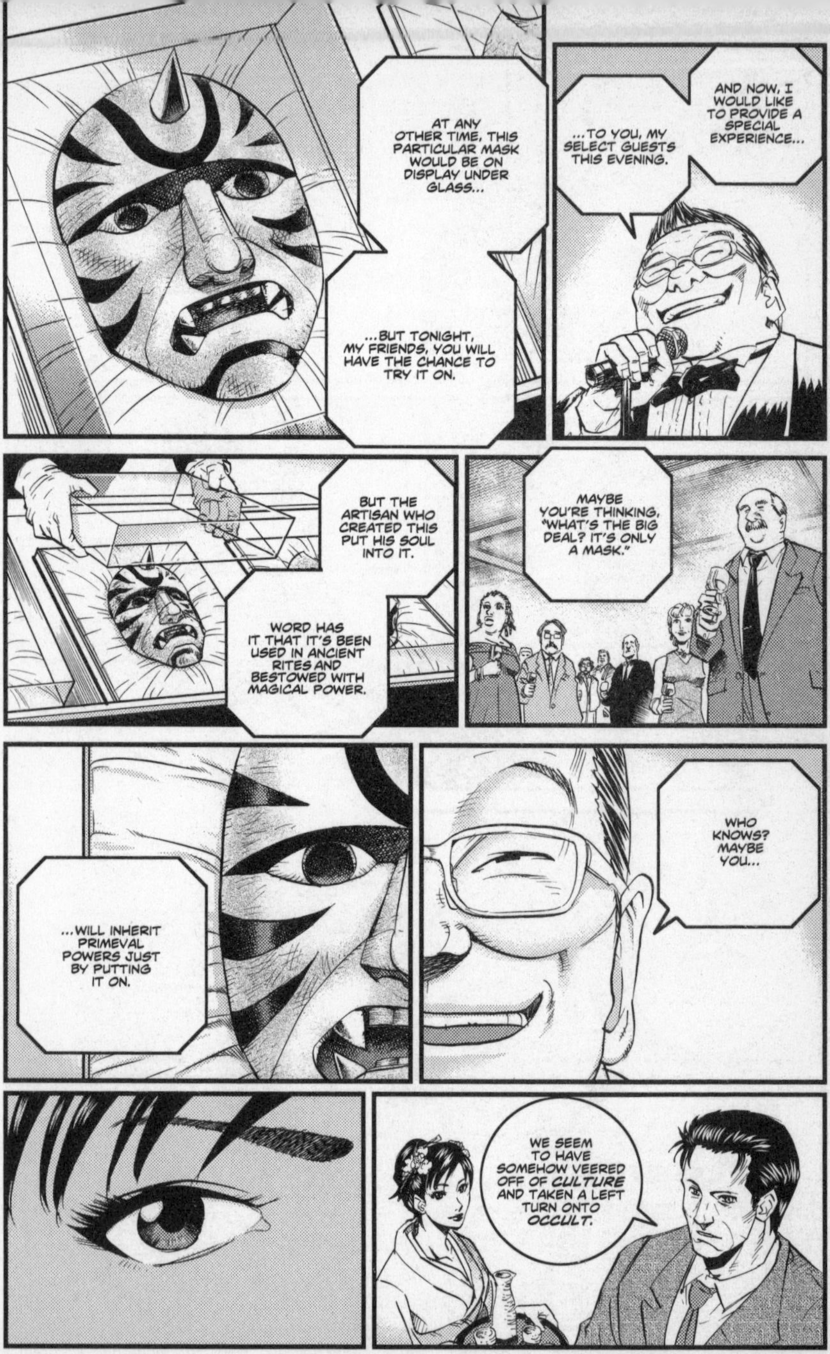
AT ANY OTHER TIME, THIS PARTICULAR MASK WOULD BE ON DISPLAY UNDER GLASS...
...BUT TONIGHT, MY FRIENDS, YOU WILL HAVE THE CHANCE TO TRY IT ON.
AND NOW, I WOULD LIKE TO PROVIDE A SPECIAL EXPERIENCE...
...TO YOU, MY SELECT GUESTS THIS EVENING.
BUT THE ARTISAN WHO CREATED THIS PUT HIS SOUL INTO IT.
WORD HAS IT THAT IT'S BEEN USED IN ANCIENT RITES AND BESTOWED WITH MAGICAL POWER.
MAYBE YOU'RE THINKING, "WHAT'S THE BIG DEAL? IT'S ONLY A MASK."
WHO KNOWS? MAYBE YOU...
...WILL INHERIT PRIMEVAL POWERS JUST BY PUTTING IT ON.
WE SEEM TO HAVE SOMEHOW VEERED OFF OF *CULTURE* AND TAKEN A LEFT TURN ONTO *OCCULT*.

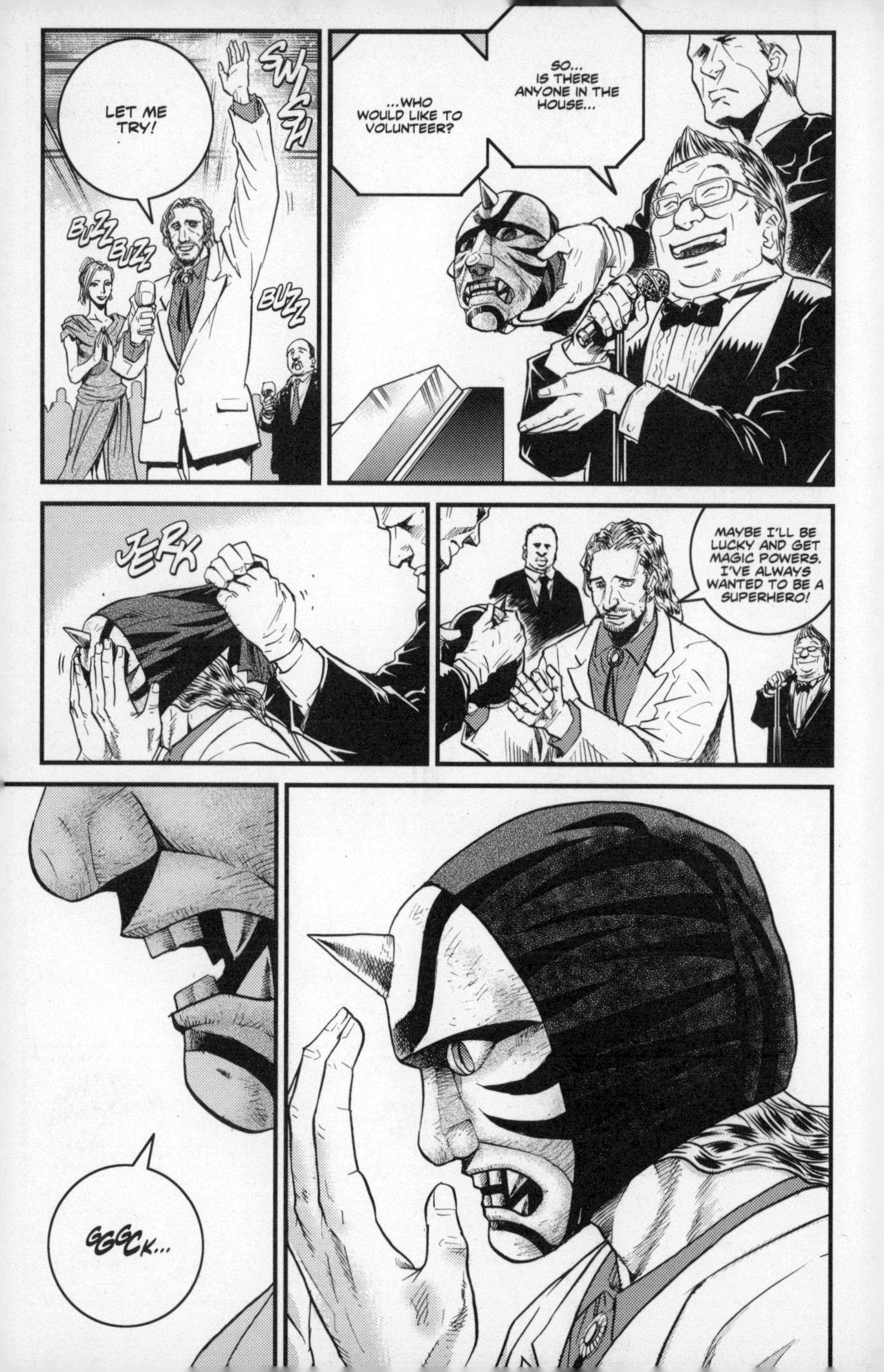
LET ME TRY!
SWISH
BUZZ BUZZ
BUZZ
SO... IS THERE ANYONE IN THE HOUSE...
...WHO WOULD LIKE TO VOLUNTEER?
JERK
MAYBE I'LL BE LUCKY AND GET MAGIC POWERS. I'VE ALWAYS WANTED TO BE A SUPERHERO!
GGGCK...

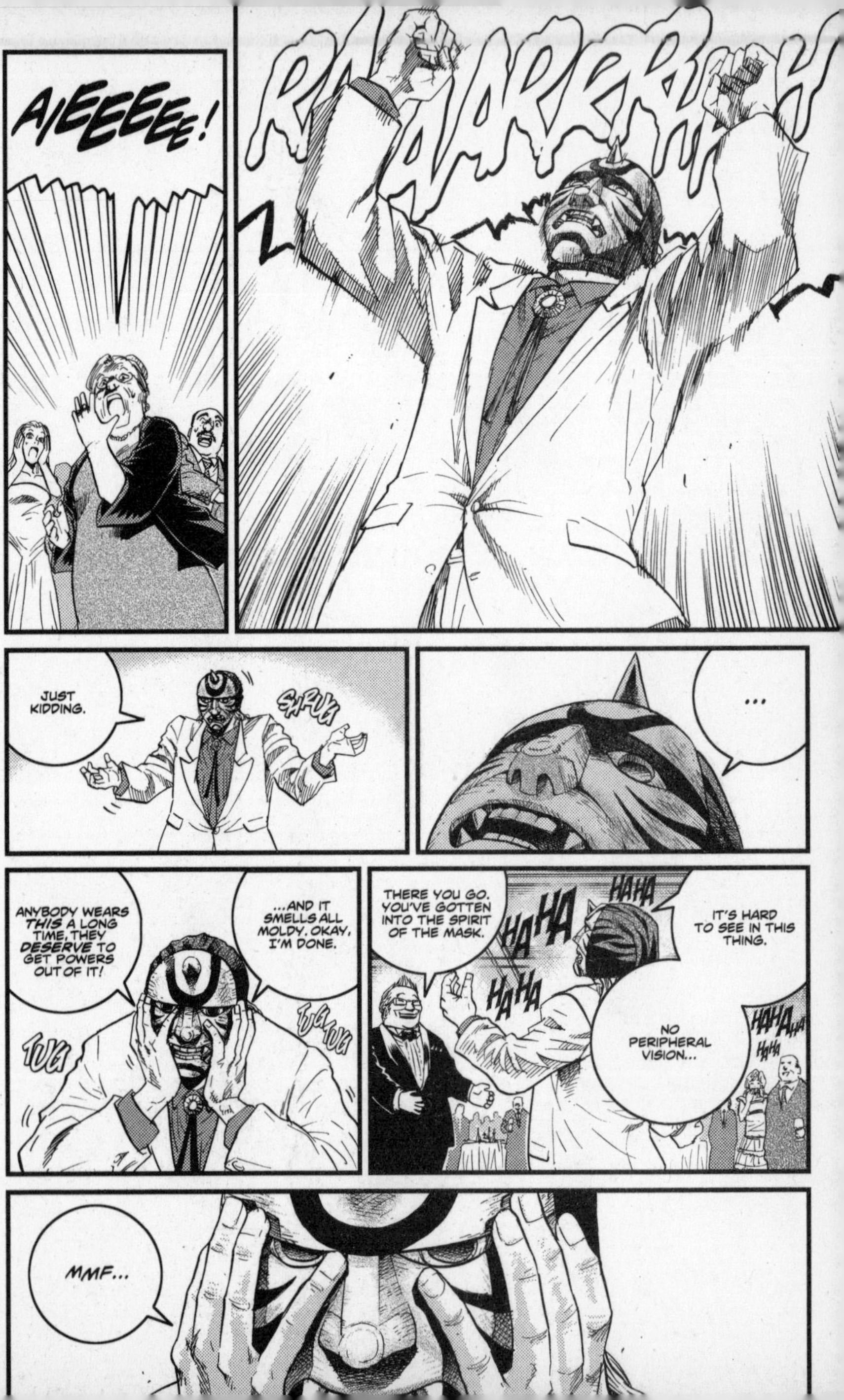
AIEEEEEE!
RAAARRRGH
JUST KIDDING.
SHRUG
...
ANYBODY WEARS THIS A LONG TIME, THEY DESERVE TO GET POWERS OUT OF IT!
...AND IT SMELLS ALL MOLDY. OKAY, I'M DONE.
TUG
TUG TUG
THERE YOU GO. YOU'VE GOTTEN INTO THE SPIRIT OF THE MASK.
HAHA
HAHA
HAHA
IT'S HARD TO SEE IN THIS THING.
NO PERIPHERAL VISION...
HAHAHA
HAHA
MMF...

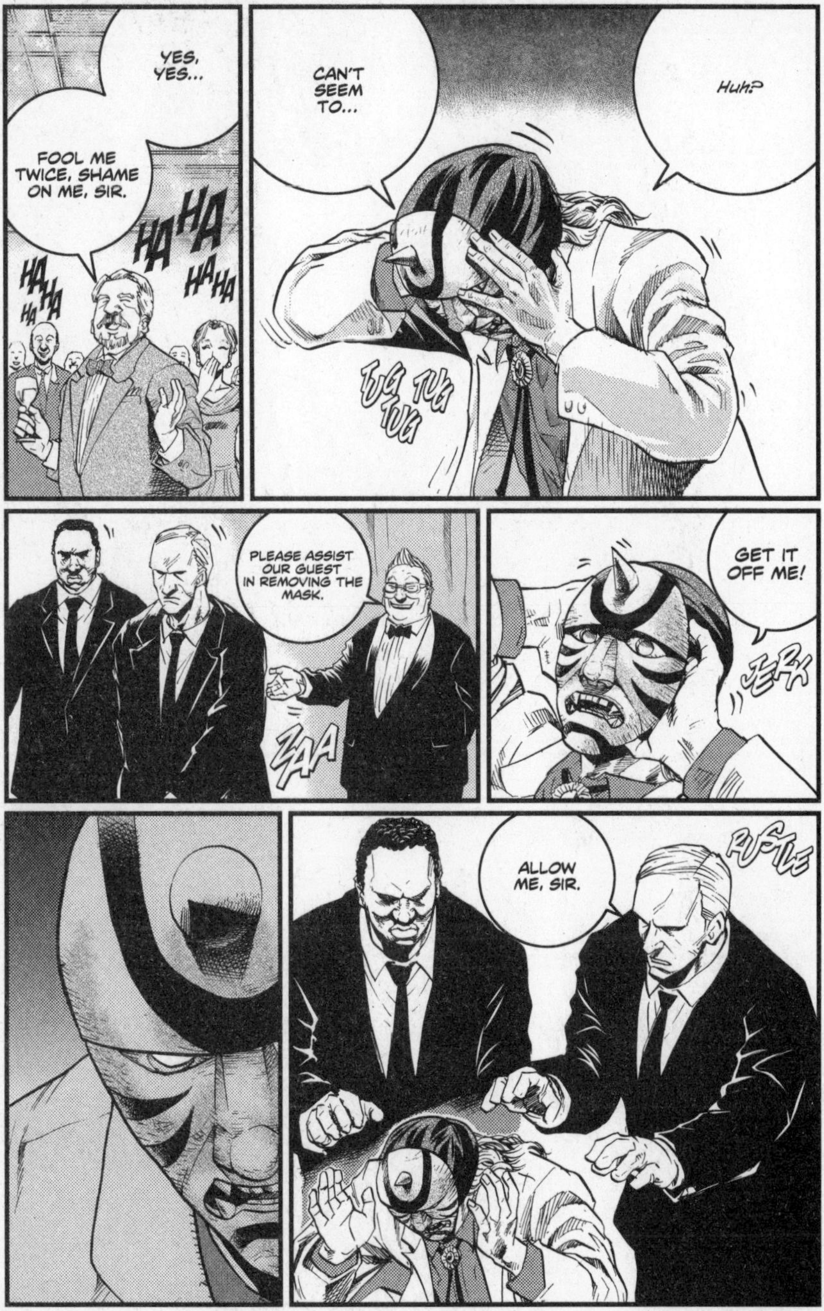
YES, YES...
FOOL ME TWICE, SHAME ON ME, SIR.
HA HA HA HA
HA HA HA HA
CAN'T SEEM TO...
Huh?
TUG TUG TUG
PLEASE ASSIST OUR GUEST IN REMOVING THE MASK.
ZAA
GET IT OFF ME!
JERK
ALLOW ME, SIR.
RUSTLE

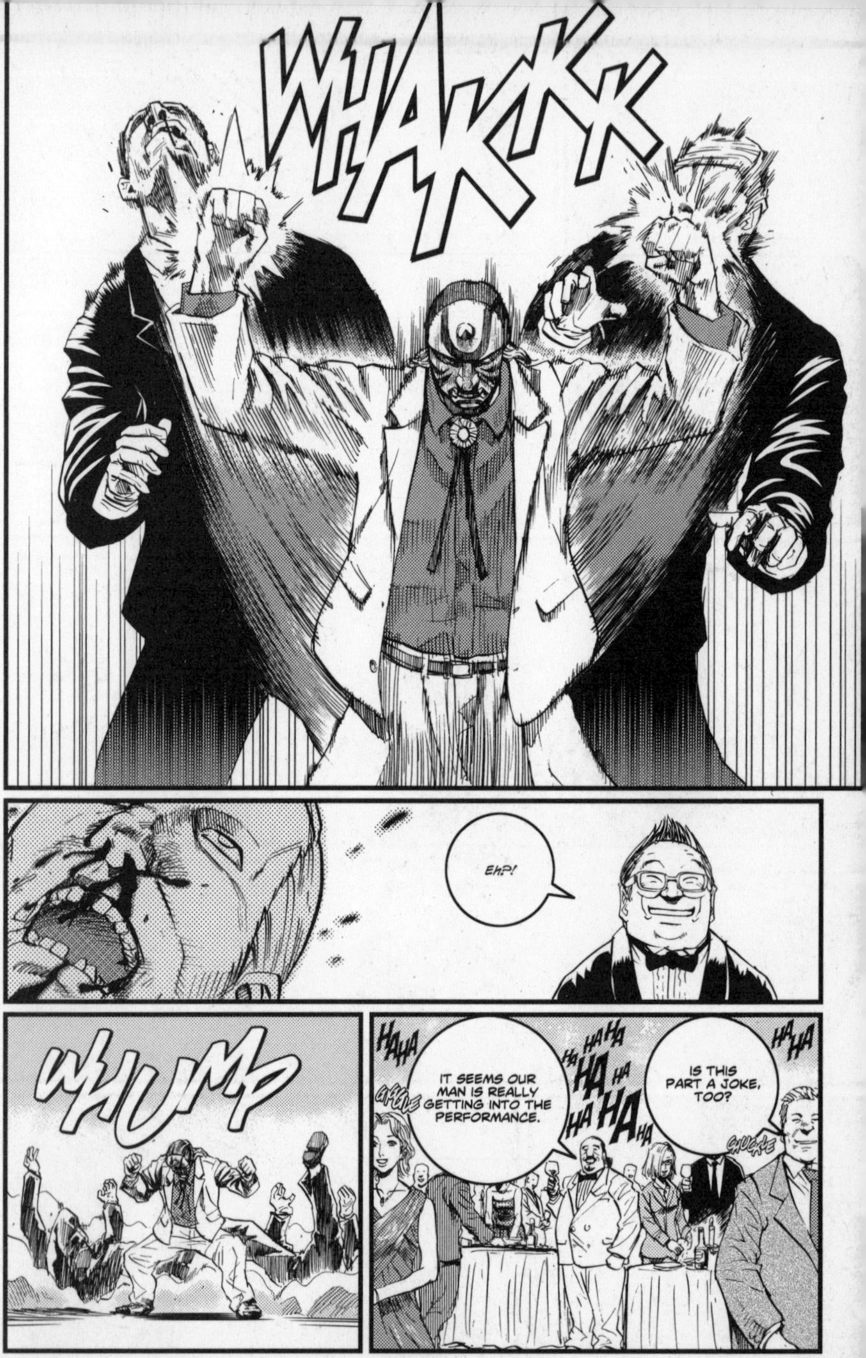
WHAKK
Eh?!
WHUMP
HAHA
GIGGLE
IT SEEMS OUR MAN IS REALLY GETTING INTO THE PERFORMANCE.
HA HA HA HA HA HA HA HA HA
IS THIS PART A JOKE, TOO?
CHUCKLE
HA HA

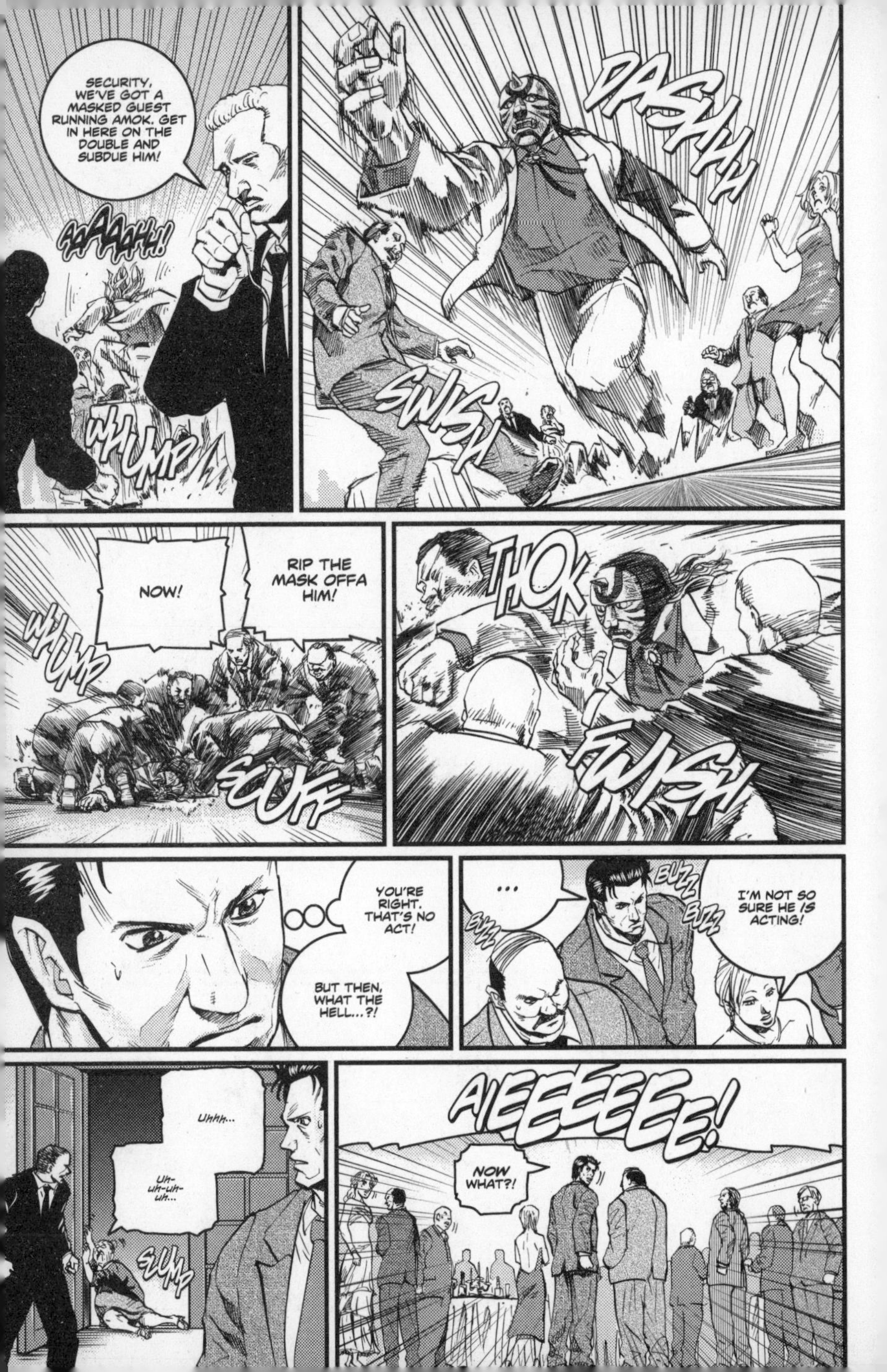
SECURITY, WE'VE GOT A MASKED GUEST RUNNING AMOK. GET IN HERE ON THE DOUBLE AND SUBDUE HIM!
AAAAAHH!
WHUMP
DASHHH
SWISH
NOW!
RIP THE MASK OFFA HIM!
WHUMP
SCUFF
THOK
FWISH
YOU'RE RIGHT. THAT'S NO ACT!
BUT THEN, WHAT THE HELL...?!
...
BUZZ BUZZ
I'M NOT SO SURE HE IS ACTING!
Uhhh...
Uh-uh-uh-uh...
SLUMP
AIEEEEEEE!
NOW WHAT?!

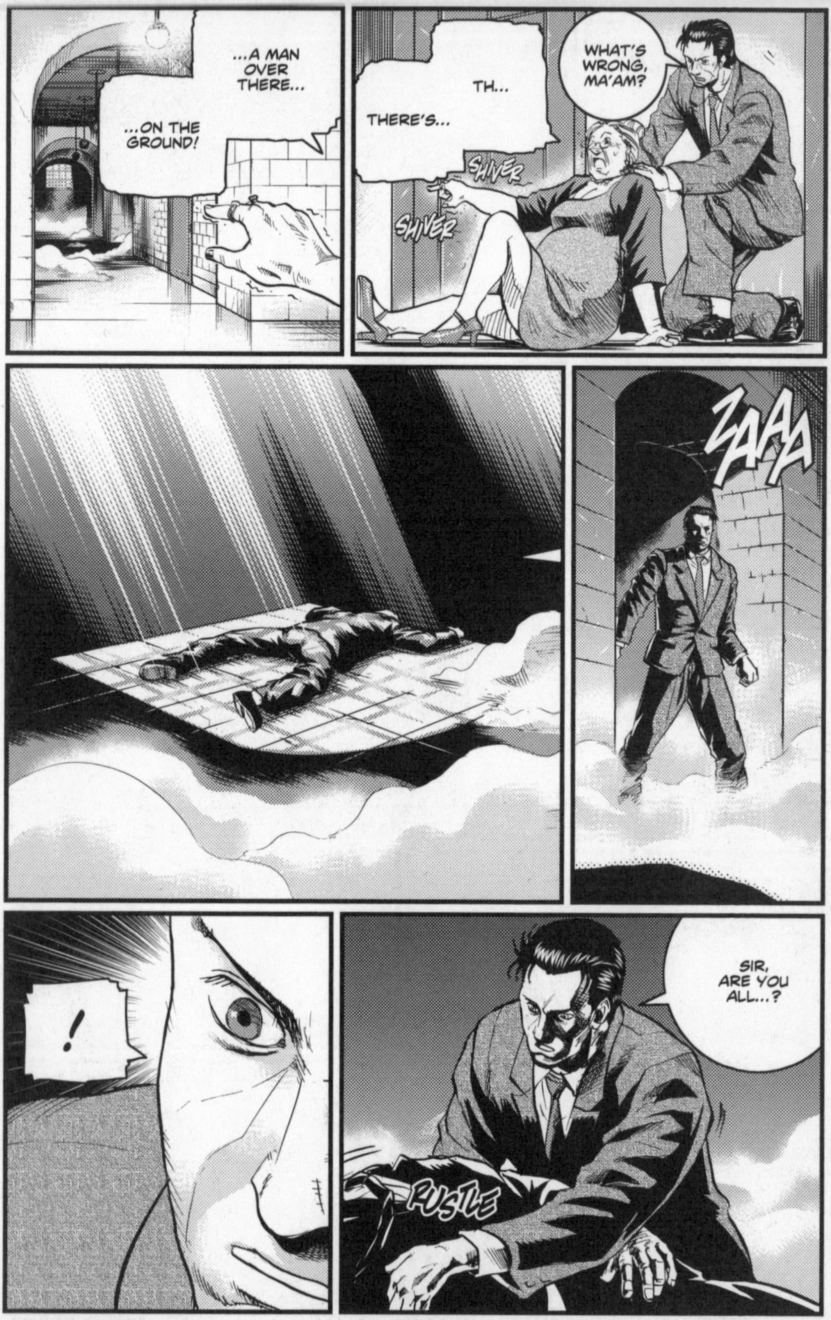
...A MAN OVER THERE...
...ON THE GROUND!
TH...
THERE'S...
WHAT'S WRONG, MA'AM?
SHIVER
SHIVER
ZAAAA
!
SIR, ARE YOU ALL...?
RUSTLE

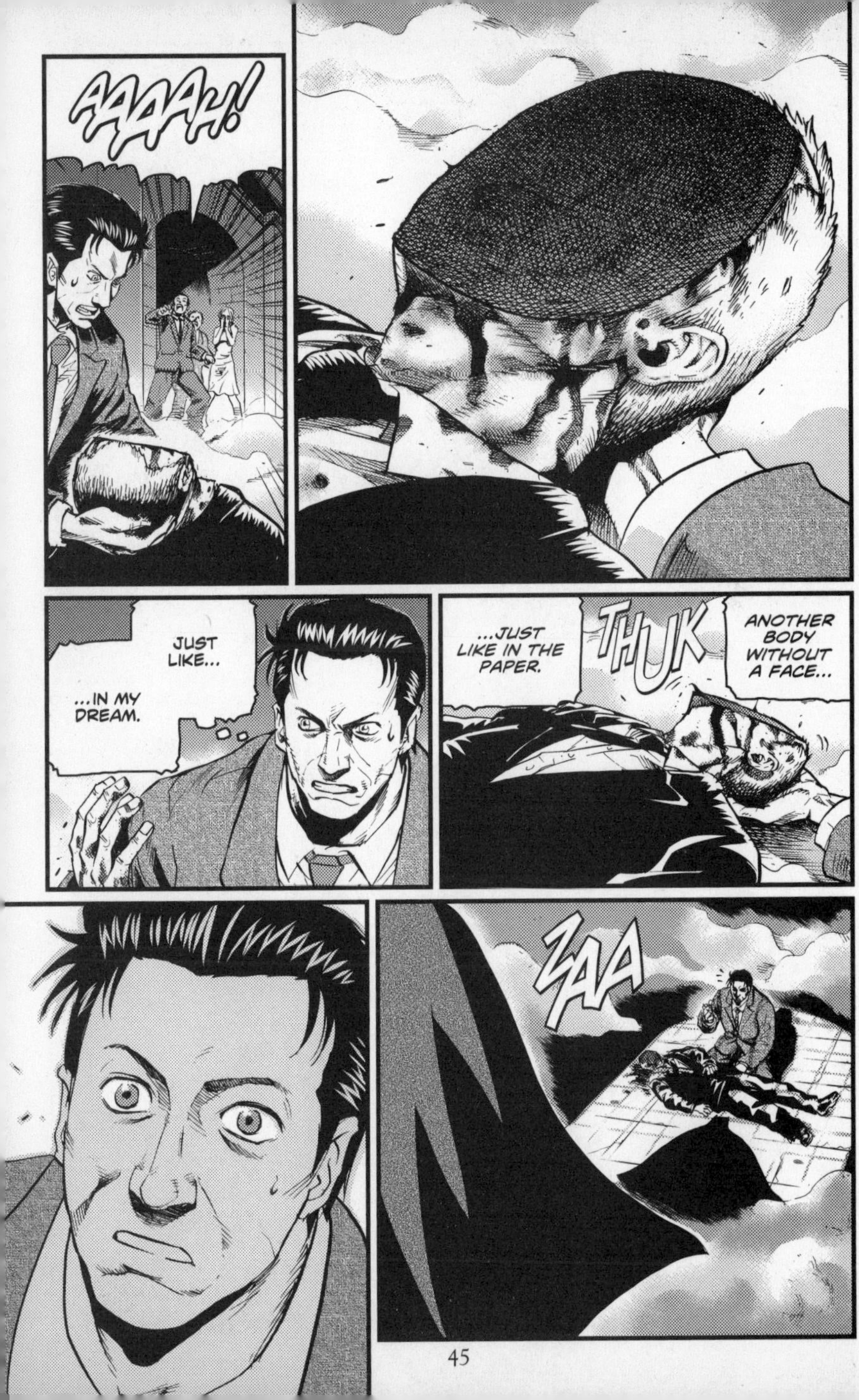
AAAAH!
JUST LIKE...
...IN MY DREAM.
...JUST LIKE IN THE PAPER.
THUK
ANOTHER BODY WITHOUT A FACE...
ZAA

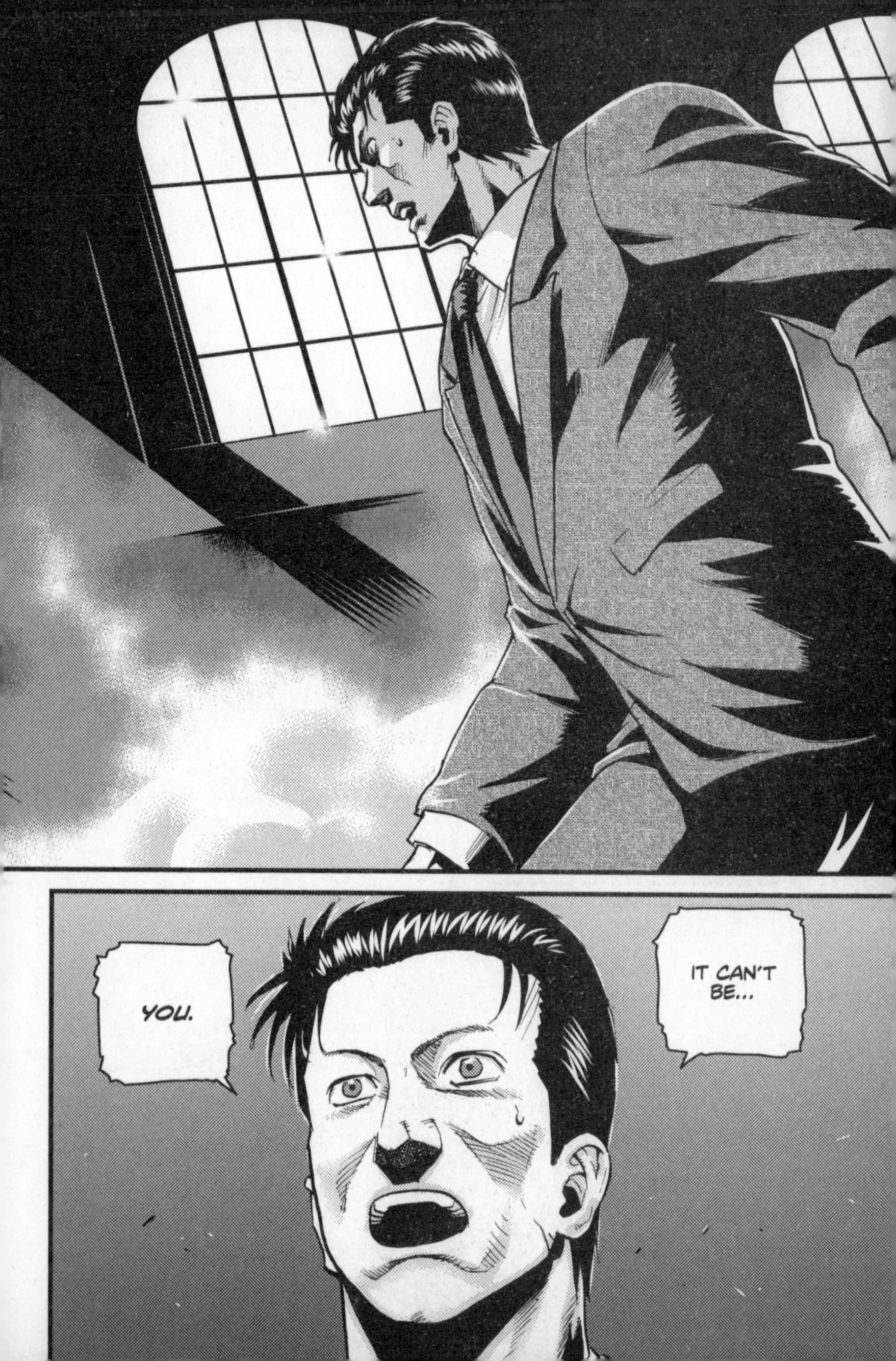
YOU.
IT CAN'T BE...

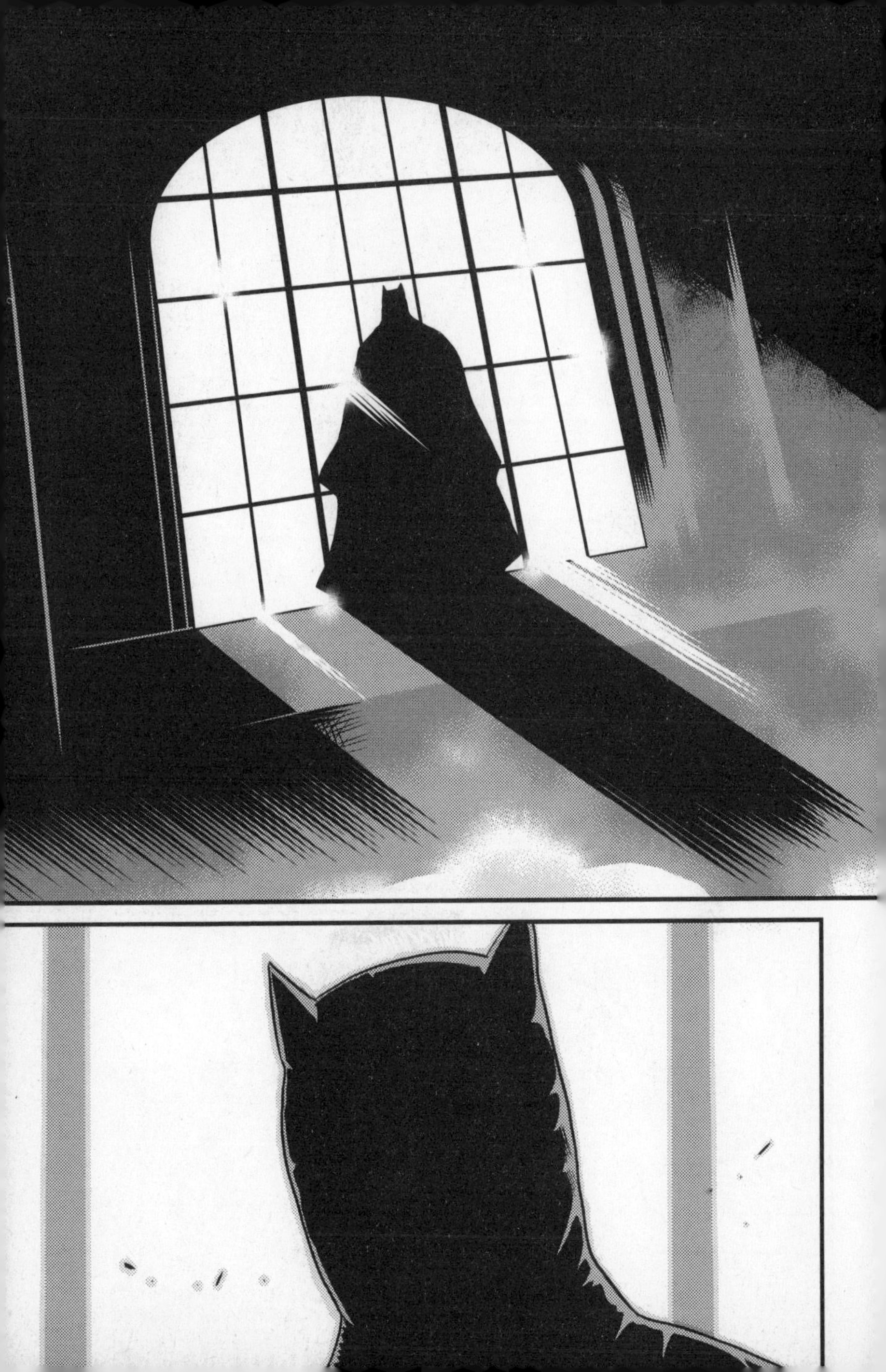

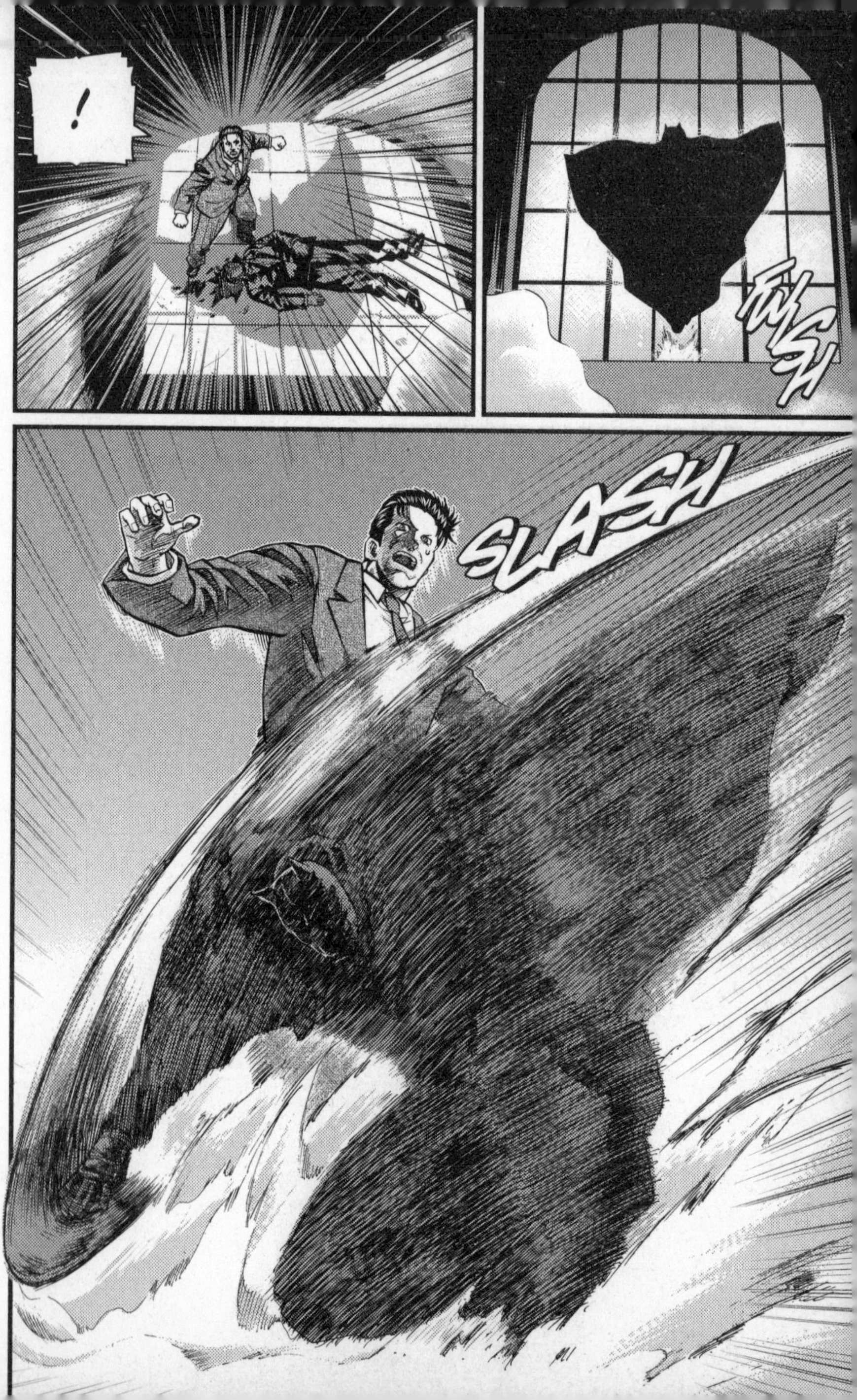
!
FWISH
SLASH

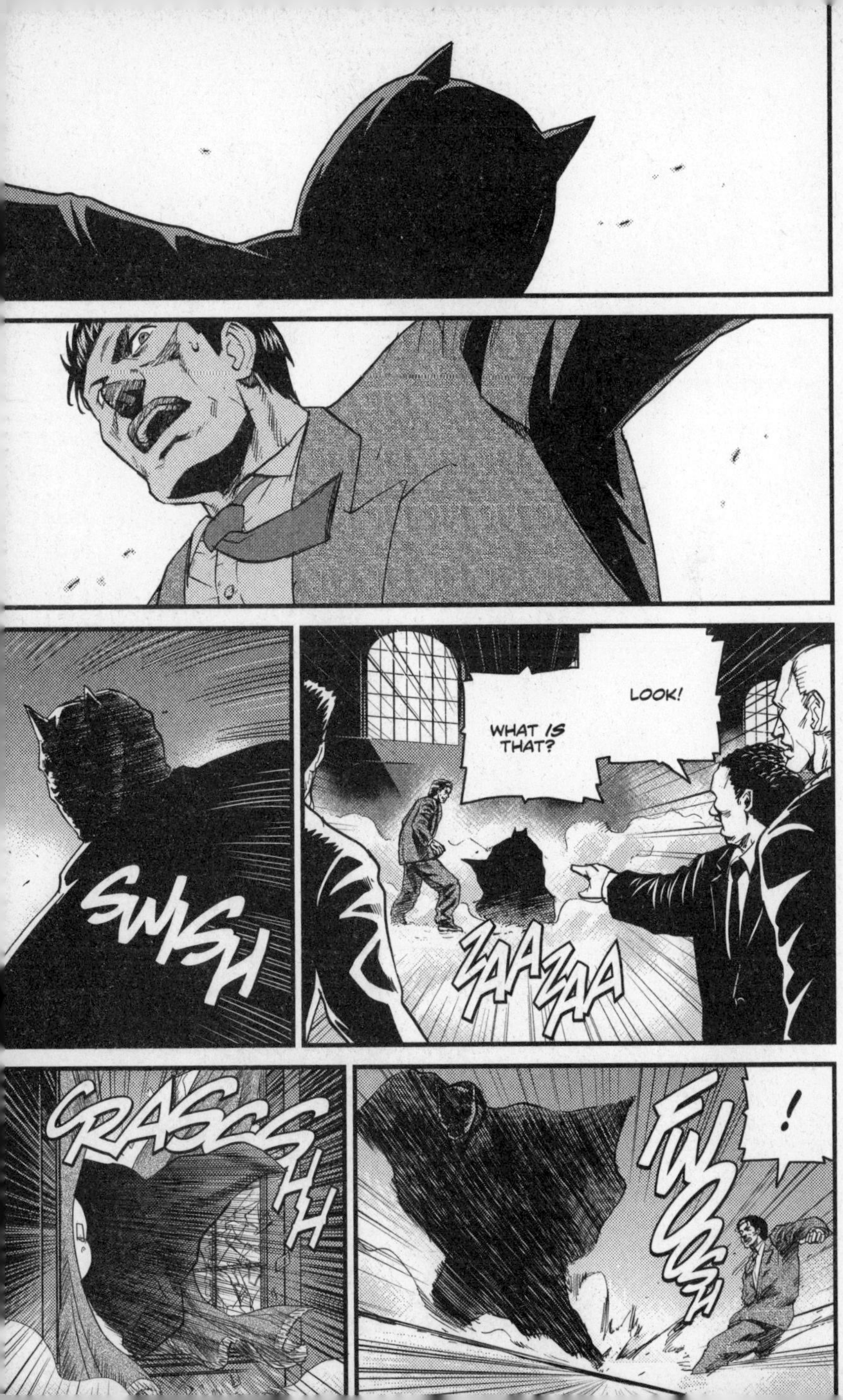
SWISH
LOOK!
WHAT IS THAT?
ZAAZAA
CRASCSHH
FWOOSH
!

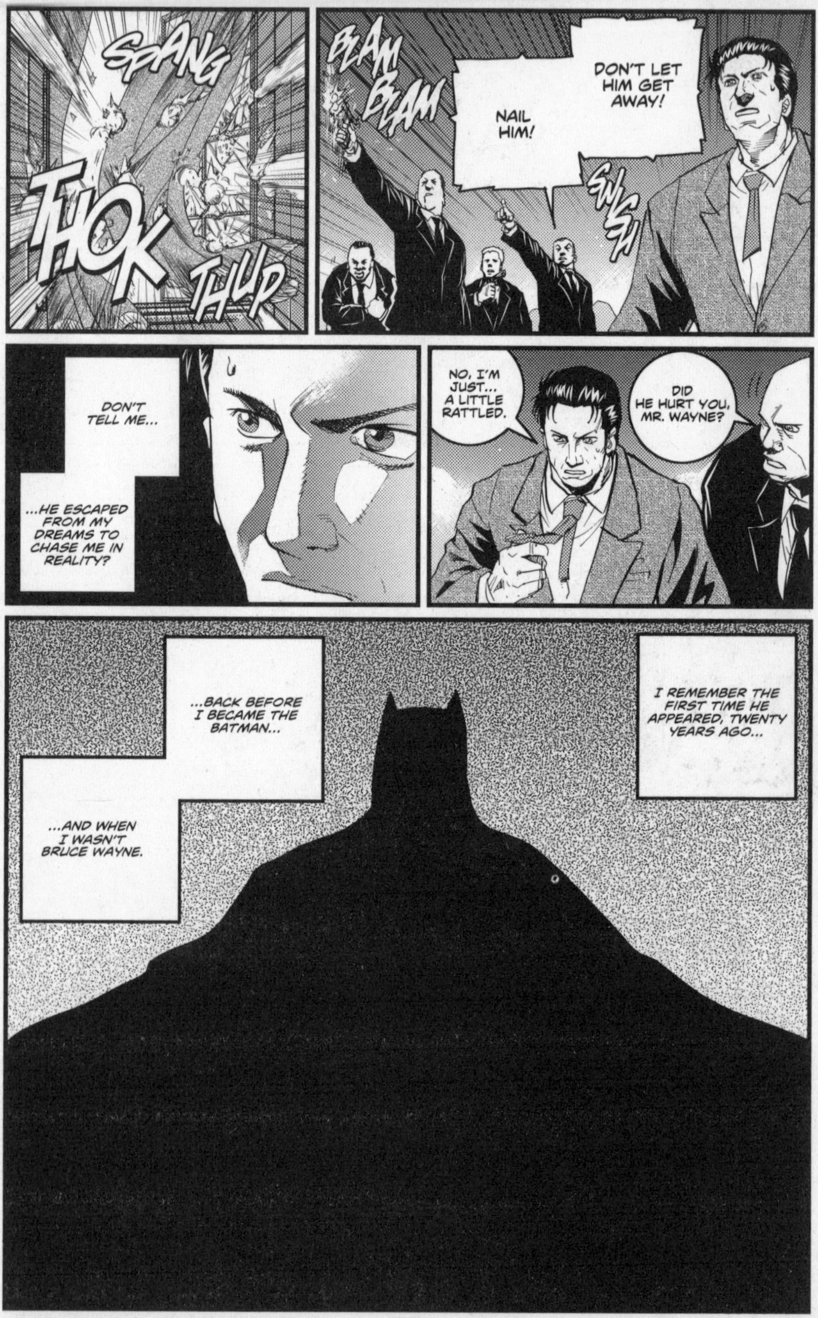
SPANG
THOK
THUD
BLAM
BLAM
DON'T LET HIM GET AWAY!
NAIL HIM!
SWISH
DON'T TELL ME...
...HE ESCAPED FROM MY DREAMS TO CHASE ME IN REALITY?
DID HE HURT YOU, MR. WAYNE?
NO, I'M JUST... A LITTLE RATTLED.
I REMEMBER THE FIRST TIME HE APPEARED, TWENTY YEARS AGO...
...BACK BEFORE I BECAME THE BATMAN...
...AND WHEN I WASN'T BRUCE WAYNE.

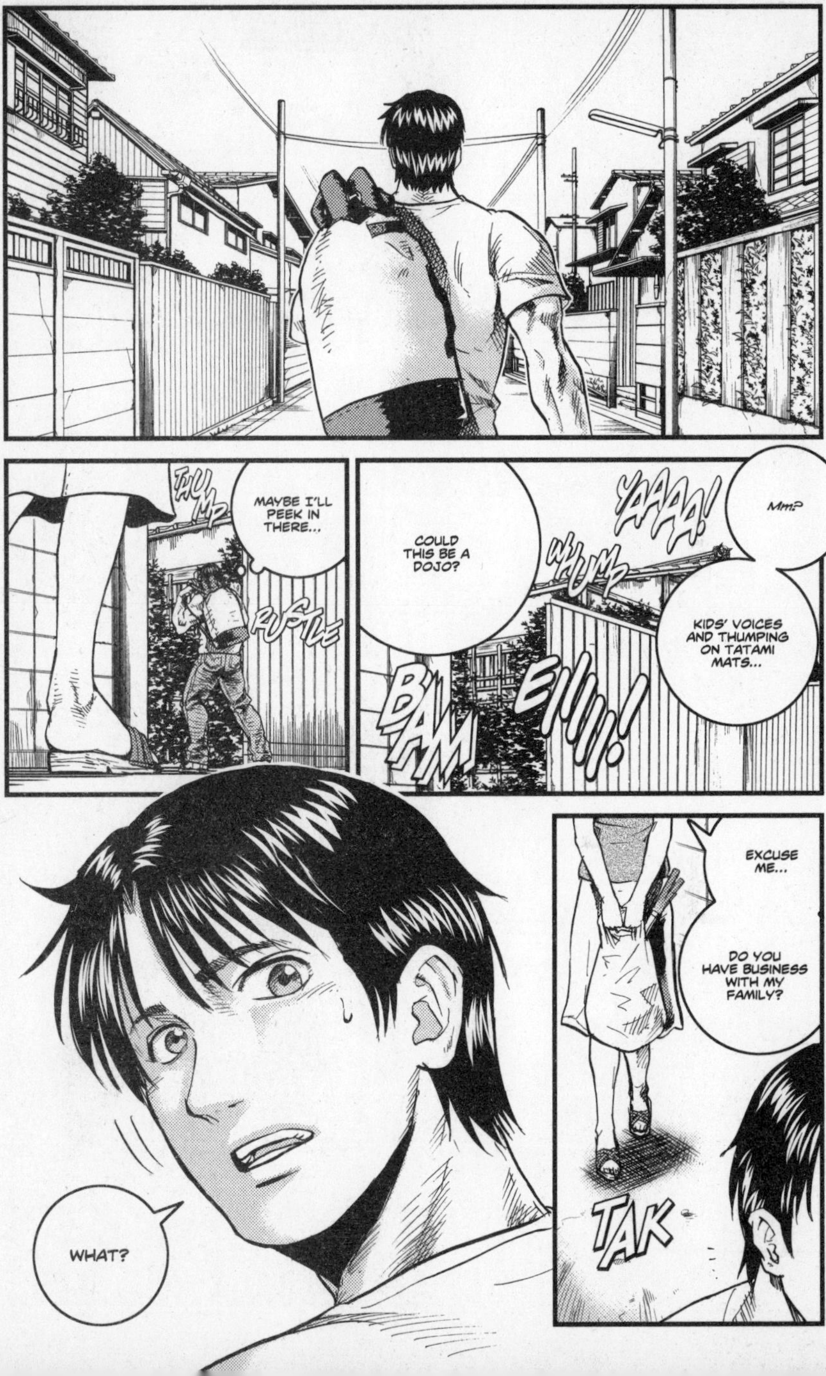
THUMP
MAYBE I'LL PEEK IN THERE...
RUSTLE
COULD THIS BE A DOJO?
YAAAA!
WHUMP
Mm?
KIDS' VOICES AND THUMPING ON TATAMI MATS...
BAM
EI!!!!!!
EXCUSE ME...
DO YOU HAVE BUSINESS WITH MY FAMILY?
TAK
WHAT?

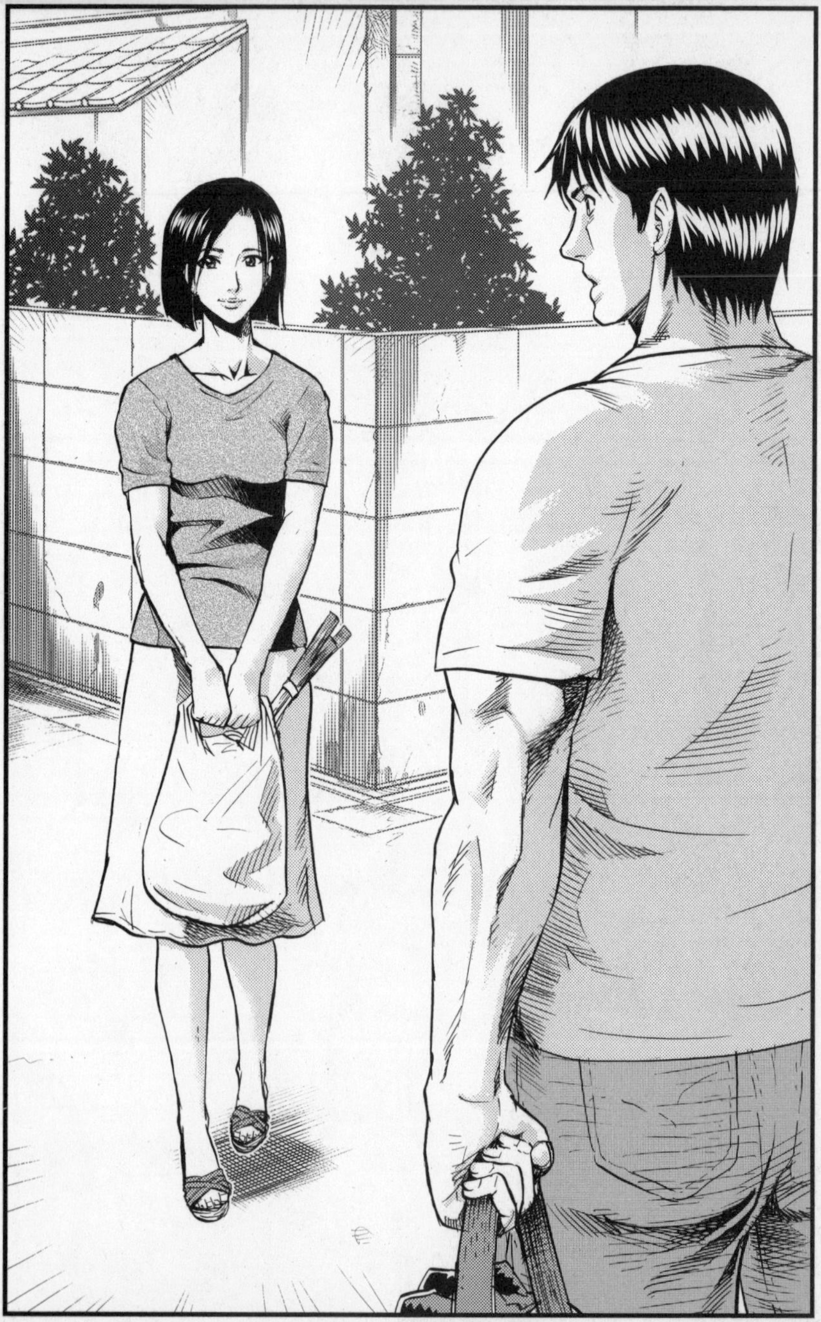

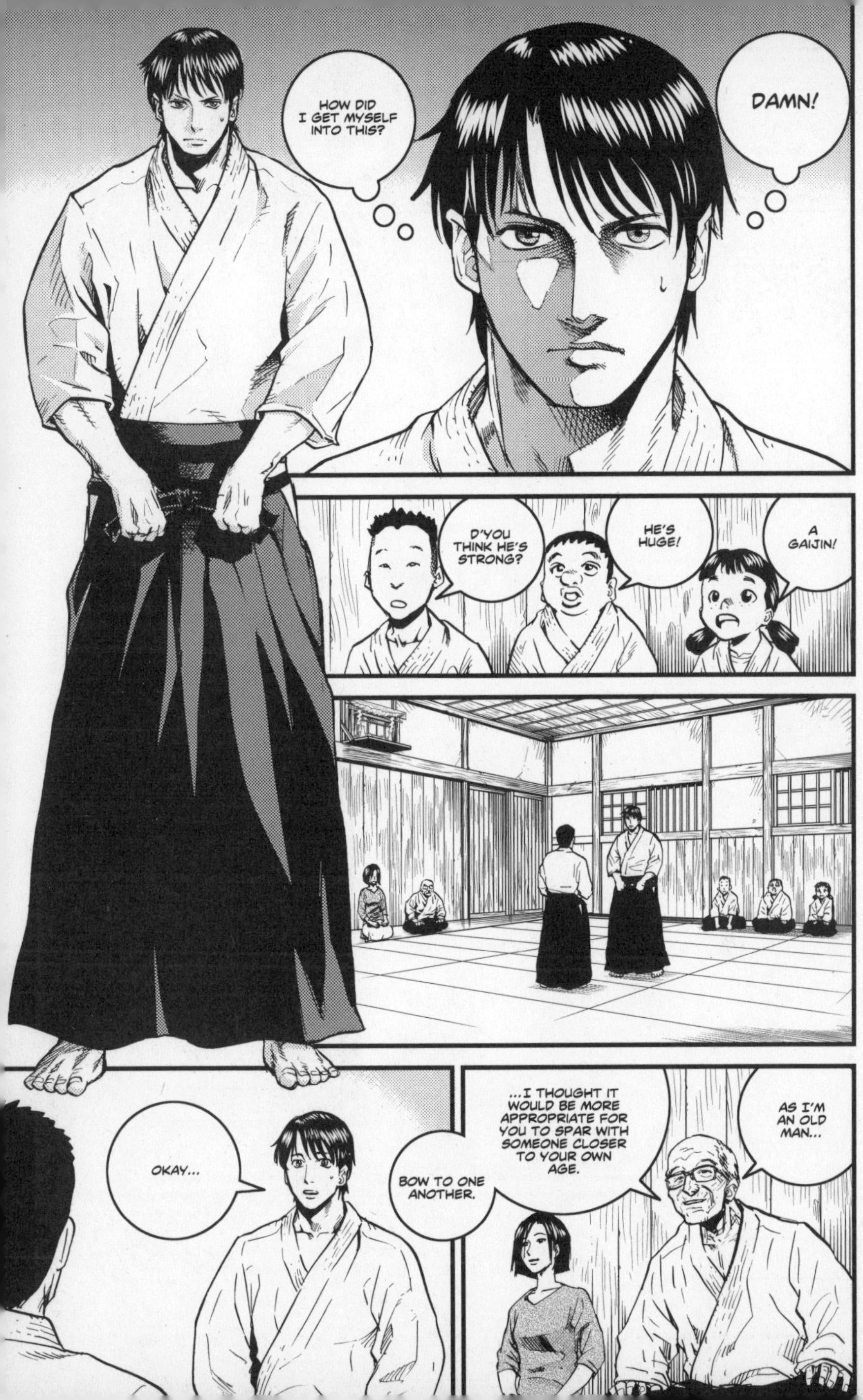
DAMN!
HOW DID I GET MYSELF INTO THIS?
A GAIJIN!
HE'S HUGE!
D'YOU THINK HE'S STRONG?
AS I'M AN OLD MAN...
...I THOUGHT IT WOULD BE MORE APPROPRIATE FOR YOU TO SPAR WITH SOMEONE CLOSER TO YOUR OWN AGE.
BOW TO ONE ANOTHER.
OKAY...

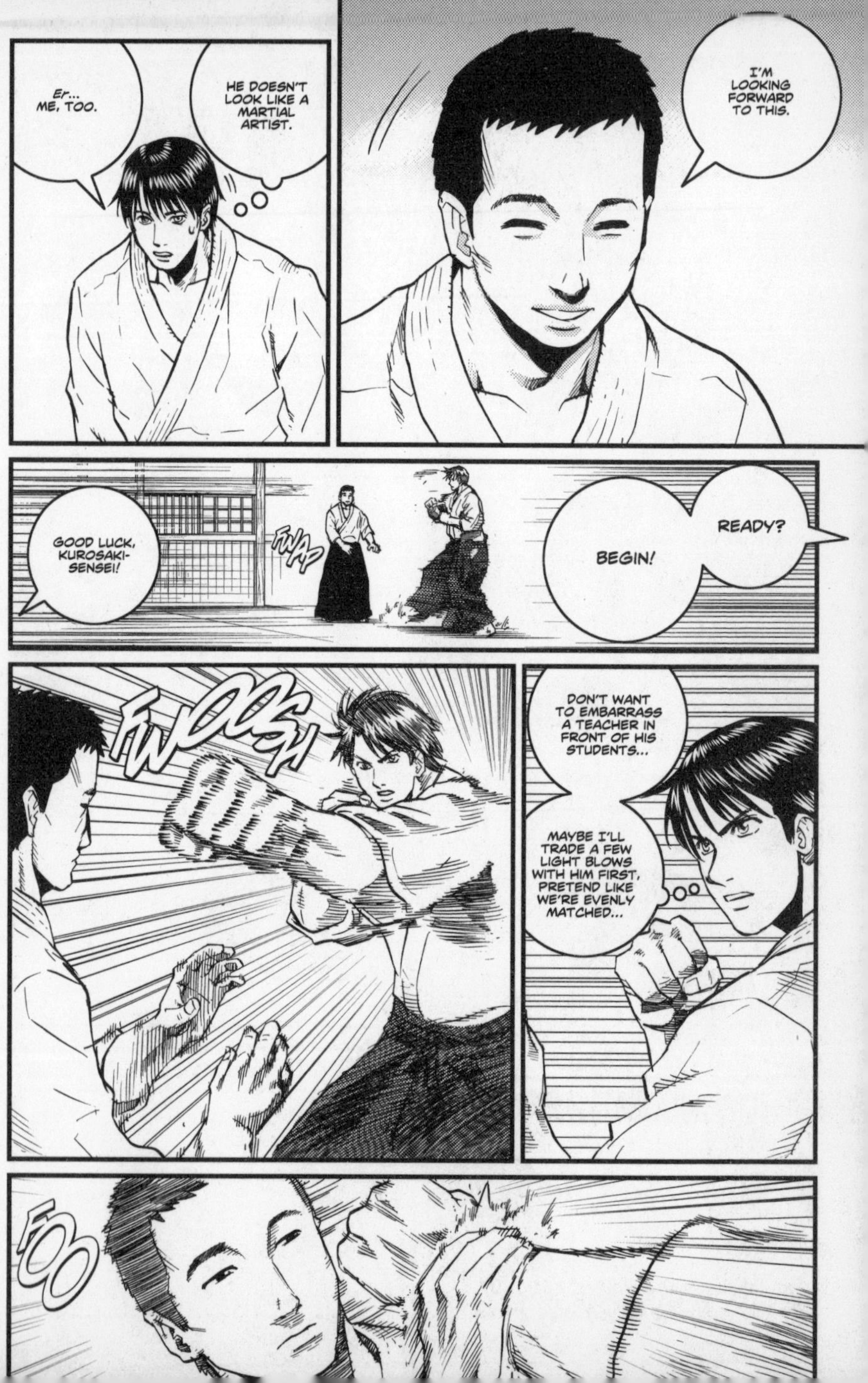
I'M LOOKING FORWARD TO THIS.
HE DOESN'T LOOK LIKE A MARTIAL ARTIST.
Er... ME, TOO.
READY?
BEGIN!
FWAP
GOOD LUCK, KUROSAKI-SENSEI!
DON'T WANT TO EMBARRASS A TEACHER IN FRONT OF HIS STUDENTS...
MAYBE I'LL TRADE A FEW LIGHT BLOWS WITH HIM FIRST, PRETEND LIKE WE'RE EVENLY MATCHED...
FWOOSH
FOO

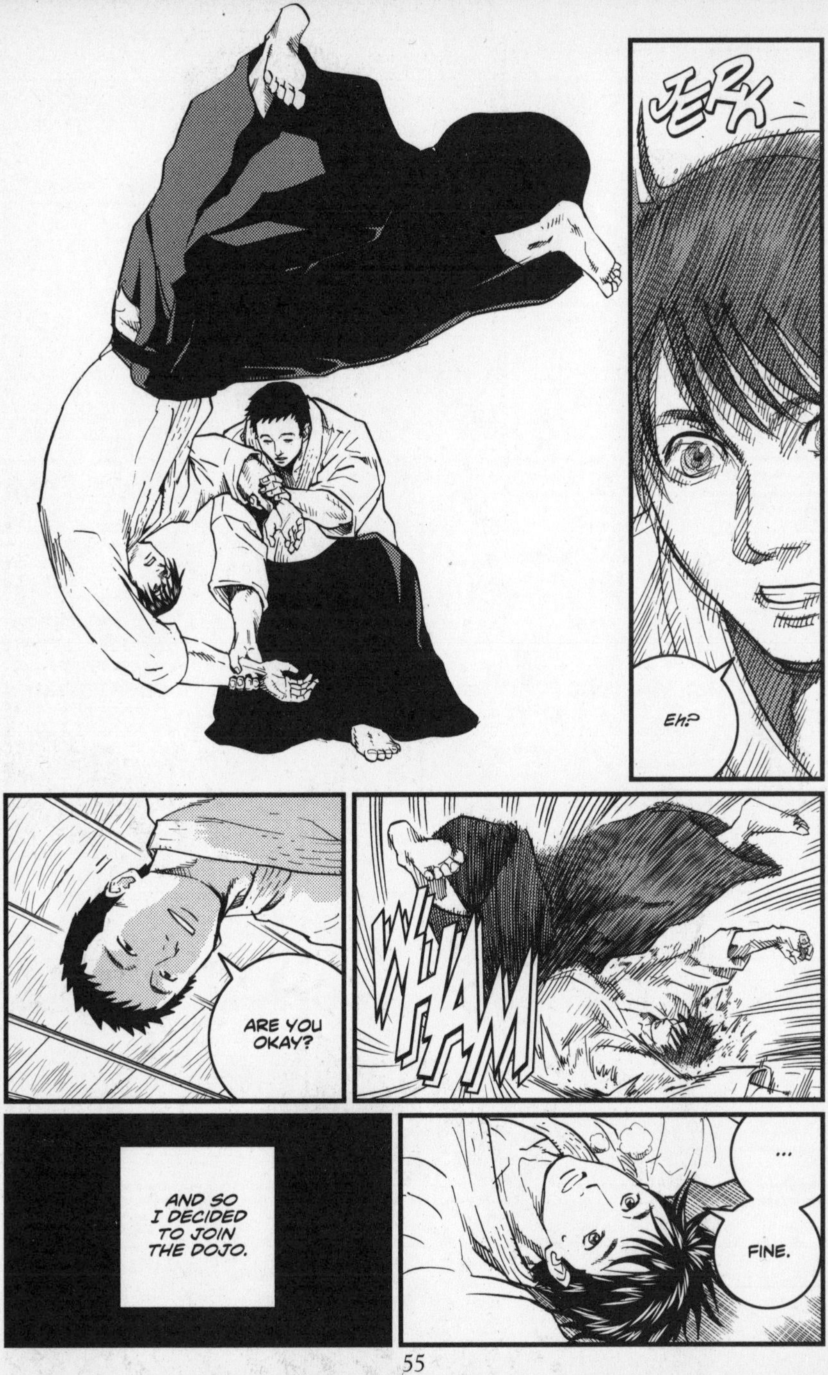
JERK
Eh?
WHAM
ARE YOU OKAY?
...
FINE.
AND SO I DECIDED TO JOIN THE DOJO.

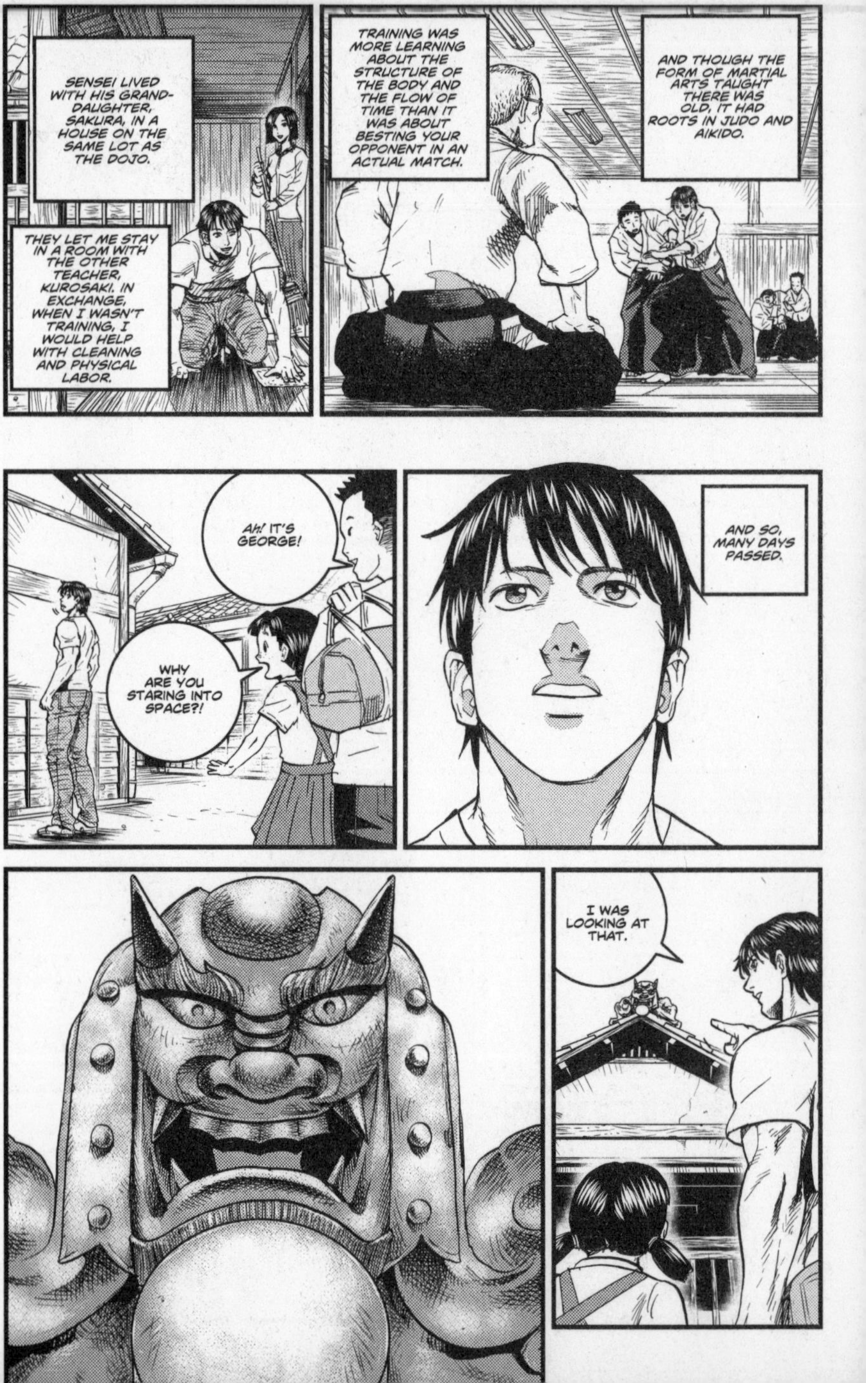
SENSEI LIVED WITH HIS GRAND-DAUGHTER, SAKURA, IN A HOUSE ON THE SAME LOT AS THE DOJO.
THEY LET ME STAY IN A ROOM WITH THE OTHER TEACHER, KUROSAKI. IN EXCHANGE, WHEN I WASN'T TRAINING, I WOULD HELP WITH CLEANING AND PHYSICAL LABOR.
TRAINING WAS MORE LEARNING ABOUT THE STRUCTURE OF THE BODY AND THE FLOW OF TIME THAN IT WAS ABOUT BESTING YOUR OPPONENT IN AN ACTUAL MATCH.
AND THOUGH THE FORM OF MARTIAL ARTS TAUGHT THERE WAS OLD, IT HAD ROOTS IN JUDO AND AIKIDO.
AH! IT'S GEORGE!
WHY ARE YOU STARING INTO SPACE?!
AND SO, MANY DAYS PASSED.
I WAS LOOKING AT THAT.

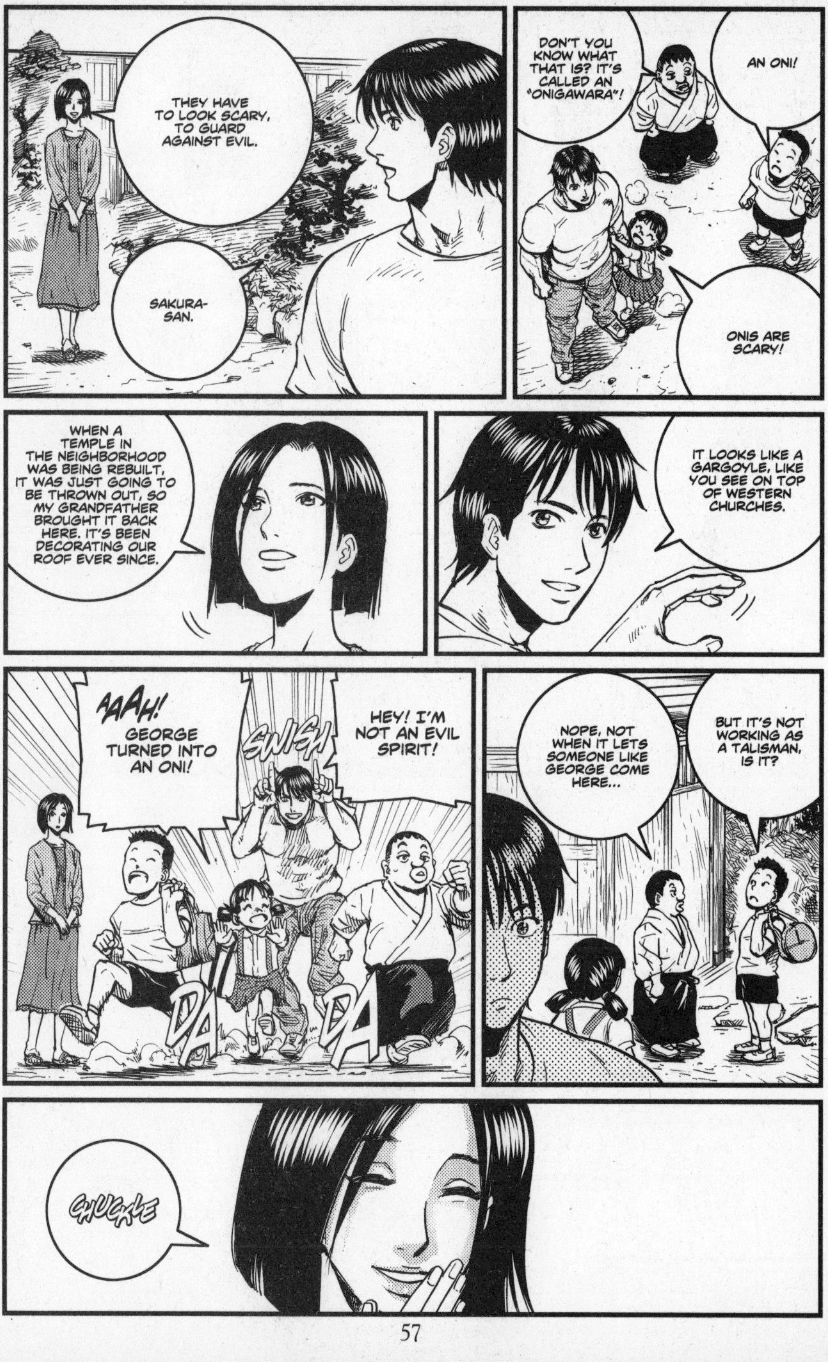

THEY HAVE TO LOOK SCARY, TO GUARD AGAINST EVIL.
SAKURA-SAN.
DON'T YOU KNOW WHAT THAT IS? IT'S CALLED AN "ONIGAWARA"!
AN ONI!
ONIS ARE SCARY!
WHEN A TEMPLE IN THE NEIGHBORHOOD WAS BEING REBUILT, IT WAS JUST GOING TO BE THROWN OUT, SO MY GRANDFATHER BROUGHT IT BACK HERE. IT'S BEEN DECORATING OUR ROOF EVER SINCE.
IT LOOKS LIKE A GARGOYLE, LIKE YOU SEE ON TOP OF WESTERN CHURCHES.
AAAH! GEORGE TURNED INTO AN ONI!
SWISH
HEY! I'M NOT AN EVIL SPIRIT!
DA
DA
BUT IT'S NOT WORKING AS A TALISMAN, IS IT?
NOPE, NOT WHEN IT LETS SOMEONE LIKE GEORGE COME HERE...
CHUCKLE

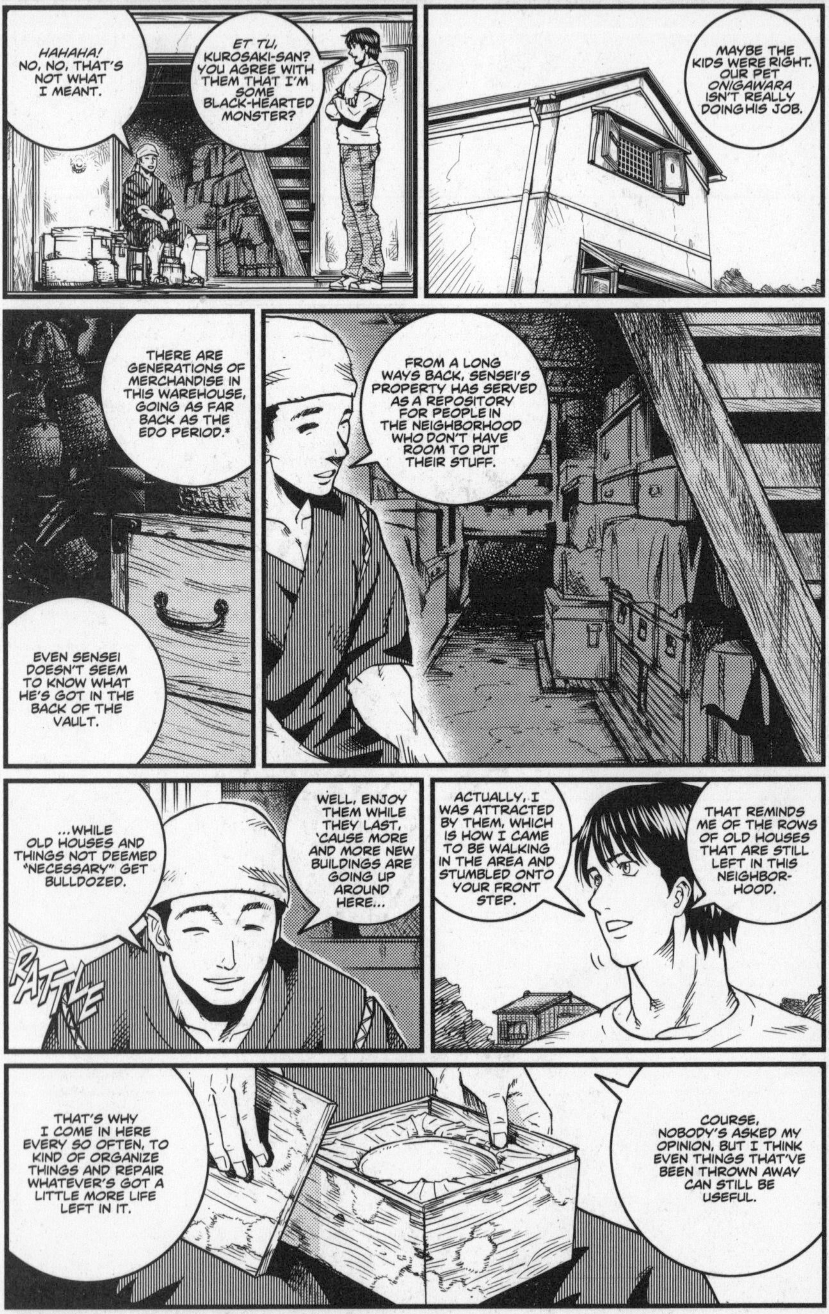
ET TU, KUROSAKI-SAN? YOU AGREE WITH THEM THAT I'M SOME BLACK-HEARTED MONSTER?
HAHAHA! NO, NO, THAT'S NOT WHAT I MEANT.
MAYBE THE KIDS WERE RIGHT. OUR PET ONIGAWARA ISN'T REALLY DOING HIS JOB.
FROM A LONG WAYS BACK, SENSEI'S PROPERTY HAS SERVED AS A REPOSITORY FOR PEOPLE IN THE NEIGHBORHOOD WHO DON'T HAVE ROOM TO PUT THEIR STUFF.
THERE ARE GENERATIONS OF MERCHANDISE IN THIS WAREHOUSE, GOING AS FAR BACK AS THE EDO PERIOD.*
EVEN SENSEI DOESN'T SEEM TO KNOW WHAT HE'S GOT IN THE BACK OF THE VAULT.
WELL, ENJOY THEM WHILE THEY LAST, 'CAUSE MORE AND MORE NEW BUILDINGS ARE GOING UP AROUND HERE...
...WHILE OLD HOUSES AND THINGS NOT DEEMED "NECESSARY" GET BULLDOZED.
RATTLE
THAT REMINDS ME OF THE ROWS OF OLD HOUSES THAT ARE STILL LEFT IN THIS NEIGHBOR-HOOD.
ACTUALLY, I WAS ATTRACTED BY THEM, WHICH IS HOW I CAME TO BE WALKING IN THE AREA AND STUMBLED ONTO YOUR FRONT STEP.
THAT'S WHY I COME IN HERE EVERY SO OFTEN, TO KIND OF ORGANIZE THINGS AND REPAIR WHATEVER'S GOT A LITTLE MORE LIFE LEFT IN IT.
COURSE, NOBODY'S ASKED MY OPINION, BUT I THINK EVEN THINGS THAT'VE BEEN THROWN AWAY CAN STILL BE USEFUL.

*EDO PERIOD - IN JAPANESE HISTORY, LASTING APP. FROM 1603-1867.

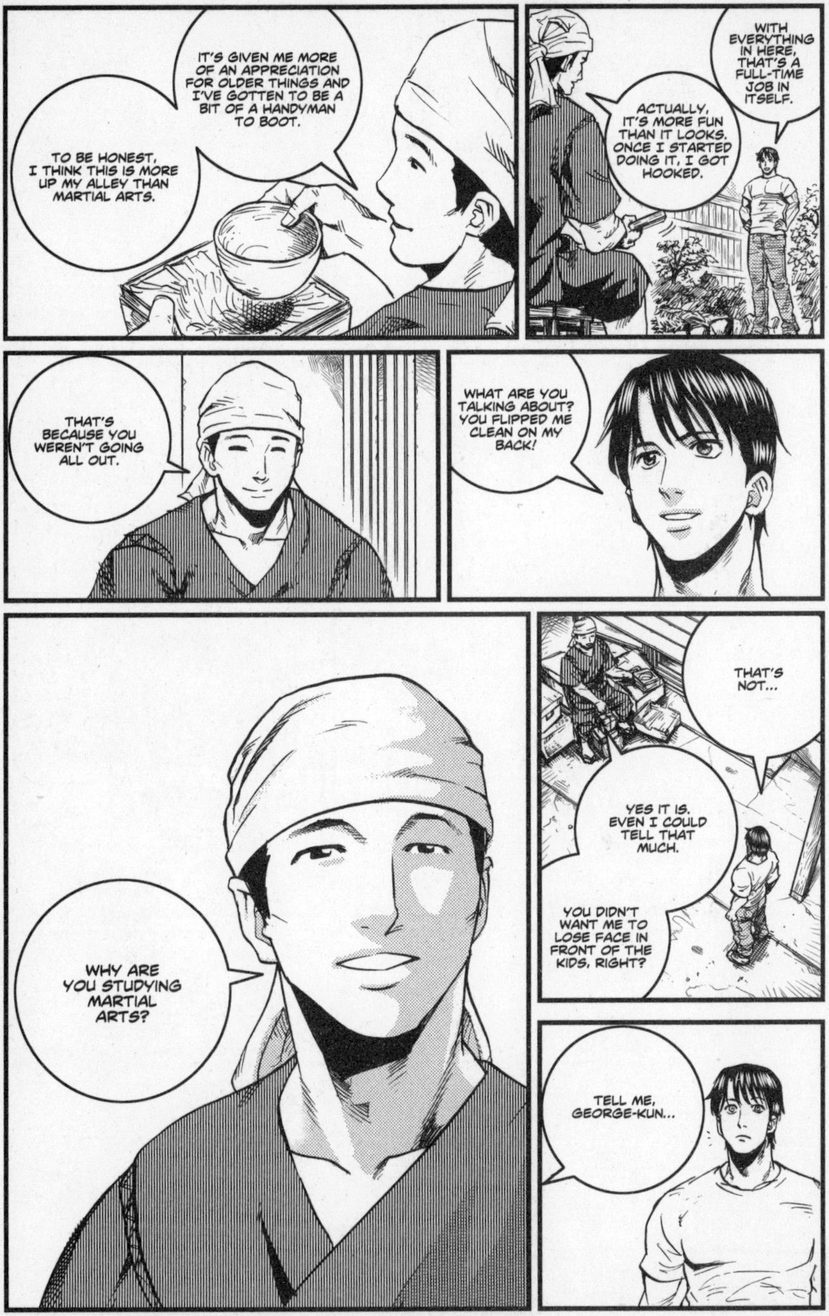
IT'S GIVEN ME MORE OF AN APPRECIATION FOR OLDER THINGS AND I'VE GOTTEN TO BE A BIT OF A HANDYMAN TO BOOT.
TO BE HONEST, I THINK THIS IS MORE UP MY ALLEY THAN MARTIAL ARTS.
WITH EVERYTHING IN HERE, THAT'S A FULL-TIME JOB IN ITSELF.
ACTUALLY, IT'S MORE FUN THAN IT LOOKS. ONCE I STARTED DOING IT, I GOT HOOKED.
THAT'S BECAUSE YOU WEREN'T GOING ALL OUT.
WHAT ARE YOU TALKING ABOUT? YOU FLIPPED ME CLEAN ON MY BACK!
THAT'S NOT...
YES IT IS. EVEN I COULD TELL THAT MUCH.
YOU DIDN'T WANT ME TO LOSE FACE IN FRONT OF THE KIDS, RIGHT?
TELL ME, GEORGE-KUN...
WHY ARE YOU STUDYING MARTIAL ARTS?

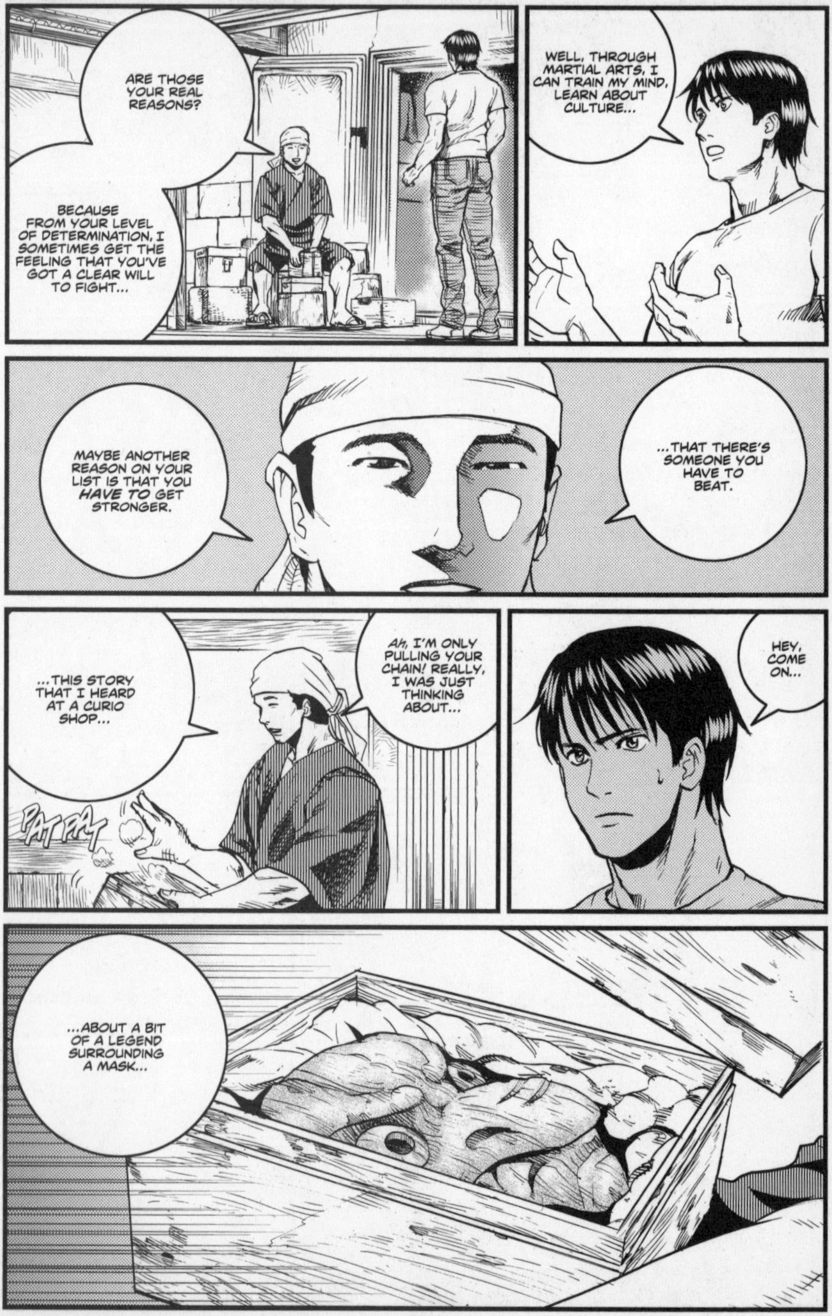

ARE THOSE YOUR REAL REASONS?
BECAUSE FROM YOUR LEVEL OF DETERMINATION, I SOMETIMES GET THE FEELING THAT YOU'VE GOT A CLEAR WILL TO FIGHT...
WELL, THROUGH MARTIAL ARTS, I CAN TRAIN MY MIND, LEARN ABOUT CULTURE...
MAYBE ANOTHER REASON ON YOUR LIST IS THAT YOU *HAVE TO* GET STRONGER.
...THAT THERE'S SOMEONE YOU HAVE TO BEAT.
Ah, I'M ONLY PULLING YOUR CHAIN! REALLY, I WAS JUST THINKING ABOUT...
...THIS STORY THAT I HEARD AT A CURIO SHOP...
PAT PAT
HEY, COME ON...
...ABOUT A BIT OF A LEGEND SURROUNDING A MASK...

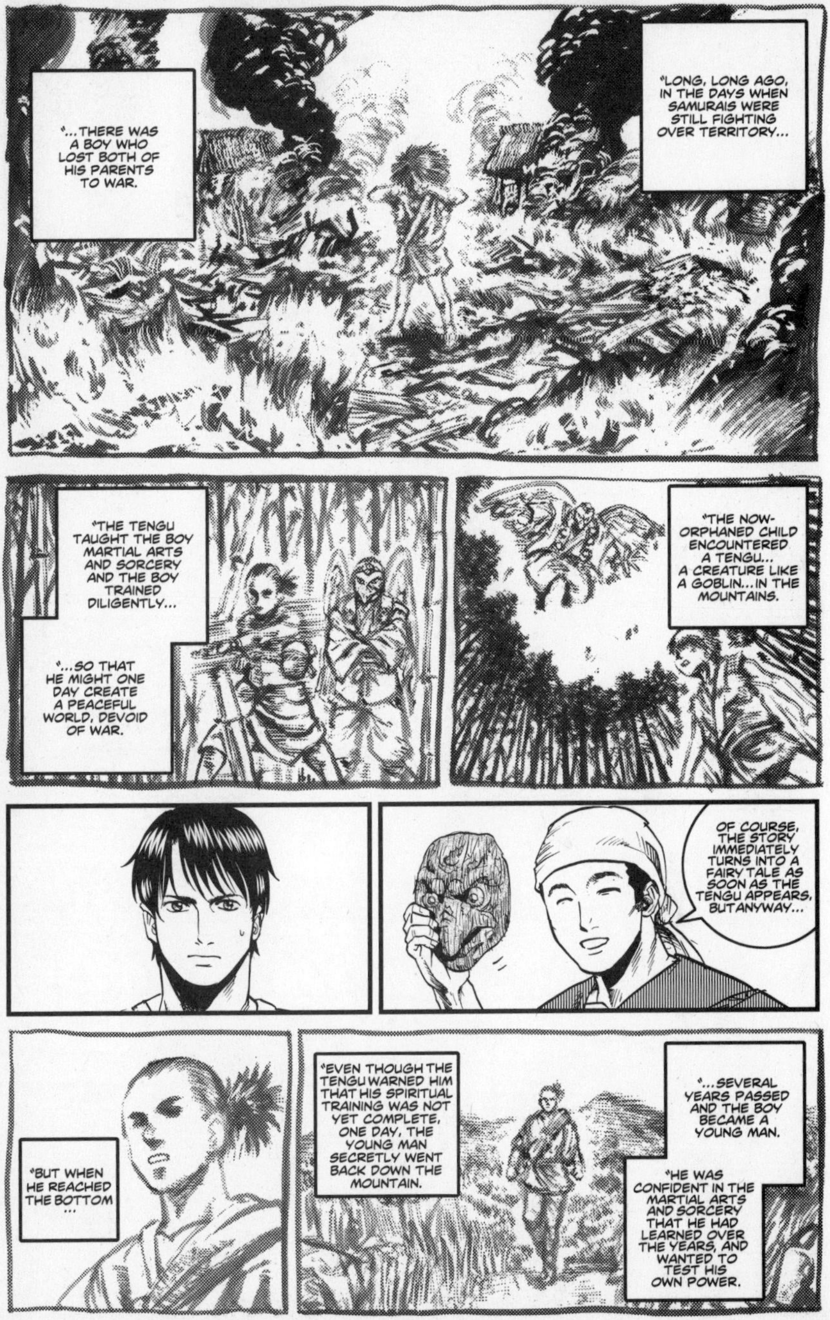
"LONG, LONG AGO, IN THE DAYS WHEN SAMURAIS WERE STILL FIGHTING OVER TERRITORY...
"...THERE WAS A BOY WHO LOST BOTH OF HIS PARENTS TO WAR.
"THE NOW-ORPHANED CHILD ENCOUNTERED A TENGU... A CREATURE LIKE A GOBLIN...IN THE MOUNTAINS.
"THE TENGU TAUGHT THE BOY MARTIAL ARTS AND SORCERY AND THE BOY TRAINED DILIGENTLY...
"...SO THAT HE MIGHT ONE DAY CREATE A PEACEFUL WORLD, DEVOID OF WAR.
OF COURSE, THE STORY IMMEDIATELY TURNS INTO A FAIRY TALE AS SOON AS THE TENGU APPEARS, BUTANYWAY...
"...SEVERAL YEARS PASSED AND THE BOY BECAME A YOUNG MAN.
"HE WAS CONFIDENT IN THE MARTIAL ARTS AND SORCERY THAT HE HAD LEARNED OVER THE YEARS, AND WANTED TO TEST HIS OWN POWER.
"EVEN THOUGH THE TENGU WARNED HIM THAT HIS SPIRITUAL TRAINING WAS NOT YET COMPLETE, ONE DAY, THE YOUNG MAN SECRETLY WENT BACK DOWN THE MOUNTAIN.
"BUT WHEN HE REACHED THE BOTTOM ...

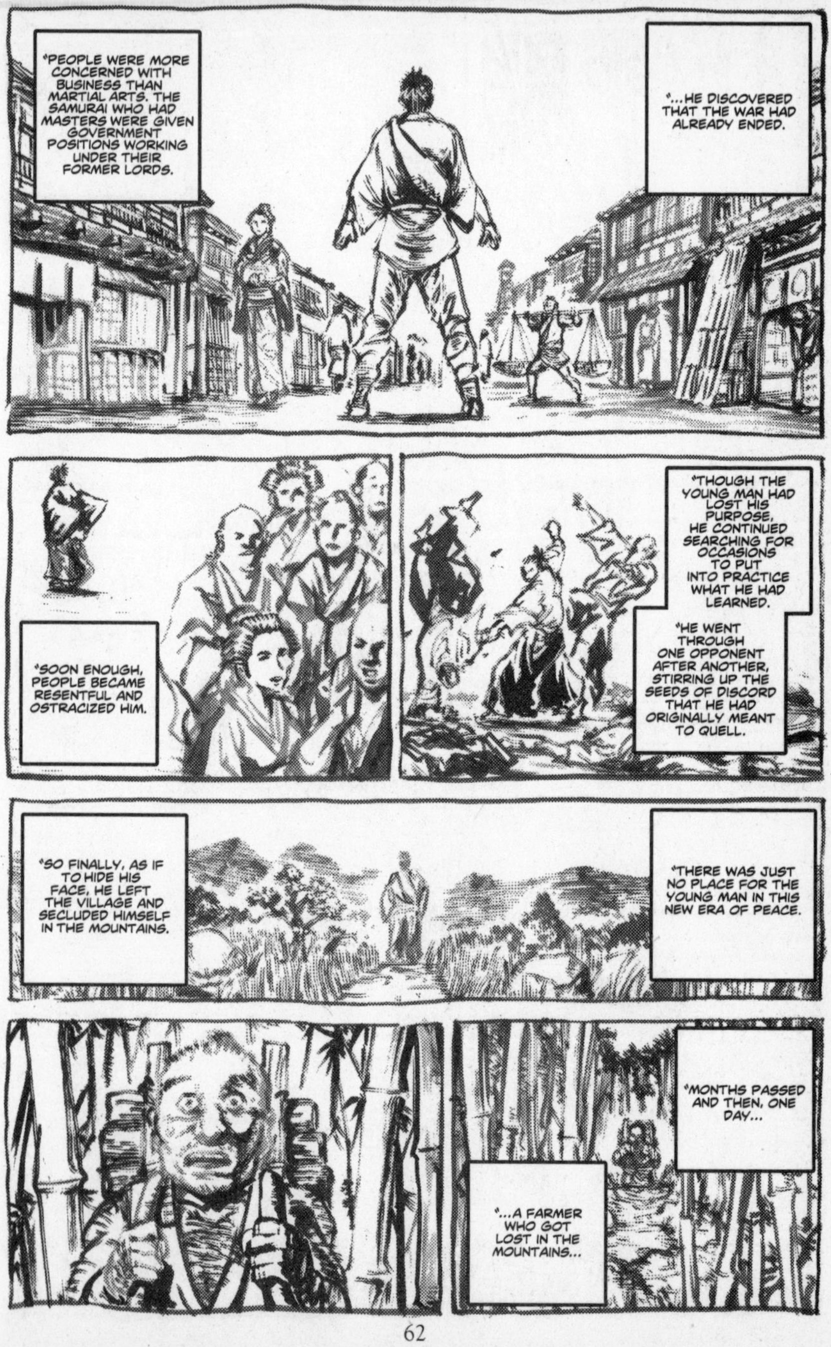
"PEOPLE WERE MORE CONCERNED WITH BUSINESS THAN MARTIAL ARTS. THE SAMURAI WHO HAD MASTERS WERE GIVEN GOVERNMENT POSITIONS WORKING UNDER THEIR FORMER LORDS.
"...HE DISCOVERED THAT THE WAR HAD ALREADY ENDED.
"SOON ENOUGH, PEOPLE BECAME RESENTFUL AND OSTRACIZED HIM.
"THOUGH THE YOUNG MAN HAD LOST HIS PURPOSE, HE CONTINUED SEARCHING FOR OCCASIONS TO PUT INTO PRACTICE WHAT HE HAD LEARNED.
"HE WENT THROUGH ONE OPPONENT AFTER ANOTHER, STIRRING UP THE SEEDS OF DISCORD THAT HE HAD ORIGINALLY MEANT TO QUELL.
"SO FINALLY, AS IF TO HIDE HIS FACE, HE LEFT THE VILLAGE AND SECLUDED HIMSELF IN THE MOUNTAINS.
"THERE WAS JUST NO PLACE FOR THE YOUNG MAN IN THIS NEW ERA OF PEACE.
"MONTHS PASSED AND THEN, ONE DAY...
"...A FARMER WHO GOT LOST IN THE MOUNTAINS...

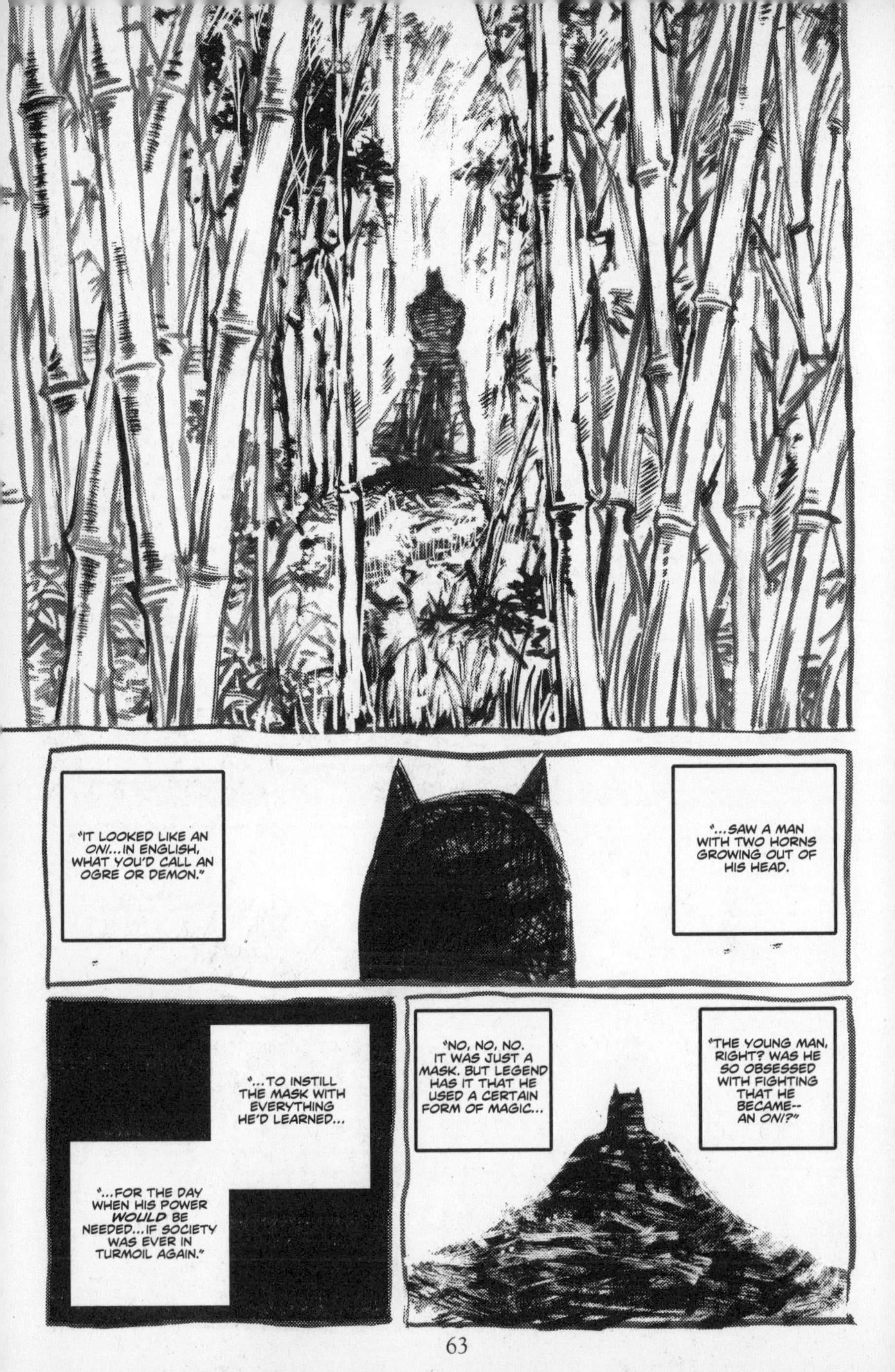
"IT LOOKED LIKE AN ONI...IN ENGLISH, WHAT YOU'D CALL AN OGRE OR DEMON."
"...SAW A MAN WITH TWO HORNS GROWING OUT OF HIS HEAD.
"...TO INSTILL THE MASK WITH EVERYTHING HE'D LEARNED...
"...FOR THE DAY WHEN HIS POWER **WOULD** BE NEEDED...IF SOCIETY WAS EVER IN TURMOIL AGAIN."
"NO, NO, NO. IT WAS JUST A MASK. BUT LEGEND HAS IT THAT HE USED A CERTAIN FORM OF MAGIC...
"THE YOUNG MAN, RIGHT? WAS HE SO OBSESSED WITH FIGHTING THAT HE BECAME-- AN ONI?"

AS IT SO HAPPENS...

...JUST THE OTHER DAY, I ACQUIRED THAT VERY SAME MASK.

THE STORY GOES THAT IF YOU PUT IT ON, YOU'RE BESTOWED WITH THE MARTIAL ARTS ABILITIES OF WHOEVER WORE IT PREVIOUSLY. IT'S LIKE A MYTHOLOGICAL OBJECT!

BY RIGHTS, IT SHOULD BELONG IN A MUSEUM...

...BUT IF YOU ACT NOW, I'LL GIVE YOU A GOOD DEAL ON IT!

ANYWAY, IF THERE REALLY WAS SUCH A MASK...

JUST THINK, YOU WOULDN'T EVER HAVE TO DO ANY MORE TRAINING!

...WOULD YOU PUT IT ON?

Uh-huh. SO THAT'S HOW YOU PALM OFF SUSPECT GOODS ON UNSUSPECTING CUSTOMERS.

EXACTLY!

...I'D CONQUER HIM WITH MY OWN!

ME, INSTEAD OF TAKING THAT ONI'S POWER...

JAB

Hmm...

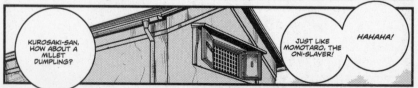

KUROSAKI-SAN, HOW ABOUT A MILLET DUMPLING?

JUST LIKE MOMOTARO, THE ONI-SLAYER!

HAHAHA!

BUT I HAVE TO REMIND MYSELF THAT I DIDN'T COME TO THIS COUNTRY TO UNWIND.

THE CLIMATE IS MILD. THE PEOPLE ARE FRIENDLY. EVERY DAY IS TRANQUIL.

BEING HERE MAKES ME FEEL AT PEACE.

MY SOLE PURPOSE IN USING A FALSE NAME, HIDING ALL SIGNS OF MY WEALTH AND COMING HERE WAS TO ACQUIRE THE SKILLS I NEED TO WAGE WAR AGAINST CRIME.

A LONG TIME AGO IN A FINE ART BOOK, I SAW A JAPANESE WOODBLOCK PRINT OF A LARGE WOODEN BRIDGE. HENCE, "GEORGE WOODBRIDGE."

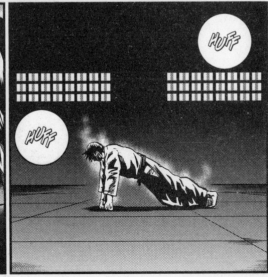

HUFF

HUFF

65

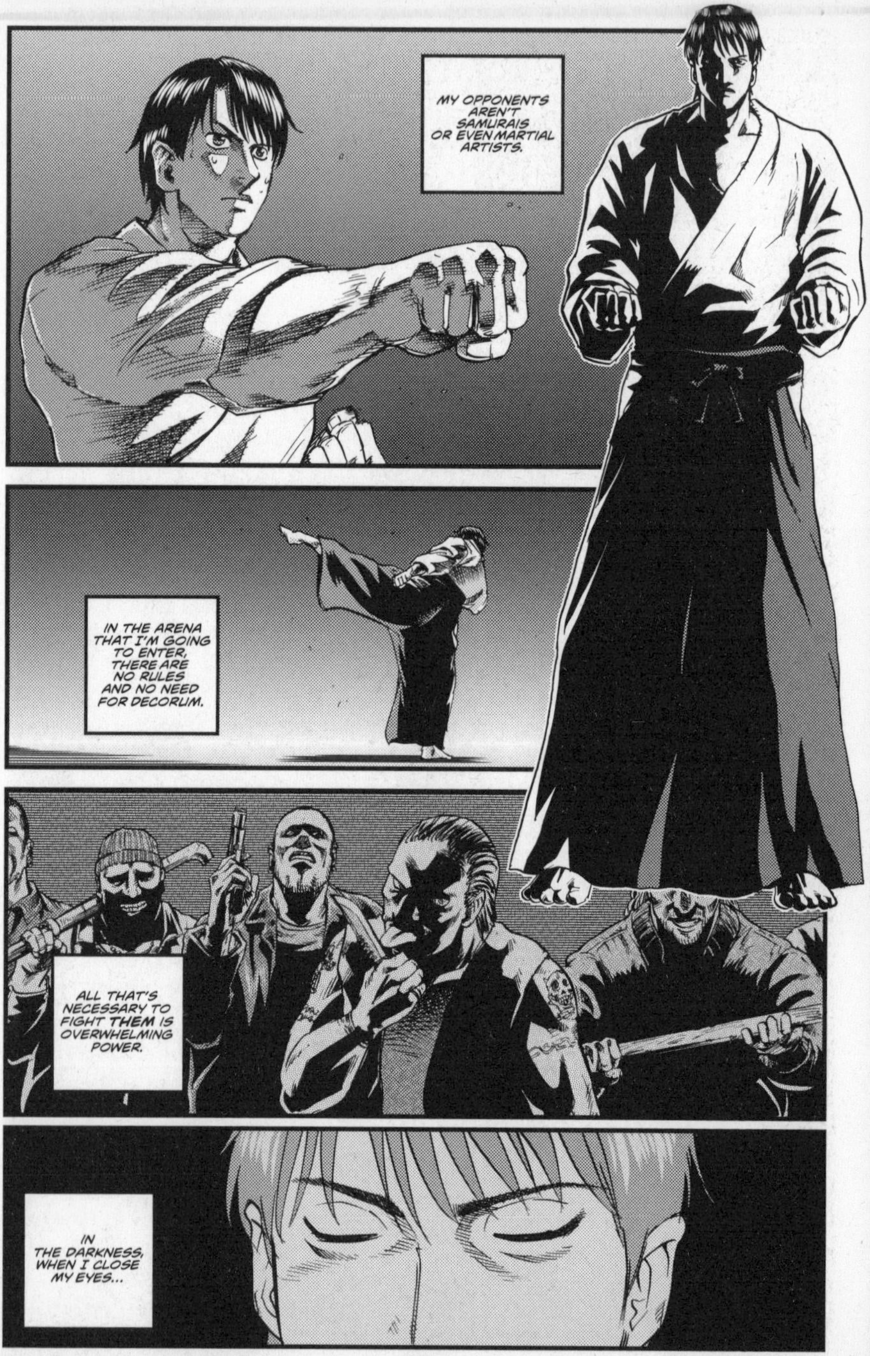
MY OPPONENTS AREN'T SAMURAIS OR EVEN MARTIAL ARTISTS.
IN THE ARENA THAT I'M GOING TO ENTER, THERE ARE NO RULES AND NO NEED FOR DECORUM.
ALL THAT'S NECESSARY TO FIGHT **THEM** IS OVERWHELMING POWER.
IN THE DARKNESS, WHEN I CLOSE MY EYES...

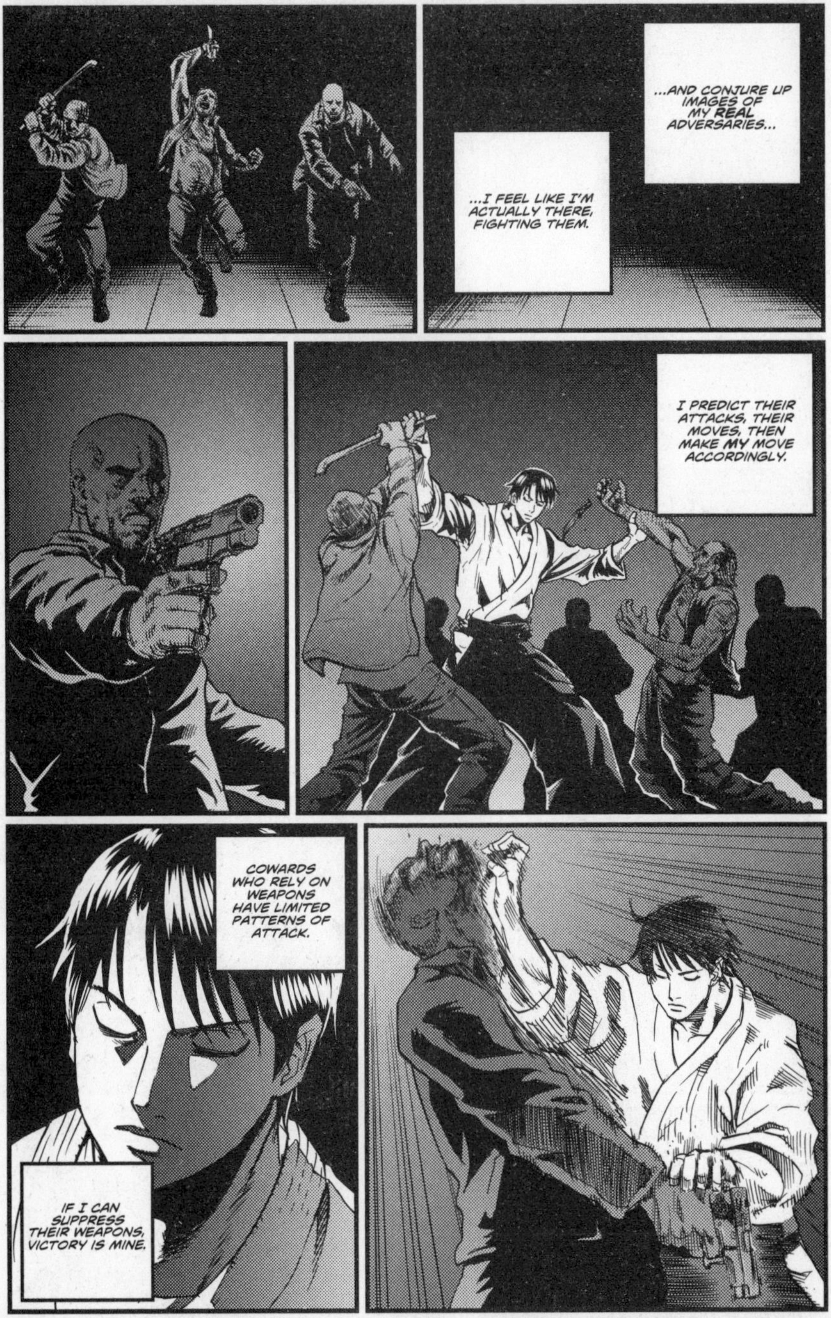
...AND CONJURE UP IMAGES OF MY REAL ADVERSARIES...
...I FEEL LIKE I'M ACTUALLY THERE, FIGHTING THEM.
I PREDICT THEIR ATTACKS, THEIR MOVES, THEN MAKE MY MOVE ACCORDINGLY.
COWARDS WHO RELY ON WEAPONS HAVE LIMITED PATTERNS OF ATTACK.
IF I CAN SUPPRESS THEIR WEAPONS, VICTORY IS MINE.

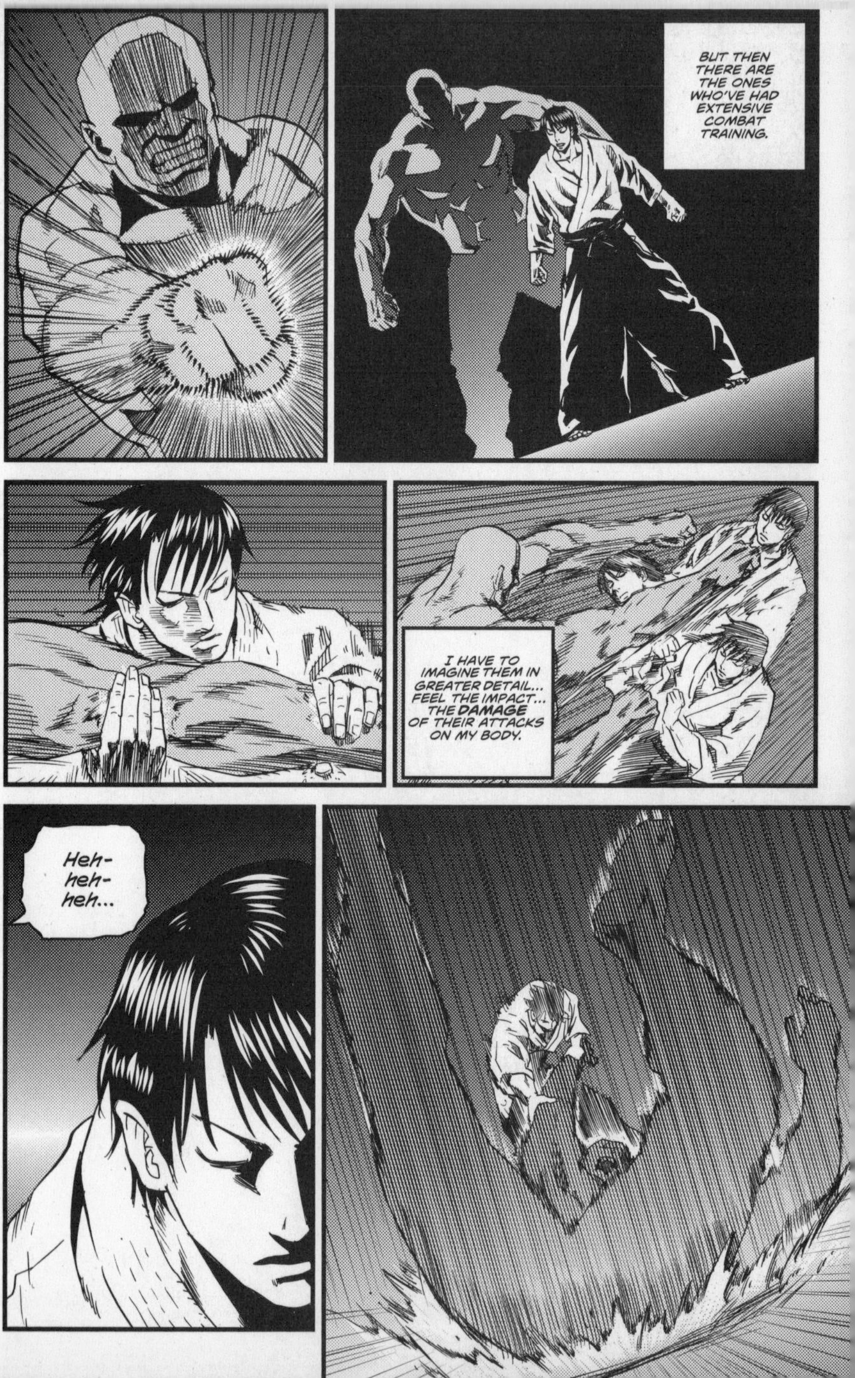
BUT THEN THERE ARE THE ONES WHO'VE HAD EXTENSIVE COMBAT TRAINING.
I HAVE TO IMAGINE THEM IN GREATER DETAIL... FEEL THE IMPACT... THE DAMAGE OF THEIR ATTACKS ON MY BODY.
Heh-heh-heh...

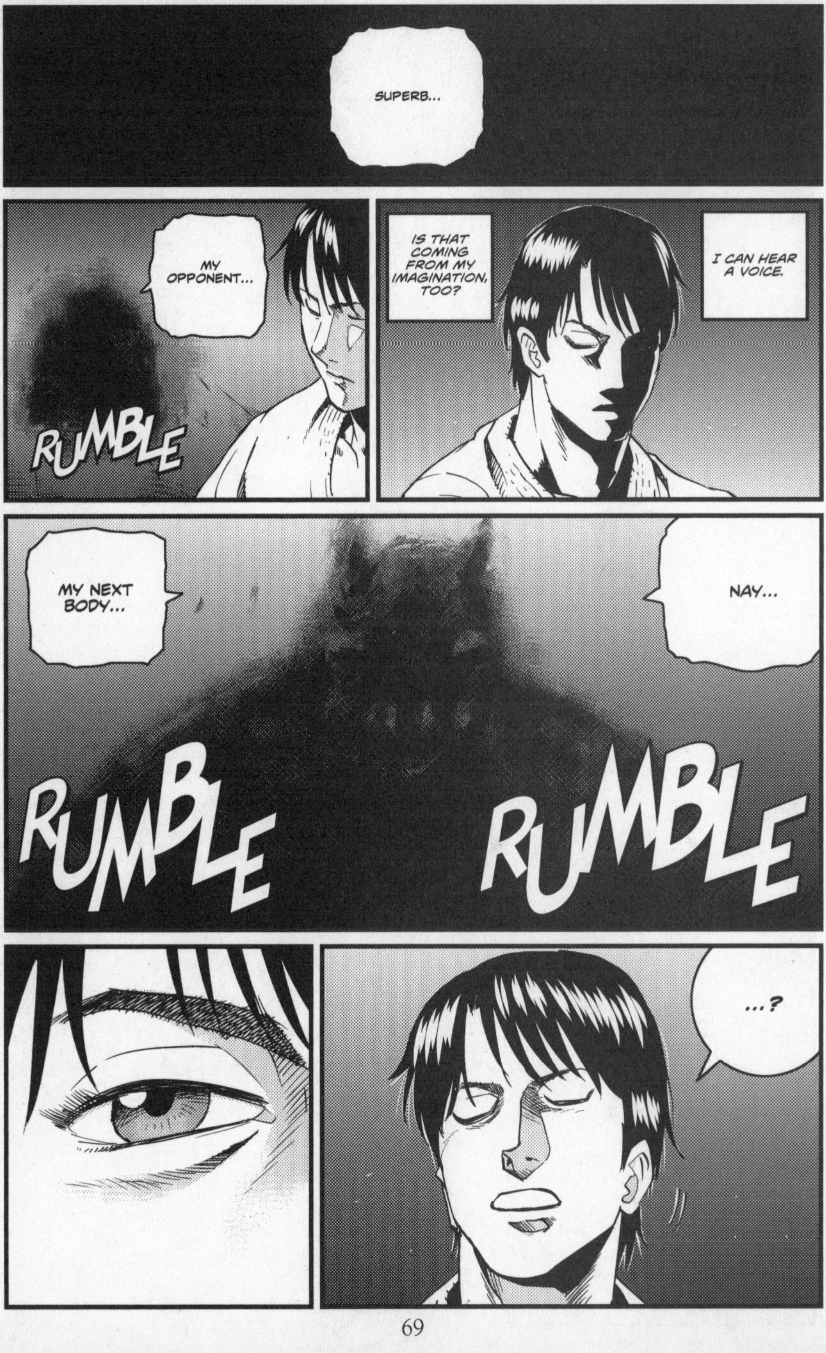
SUPERB...
I CAN HEAR A VOICE.
IS THAT COMING FROM MY IMAGINATION, TOO?
MY OPPONENT...
RUMBLE
NAY...
MY NEXT BODY...
RUMBLE
RUMBLE
...?

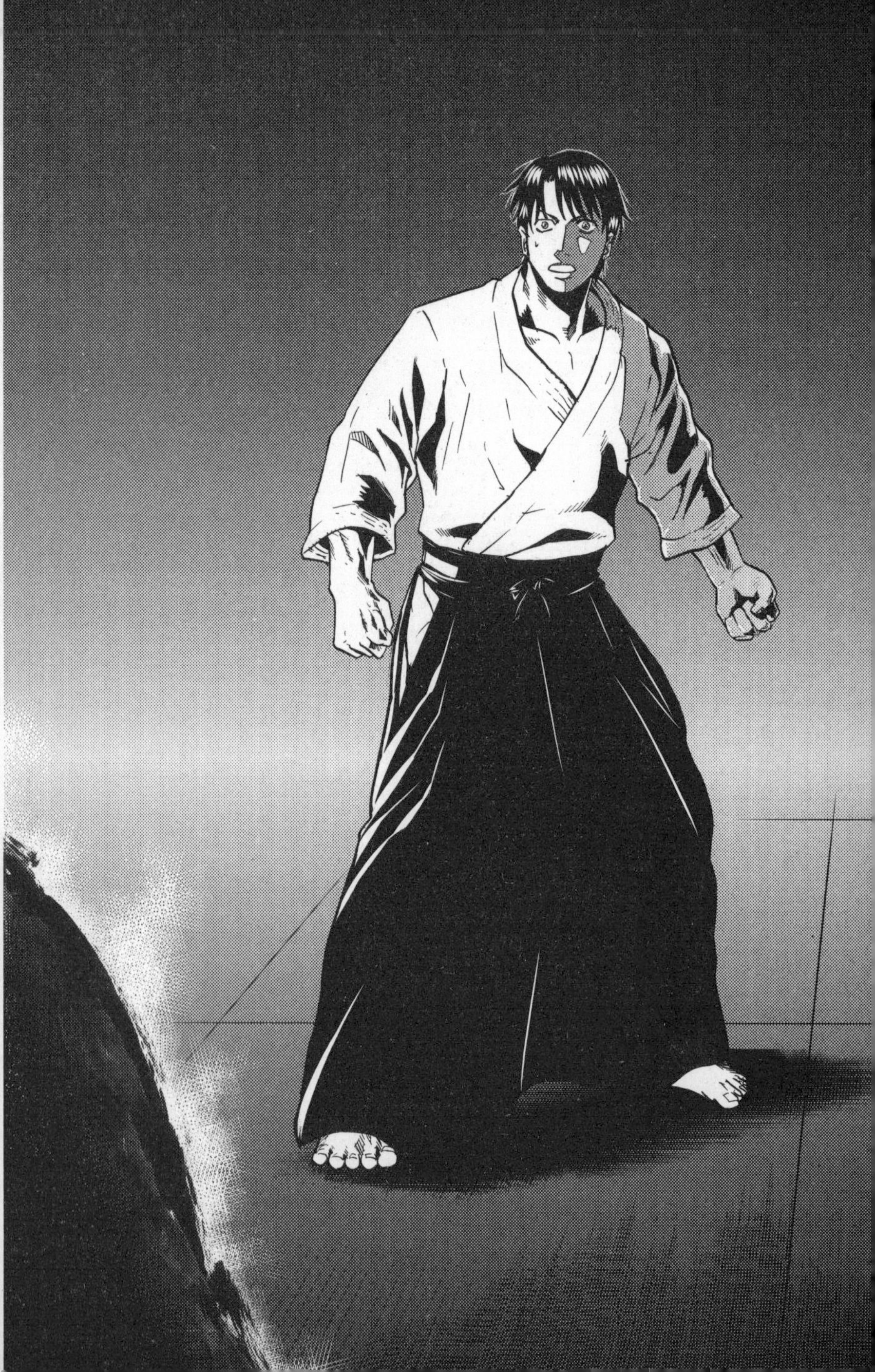

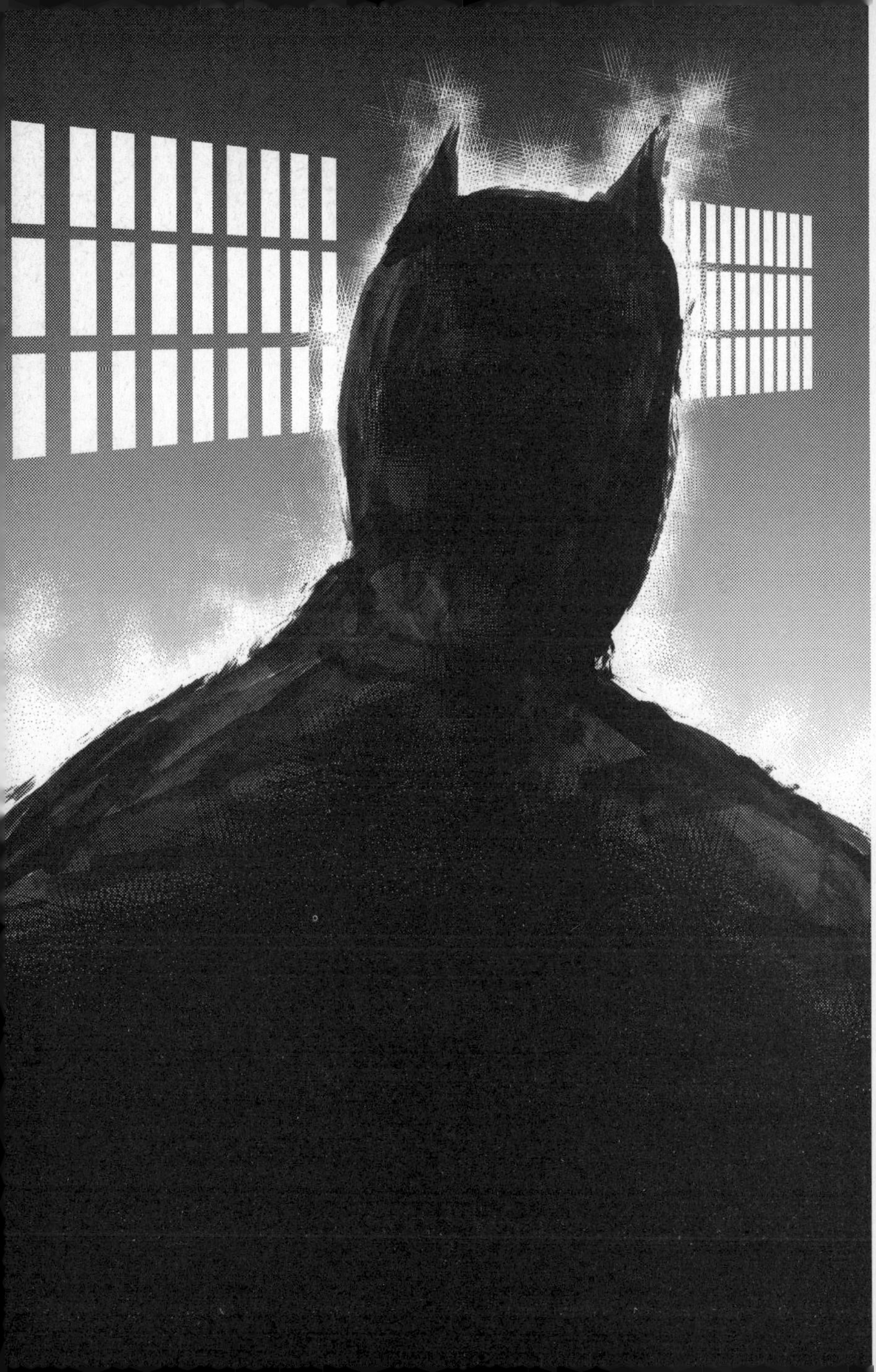

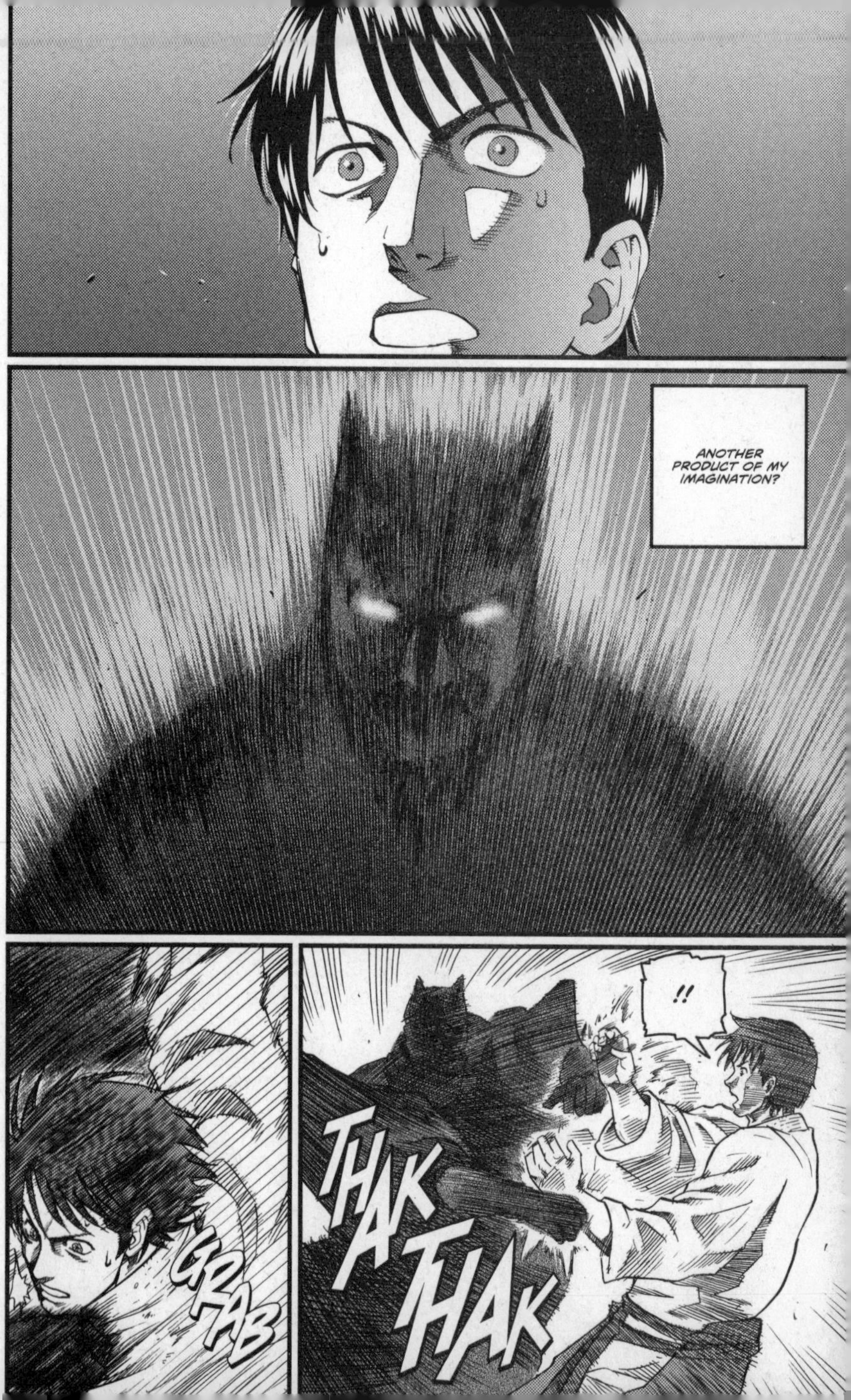
ANOTHER PRODUCT OF MY IMAGINATION?
!!
THAK THAK
GRAB

WHUD

YOU'RE STILL SOFT, BOY...YOU NEED TO BECOME STRONGER TO BE OF ANY USE TO ME.

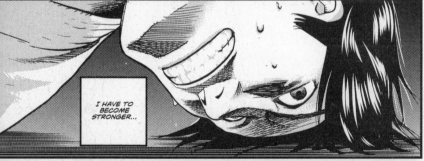

I HAVE TO BECOME STRONGER...

...TO FIGHT CRIME...TO FIGHT...EVIL...

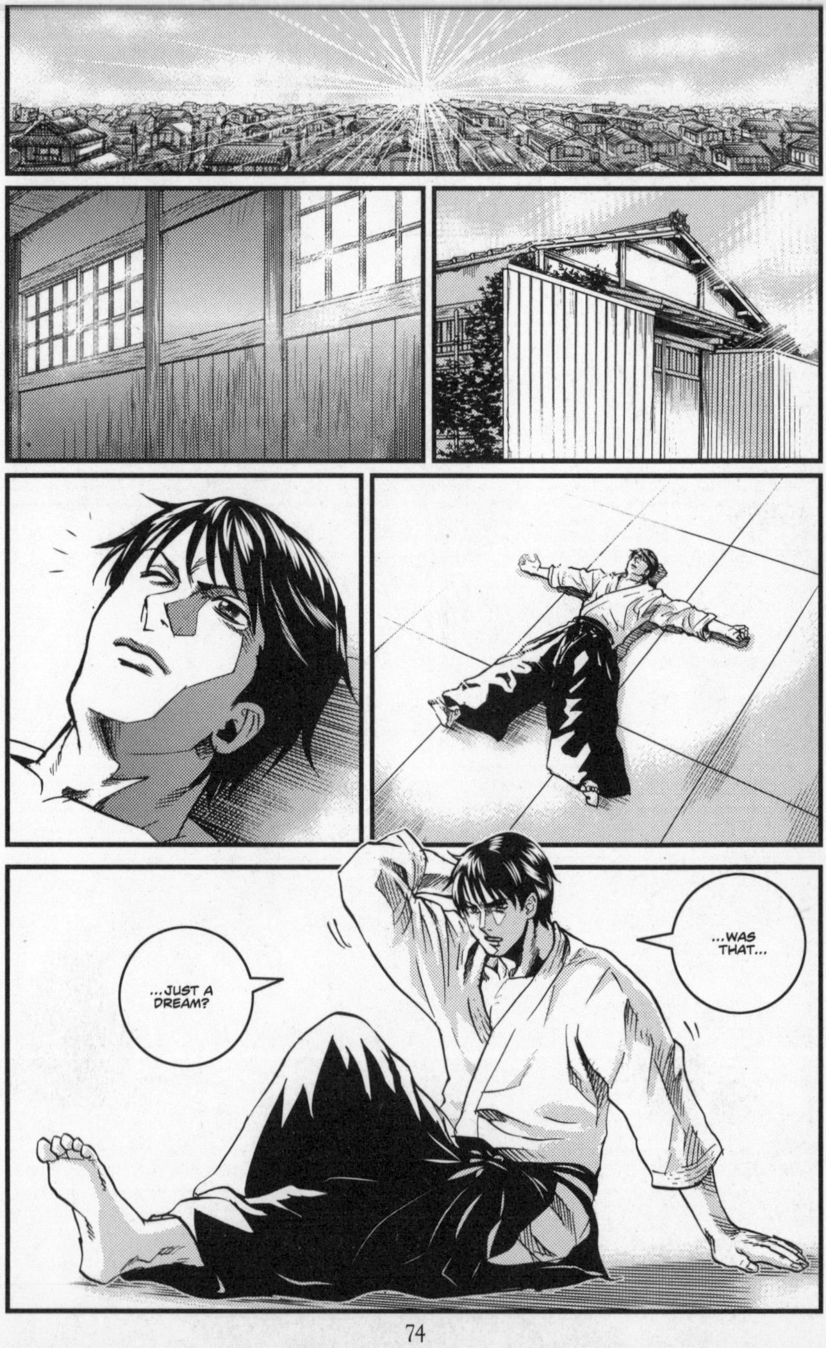
...WAS THAT...
...JUST A DREAM?

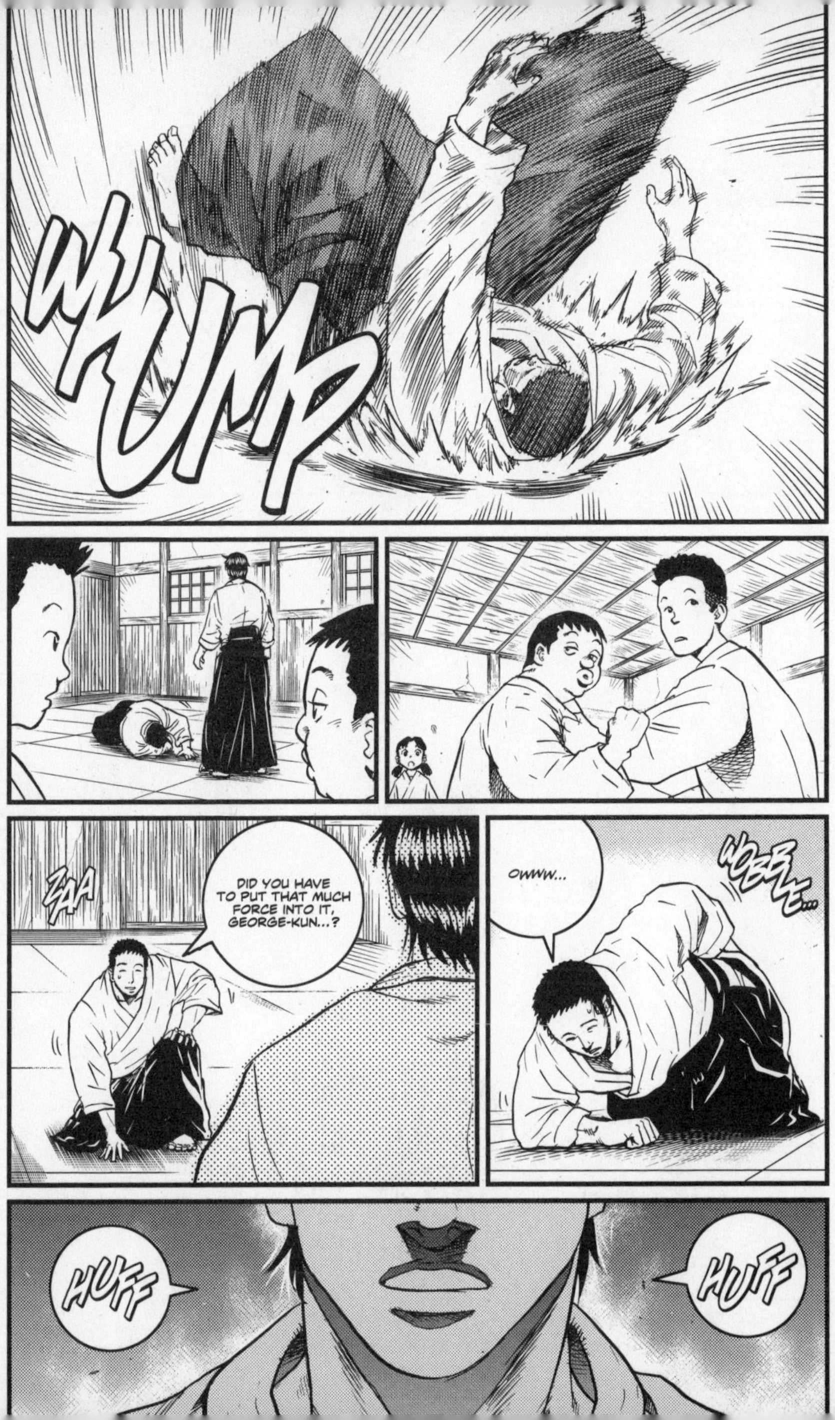
WHUMP
ZAA
DID YOU HAVE TO PUT THAT MUCH FORCE INTO IT, GEORGE-KUN...?
WOBBLE...
OWWW...
HUFF
HUFF

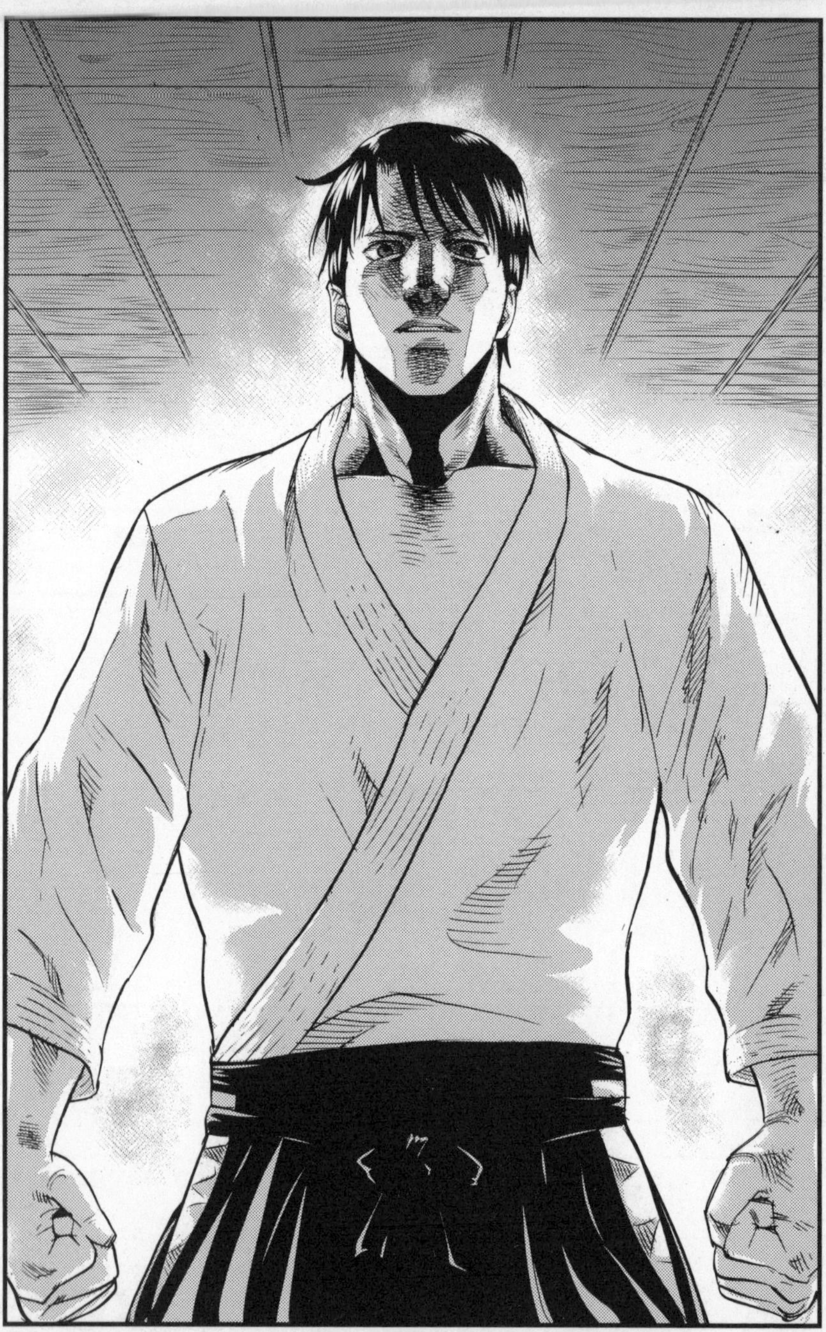

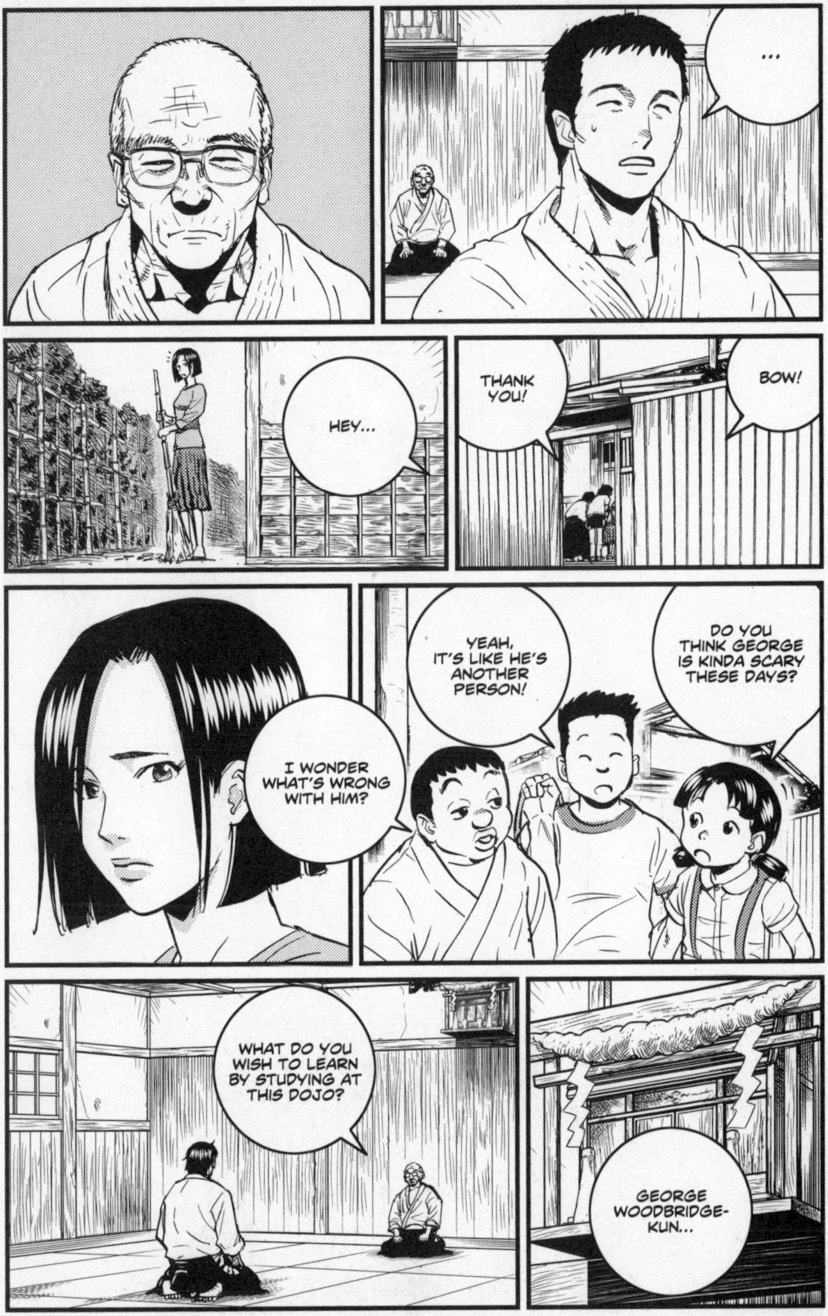
...
HEY...
BOW!
THANK YOU!
DO YOU THINK GEORGE IS KINDA SCARY THESE DAYS?
YEAH, IT'S LIKE HE'S ANOTHER PERSON!
I WONDER WHAT'S WRONG WITH HIM?
WHAT DO YOU WISH TO LEARN BY STUDYING AT THIS DOJO?
GEORGE WOODBRIDGE-KUN...

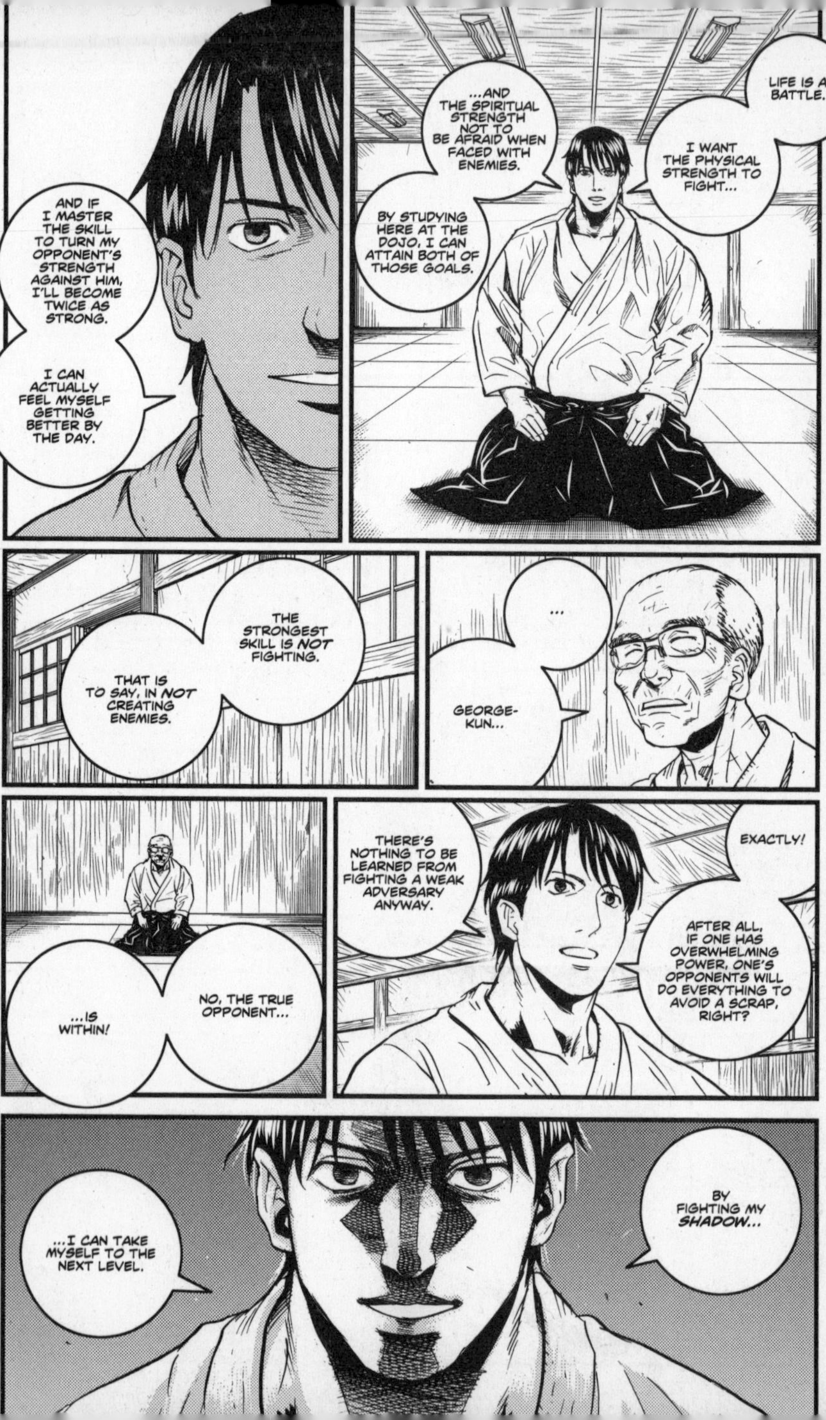
LIFE IS A BATTLE.
I WANT THE PHYSICAL STRENGTH TO FIGHT...
...AND THE SPIRITUAL STRENGTH NOT TO BE AFRAID WHEN FACED WITH ENEMIES.
BY STUDYING HERE AT THE DOJO, I CAN ATTAIN BOTH OF THOSE GOALS.
AND IF I MASTER THE SKILL TO TURN MY OPPONENT'S STRENGTH AGAINST HIM, I'LL BECOME TWICE AS STRONG.
I CAN ACTUALLY FEEL MYSELF GETTING BETTER BY THE DAY.
...
GEORGE-KUN...
THE STRONGEST SKILL IS *NOT* FIGHTING.
THAT IS TO SAY, IN *NOT* CREATING ENEMIES.
EXACTLY!
AFTER ALL, IF ONE HAS OVERWHELMING POWER, ONE'S OPPONENTS WILL DO EVERYTHING TO AVOID A SCRAP, RIGHT?
THERE'S NOTHING TO BE LEARNED FROM FIGHTING A WEAK ADVERSARY ANYWAY.
NO, THE TRUE OPPONENT...
...IS WITHIN!
BY FIGHTING MY *SHADOW*...
...I CAN TAKE MYSELF TO THE NEXT LEVEL.

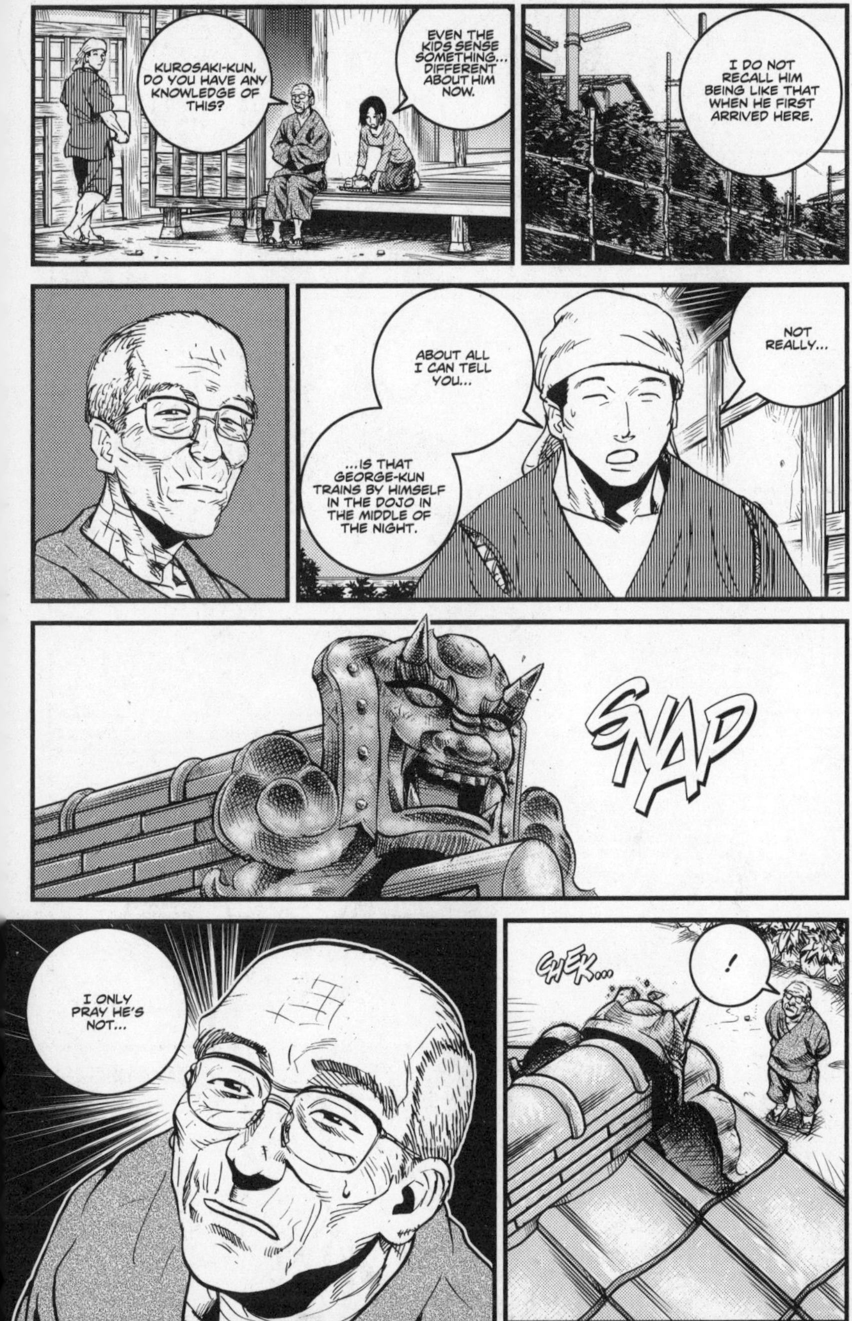
KUROSAKI-KUN, DO YOU HAVE ANY KNOWLEDGE OF THIS?
EVEN THE KIDS SENSE SOMETHING... DIFFERENT ABOUT HIM NOW.
I DO NOT RECALL HIM BEING LIKE THAT WHEN HE FIRST ARRIVED HERE.
NOT REALLY...
ABOUT ALL I CAN TELL YOU...
...IS THAT GEORGE-KUN TRAINS BY HIMSELF IN THE DOJO IN THE MIDDLE OF THE NIGHT.
SNAP
I ONLY PRAY HE'S NOT...
CHEK...
!

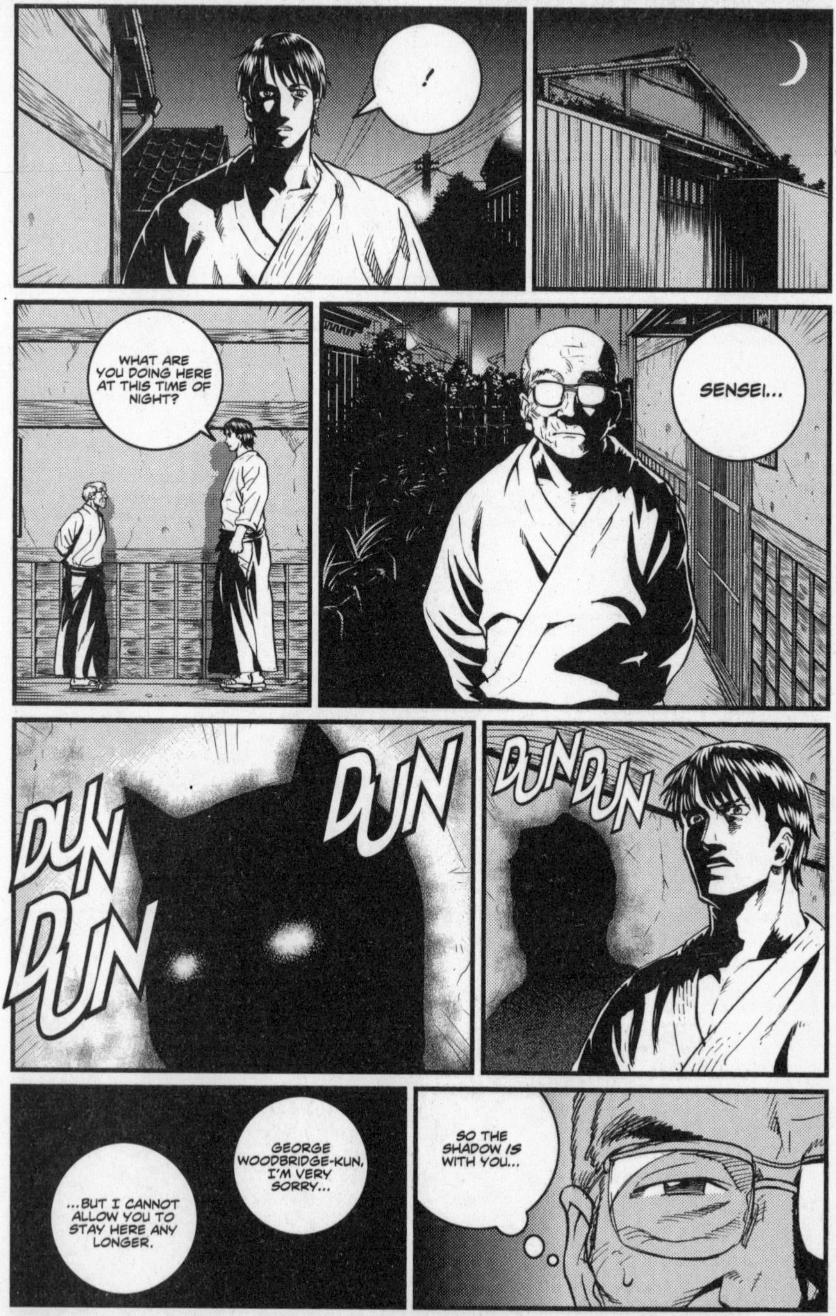
!
WHAT ARE YOU DOING HERE AT THIS TIME OF NIGHT?
SENSEI...
DUN DUN
DUN
DUN DUN
GEORGE WOODBRIDGE-KUN, I'M VERY SORRY...
...BUT I CANNOT ALLOW YOU TO STAY HERE ANY LONGER.
SO THE SHADOW IS WITH YOU...

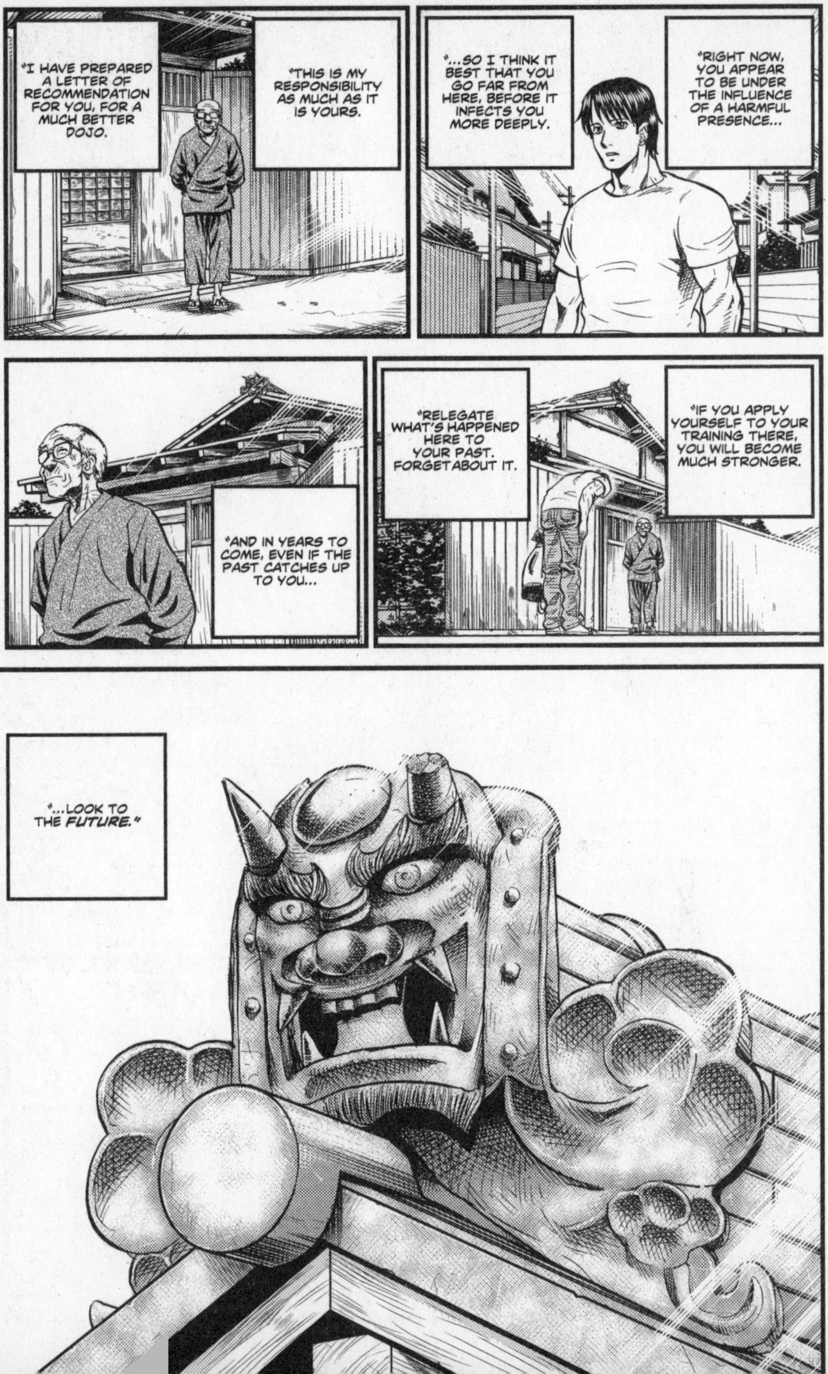

"I HAVE PREPARED A LETTER OF RECOMMENDATION FOR YOU, FOR A MUCH BETTER DOJO.
"THIS IS MY RESPONSIBILITY AS MUCH AS IT IS YOURS.
"RIGHT NOW, YOU APPEAR TO BE UNDER THE INFLUENCE OF A HARMFUL PRESENCE...
"...SO I THINK IT BEST THAT YOU GO FAR FROM HERE, BEFORE IT INFECTS YOU MORE DEEPLY.
"IF YOU APPLY YOURSELF TO YOUR TRAINING THERE, YOU WILL BECOME MUCH STRONGER.
"RELEGATE WHAT'S HAPPENED HERE TO YOUR PAST. FORGET ABOUT IT.
"AND IN YEARS TO COME, EVEN IF THE PAST CATCHES UP TO YOU...
"...LOOK TO THE *FUTURE*."

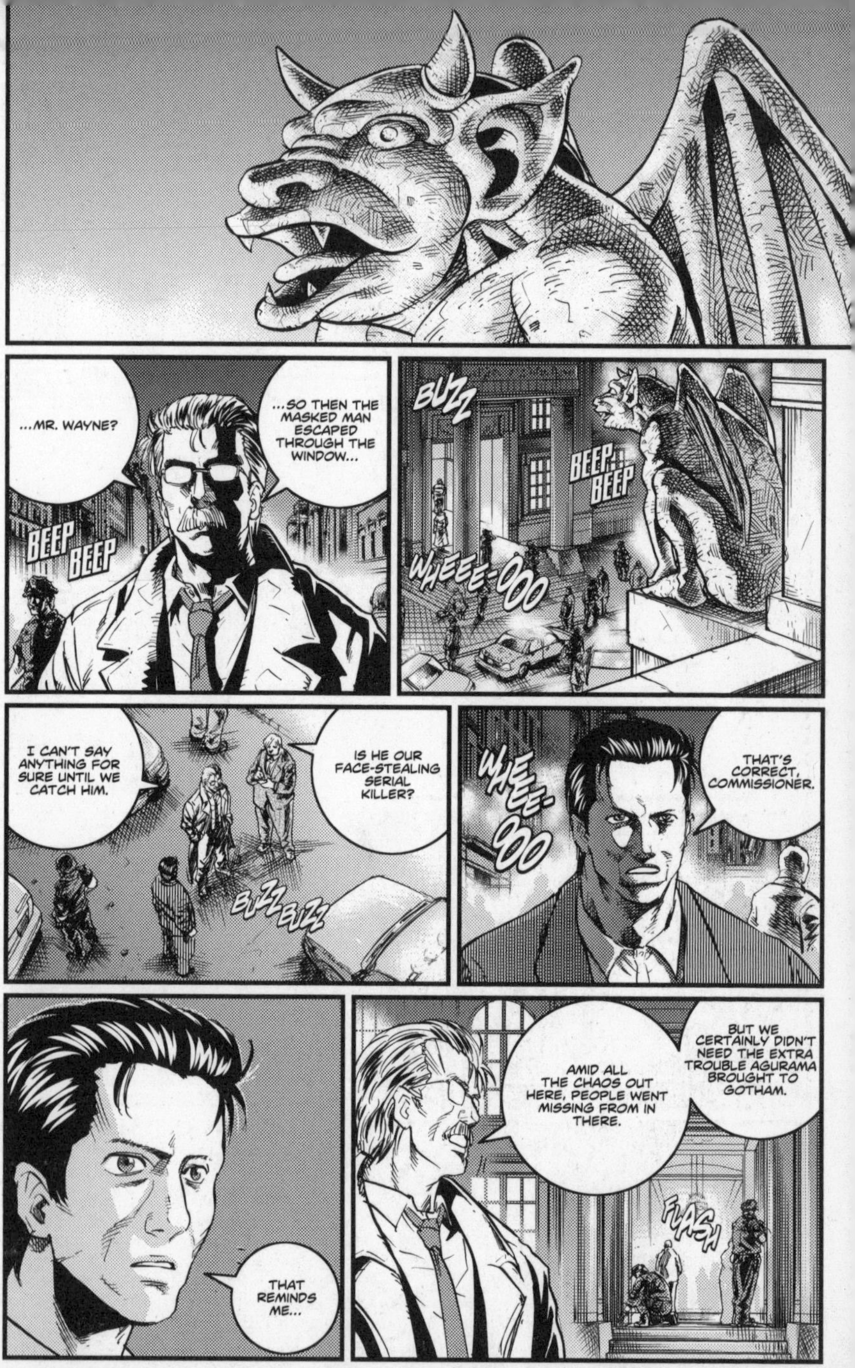
...SO THEN THE MASKED MAN ESCAPED THROUGH THE WINDOW...
...MR. WAYNE?
BEEP BEEP
BUZZ
BEEP BEEP
WHEEE-OOO
IS HE OUR FACE-STEALING SERIAL KILLER?
I CAN'T SAY ANYTHING FOR SURE UNTIL WE CATCH HIM.
BUZZ BUZZ
WHEEE-OOO
THAT'S CORRECT, COMMISSIONER.
THAT REMINDS ME...
BUT WE CERTAINLY DIDN'T NEED THE EXTRA TROUBLE AGURAMA BROUGHT TO GOTHAM.
AMID ALL THE CHAOS OUT HERE, PEOPLE WENT MISSING FROM IN THERE.
FLASH

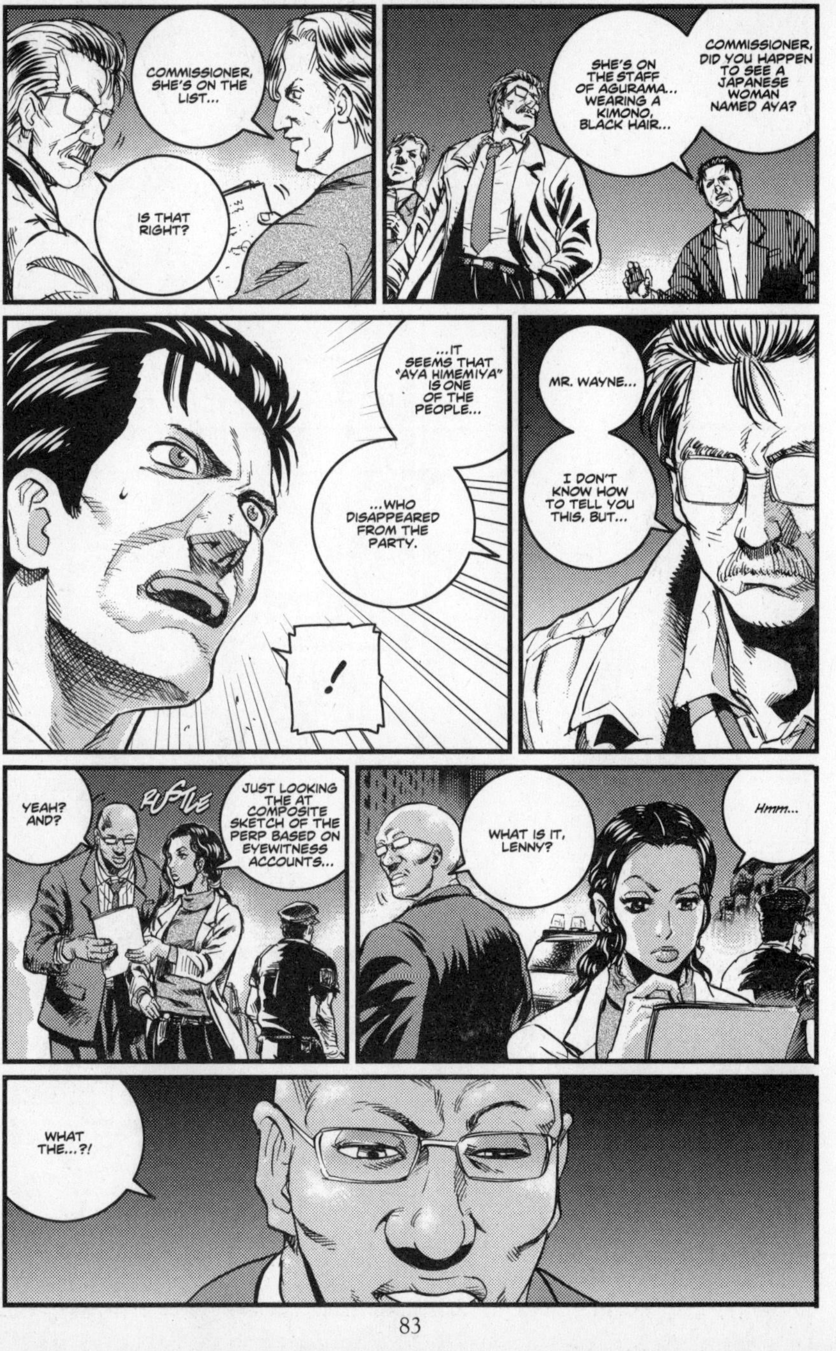
COMMISSIONER, SHE'S ON THE LIST...
IS THAT RIGHT?
COMMISSIONER, DID YOU HAPPEN TO SEE A JAPANESE WOMAN NAMED AYA?
SHE'S ON THE STAFF OF AGURAMA... WEARING A KIMONO, BLACK HAIR...
MR. WAYNE...
I DON'T KNOW HOW TO TELL YOU THIS, BUT...
...IT SEEMS THAT "AYA HIMEMIYA" IS ONE OF THE PEOPLE...
...WHO DISAPPEARED FROM THE PARTY.
!
YEAH? AND?
RUSTLE
JUST LOOKING THE AT COMPOSITE SKETCH OF THE PERP BASED ON EYEWITNESS ACCOUNTS...
Hmm...
WHAT IS IT, LENNY?
WHAT THE...?!

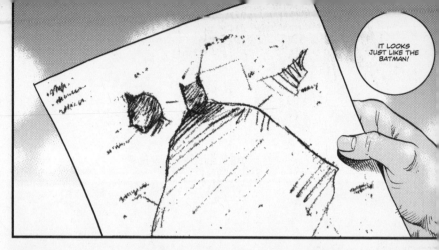

IT LOOKS JUST LIKE THE BATMAN!

ALFRED!

TAK

AFTER I CALLED, DID YOU FIND OUT ANYTHING?

WELCOME HOME, MASTER BRUCE.

RUMBLE

RUSTLE

...BUT I DID PICK UP SOMETHING INTRIGUING.

WHAT'S THAT?

I DIDN'T HAVE TIME TO QUESTION PEOPLE WHO LIVED THERE BACK THEN...

A BIT. ROUGHLY TWENTY YEARS AGO, A PARCEL OF LAND IN JAPAN THAT INCLUDES THE DOJO YOU INQUIRED ABOUT WAS PART OF A LARGE-SCALE REDEVELOPMENT PROJECT.

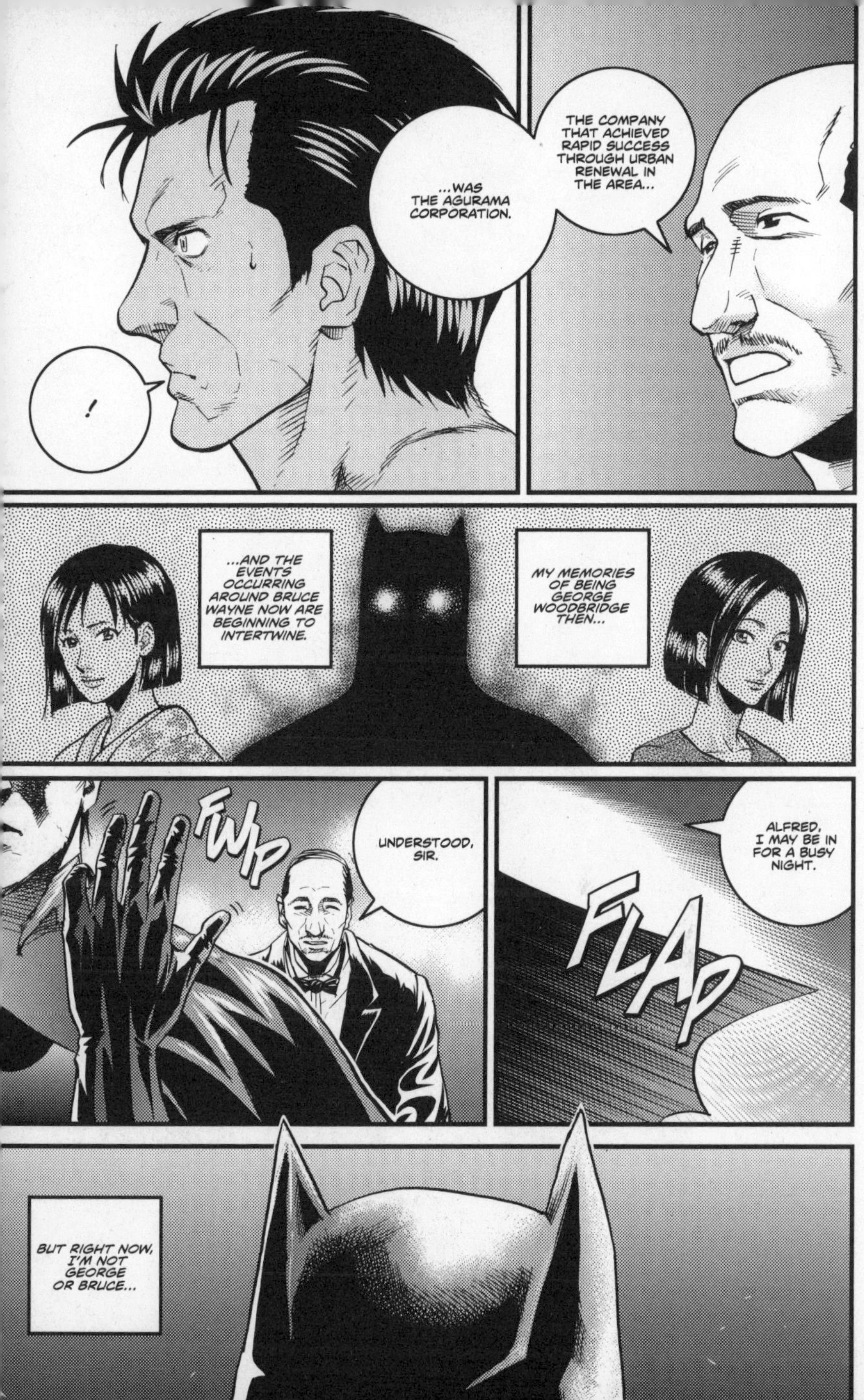
THE COMPANY THAT ACHIEVED RAPID SUCCESS THROUGH URBAN RENEWAL IN THE AREA...
...WAS THE AGURAMA CORPORATION.
!
...AND THE EVENTS OCCURRING AROUND BRUCE WAYNE NOW ARE BEGINNING TO INTERTWINE.
MY MEMORIES OF BEING GEORGE WOODBRIDGE THEN...
ALFRED, I MAY BE IN FOR A BUSY NIGHT.
FLAP
UNDERSTOOD, SIR.
FWIP
BUT RIGHT NOW, I'M NOT GEORGE OR BRUCE...

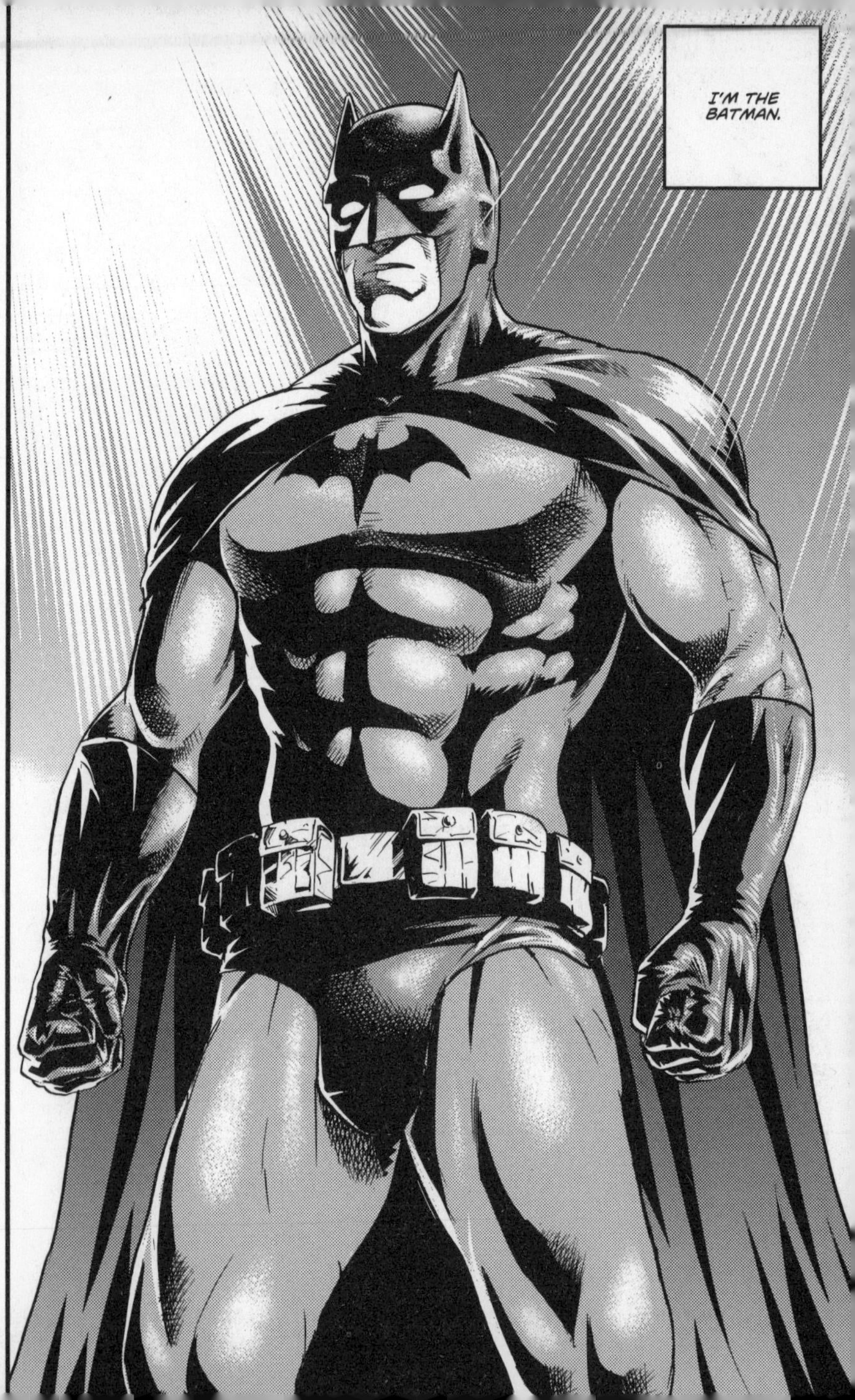
I'M THE BATMAN.

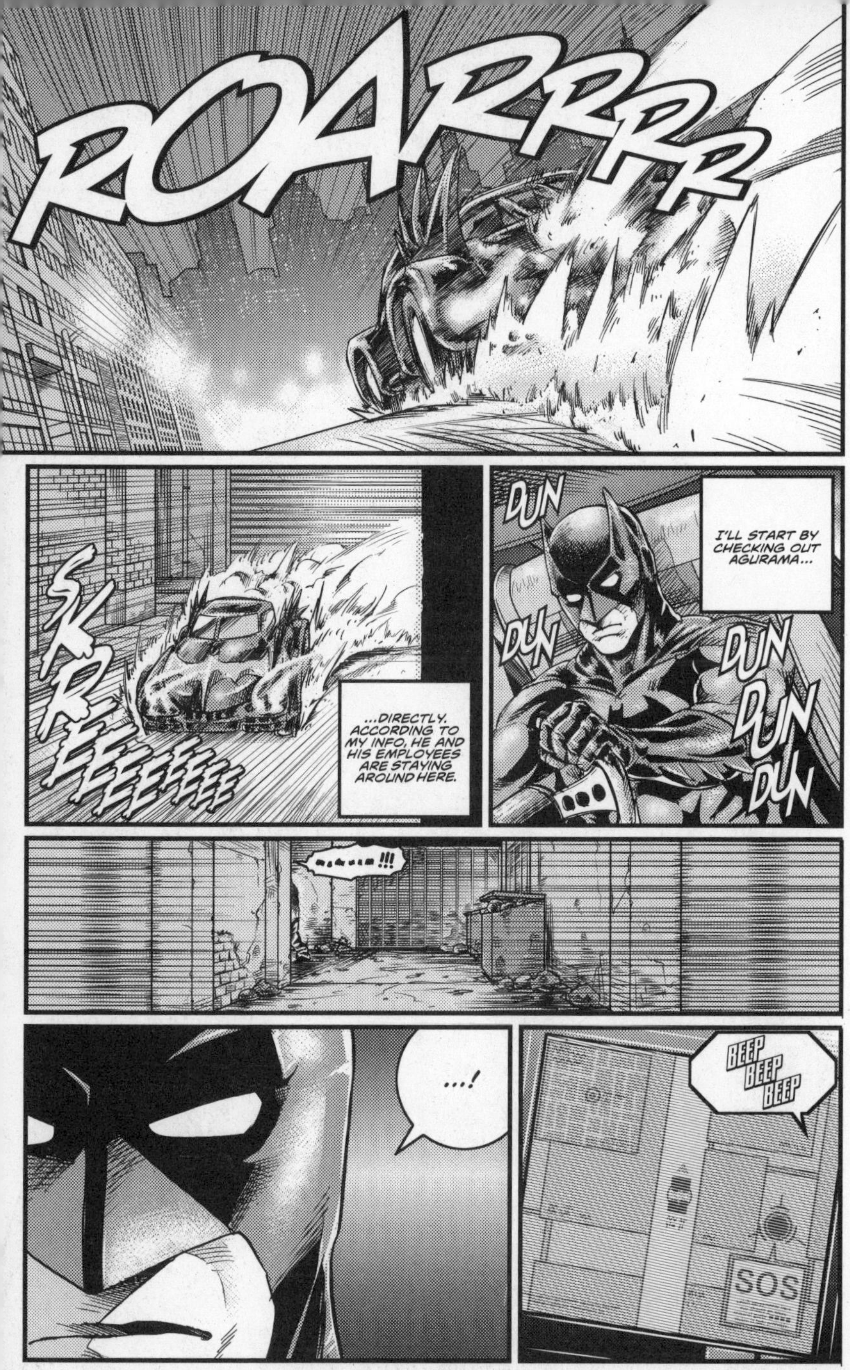
ROARRRR
SKREEEEEEEEEE
...DIRECTLY. ACCORDING TO MY INFO, HE AND HIS EMPLOYEES ARE STAYING AROUND HERE.
DUN
I'LL START BY CHECKING OUT AGURAMA...
DUN
DUN DUN DUN DUN
...!
BEEP BEEP BEEP
SOS

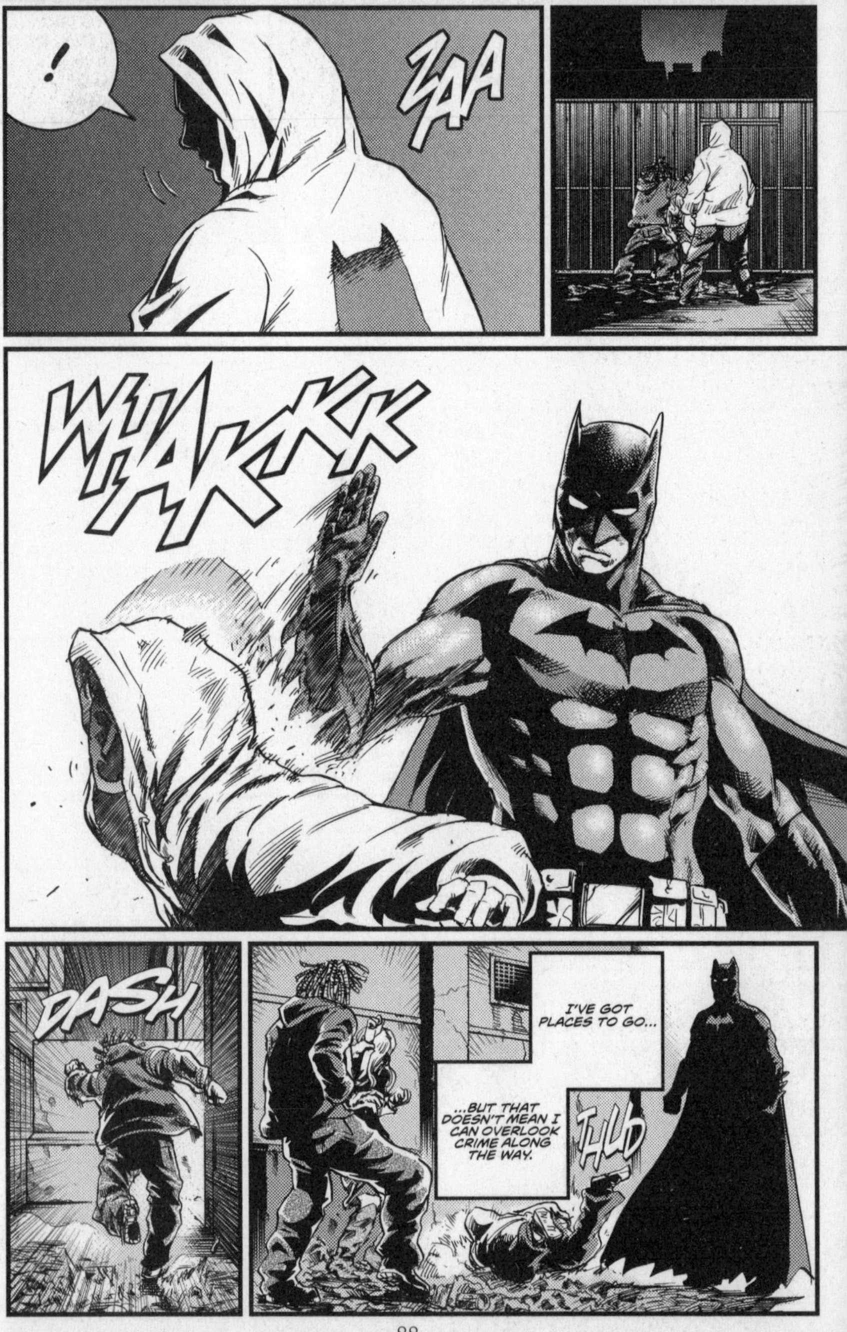
!
ZAA
WHAKKK
DASH
I'VE GOT PLACES TO GO...
...BUT THAT DOESN'T MEAN I CAN OVERLOOK CRIME ALONG THE WAY.
THUD

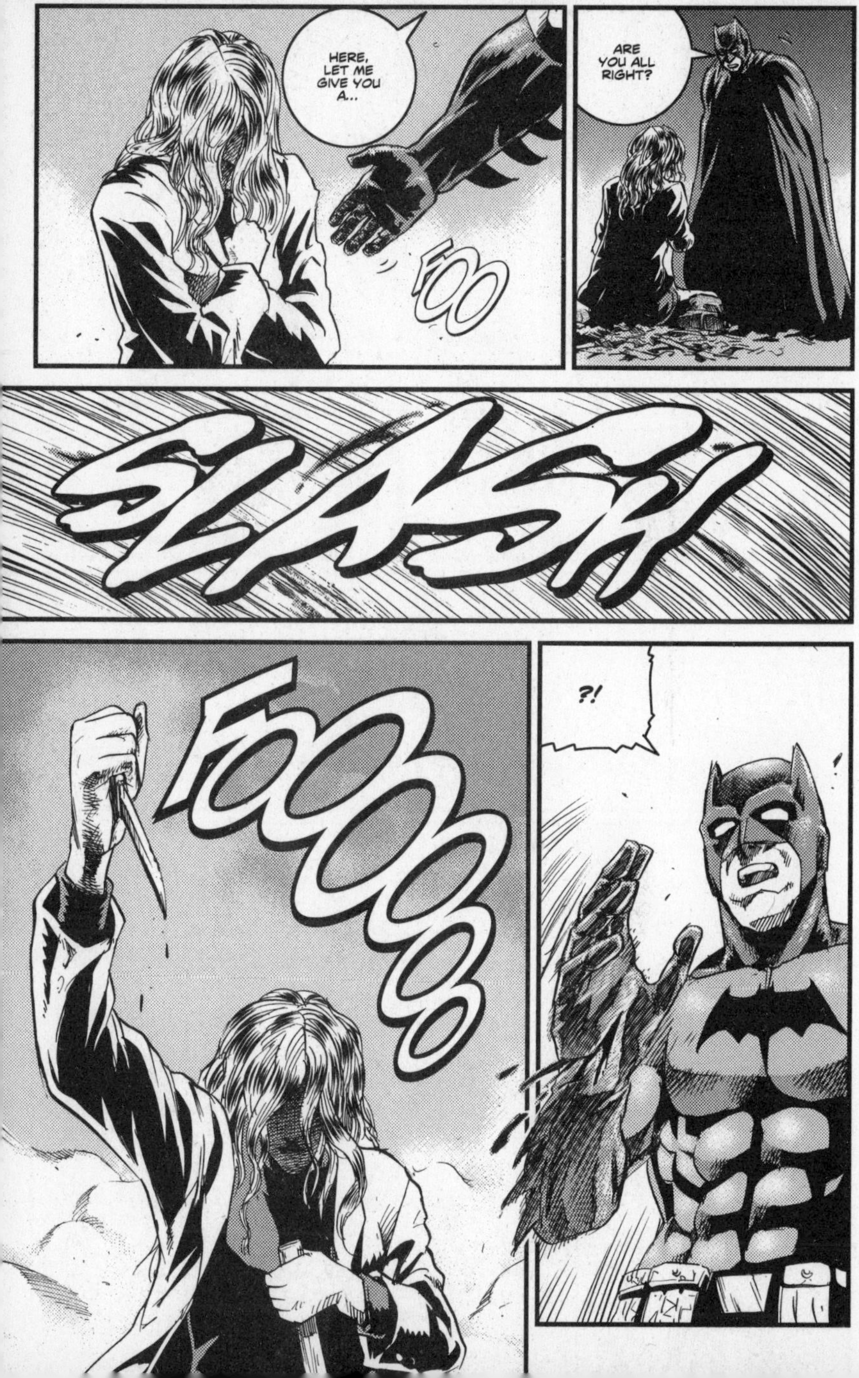
HERE, LET ME GIVE YOU A...
FOO
ARE YOU ALL RIGHT?
SLASH
FOOOOOO
?!

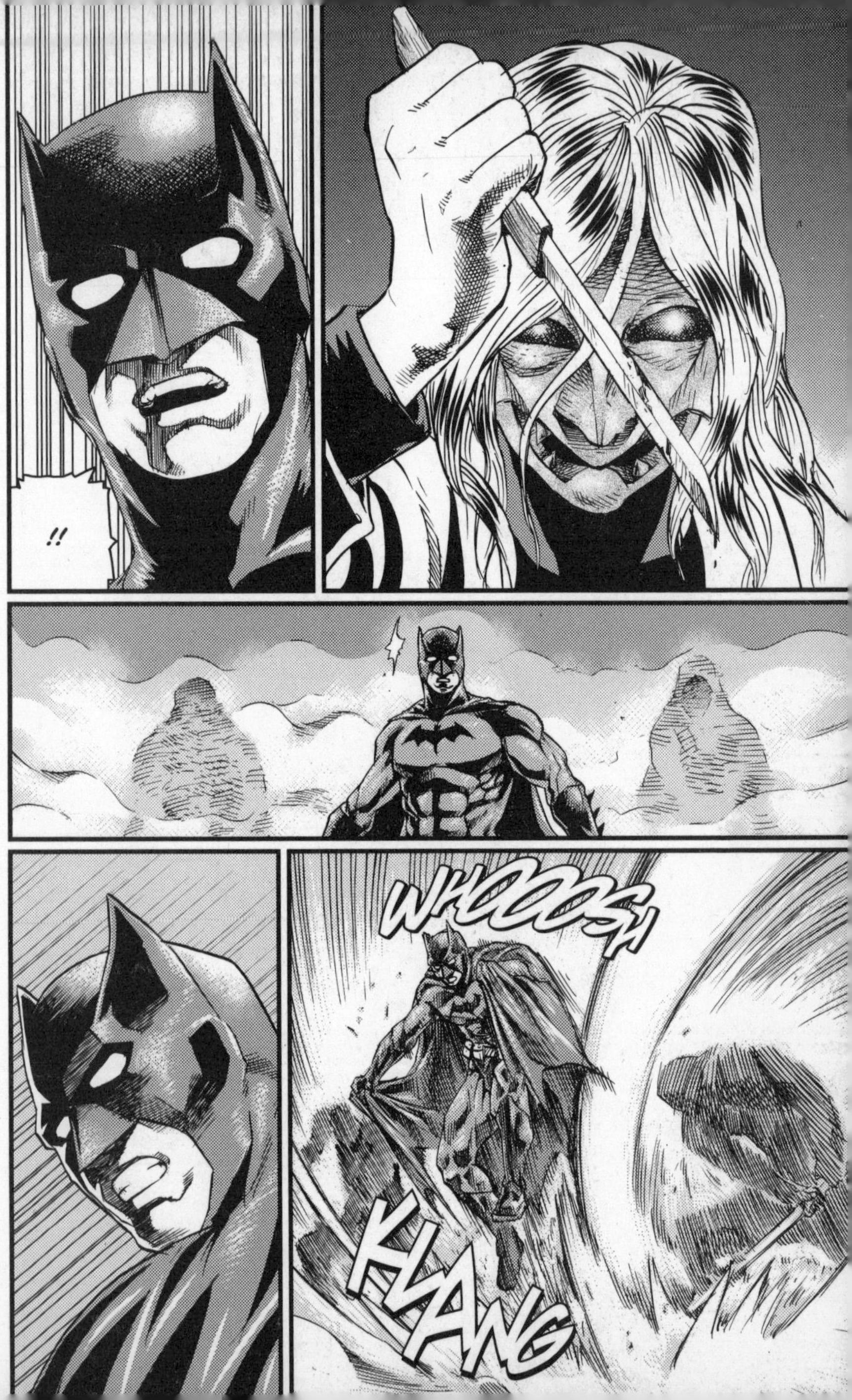
!!
WHOOOSH
KLANG

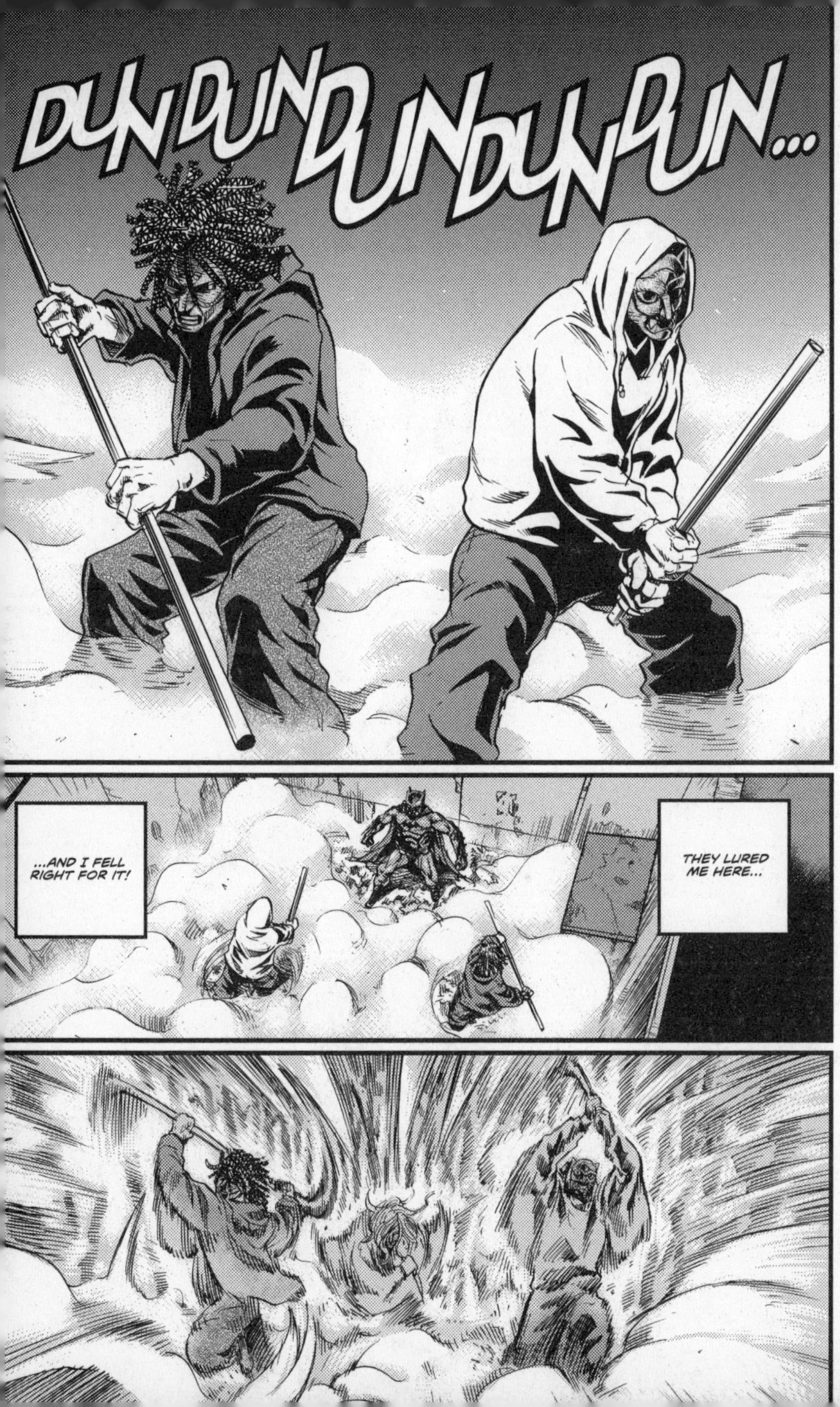
DUN DUN DUN DUN DUN...
THEY LURED ME HERE...
...AND I FELL RIGHT FOR IT!

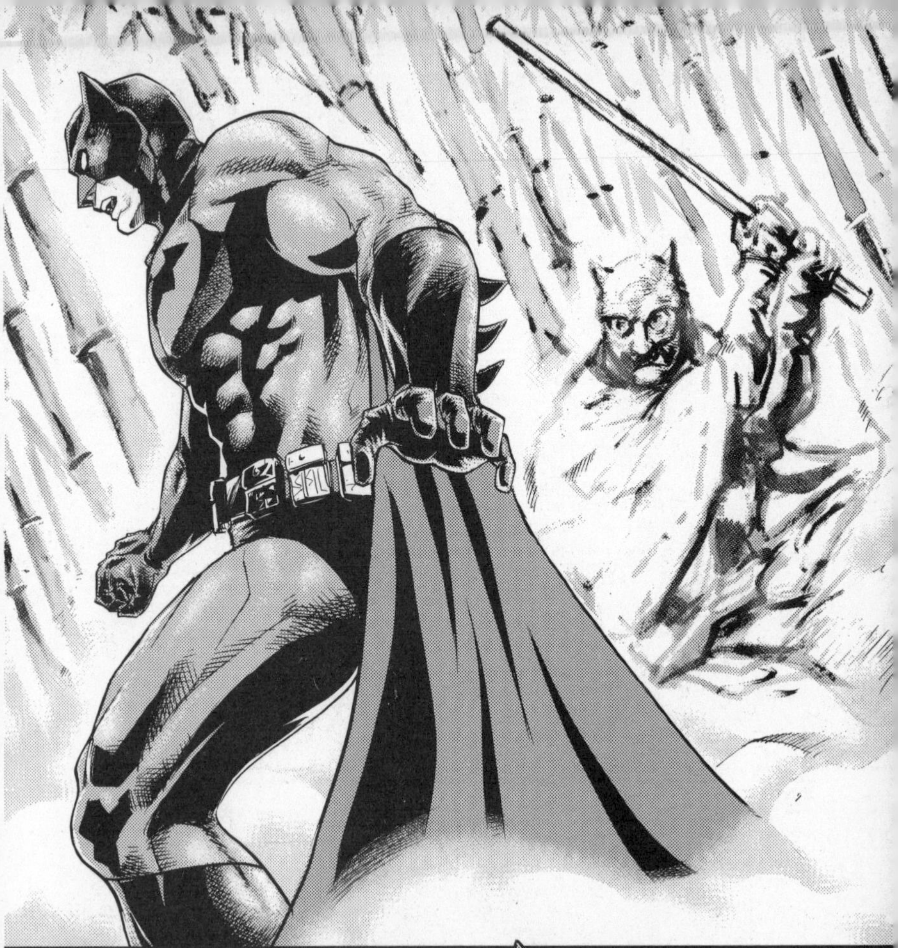
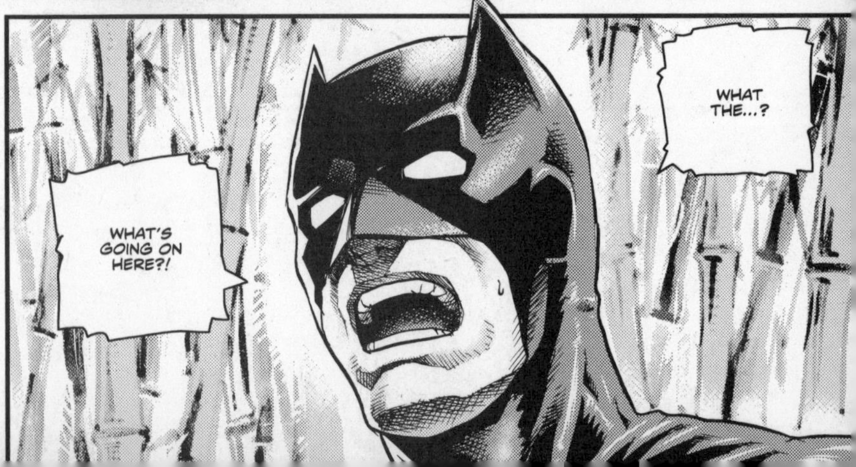
WHAT THE...?
WHAT'S GOING ON HERE?!

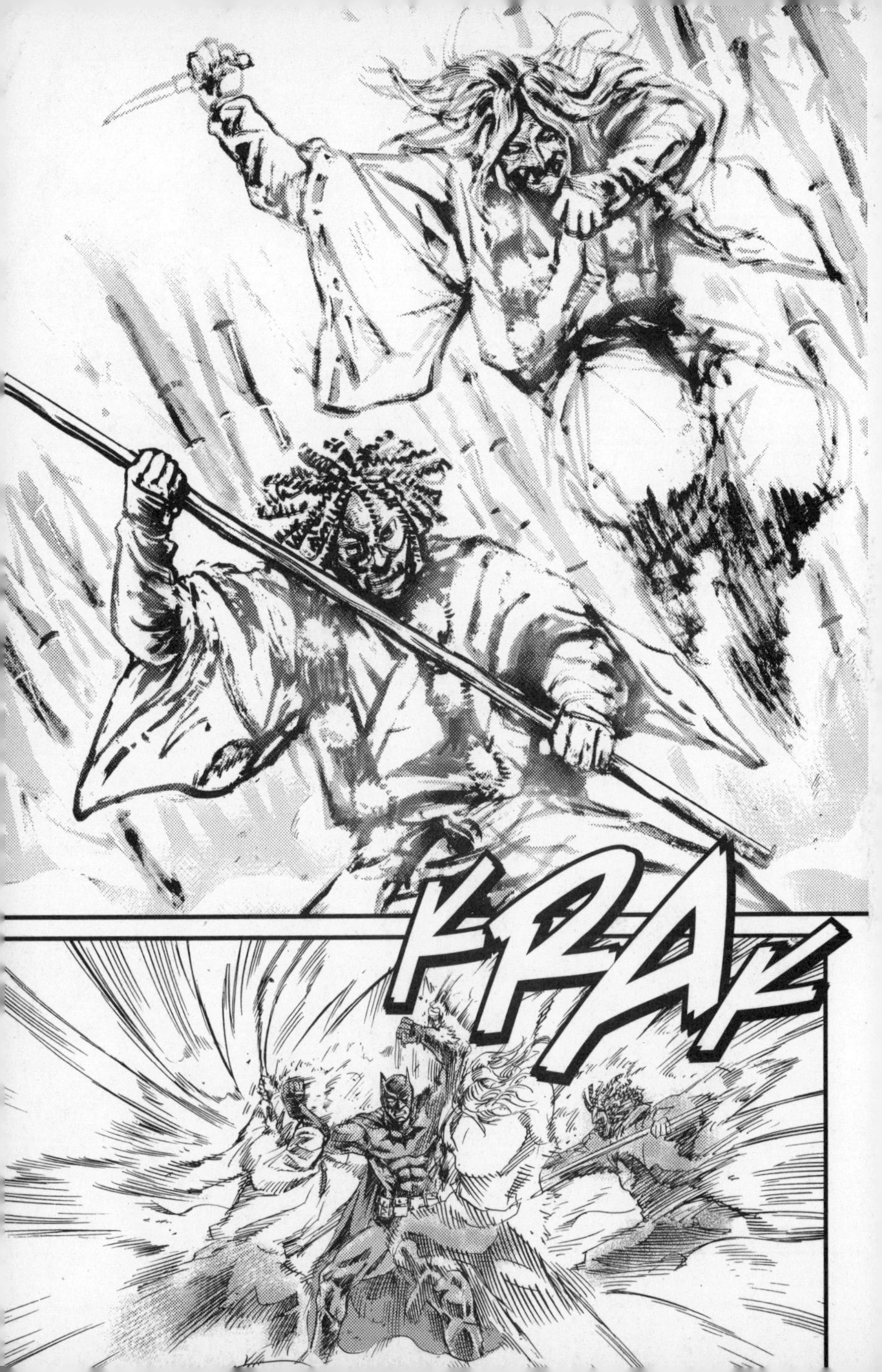
KRAK

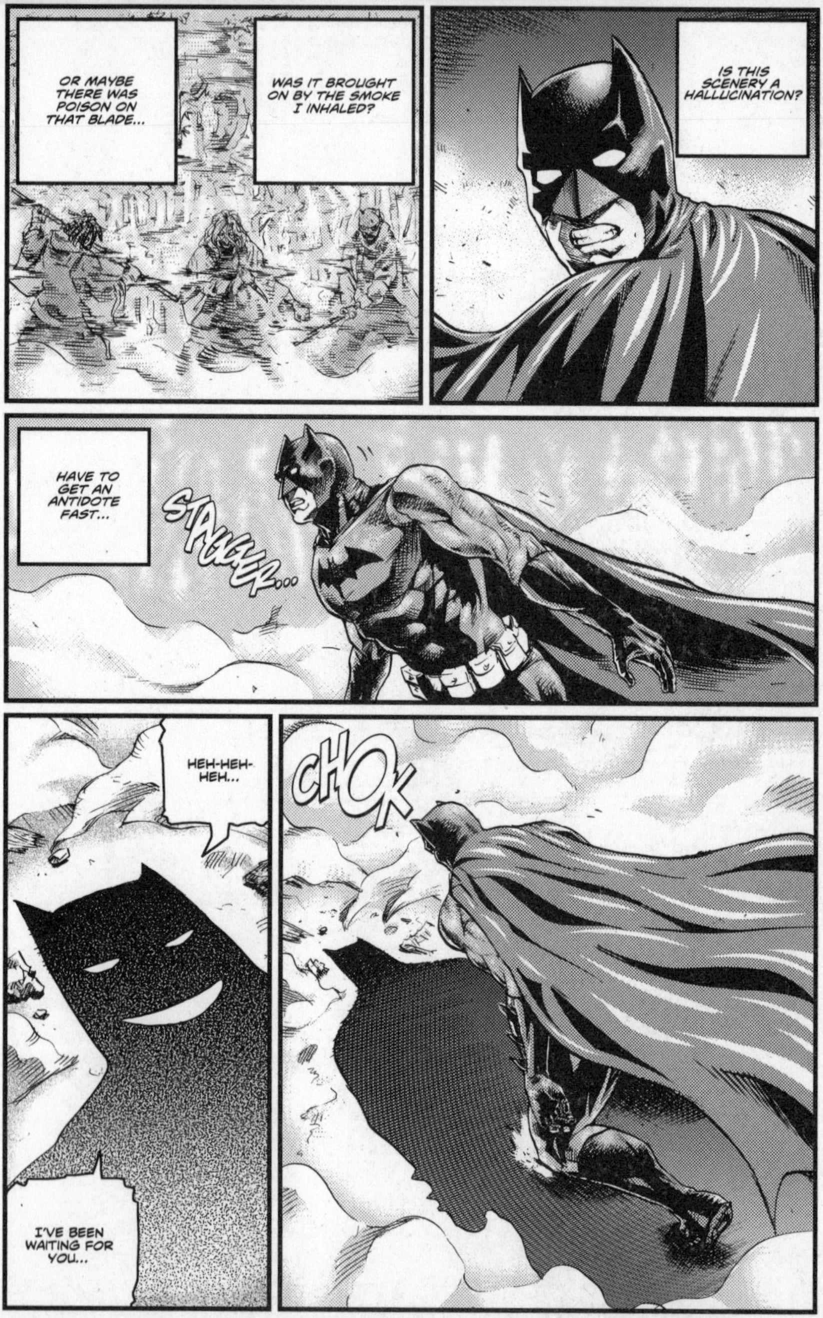
OR MAYBE THERE WAS POISON ON THAT BLADE...
WAS IT BROUGHT ON BY THE SMOKE I INHALED?
IS THIS SCENERY A HALLUCINATION?
HAVE TO GET AN ANTIDOTE FAST...
STAGGER...
HEH-HEH-HEH...
I'VE BEEN WAITING FOR YOU...
CHOK

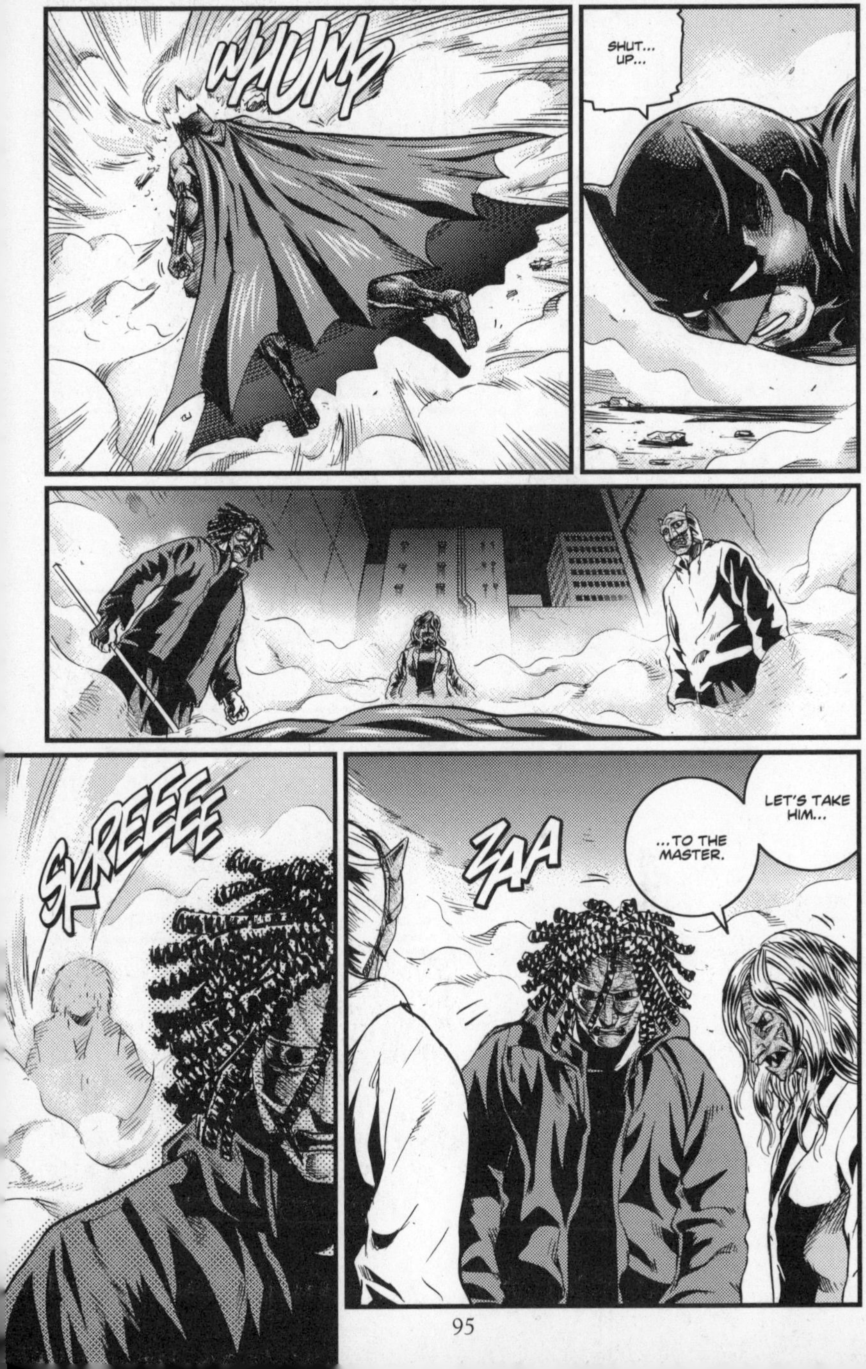
WHUMP
SHUT... UP...
SKREEEE
ZAA
LET'S TAKE HIM...
...TO THE MASTER.

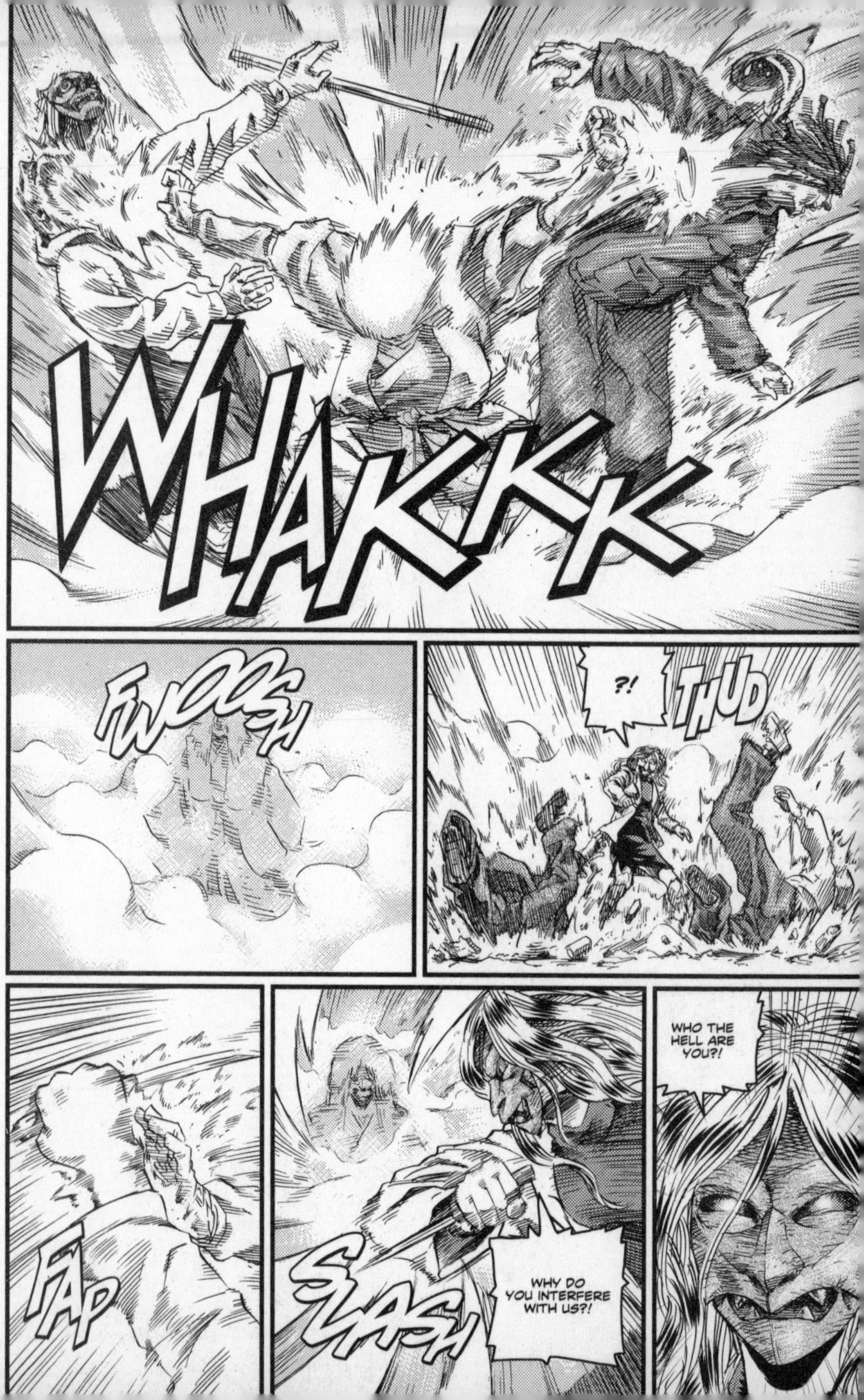
WHAKKK
FWOOSH
?!
THUD
FAP
SLASH
WHY DO YOU INTERFERE WITH US?!
WHO THE HELL ARE YOU?!

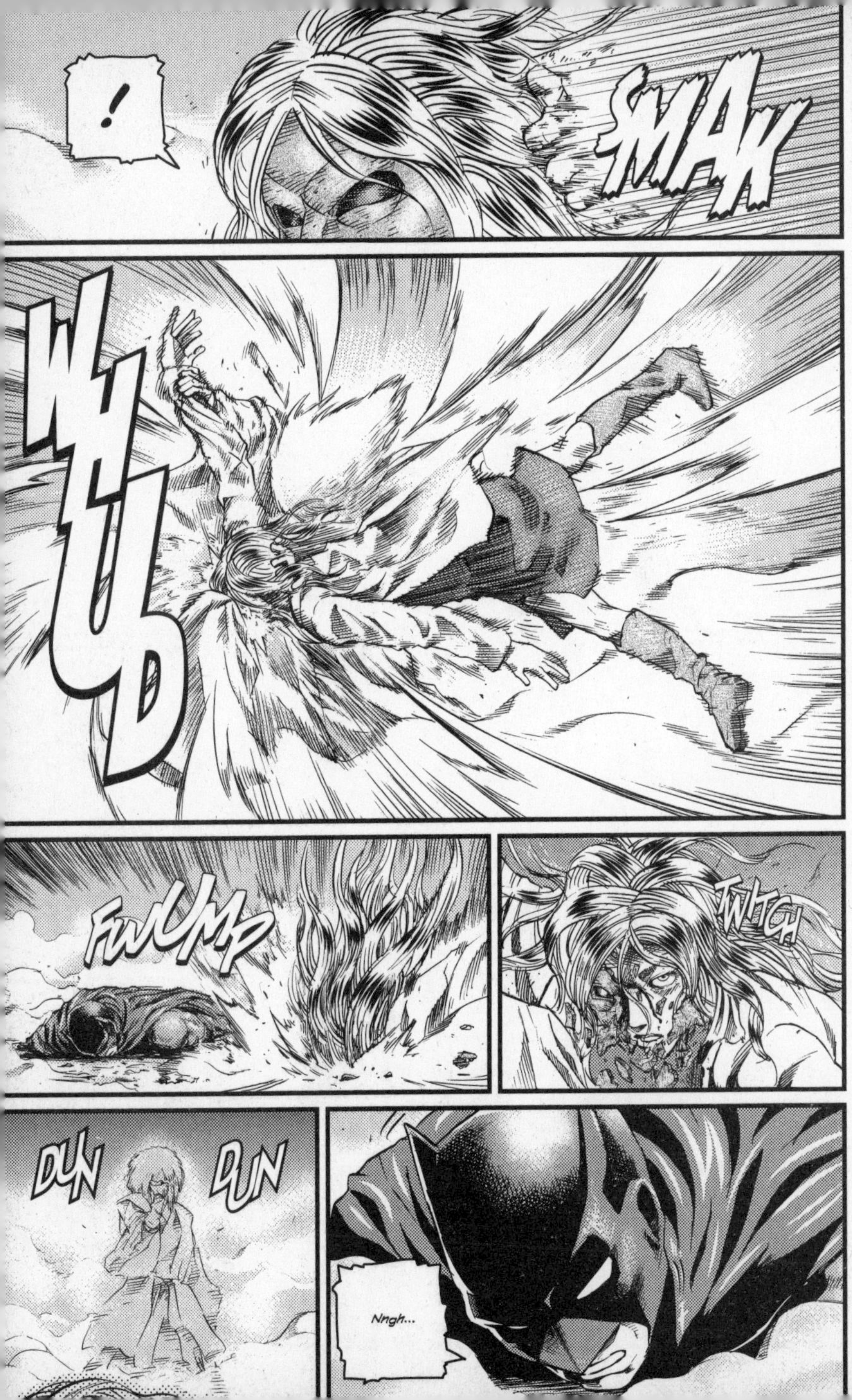

!
SMAK
WHUD
FWUMP
TWITCH
DUN DUN
Nngh...

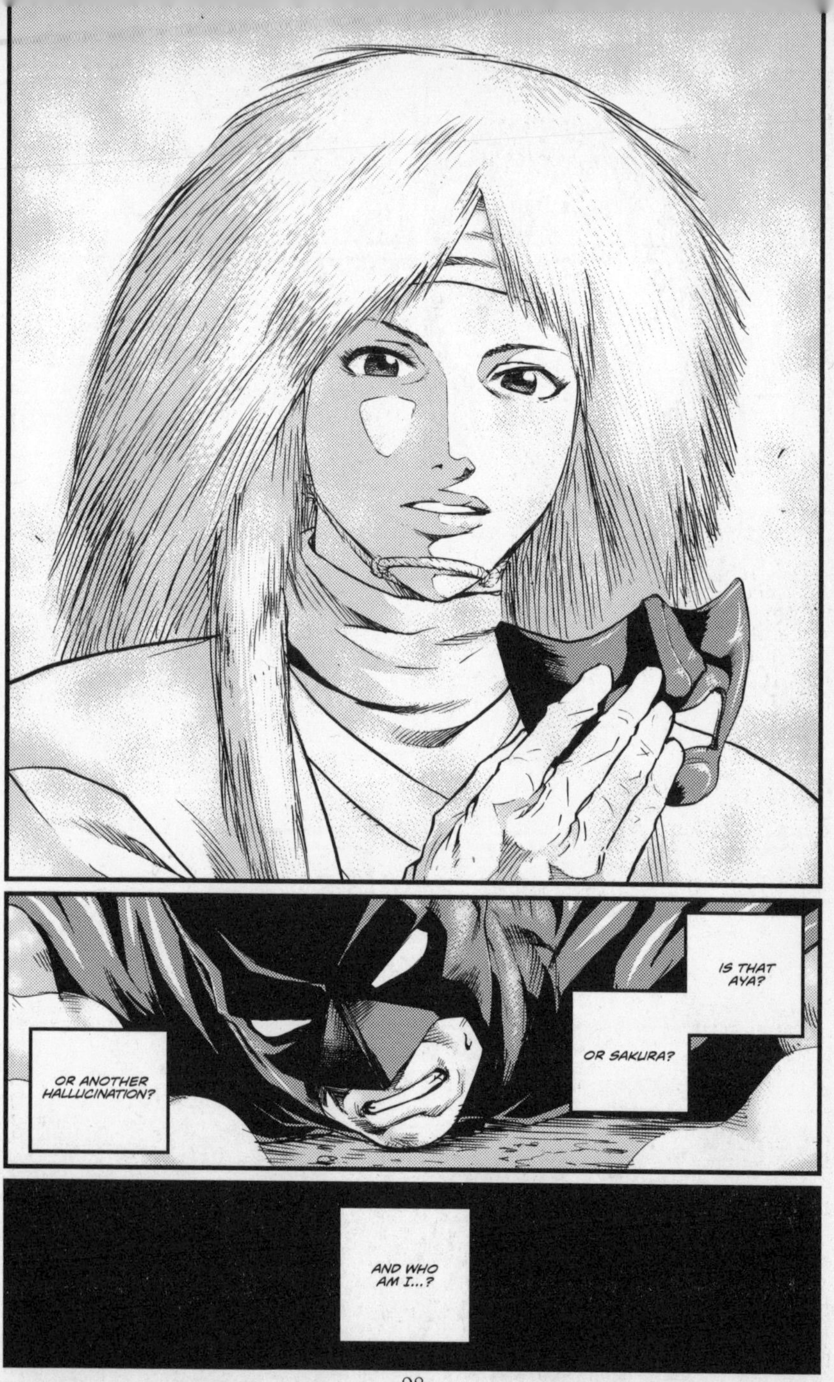
IS THAT AYA?
OR SAKURA?
OR ANOTHER HALLUCINATION?
AND WHO AM I...?

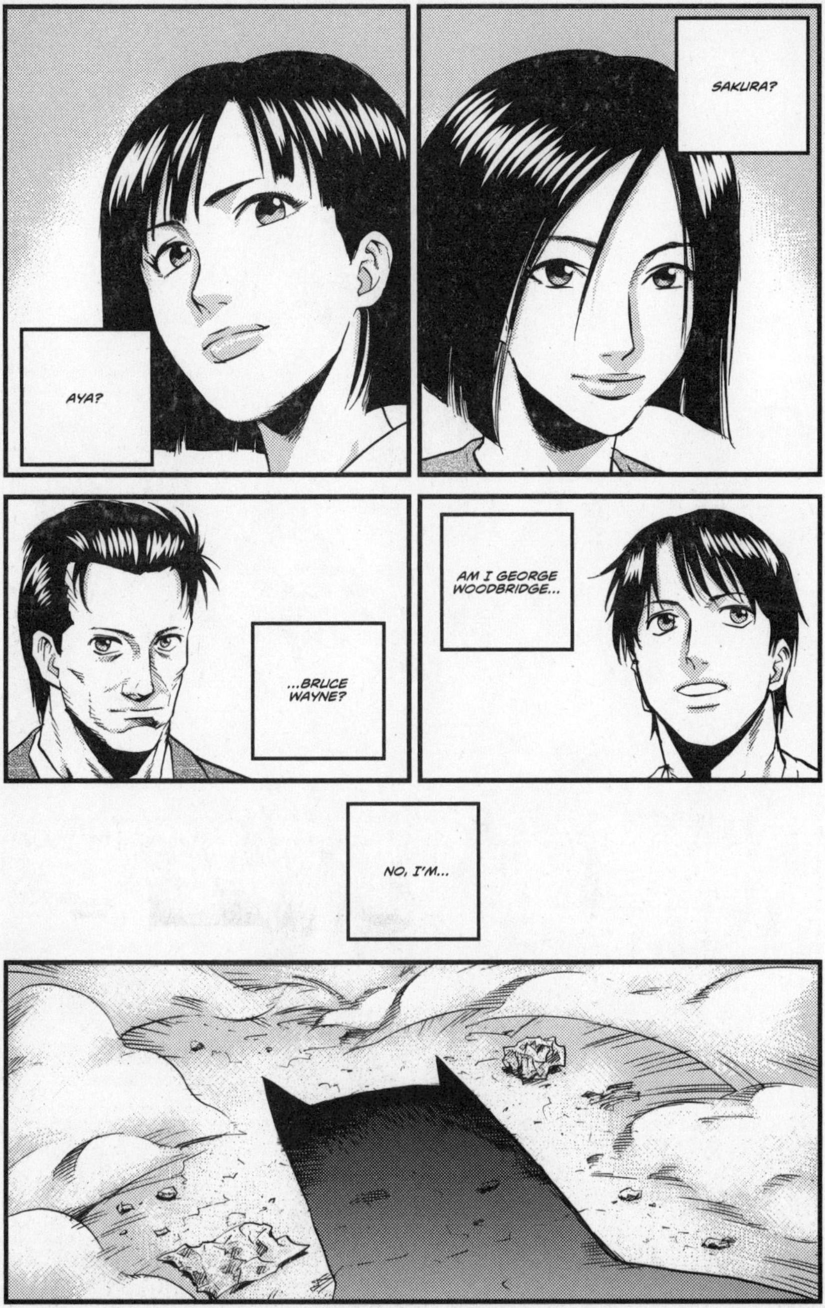
AYA?
SAKURA?
...BRUCE WAYNE?
AM I GEORGE WOODBRIDGE...
NO, I'M...

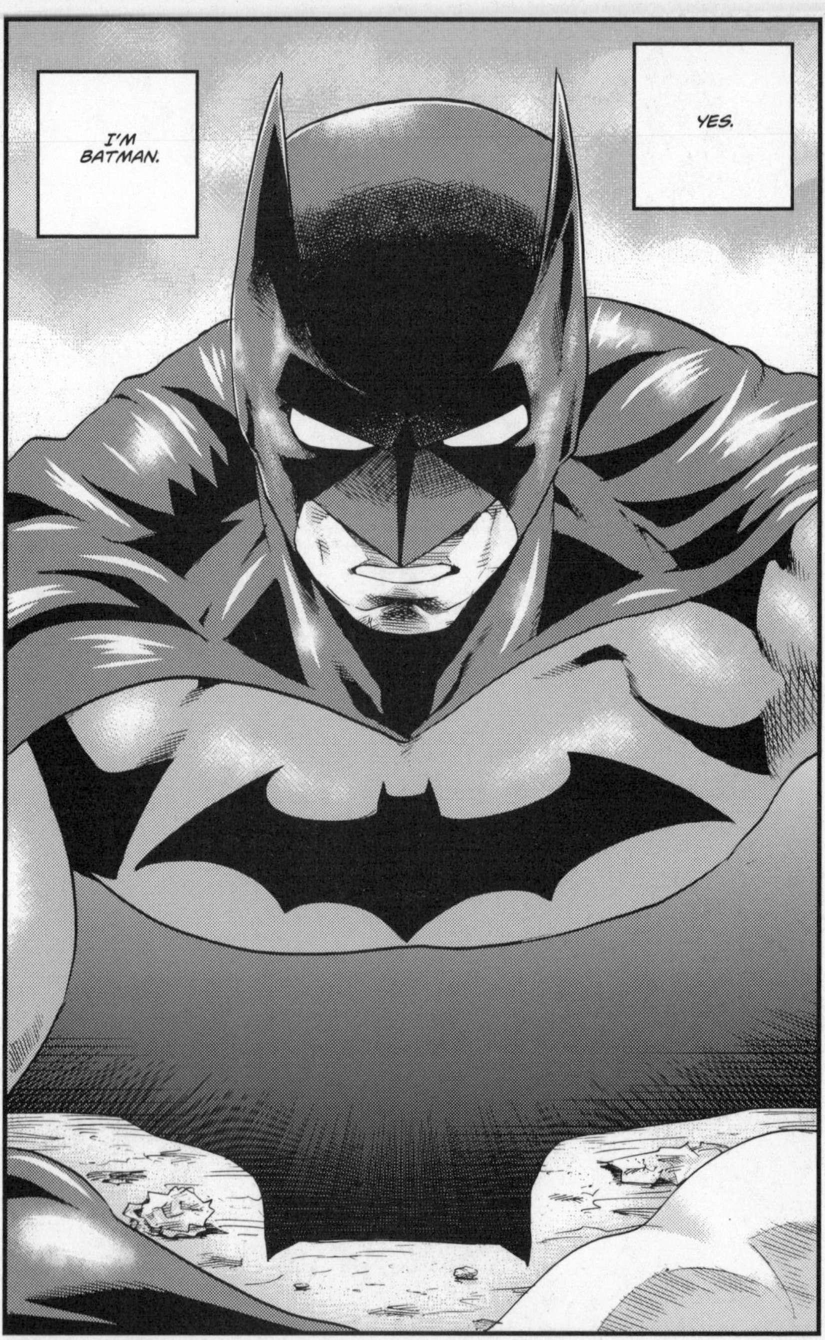
I'M BATMAN.
YES.

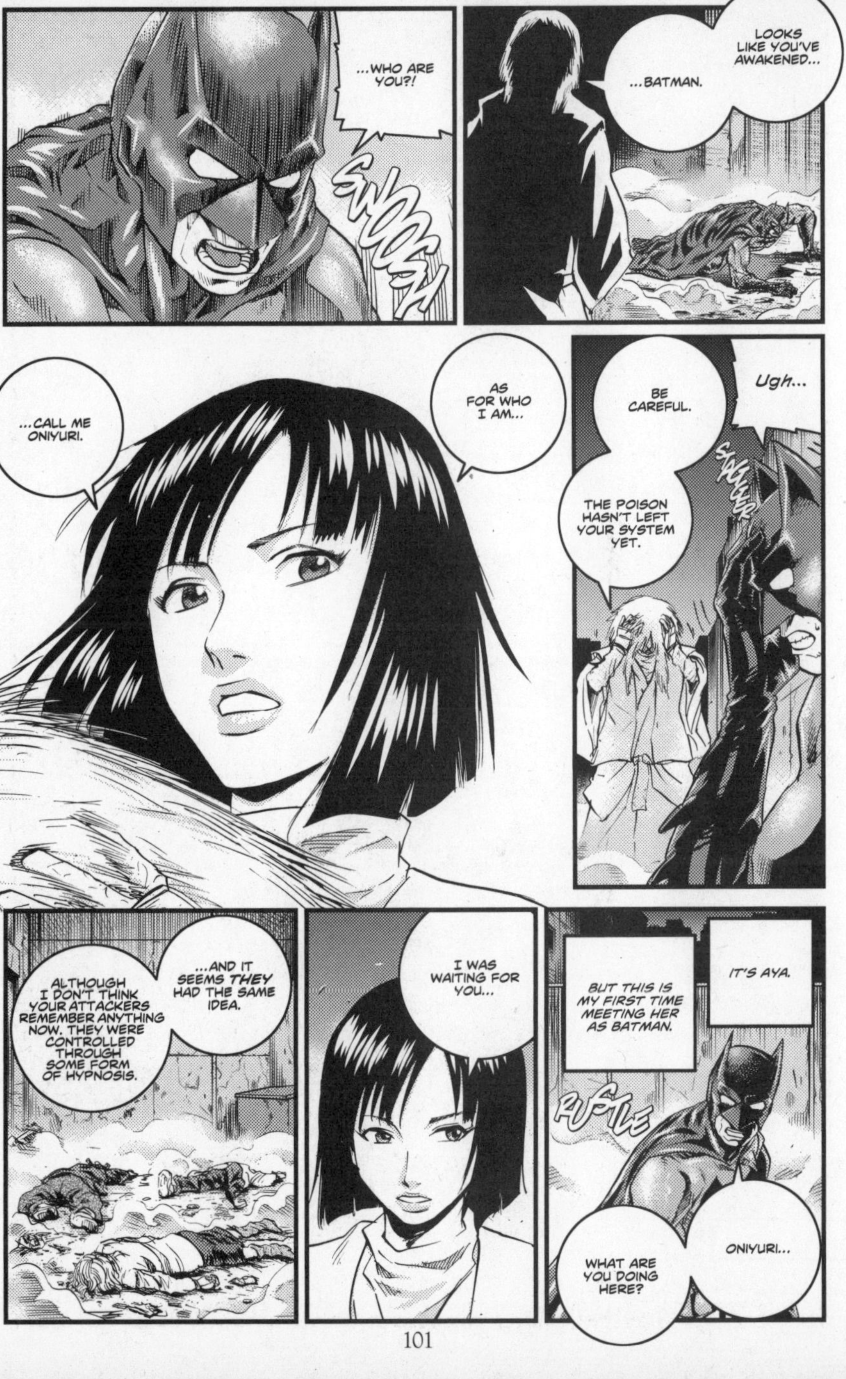
...WHO ARE YOU?!
SWOOSH
LOOKS LIKE YOU'VE AWAKENED...
...BATMAN.
AS FOR WHO I AM...
...CALL ME ONIYURI.
Ugh...
BE CAREFUL.
THE POISON HASN'T LEFT YOUR SYSTEM YET.
STAGGER
ALTHOUGH I DON'T THINK YOUR ATTACKERS REMEMBER ANYTHING NOW. THEY WERE CONTROLLED THROUGH SOME FORM OF HYPNOSIS.
...AND IT SEEMS THEY HAD THE SAME IDEA.
I WAS WAITING FOR YOU...
IT'S AYA.
BUT THIS IS MY FIRST TIME MEETING HER AS BATMAN.
RUSTLE
ONIYURI...
WHAT ARE YOU DOING HERE?

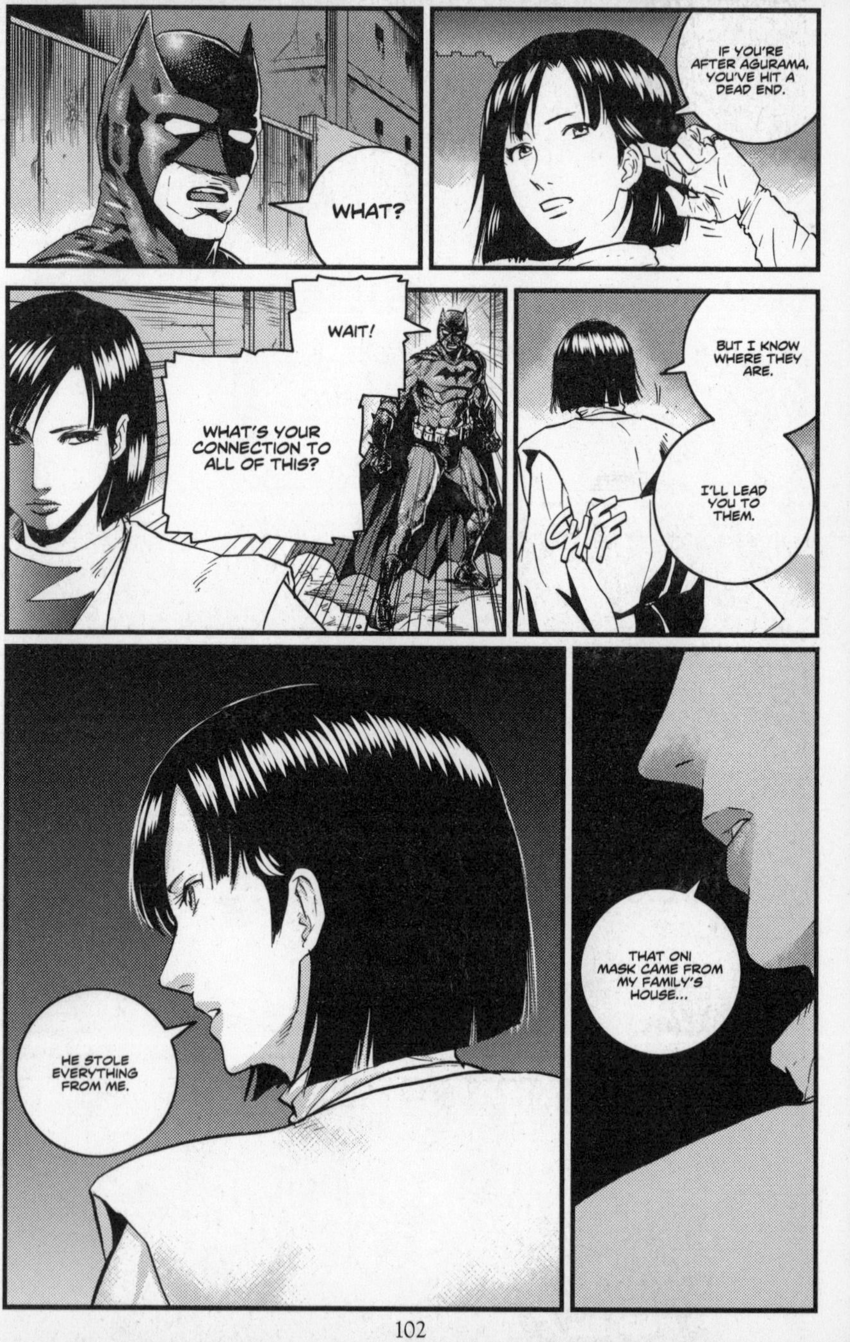
WHAT?
IF YOU'RE AFTER AGURAMA, YOU'VE HIT A DEAD END.
WAIT!
WHAT'S YOUR CONNECTION TO ALL OF THIS?
BUT I KNOW WHERE THEY ARE.
I'LL LEAD YOU TO THEM.
CHFF
THAT ONI MASK CAME FROM MY FAMILY'S HOUSE...
HE STOLE EVERYTHING FROM ME.

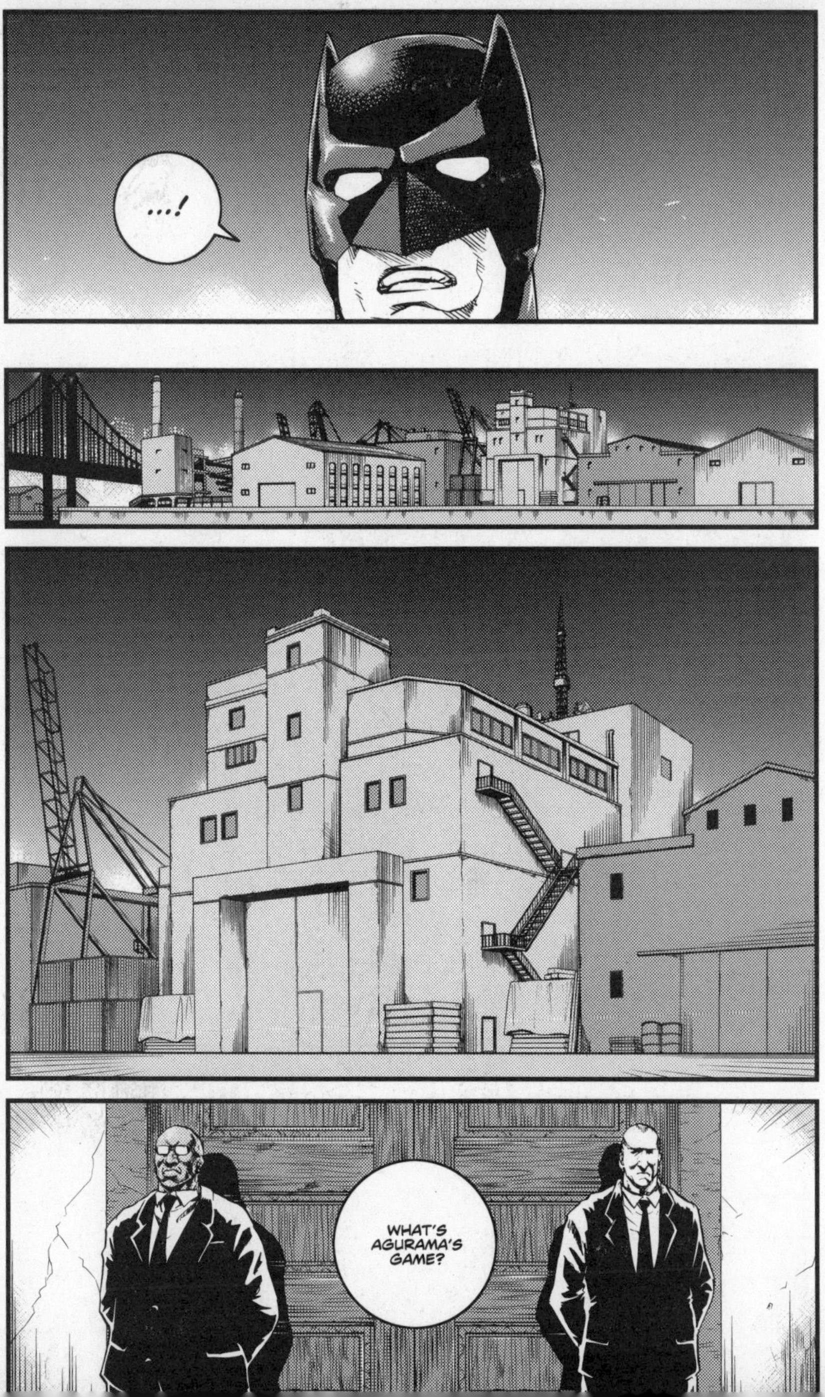
...!
WHAT'S AGURAMA'S GAME?

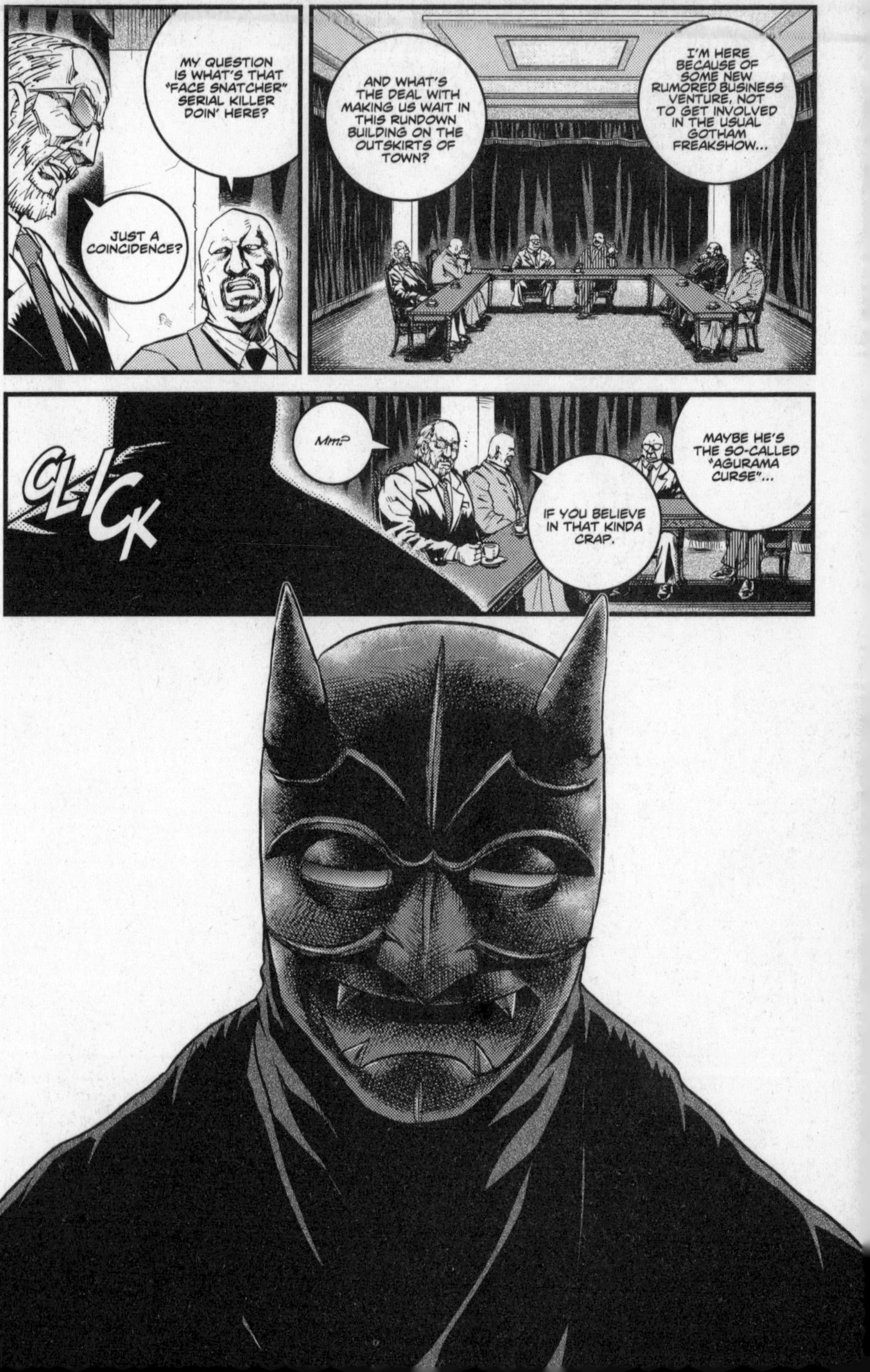
MY QUESTION IS WHAT'S THAT "FACE SNATCHER" SERIAL KILLER DOIN' HERE?
JUST A COINCIDENCE?
AND WHAT'S THE DEAL WITH MAKING US WAIT IN THIS RUNDOWN BUILDING ON THE OUTSKIRTS OF TOWN?
I'M HERE BECAUSE OF SOME NEW RUMORED BUSINESS VENTURE, NOT TO GET INVOLVED IN THE USUAL GOTHAM FREAKSHOW...
CLICK
Mm?
MAYBE HE'S THE SO-CALLED "AGURAMA CURSE"...
IF YOU BELIEVE IN THAT KINDA CRAP.

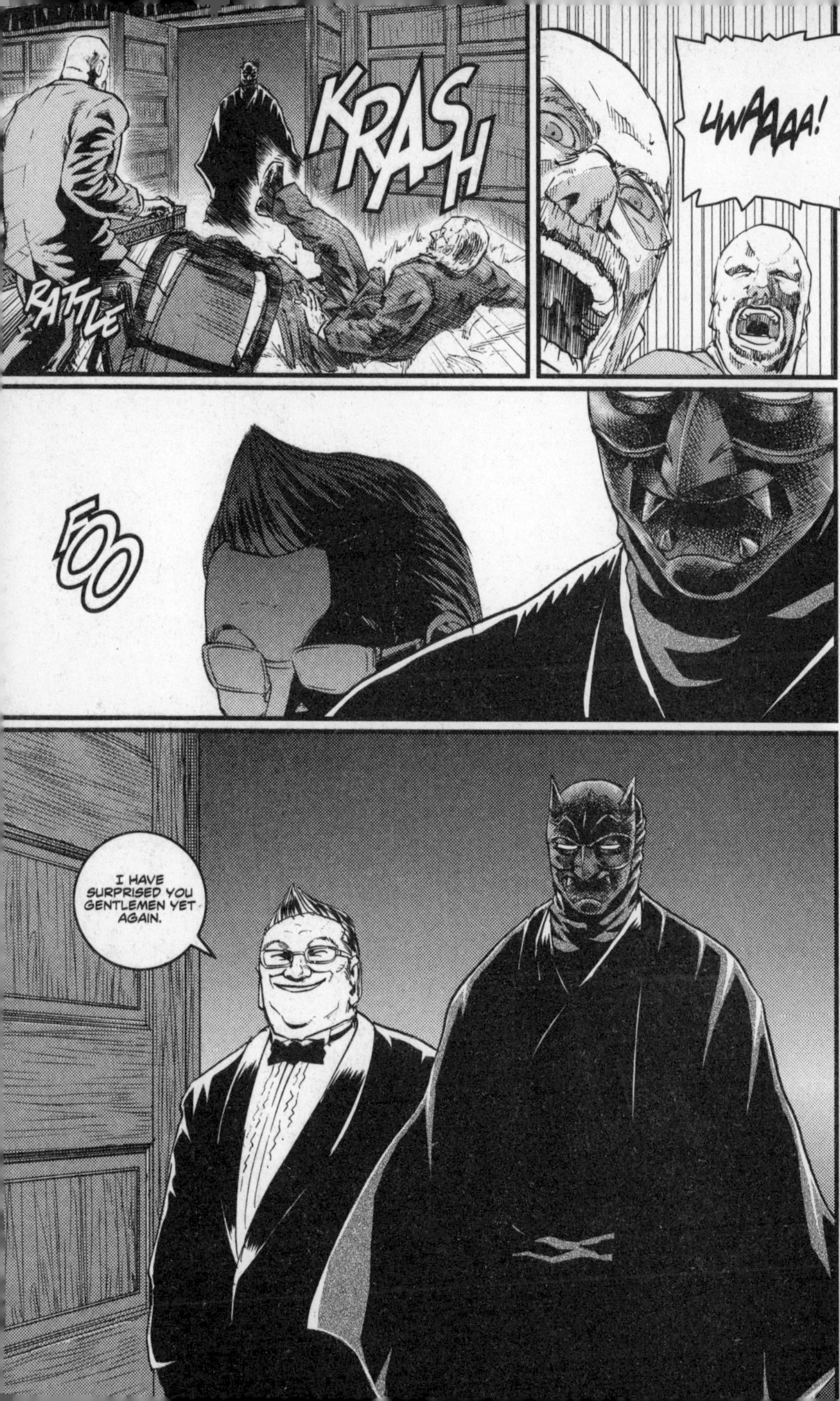
KRASH
RATTLE
UWAAAA!
FOO
I HAVE SURPRISED YOU GENTLEMEN YET AGAIN.

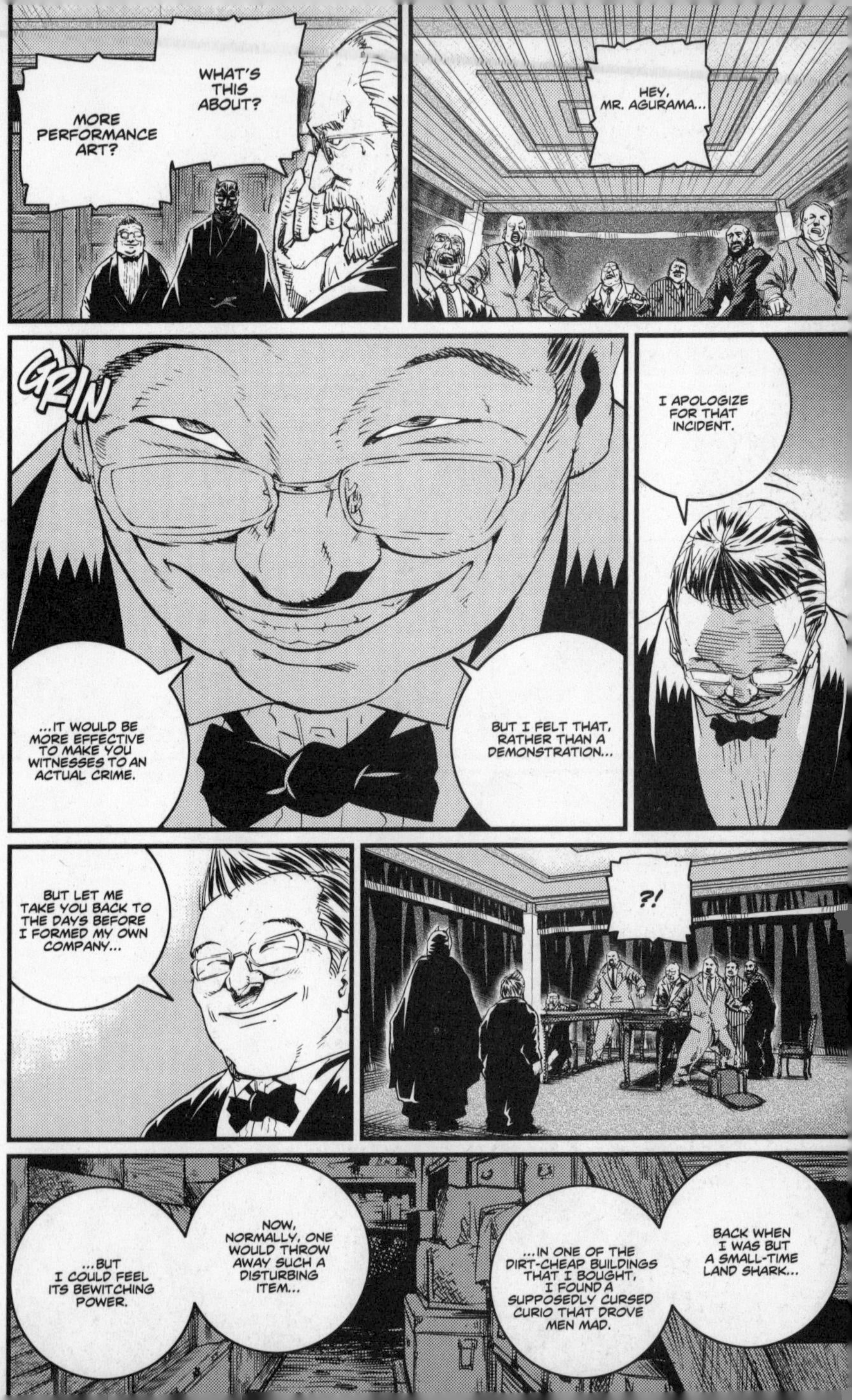
HEY, MR. AGURAMA...
WHAT'S THIS ABOUT?
MORE PERFORMANCE ART?
I APOLOGIZE FOR THAT INCIDENT.
GRIN
BUT I FELT THAT, RATHER THAN A DEMONSTRATION...
...IT WOULD BE MORE EFFECTIVE TO MAKE YOU WITNESSES TO AN ACTUAL CRIME.
?!
BUT LET ME TAKE YOU BACK TO THE DAYS BEFORE I FORMED MY OWN COMPANY...
BACK WHEN I WAS BUT A SMALL-TIME LAND SHARK...
...IN ONE OF THE DIRT-CHEAP BUILDINGS THAT I BOUGHT, I FOUND A SUPPOSEDLY CURSED CURIO THAT DROVE MEN MAD.
NOW, NORMALLY, ONE WOULD THROW AWAY SUCH A DISTURBING ITEM...
...BUT I COULD FEEL ITS BEWITCHING POWER.

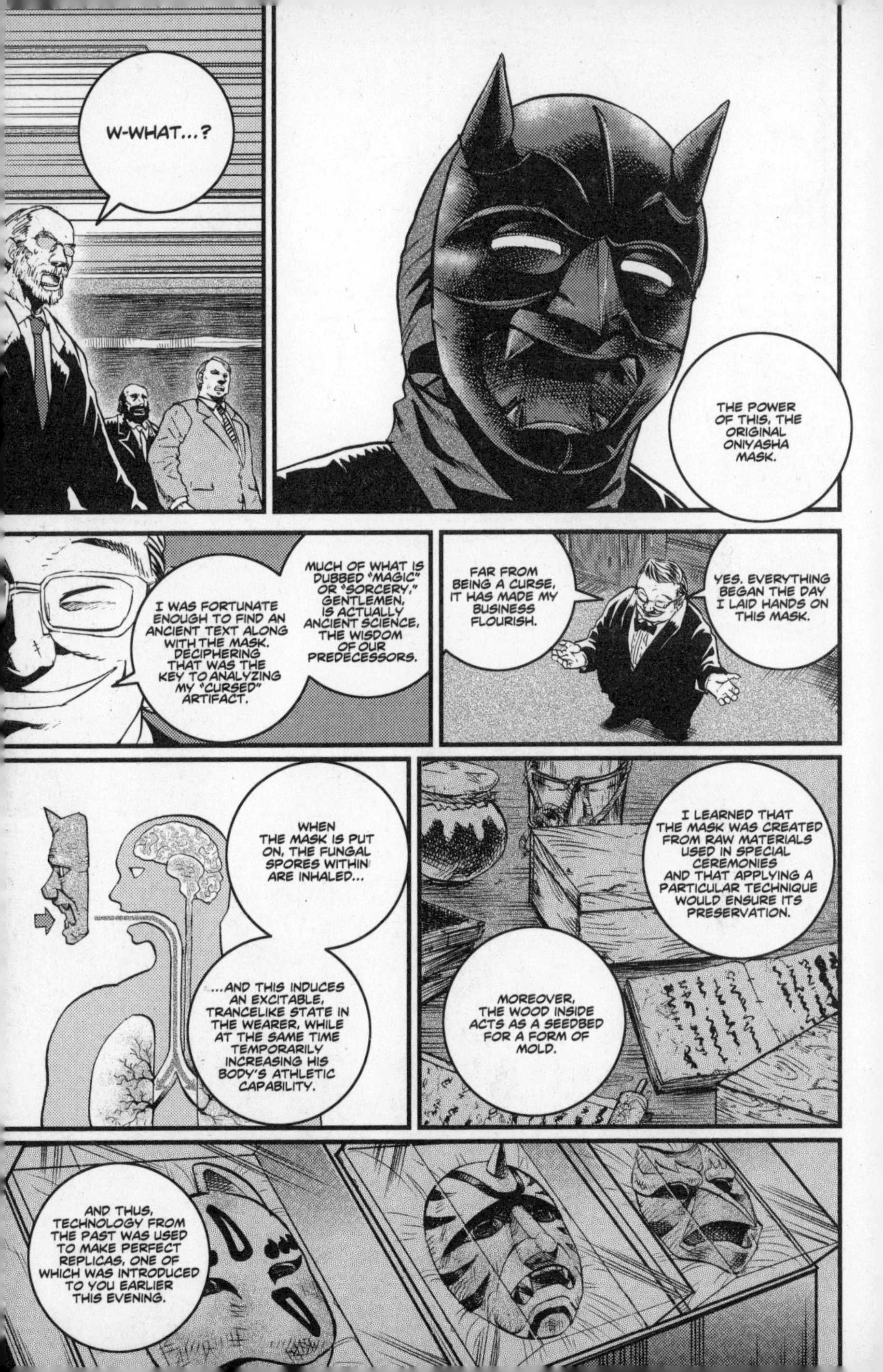
W-WHAT...?
THE POWER OF THIS, THE ORIGINAL ONIYASHA MASK.
I WAS FORTUNATE ENOUGH TO FIND AN ANCIENT TEXT ALONG WITH THE MASK. DECIPHERING THAT WAS THE KEY TO ANALYZING MY "CURSED" ARTIFACT.
MUCH OF WHAT IS DUBBED "MAGIC" OR "SORCERY," GENTLEMEN, IS ACTUALLY ANCIENT SCIENCE, THE WISDOM OF OUR PREDECESSORS.
FAR FROM BEING A CURSE, IT HAS MADE MY BUSINESS FLOURISH.
YES. EVERYTHING BEGAN THE DAY I LAID HANDS ON THIS MASK.
WHEN THE MASK IS PUT ON, THE FUNGAL SPORES WITHIN ARE INHALED...
...AND THIS INDUCES AN EXCITABLE, TRANCELIKE STATE IN THE WEARER, WHILE AT THE SAME TIME TEMPORARILY INCREASING HIS BODY'S ATHLETIC CAPABILITY.
I LEARNED THAT THE MASK WAS CREATED FROM RAW MATERIALS USED IN SPECIAL CEREMONIES AND THAT APPLYING A PARTICULAR TECHNIQUE WOULD ENSURE ITS PRESERVATION.
MOREOVER, THE WOOD INSIDE ACTS AS A SEEDBED FOR A FORM OF MOLD.
AND THUS, TECHNOLOGY FROM THE PAST WAS USED TO MAKE PERFECT REPLICAS, ONE OF WHICH WAS INTRODUCED TO YOU EARLIER THIS EVENING.

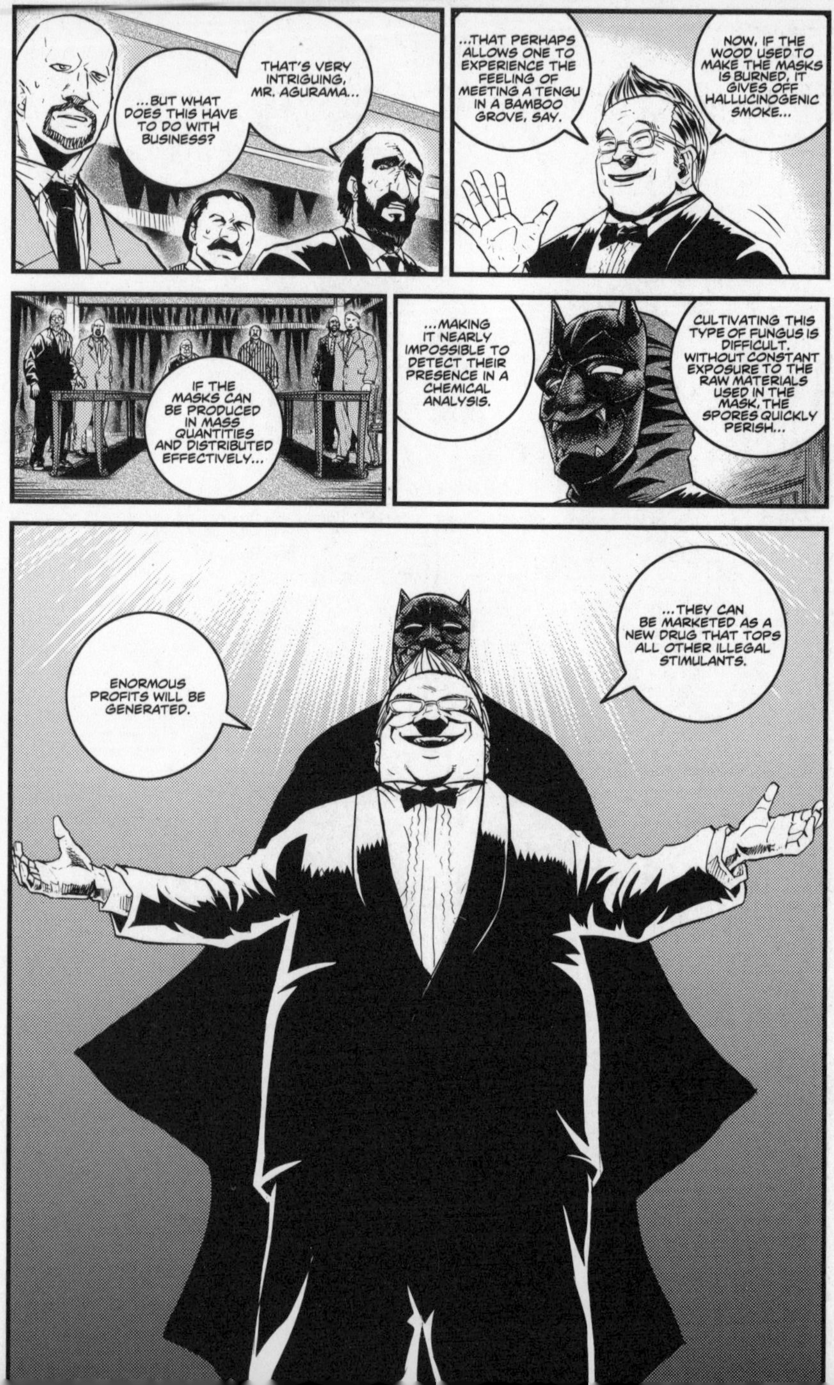
THAT'S VERY INTRIGUING, MR. AGURAMA...
...BUT WHAT DOES THIS HAVE TO DO WITH BUSINESS?
NOW, IF THE WOOD USED TO MAKE THE MASKS IS BURNED, IT GIVES OFF HALLUCINOGENIC SMOKE...
...THAT PERHAPS ALLOWS ONE TO EXPERIENCE THE FEELING OF MEETING A TENGU IN A BAMBOO GROVE, SAY.
IF THE MASKS CAN BE PRODUCED IN MASS QUANTITIES AND DISTRIBUTED EFFECTIVELY...
CULTIVATING THIS TYPE OF FUNGUS IS DIFFICULT. WITHOUT CONSTANT EXPOSURE TO THE RAW MATERIALS USED IN THE MASK, THE SPORES QUICKLY PERISH...
...MAKING IT NEARLY IMPOSSIBLE TO DETECT THEIR PRESENCE IN A CHEMICAL ANALYSIS.
...THEY CAN BE MARKETED AS A NEW DRUG THAT TOPS ALL OTHER ILLEGAL STIMULANTS.
ENORMOUS PROFITS WILL BE GENERATED.

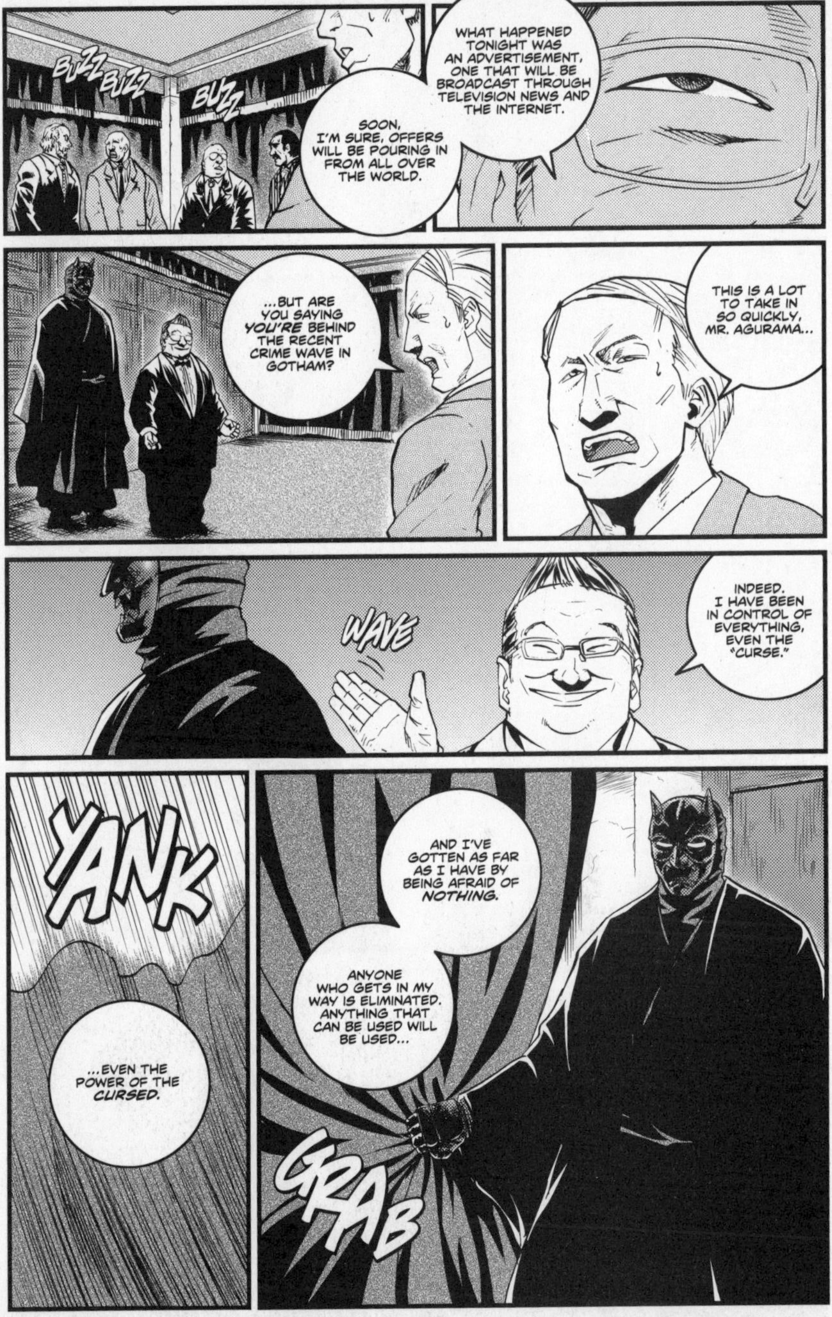
BUZZ
BUZZ
BUZZ
WHAT HAPPENED TONIGHT WAS AN ADVERTISEMENT, ONE THAT WILL BE BROADCAST THROUGH TELEVISION NEWS AND THE INTERNET.
SOON, I'M SURE, OFFERS WILL BE POURING IN FROM ALL OVER THE WORLD.
...BUT ARE YOU SAYING *YOU'RE* BEHIND THE RECENT CRIME WAVE IN GOTHAM?
THIS IS A LOT TO TAKE IN SO QUICKLY, MR. AGURAMA...
WAVE
INDEED. I HAVE BEEN IN CONTROL OF EVERYTHING, EVEN THE "CURSE."
YANK
AND I'VE GOTTEN AS FAR AS I HAVE BY BEING AFRAID OF *NOTHING.*
ANYONE WHO GETS IN MY WAY IS ELIMINATED. ANYTHING THAT CAN BE USED WILL BE USED...
...EVEN THE POWER OF THE *CURSED.*
GRAB

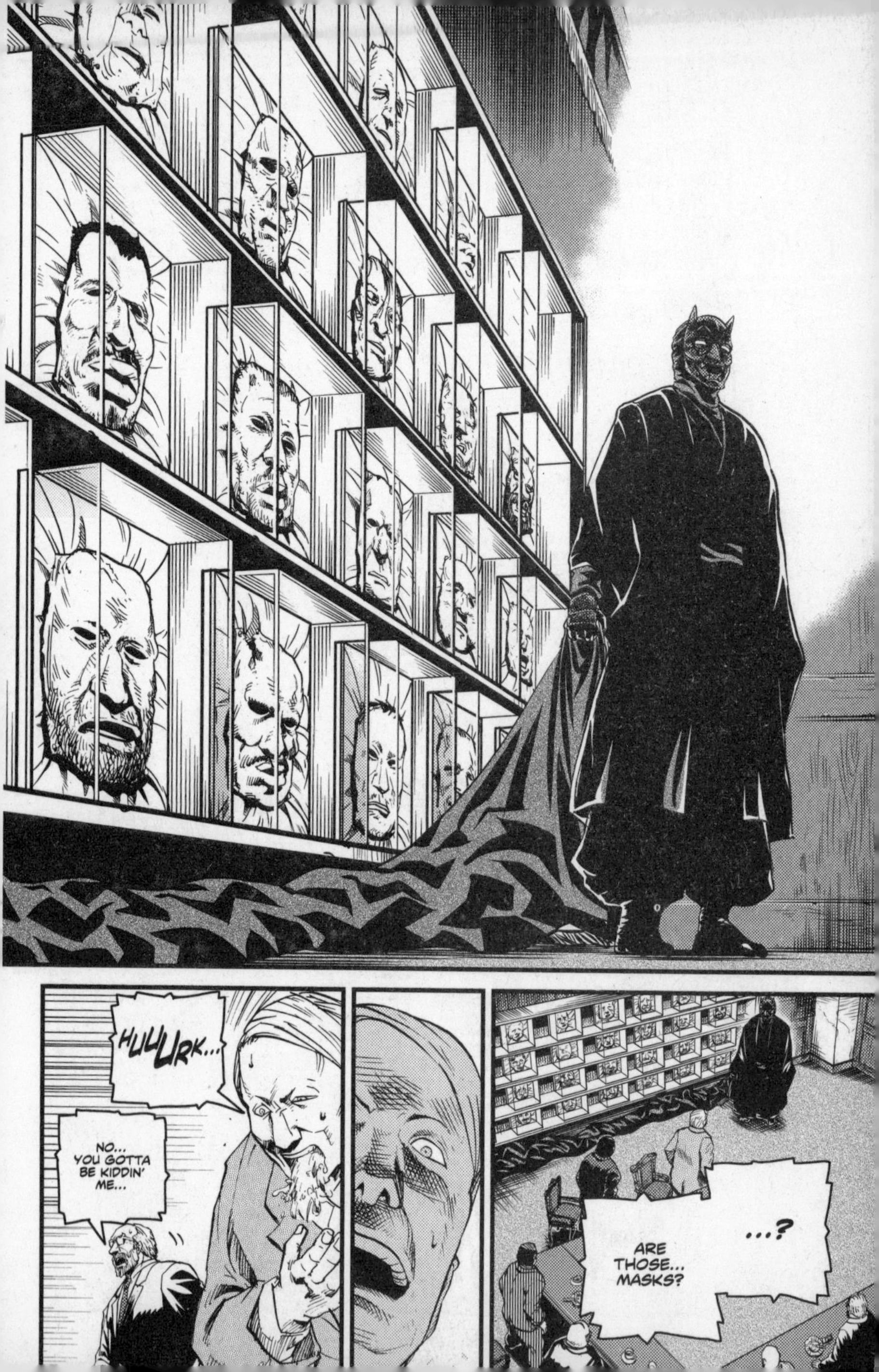
HUUURK...
NO... YOU GOTTA BE KIDDIN' ME...
...?
ARE THOSE... MASKS?

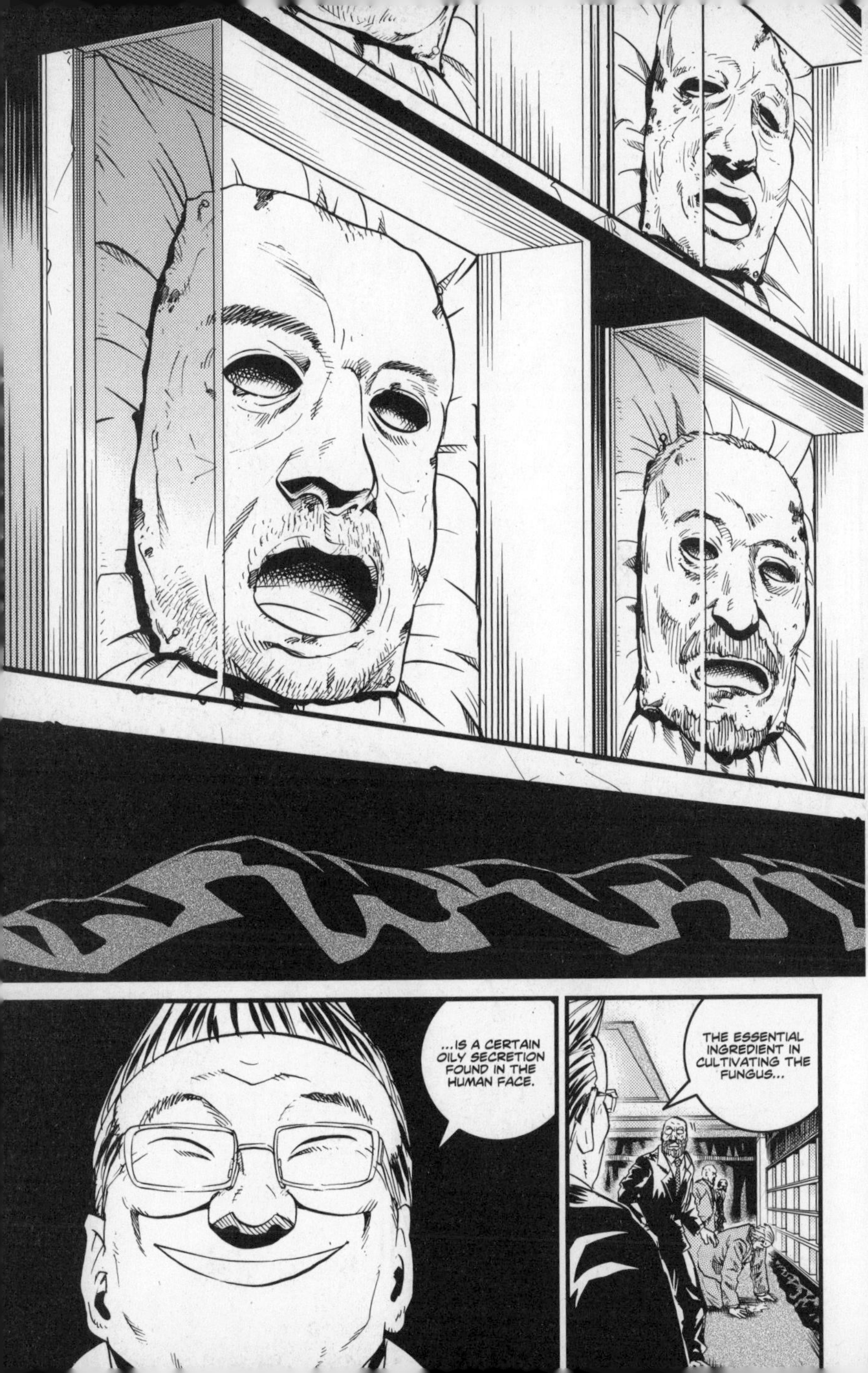
...IS A CERTAIN OILY SECRETION FOUND IN THE HUMAN FACE.
THE ESSENTIAL INGREDIENT IN CULTIVATING THE FUNGUS...

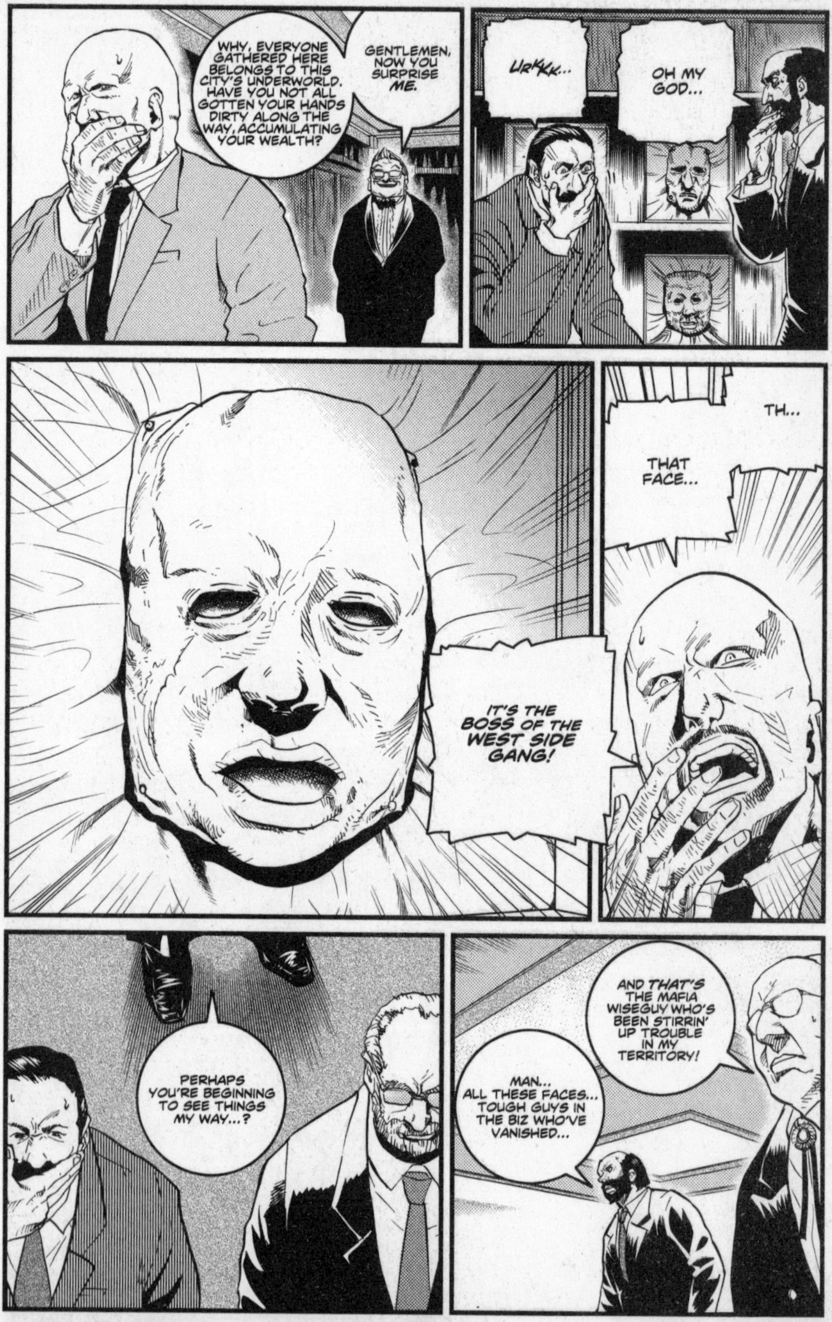

WHY, EVERYONE GATHERED HERE BELONGS TO THIS CITY'S UNDERWORLD. HAVE YOU NOT ALL GOTTEN YOUR HANDS DIRTY ALONG THE WAY, ACCUMULATING YOUR WEALTH?
GENTLEMEN, NOW YOU SURPRISE ME.
URKKK...
OH MY GOD...
TH...
THAT FACE...
IT'S THE BOSS OF THE WEST SIDE GANG!
PERHAPS YOU'RE BEGINNING TO SEE THINGS MY WAY...?
AND THAT'S THE MAFIA WISEGUY WHO'S BEEN STIRRIN' UP TROUBLE IN MY TERRITORY!
MAN... ALL THESE FACES... TOUGH GUYS IN THE BIZ WHO'VE VANISHED...

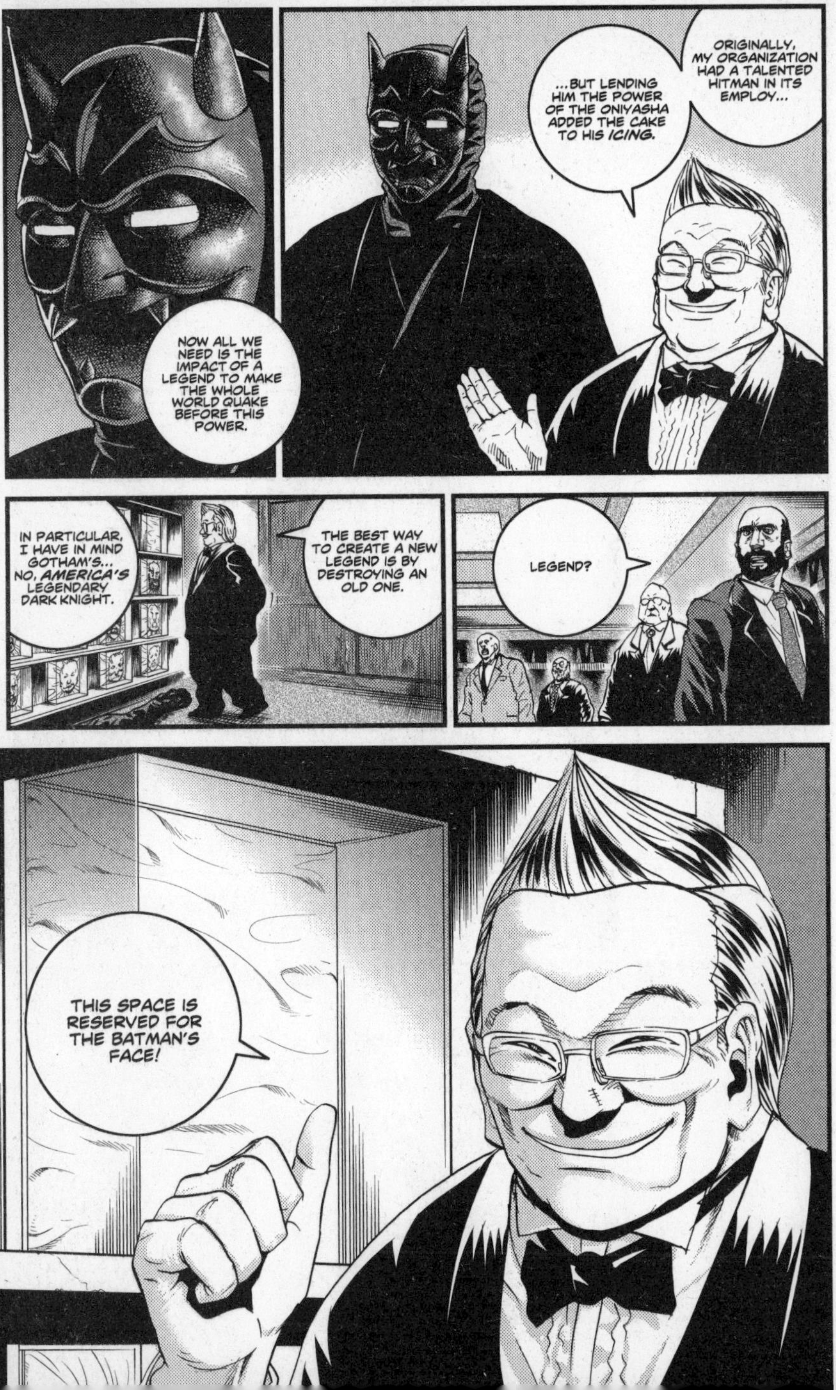
ORIGINALLY, MY ORGANIZATION HAD A TALENTED HITMAN IN ITS EMPLOY...
...BUT LENDING HIM THE POWER OF THE ONIYASHA ADDED THE CAKE TO HIS *ICING*.
NOW ALL WE NEED IS THE IMPACT OF A LEGEND TO MAKE THE WHOLE WORLD QUAKE BEFORE THIS POWER.
LEGEND?
THE BEST WAY TO CREATE A NEW LEGEND IS BY DESTROYING AN OLD ONE.
IN PARTICULAR, I HAVE IN MIND GOTHAM'S... NO, ***AMERICA'S*** LEGENDARY DARK KNIGHT.
THIS SPACE IS RESERVED FOR THE BATMAN'S FACE!

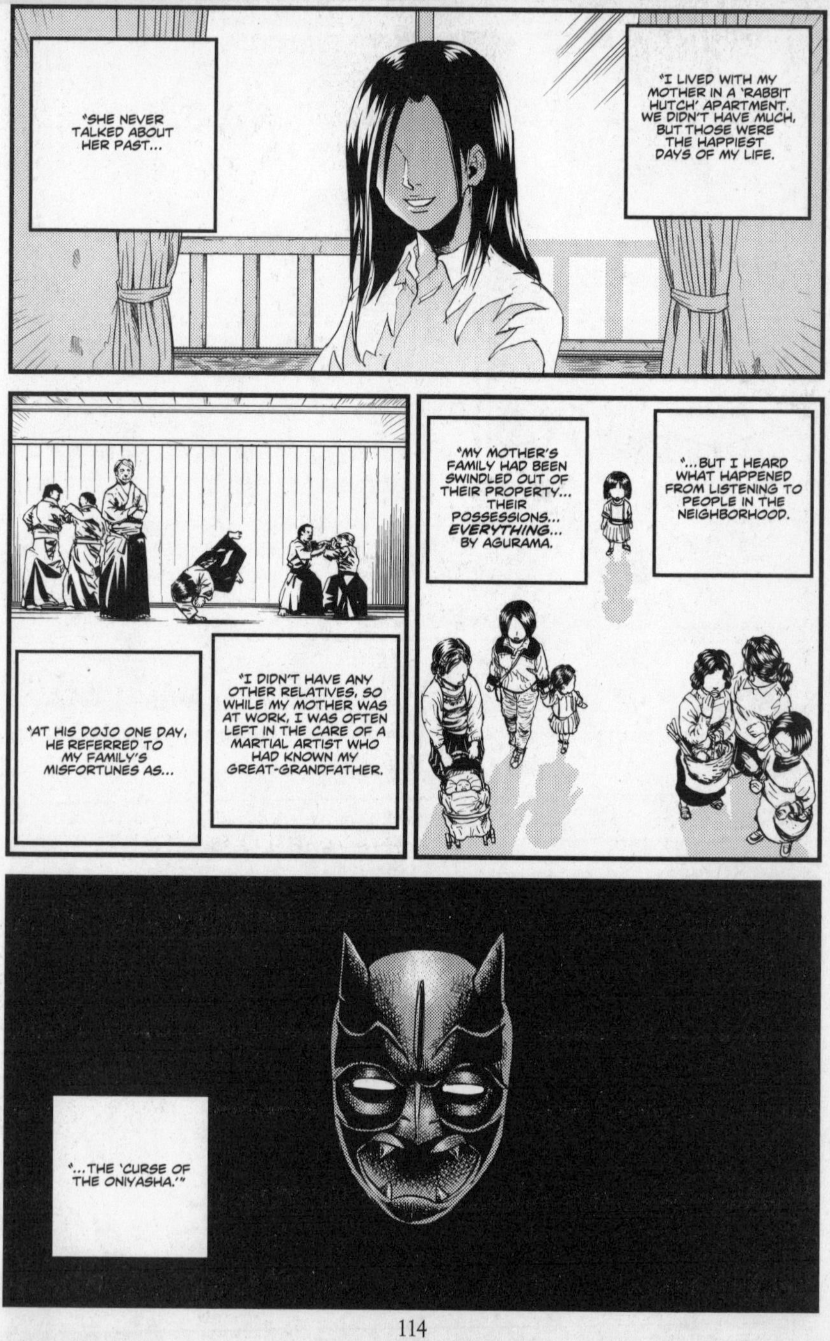
"SHE NEVER TALKED ABOUT HER PAST...
"I LIVED WITH MY MOTHER IN A 'RABBIT HUTCH' APARTMENT. WE DIDN'T HAVE MUCH, BUT THOSE WERE THE HAPPIEST DAYS OF MY LIFE.
"...BUT I HEARD WHAT HAPPENED FROM LISTENING TO PEOPLE IN THE NEIGHBORHOOD.
"MY MOTHER'S FAMILY HAD BEEN SWINDLED OUT OF THEIR PROPERTY... THEIR POSSESSIONS... EVERYTHING... BY AGURAMA.
"I DIDN'T HAVE ANY OTHER RELATIVES, SO WHILE MY MOTHER WAS AT WORK, I WAS OFTEN LEFT IN THE CARE OF A MARTIAL ARTIST WHO HAD KNOWN MY GREAT-GRANDFATHER.
"AT HIS DOJO ONE DAY, HE REFERRED TO MY FAMILY'S MISFORTUNES AS...
"...THE 'CURSE OF THE ONIYASHA.'"

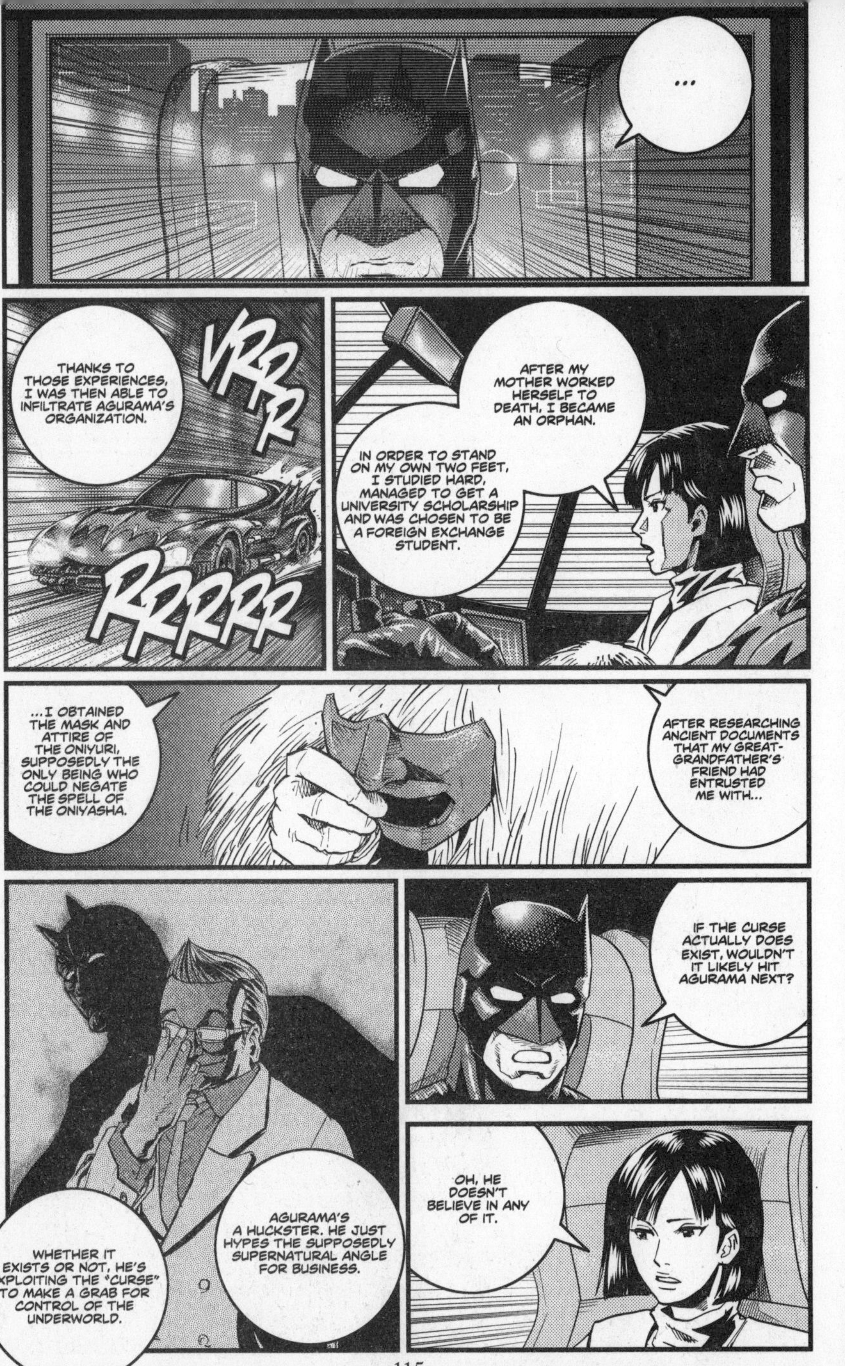
...
THANKS TO THOSE EXPERIENCES, I WAS THEN ABLE TO INFILTRATE AGURAMA'S ORGANIZATION.
VRRR
RRRRR
AFTER MY MOTHER WORKED HERSELF TO DEATH, I BECAME AN ORPHAN.
IN ORDER TO STAND ON MY OWN TWO FEET, I STUDIED HARD, MANAGED TO GET A UNIVERSITY SCHOLARSHIP AND WAS CHOSEN TO BE A FOREIGN EXCHANGE STUDENT.
AFTER RESEARCHING ANCIENT DOCUMENTS THAT MY GREAT-GRANDFATHER'S FRIEND HAD ENTRUSTED ME WITH...
...I OBTAINED THE MASK AND ATTIRE OF THE ONIYURI, SUPPOSEDLY THE ONLY BEING WHO COULD NEGATE THE SPELL OF THE ONIYASHA.
IF THE CURSE ACTUALLY DOES EXIST, WOULDN'T IT LIKELY HIT AGURAMA NEXT?
OH, HE DOESN'T BELIEVE IN ANY OF IT.
AGURAMA'S A HUCKSTER. HE JUST HYPES THE SUPPOSEDLY SUPERNATURAL ANGLE FOR BUSINESS.
WHETHER IT EXISTS OR NOT, HE'S EXPLOITING THE "CURSE" TO MAKE A GRAB FOR CONTROL OF THE UNDERWORLD.

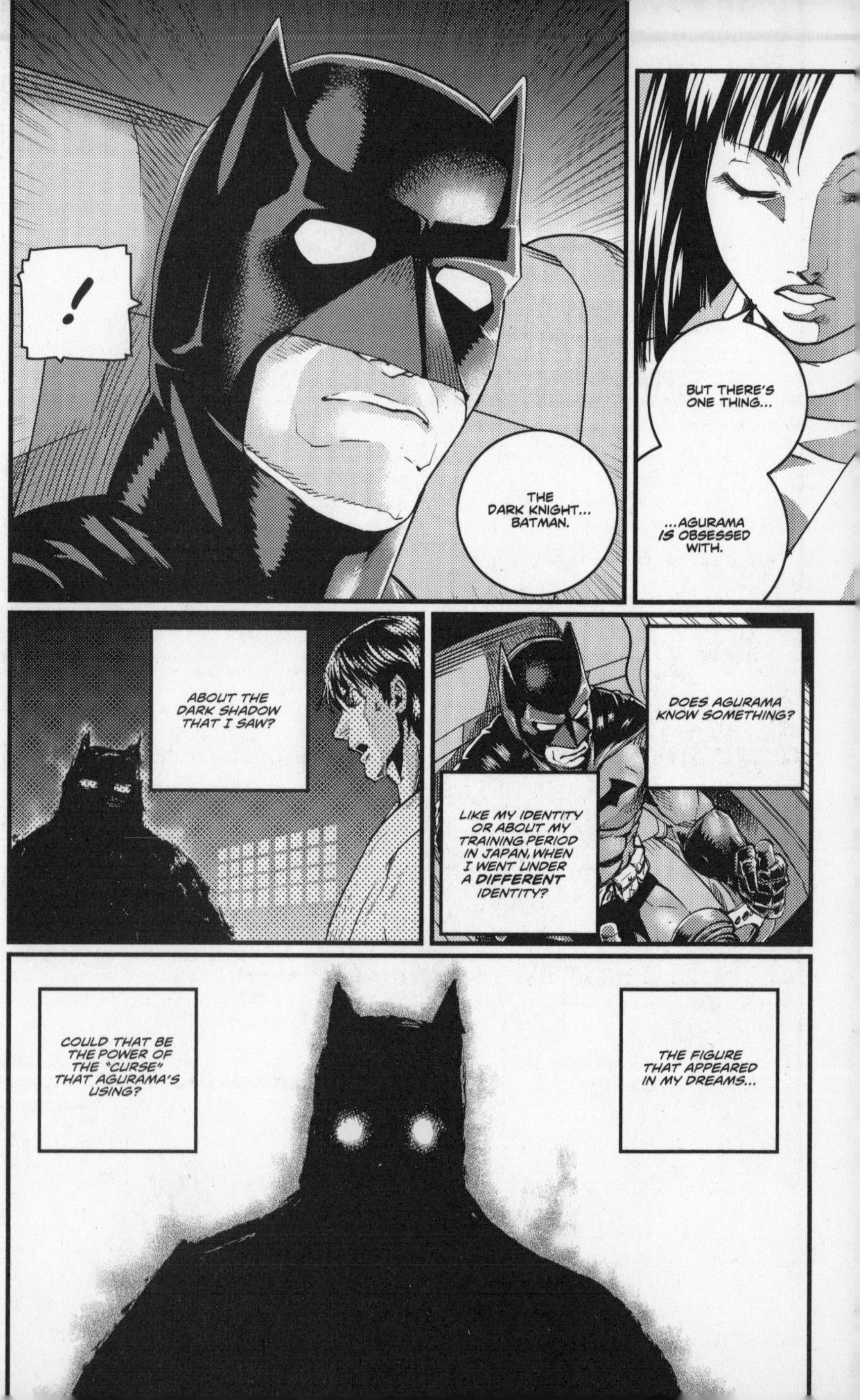
!
THE DARK KNIGHT... BATMAN.
BUT THERE'S ONE THING...
...AGURAMA IS OBSESSED WITH.
ABOUT THE DARK SHADOW THAT I SAW?
DOES AGURAMA KNOW SOMETHING?
LIKE MY IDENTITY OR ABOUT MY TRAINING PERIOD IN JAPAN, WHEN I WENT UNDER A DIFFERENT IDENTITY?
COULD THAT BE THE POWER OF THE "CURSE" THAT AGURAMA'S USING?
THE FIGURE THAT APPEARED IN MY DREAMS...

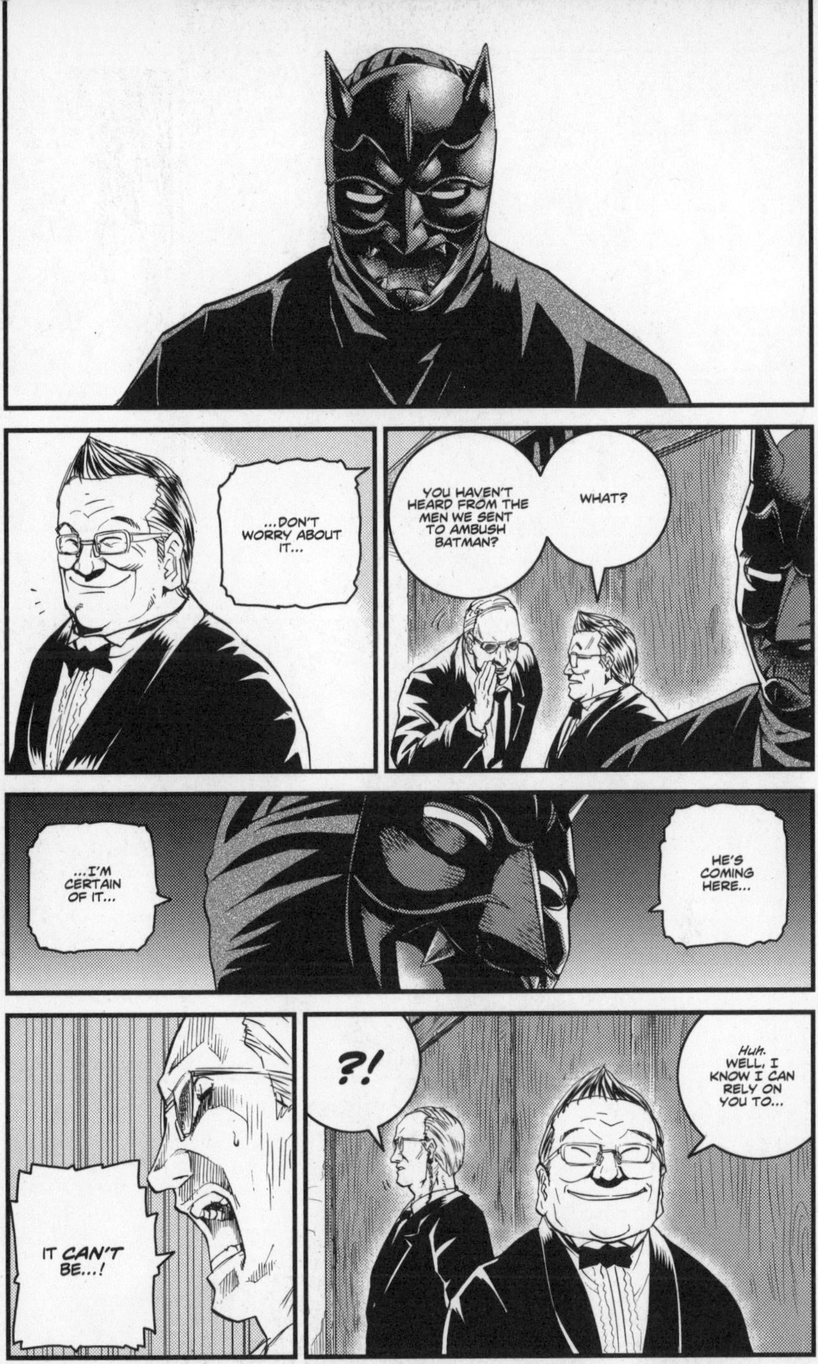
...DON'T WORRY ABOUT IT...
YOU HAVEN'T HEARD FROM THE MEN WE SENT TO AMBUSH BATMAN?
WHAT?
HE'S COMING HERE...
...I'M CERTAIN OF IT...
Huh. WELL, I KNOW I CAN RELY ON YOU TO...
?!
IT CAN'T BE...!

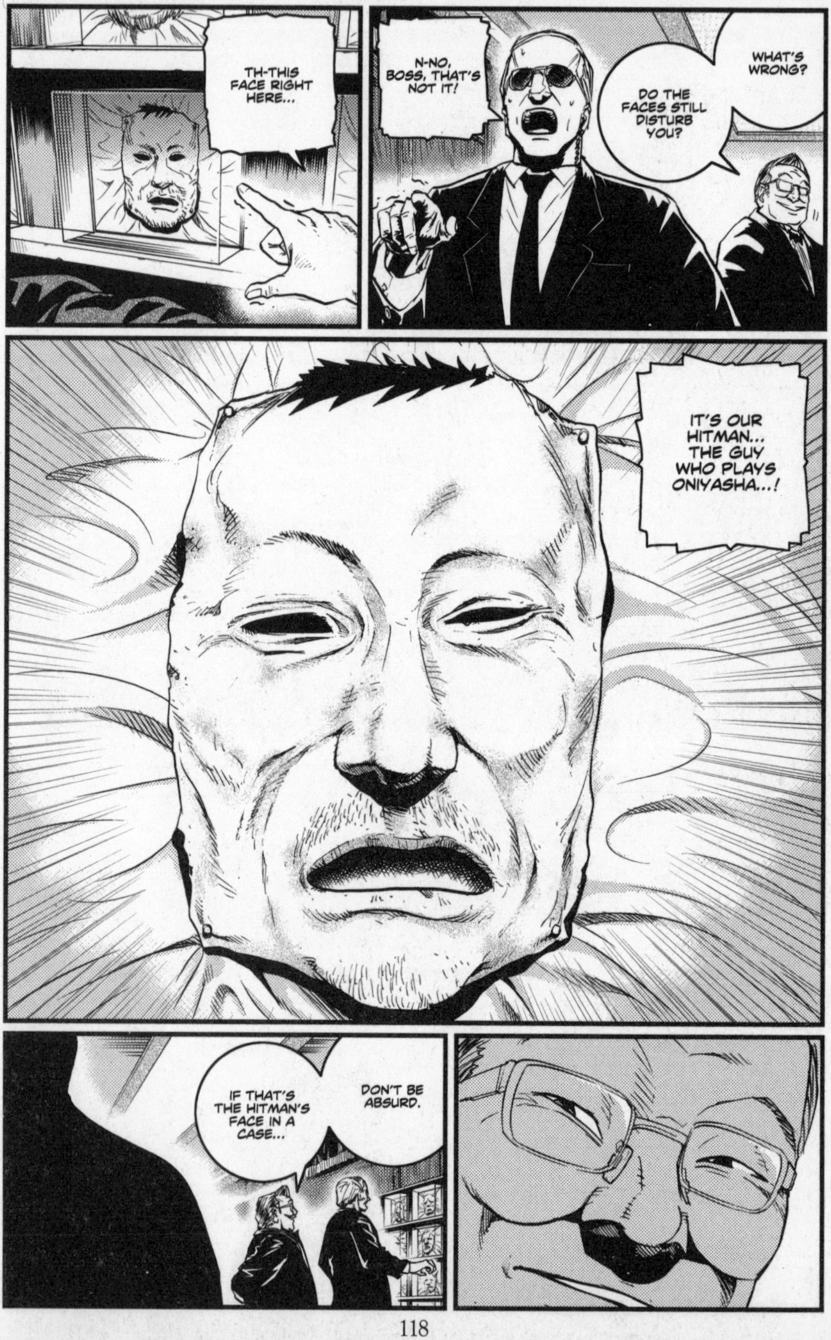
TH-THIS FACE RIGHT HERE...
N-NO, BOSS, THAT'S NOT IT!
WHAT'S WRONG?
DO THE FACES STILL DISTURB YOU?
IT'S OUR HITMAN... THE GUY WHO PLAYS ONIYASHA...!
DON'T BE ABSURD.
IF THAT'S THE HITMAN'S FACE IN A CASE...

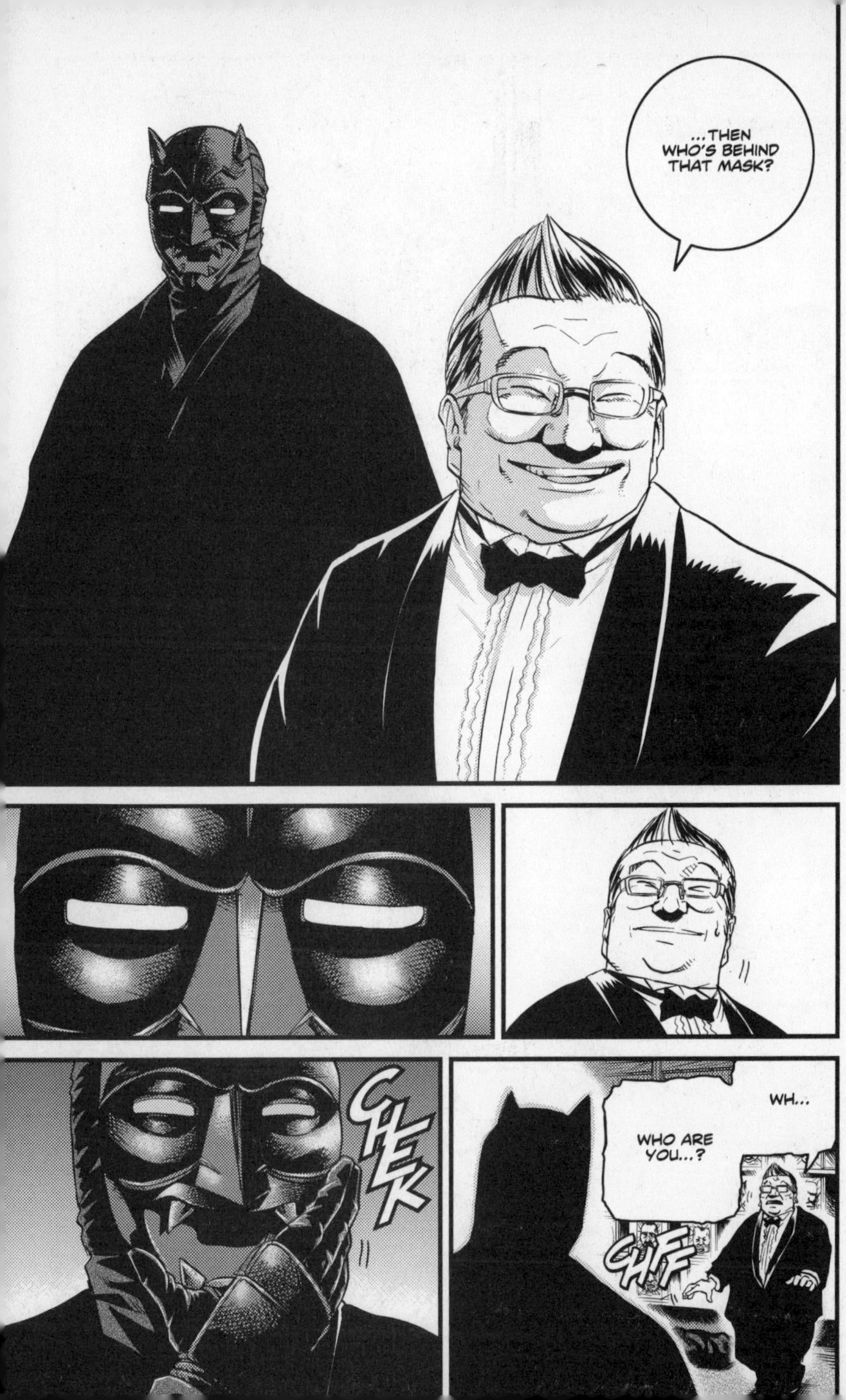
...THEN WHO'S BEHIND THAT MASK?
CHEK
WH...
WHO ARE YOU...?
CHF

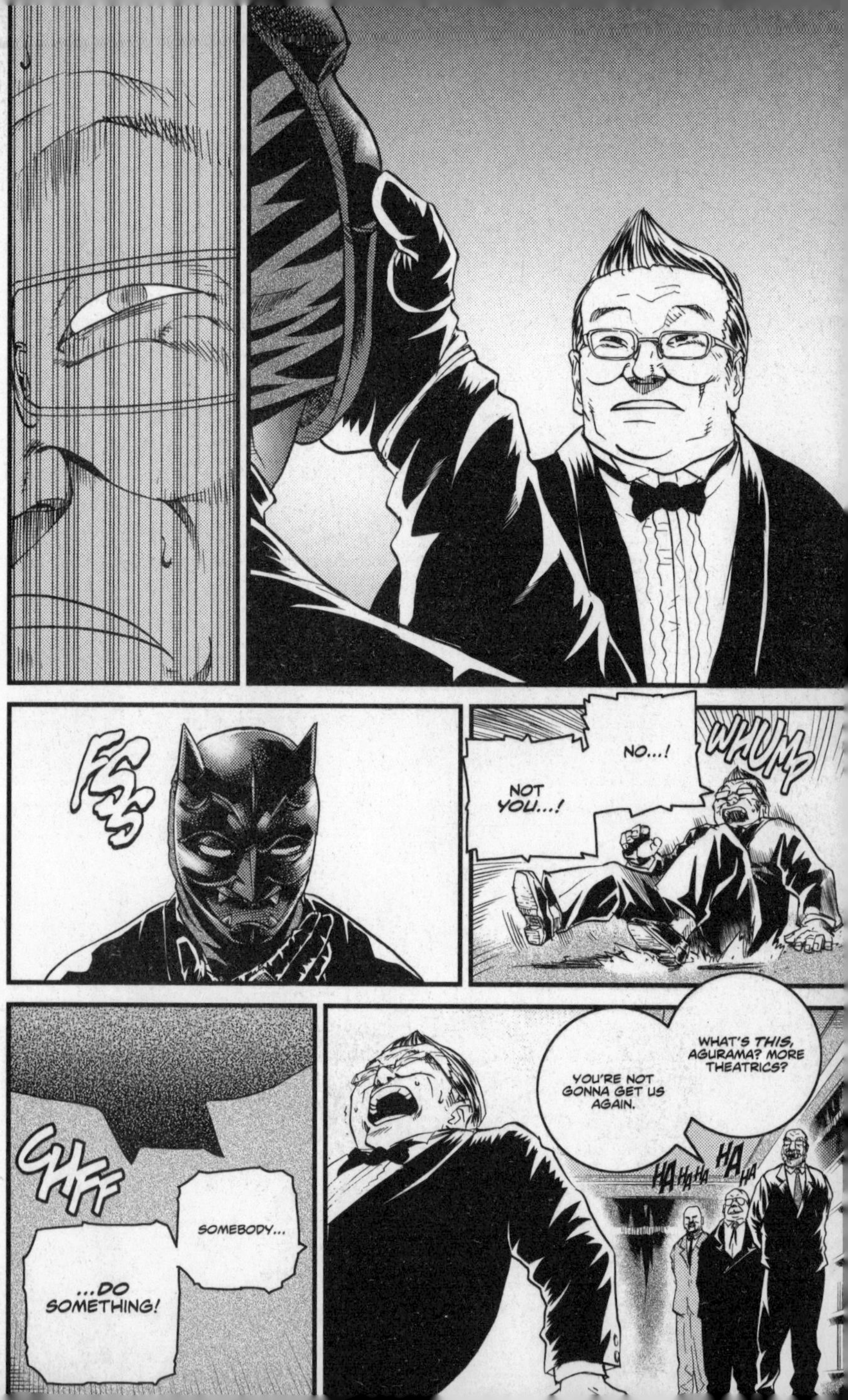
FSSS
NO...!
NOT YOU...!
WHUMP
WHAT'S THIS, AGURAMA? MORE THEATRICS?
YOU'RE NOT GONNA GET US AGAIN.
HA HA HA HA HA HA
CHFF
SOMEBODY...
...DO SOMETHING!

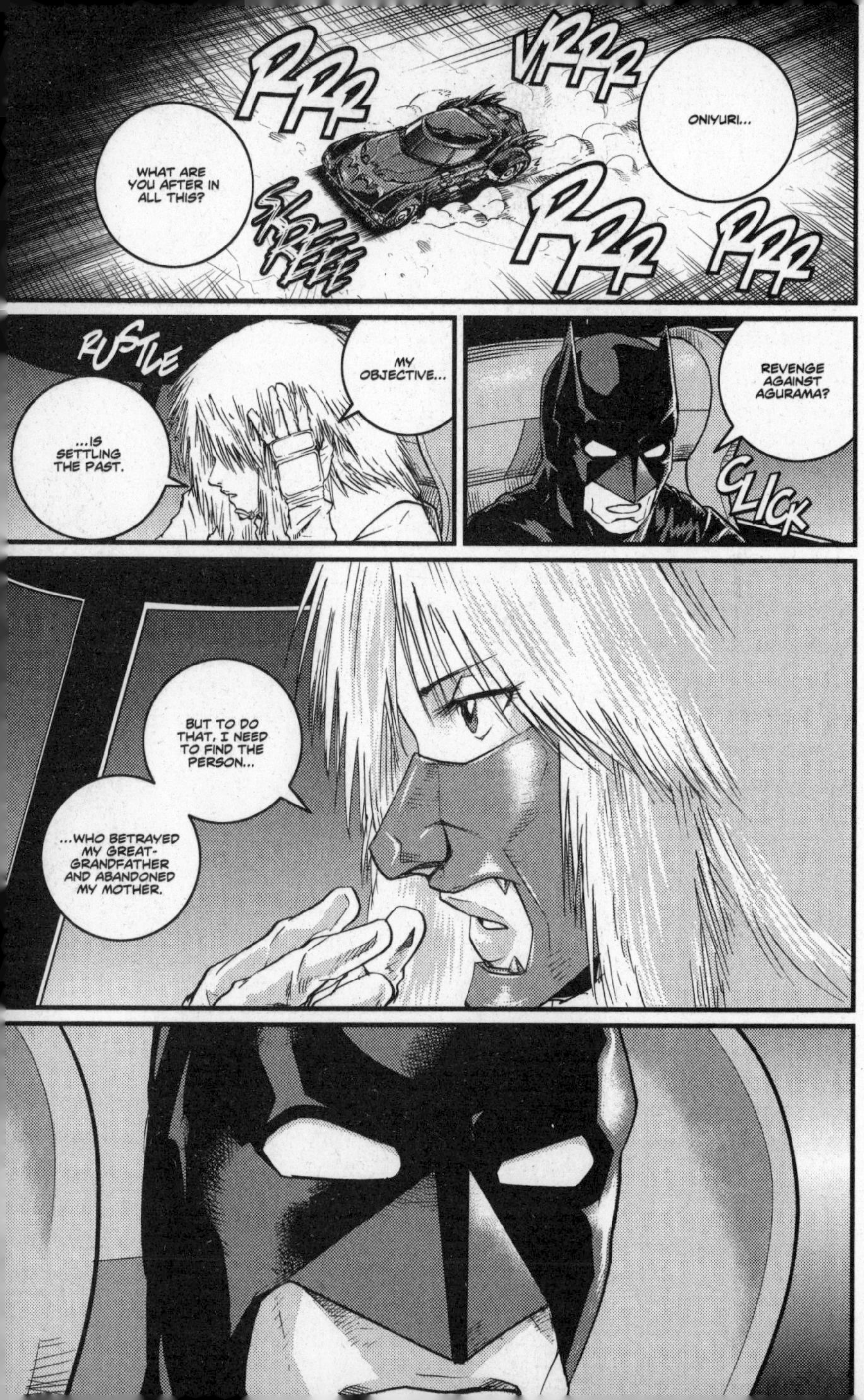
RRR
VRRR
ONIYURI...
WHAT ARE YOU AFTER IN ALL THIS?
SKREEEE
RRR
RRR
RUSTLE
MY OBJECTIVE...
...IS SETTLING THE PAST.
REVENGE AGAINST AGURAMA?
CLICK
BUT TO DO THAT, I NEED TO FIND THE PERSON...
...WHO BETRAYED MY GREAT-GRANDFATHER AND ABANDONED MY MOTHER.

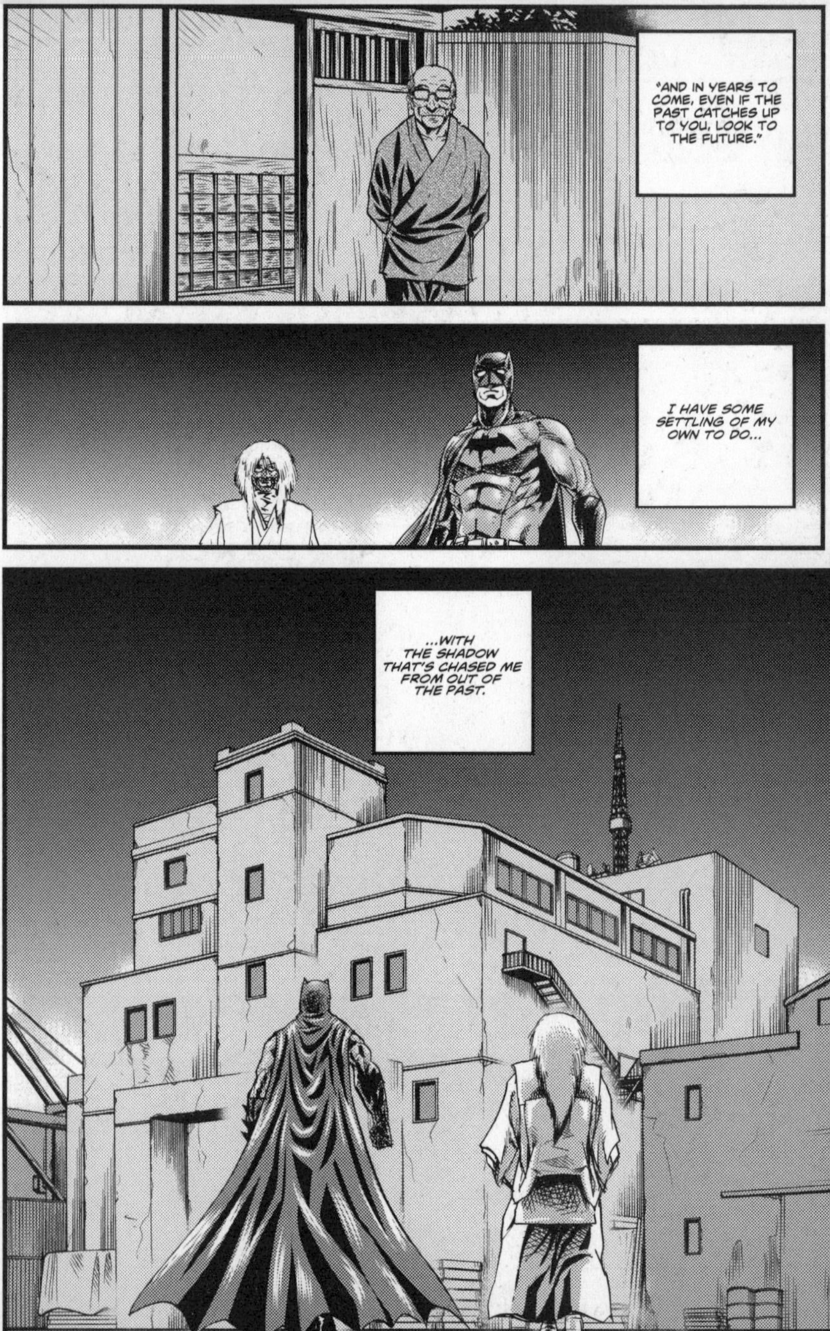
"AND IN YEARS TO COME, EVEN IF THE PAST CATCHES UP TO YOU, LOOK TO THE FUTURE."
I HAVE SOME SETTLING OF MY OWN TO DO...
...WITH THE SHADOW THAT'S CHASED ME FROM OUT OF THE PAST.

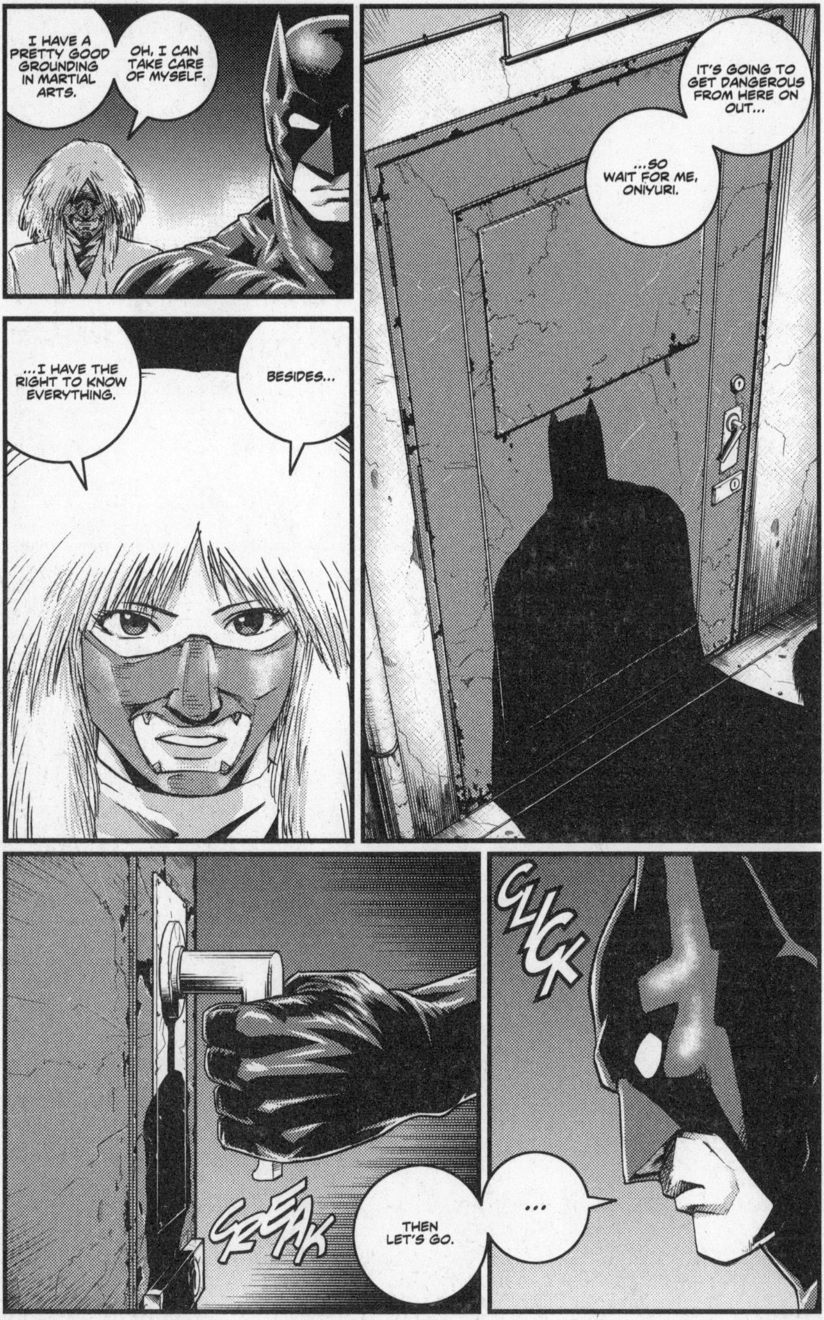
IT'S GOING TO GET DANGEROUS FROM HERE ON OUT...
...SO WAIT FOR ME, ONIYURI.
OH, I CAN TAKE CARE OF MYSELF.
I HAVE A PRETTY GOOD GROUNDING IN MARTIAL ARTS.
BESIDES...
...I HAVE THE RIGHT TO KNOW EVERYTHING.
CREAK
CLICK
...
THEN LET'S GO.

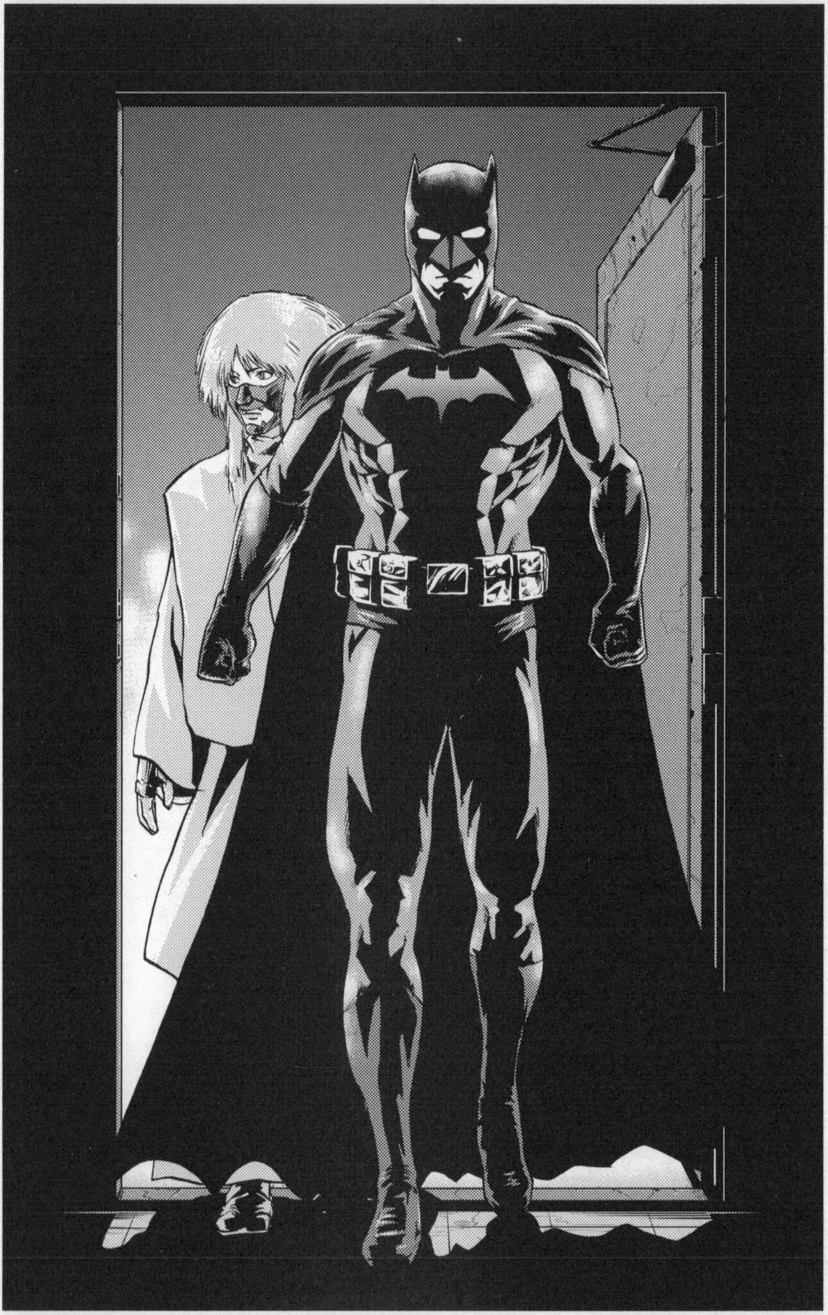

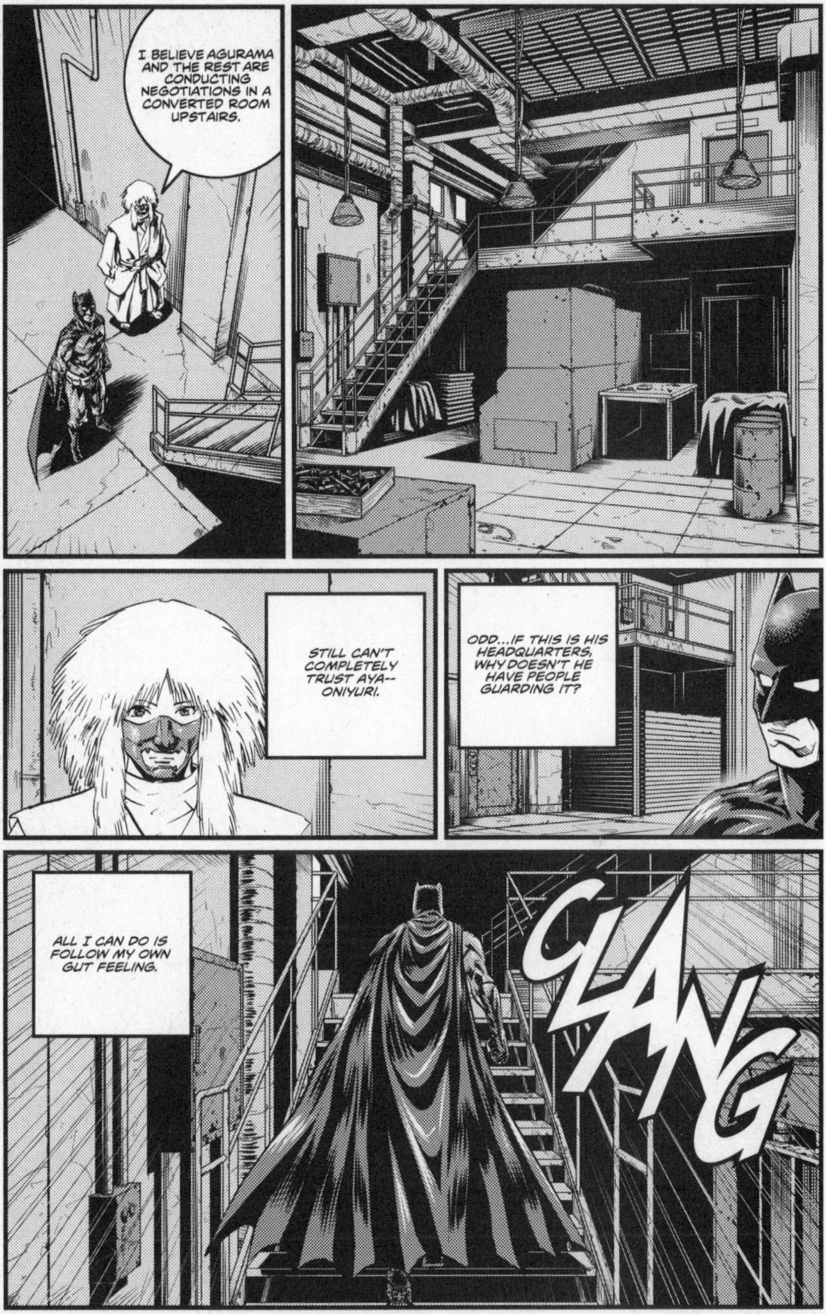
I BELIEVE AGURAMA AND THE REST ARE CONDUCTING NEGOTIATIONS IN A CONVERTED ROOM UPSTAIRS.
STILL CAN'T COMPLETELY TRUST AYA-- ONIYURI.
ODD...IF THIS IS HIS HEADQUARTERS, WHY DOESN'T HE HAVE PEOPLE GUARDING IT?
ALL I CAN DO IS FOLLOW MY OWN GUT FEELING.
CLANG

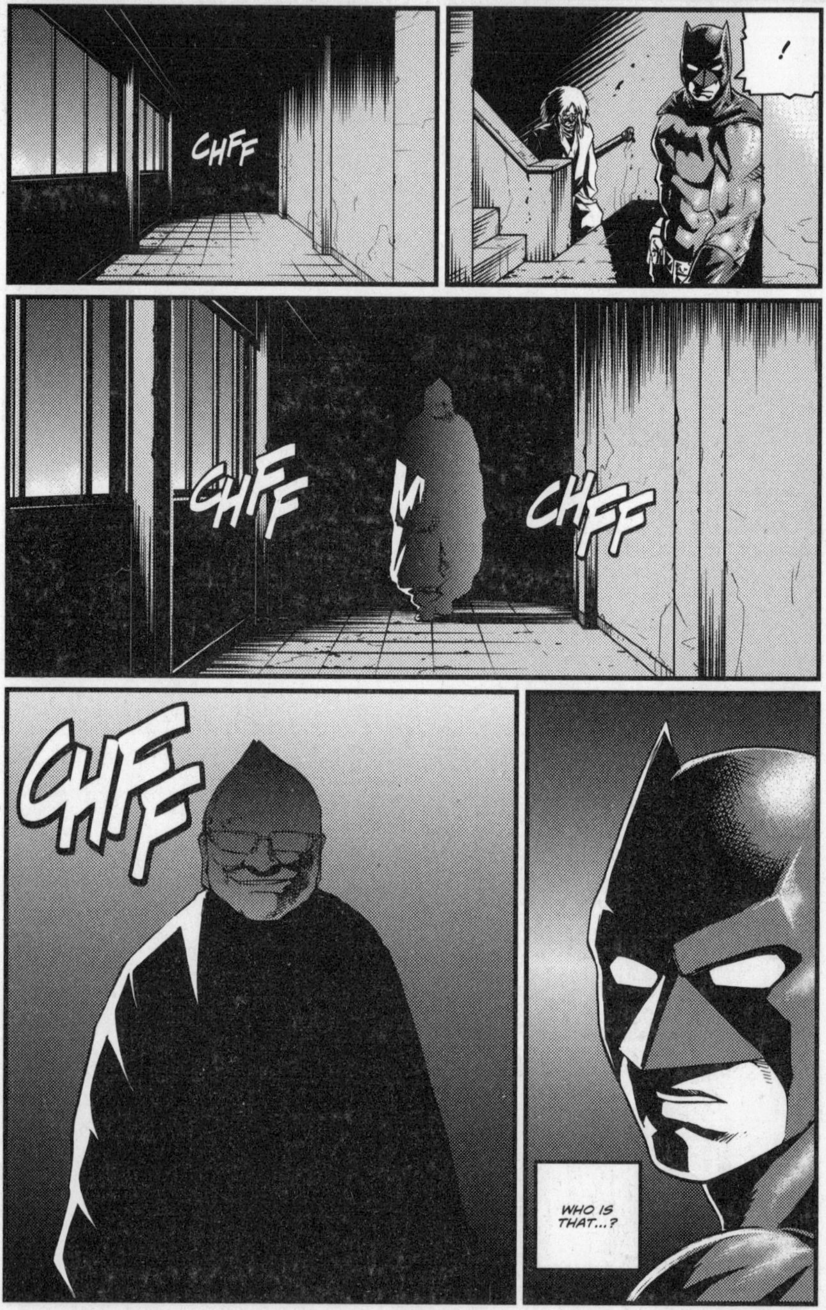
CHFF
!
CHFF
CHFF
CHFF
WHO IS THAT...?

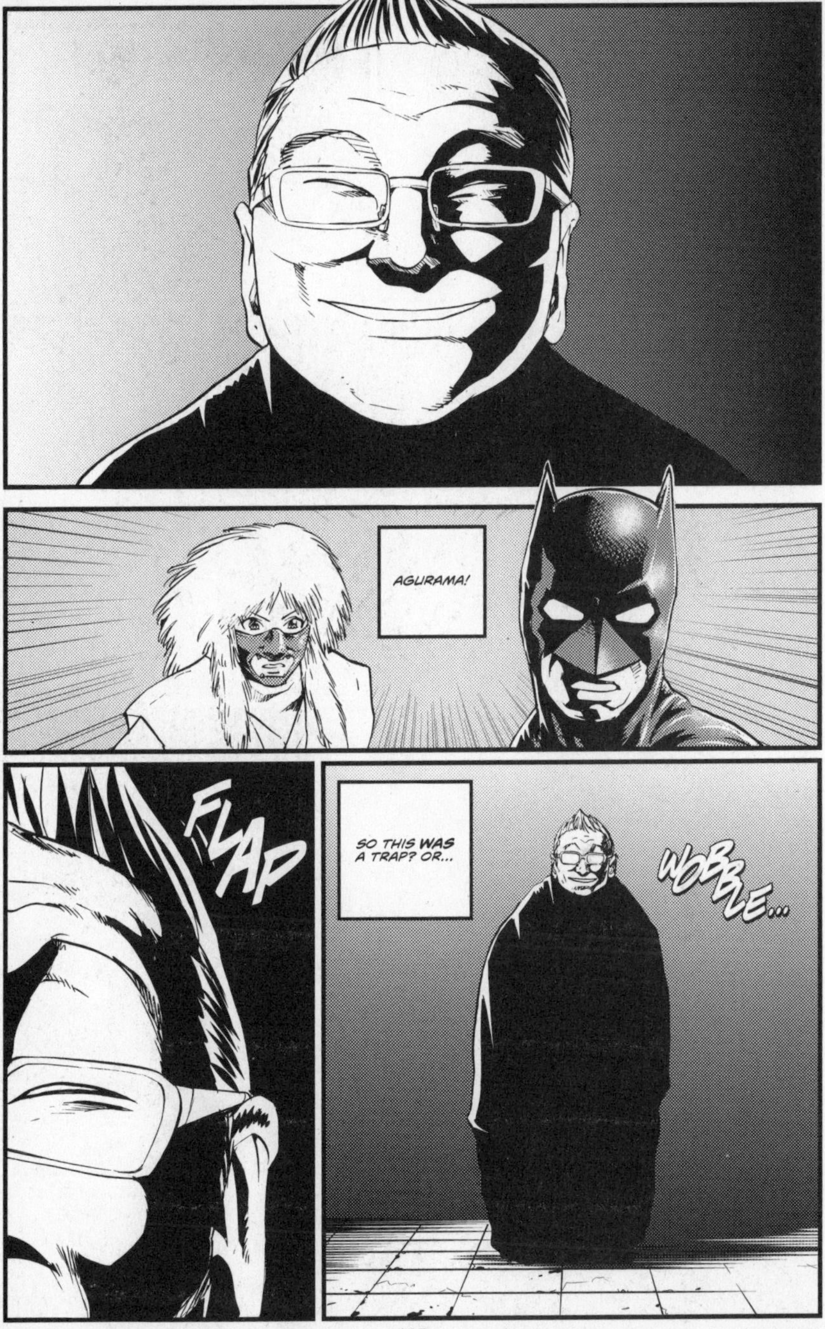
AGURAMA!
FLAP
SO THIS WAS A TRAP? OR...
WOBBLE...

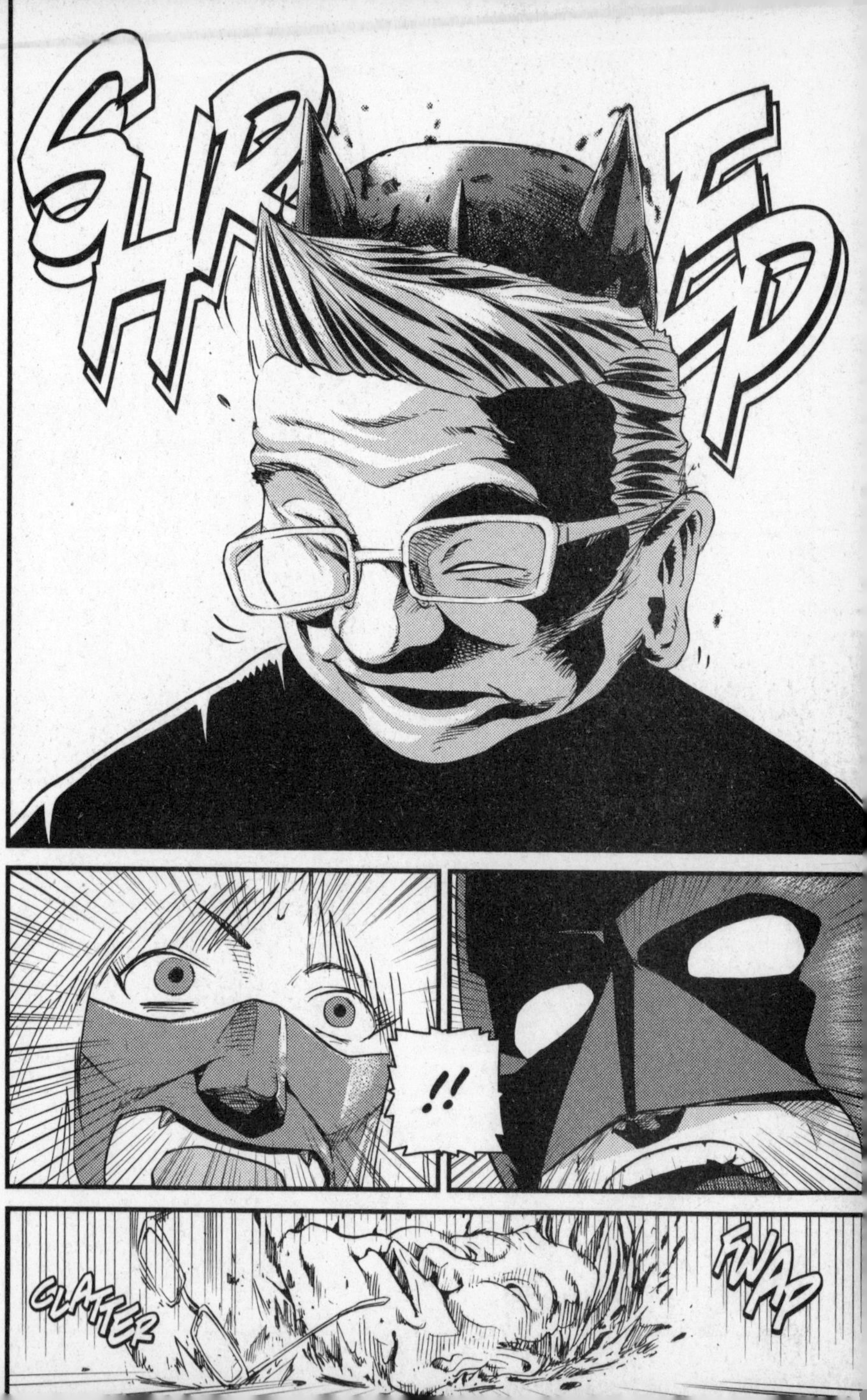
SHRED
!!
CLATTER
FWAP

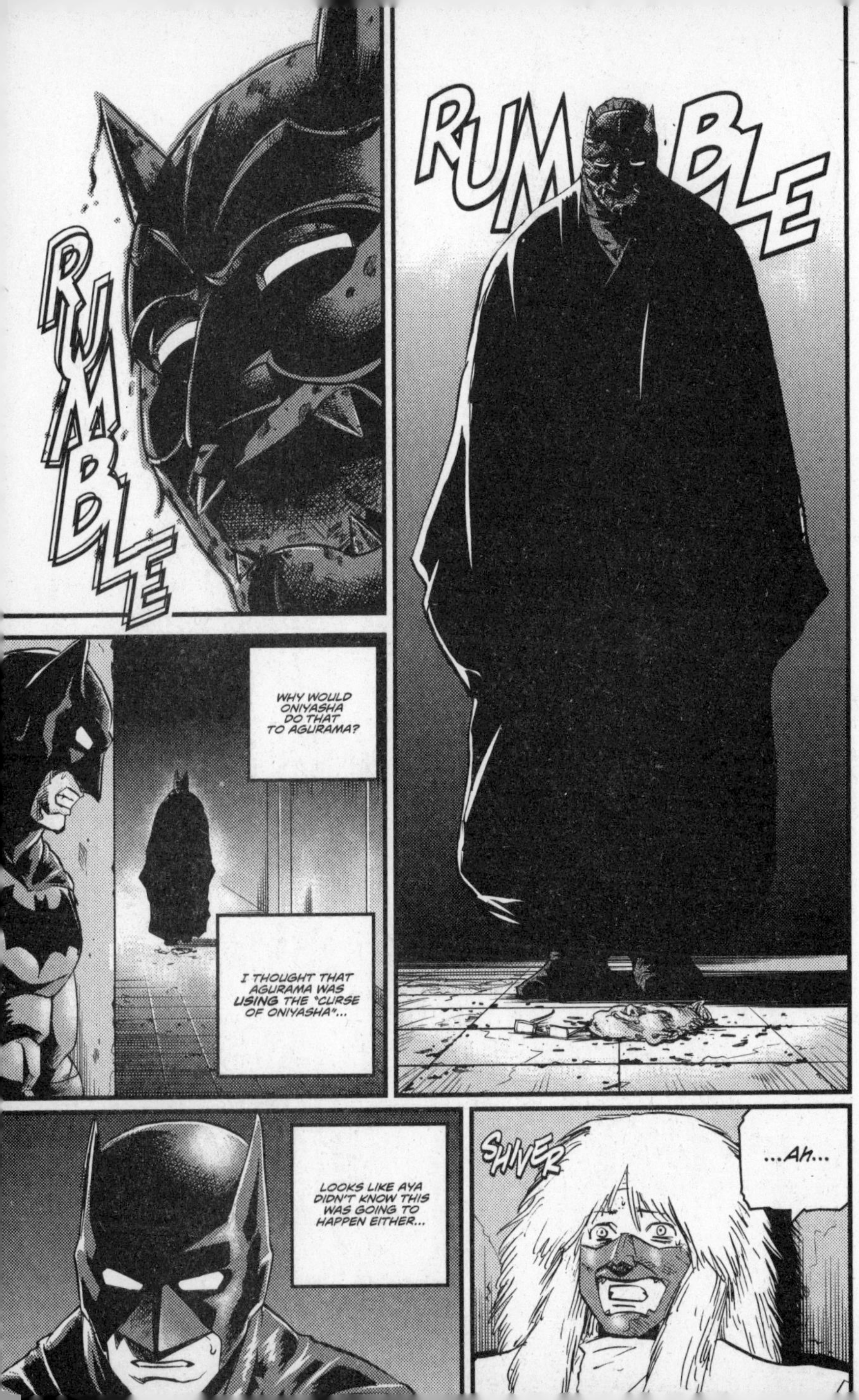
RUMBLE
RUMBLE
WHY WOULD ONIYASHA DO THAT TO AGURAMA?
I THOUGHT THAT AGURAMA WAS USING THE "CURSE OF ONIYASHA"...
LOOKS LIKE AYA DIDN'T KNOW THIS WAS GOING TO HAPPEN EITHER...
SHIVER
...Ah...

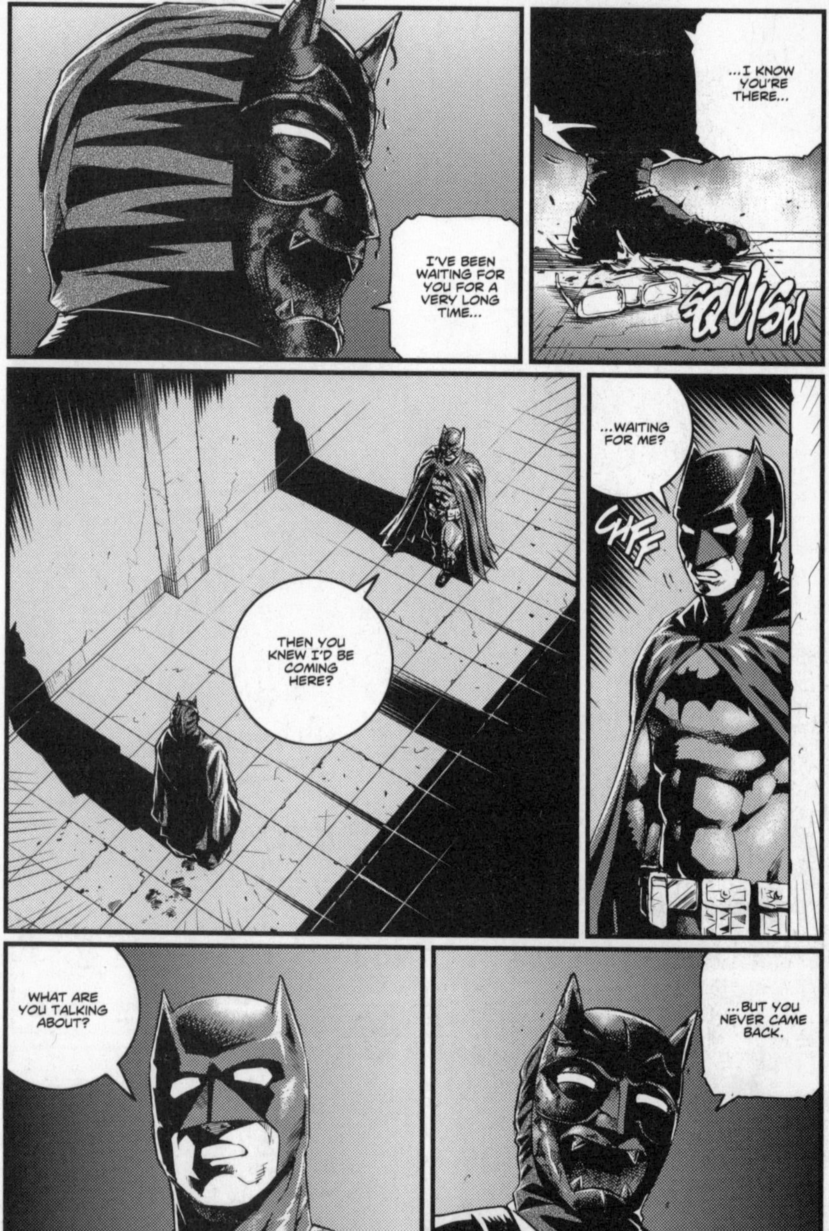
I'VE BEEN WAITING FOR YOU FOR A VERY LONG TIME...
...I KNOW YOU'RE THERE...
SQUISH
...WAITING FOR ME?
CHFF
THEN YOU KNEW I'D BE COMING HERE?
WHAT ARE YOU TALKING ABOUT?
...BUT YOU NEVER CAME BACK.

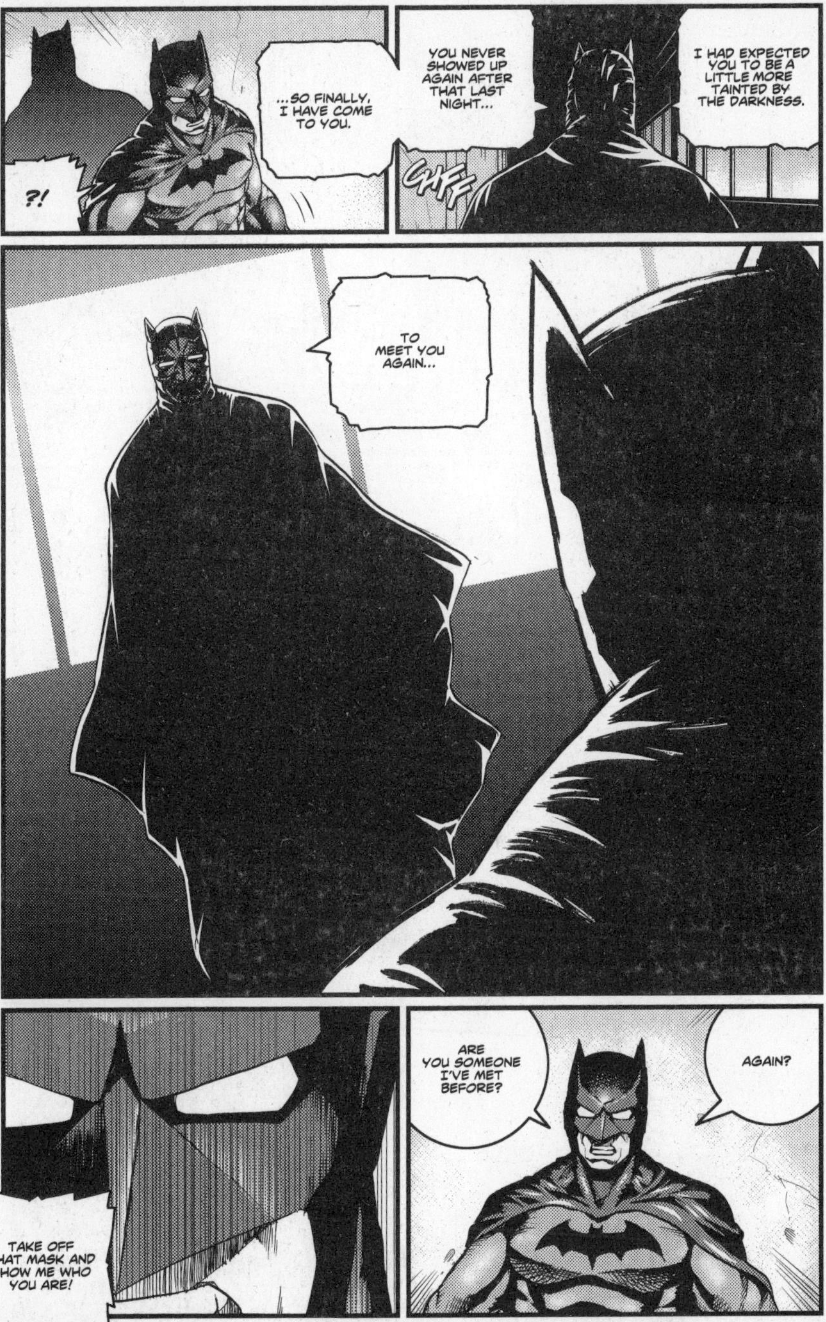

?!
...SO FINALLY, I HAVE COME TO YOU.
YOU NEVER SHOWED UP AGAIN AFTER THAT LAST NIGHT...
I HAD EXPECTED YOU TO BE A LITTLE MORE TAINTED BY THE DARKNESS.
CHFF
TO MEET YOU AGAIN...
TAKE OFF THAT MASK AND SHOW ME WHO YOU ARE!
ARE YOU SOMEONE I'VE MET BEFORE?
AGAIN?

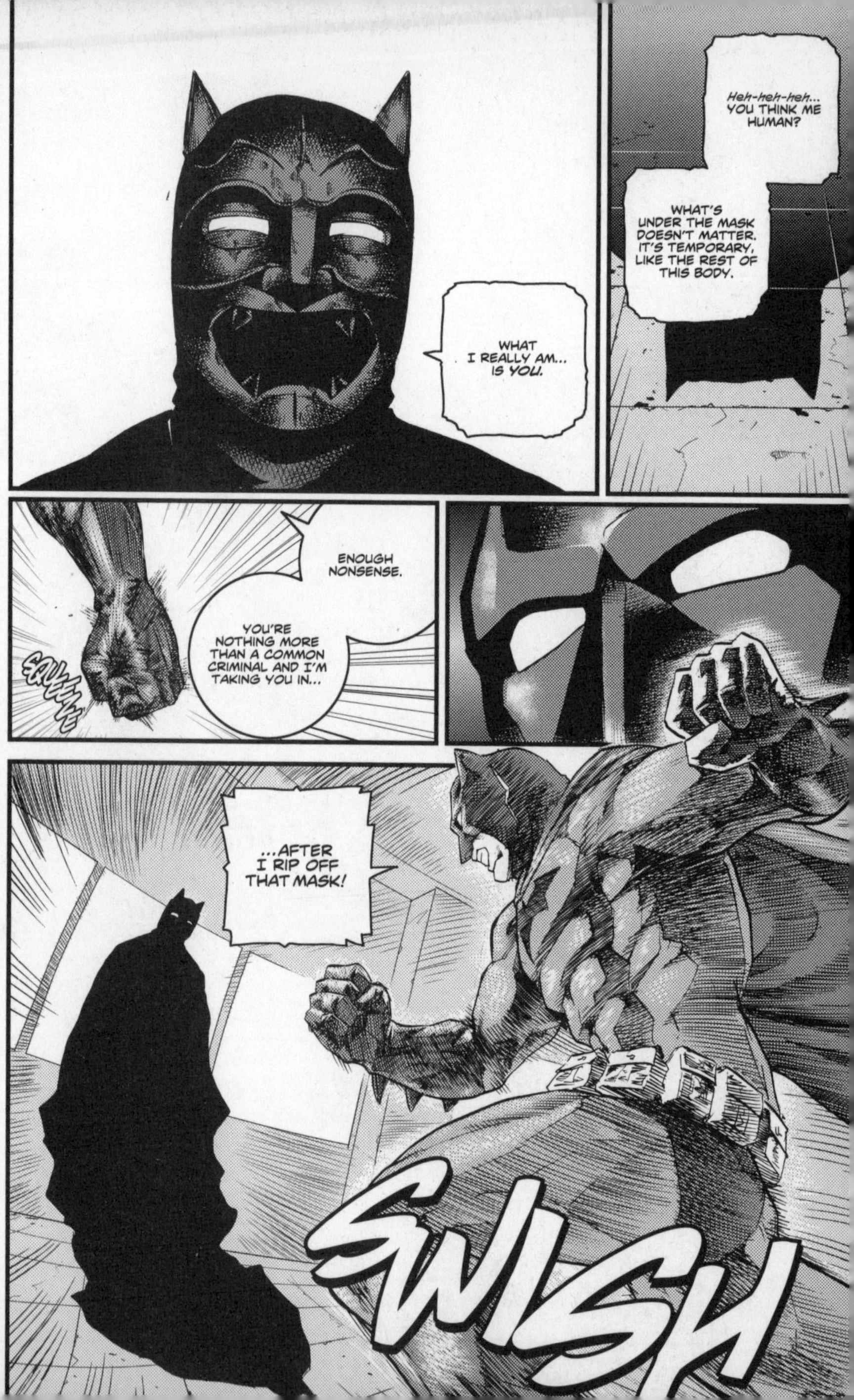
WHAT I REALLY AM... IS YOU.
Heh-heh-heh... YOU THINK ME HUMAN?
WHAT'S UNDER THE MASK DOESN'T MATTER. IT'S TEMPORARY, LIKE THE REST OF THIS BODY.
ENOUGH NONSENSE.
YOU'RE NOTHING MORE THAN A COMMON CRIMINAL AND I'M TAKING YOU IN...
SQUEEEZE
...AFTER I RIP OFF THAT MASK!
SWISH

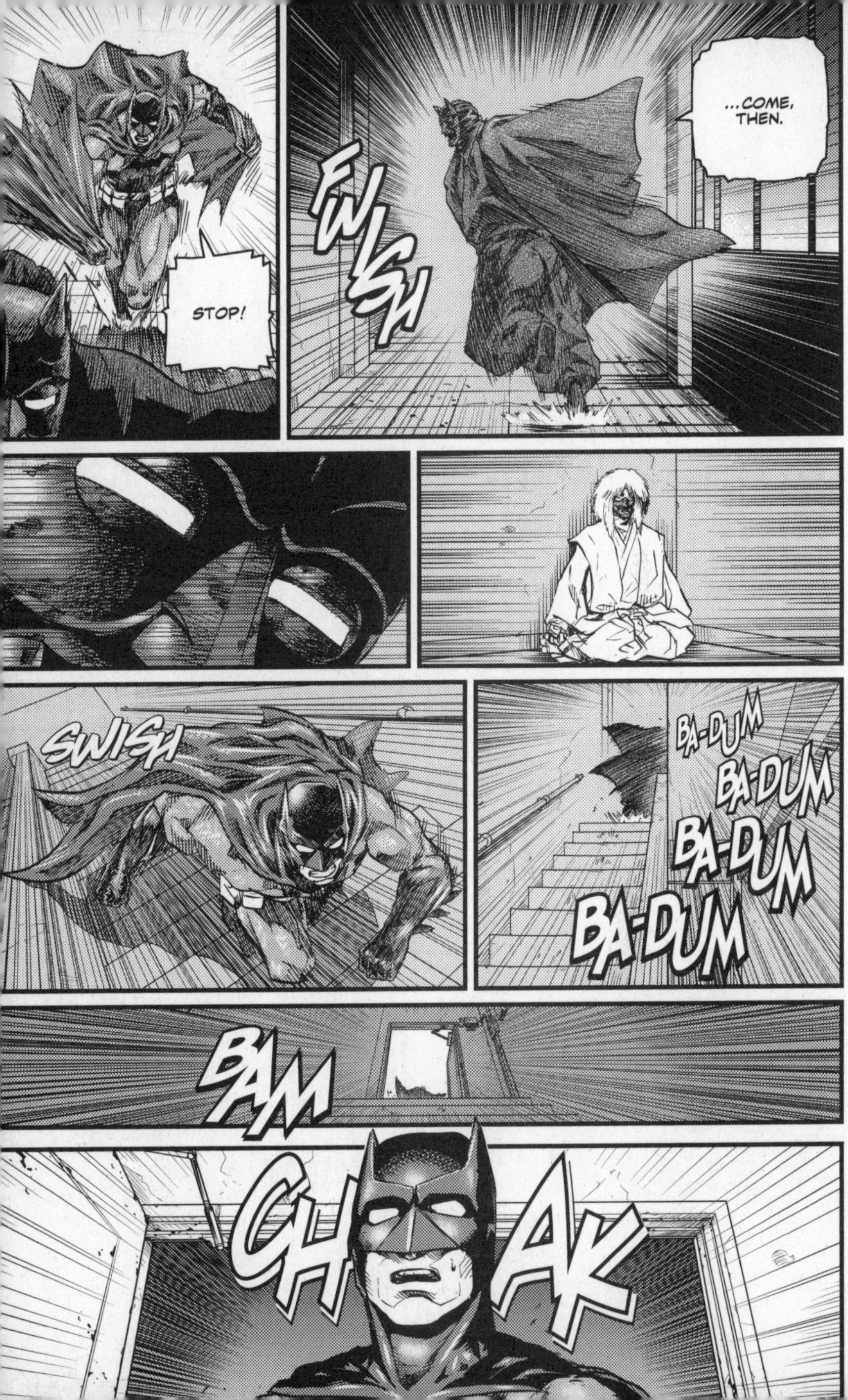
STOP!
FWISH
...COME, THEN.
SWISH
BA-DUM
BA-DUM
BA-DUM
BA-DUM
BAM
CHAK

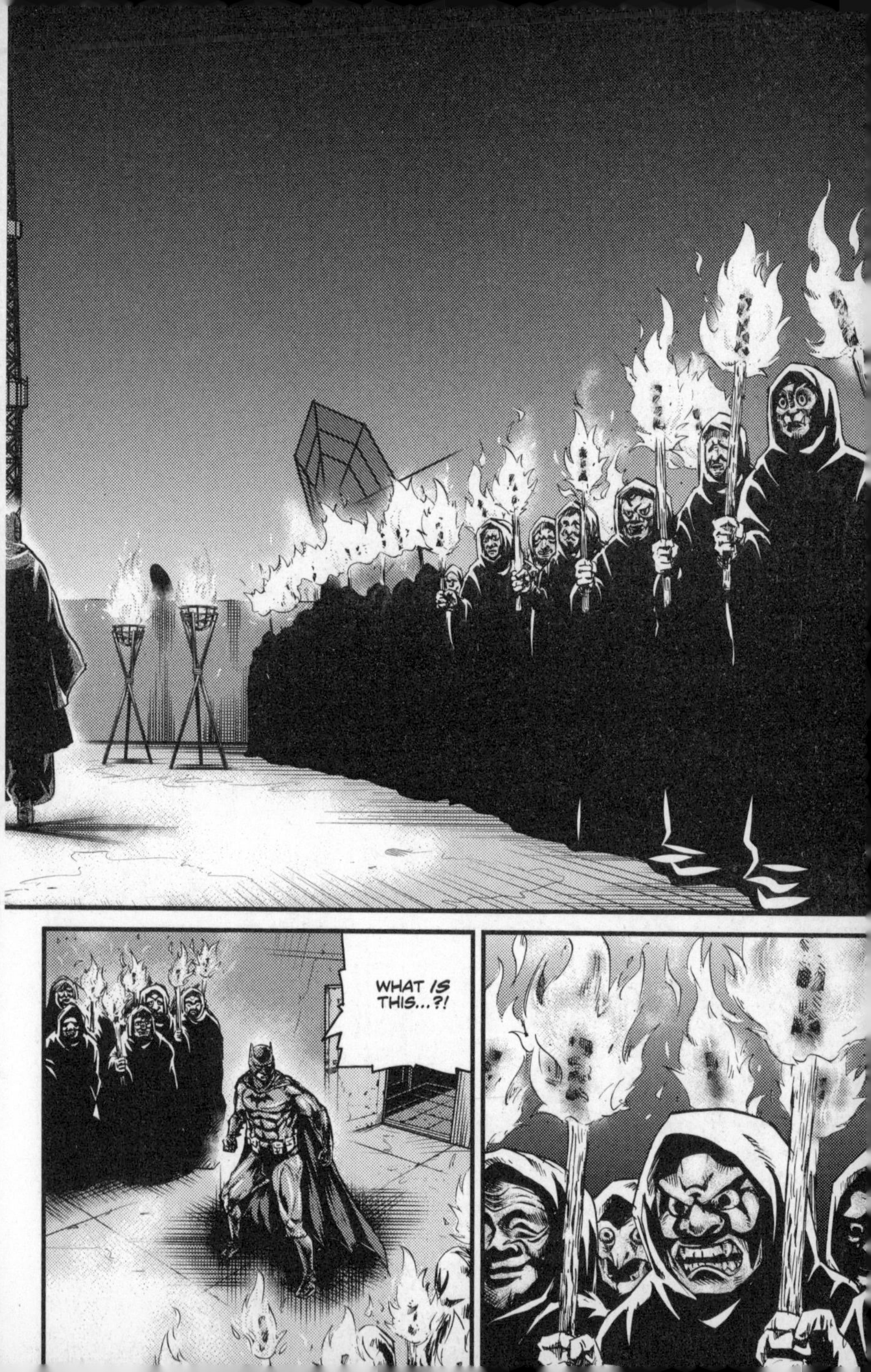
WHAT IS THIS...?!

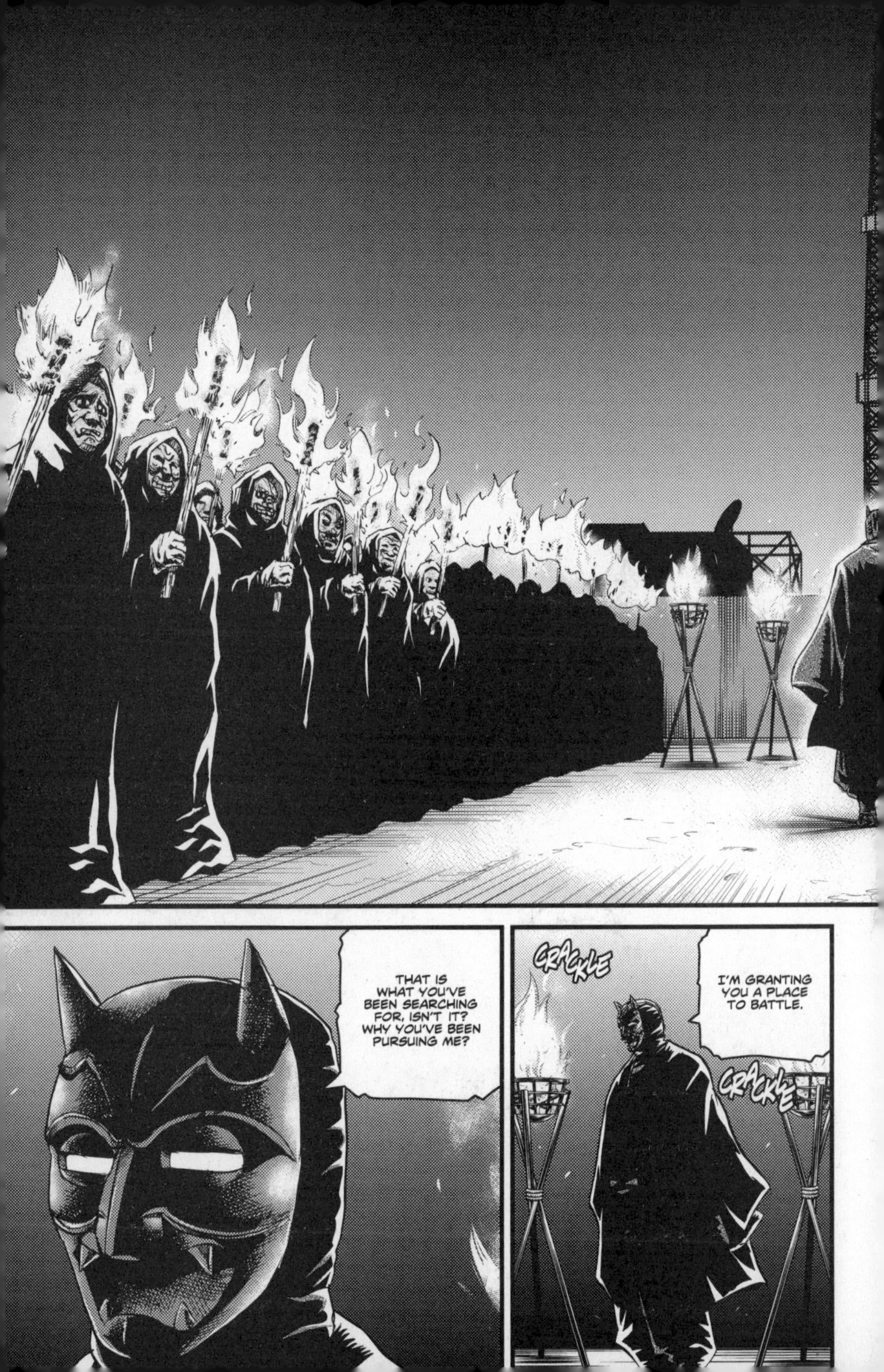
THAT IS WHAT YOU'VE BEEN SEARCHING FOR, ISN'T IT? WHY YOU'VE BEEN PURSUING ME?
CRACKLE
I'M GRANTING YOU A PLACE TO BATTLE.
CRACKLE

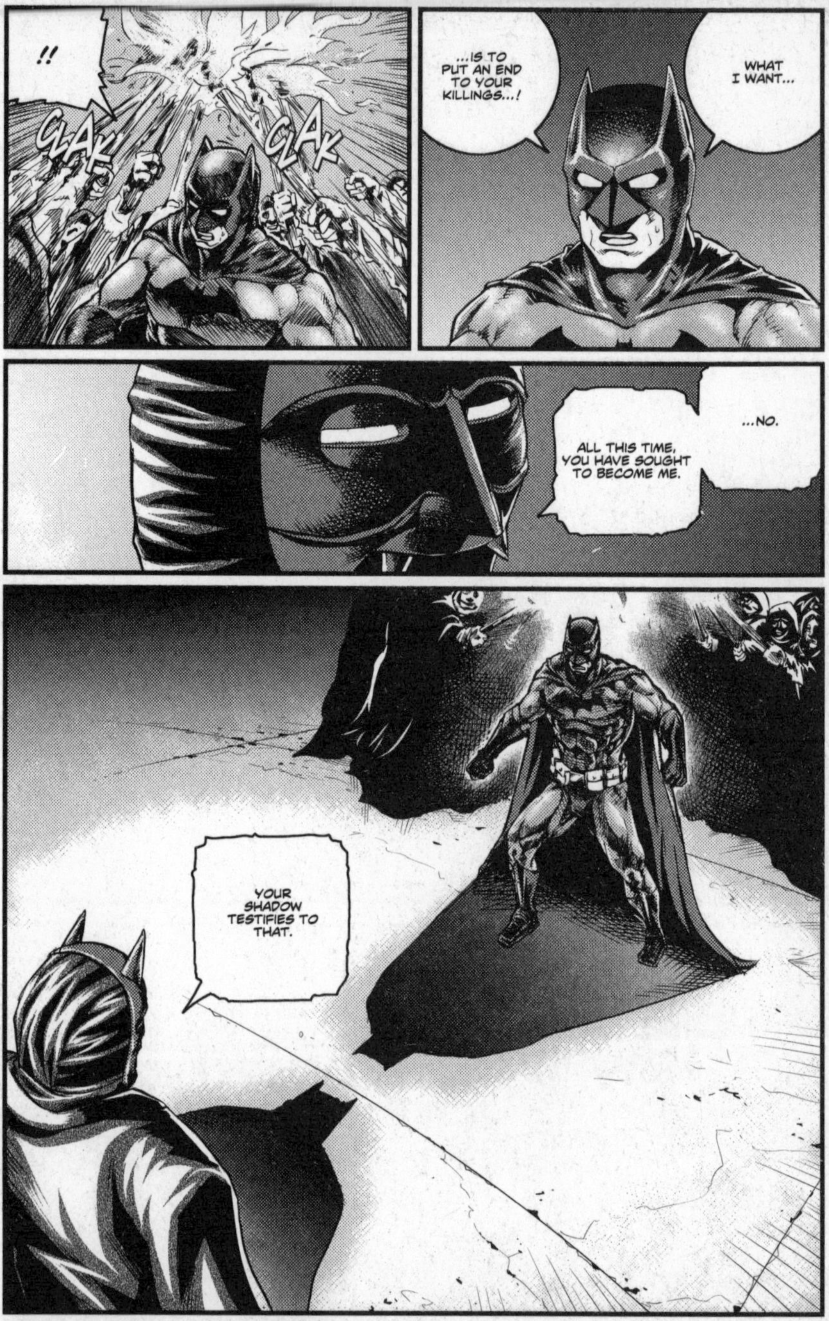
WHAT I WANT...
...IS TO PUT AN END TO YOUR KILLINGS...!
!!
CLAK
CLAK
...NO.
ALL THIS TIME, YOU HAVE SOUGHT TO BECOME ME.
YOUR SHADOW TESTIFIES TO THAT.

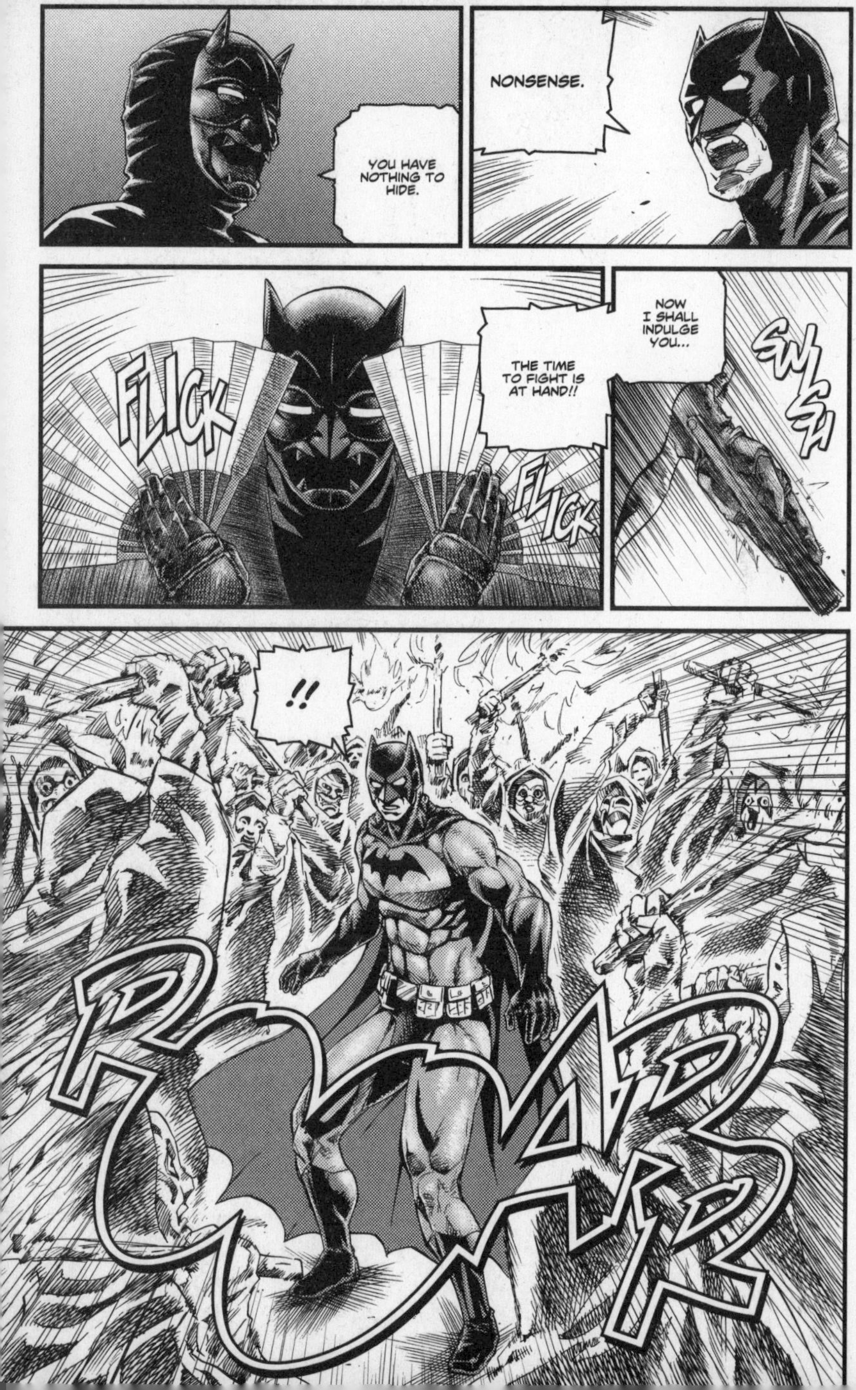
YOU HAVE NOTHING TO HIDE.
NONSENSE.
FLICK
FLICK
THE TIME TO FIGHT IS AT HAND!!
NOW I SHALL INDULGE YOU...
SWISH
!!
ROAR
ROAR

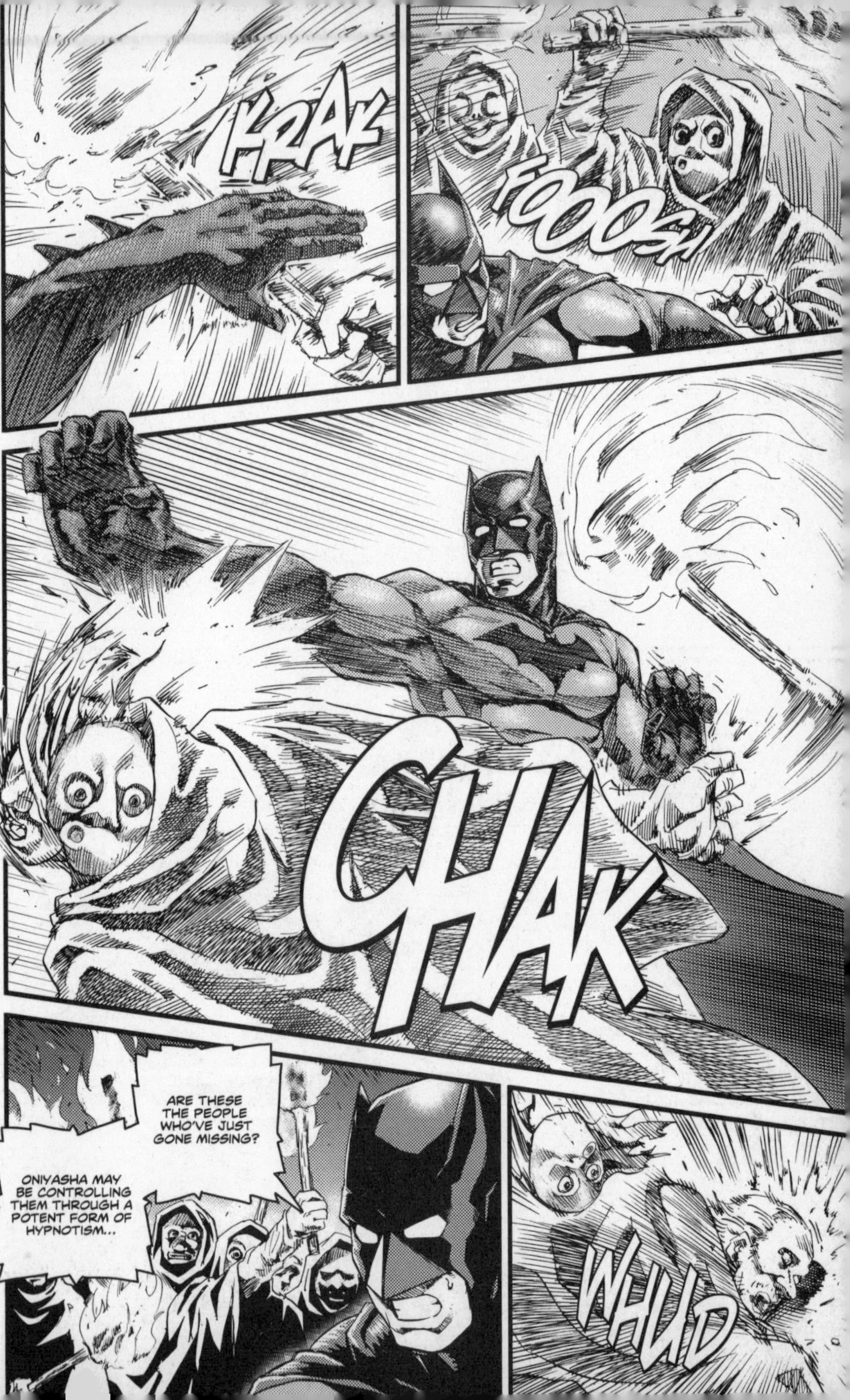
KRAK
FOOOSH
CHAK
ARE THESE THE PEOPLE WHO'VE JUST GONE MISSING?
ONIYASHA MAY BE CONTROLLING THEM THROUGH A POTENT FORM OF HYPNOTISM...
WHUD

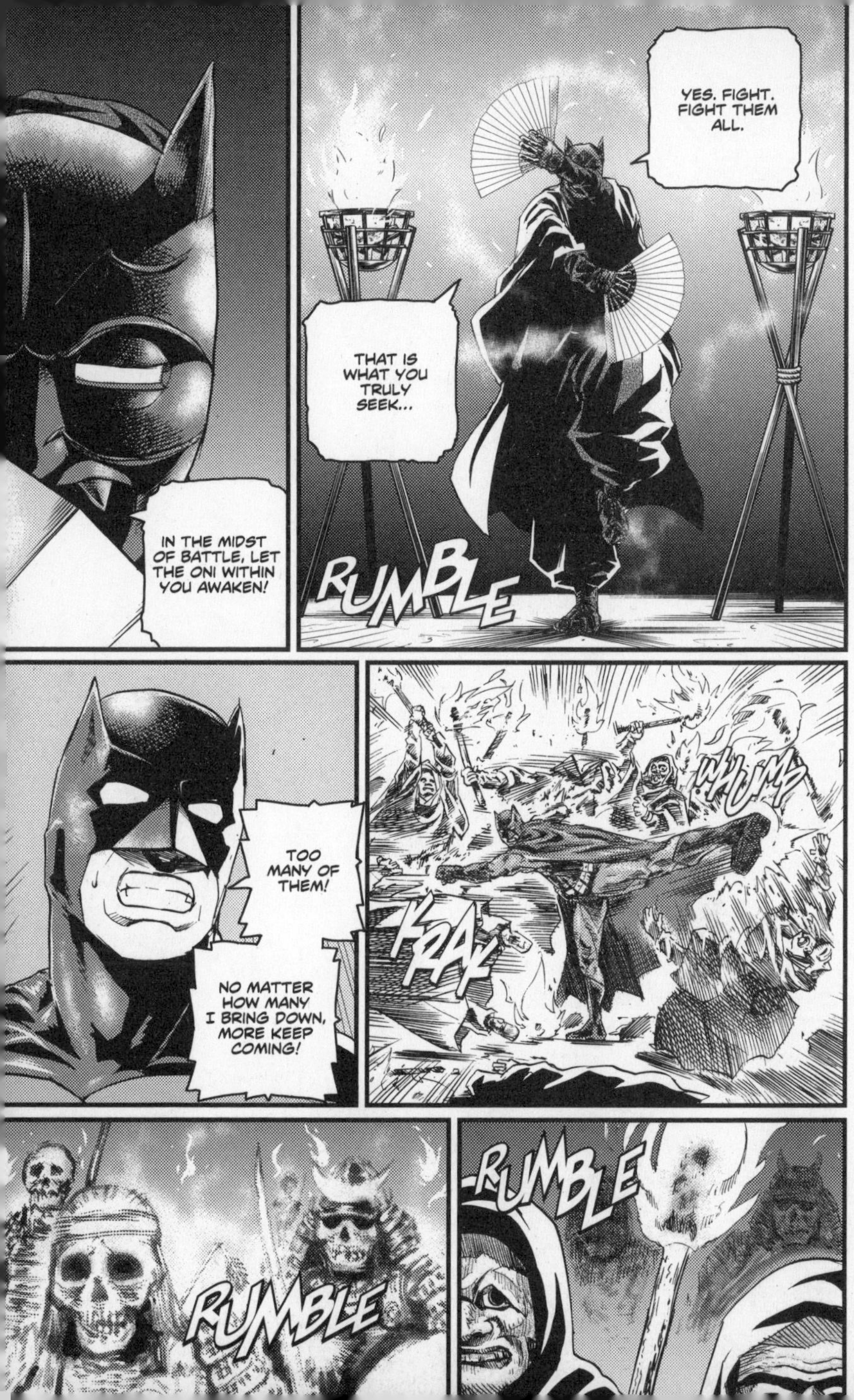

YES. FIGHT. FIGHT THEM ALL.
THAT IS WHAT YOU TRULY SEEK...
IN THE MIDST OF BATTLE, LET THE ONI WITHIN YOU AWAKEN!
RUMBLE
TOO MANY OF THEM!
NO MATTER HOW MANY I BRING DOWN, MORE KEEP COMING!
WHUMP
KRAK
RUMBLE
RUMBLE

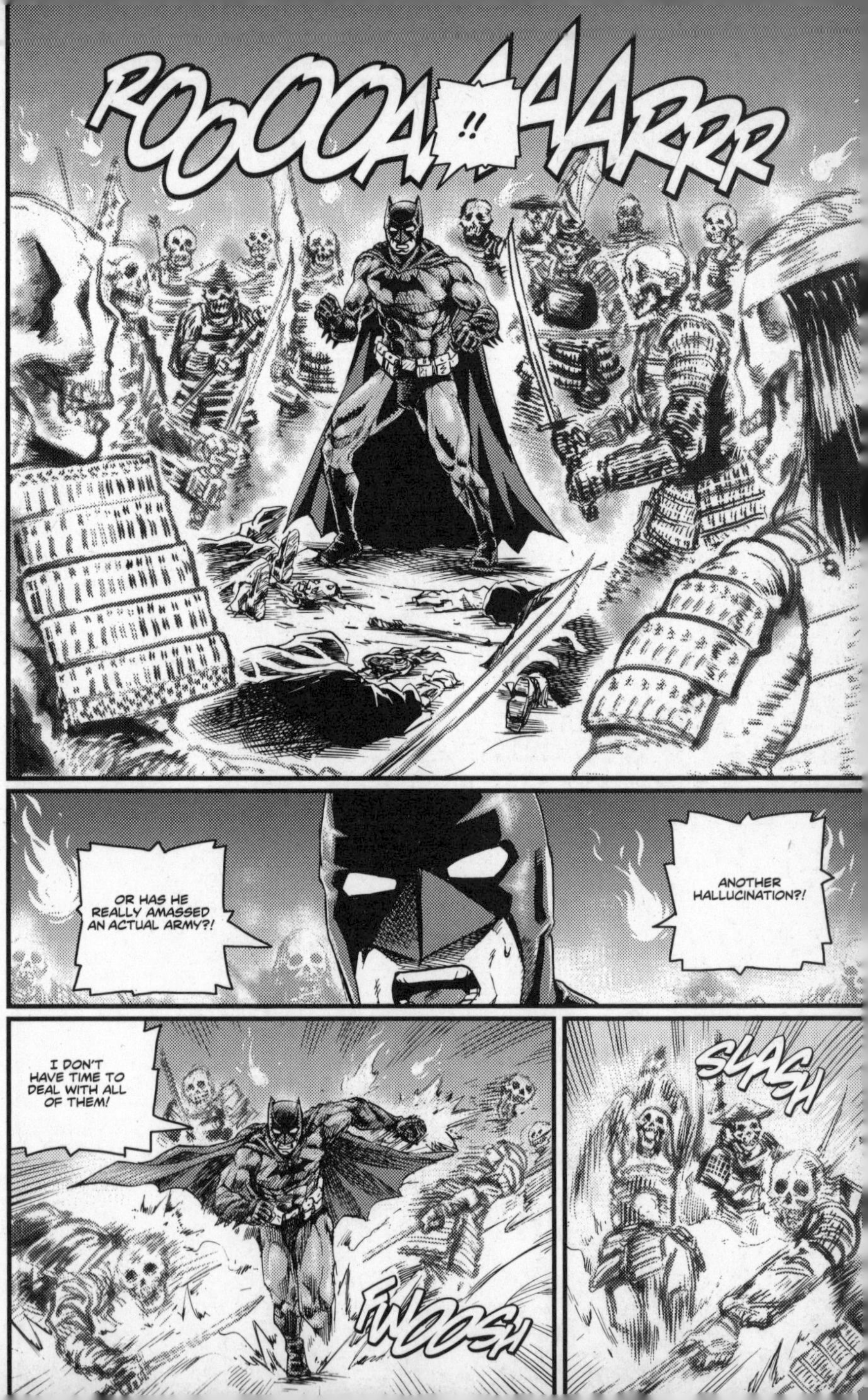
ROOOOOAAAAARRRR
!!
ANOTHER HALLUCINATION?!
OR HAS HE REALLY AMASSED AN ACTUAL ARMY?!
I DON'T HAVE TIME TO DEAL WITH ALL OF THEM!
FWOOSH
SLASH

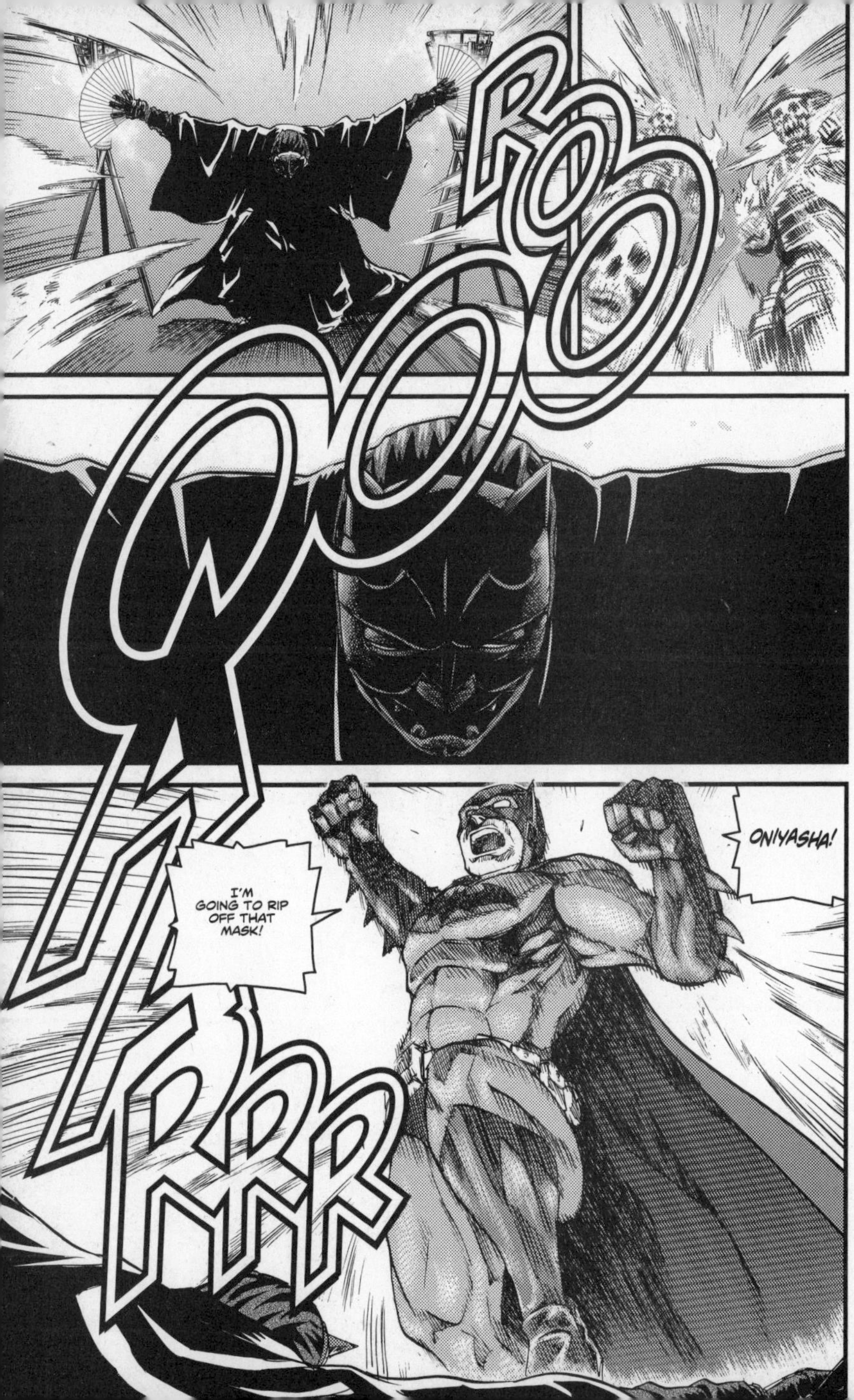
ROOOO
ONIYASHA!
I'M GOING TO RIP OFF THAT MASK!
RRRR

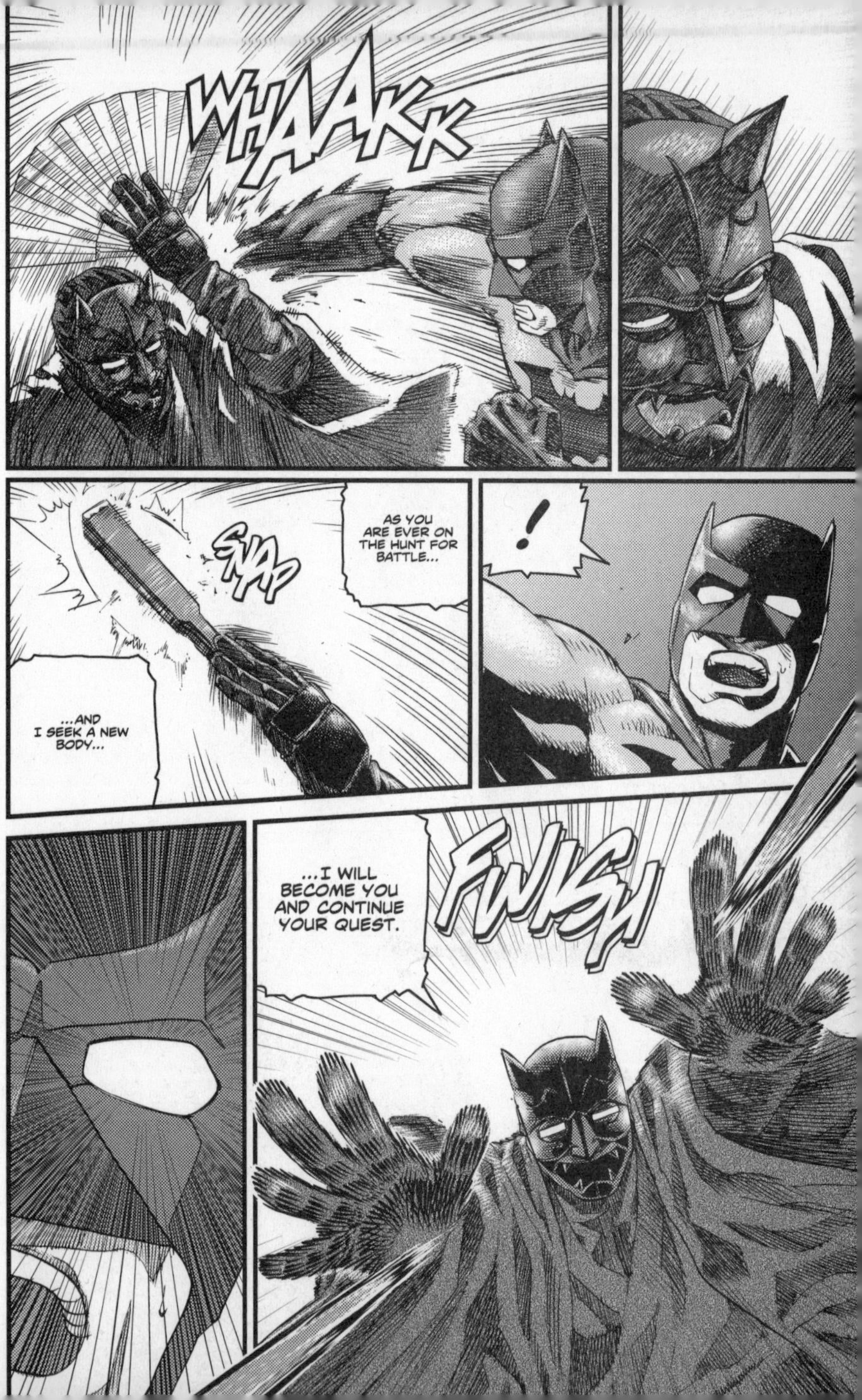
WHAAKK
SNAP
AS YOU ARE EVER ON THE HUNT FOR BATTLE...
...AND I SEEK A NEW BODY...
!
...I WILL BECOME YOU AND CONTINUE YOUR QUEST.
FWISH

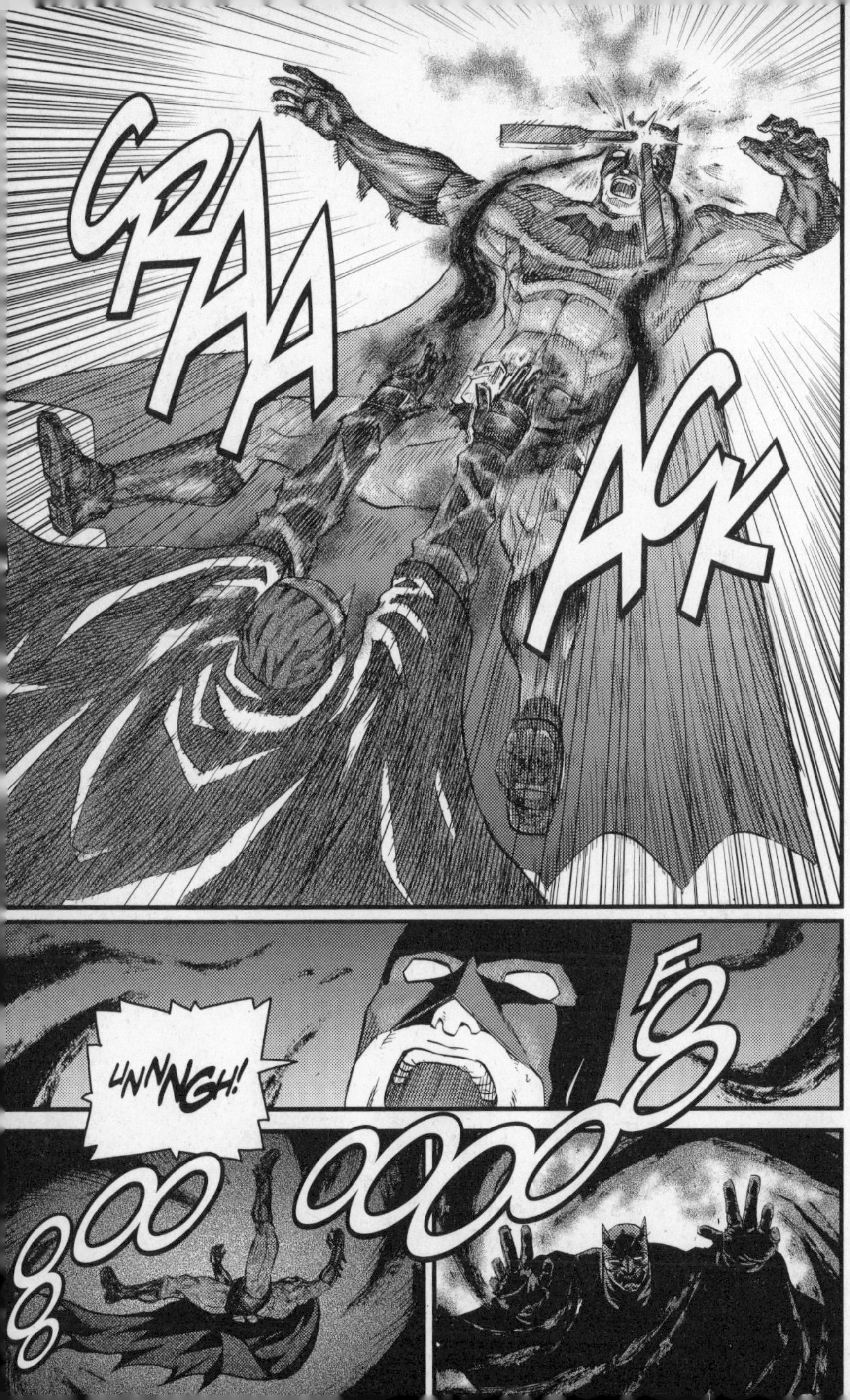

CRAAAACK
UNNNGH!
OOOOOOOOOOOOOOOOO

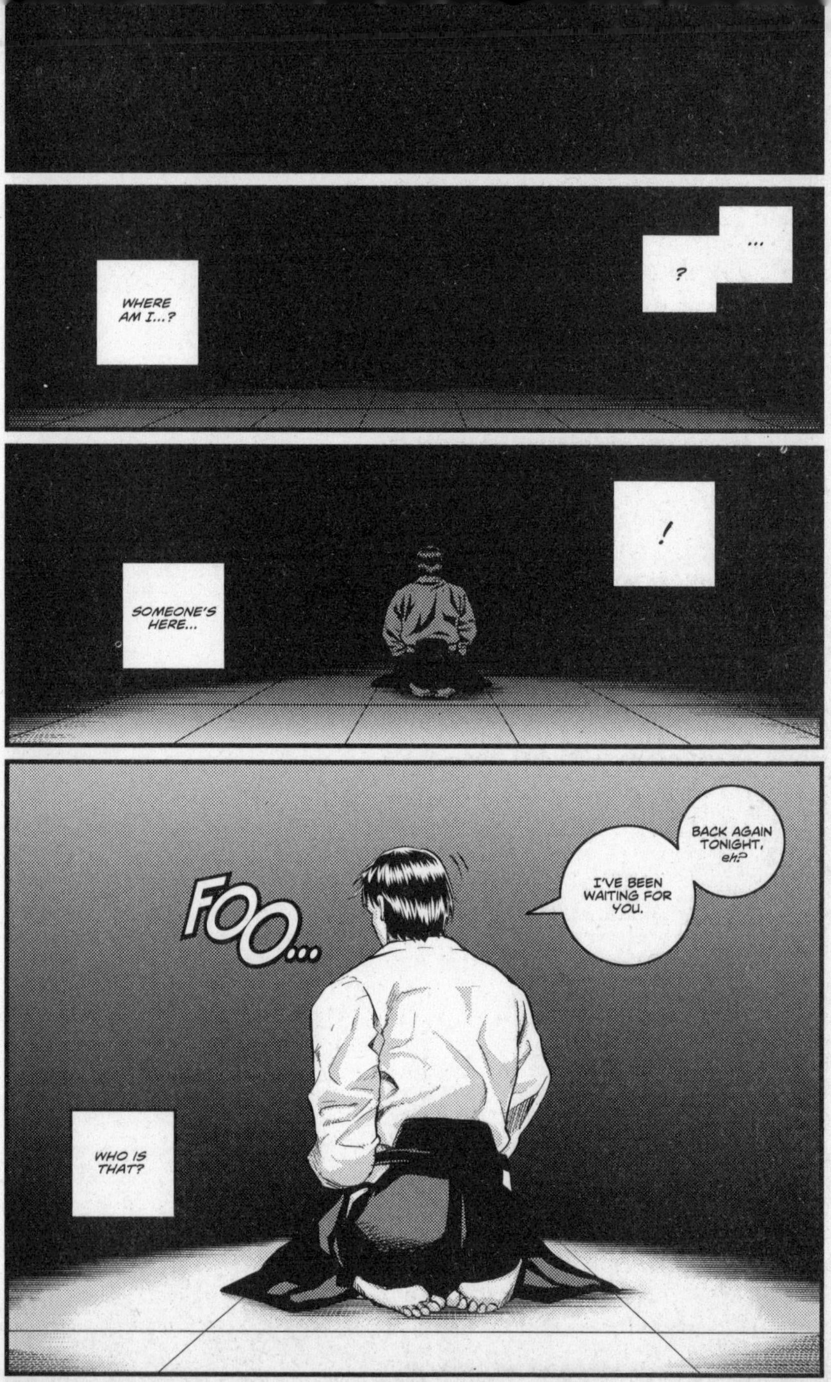

...
?
WHERE AM I...?
!
SOMEONE'S HERE...
BACK AGAIN TONIGHT, eh?
I'VE BEEN WAITING FOR YOU.
FOO...
WHO IS THAT?

?!

...THEN WHO AM I?

BUT IF THAT'S ME...

...ME?!

NO...IT CAN'T BE...

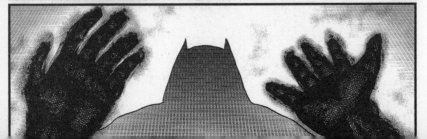

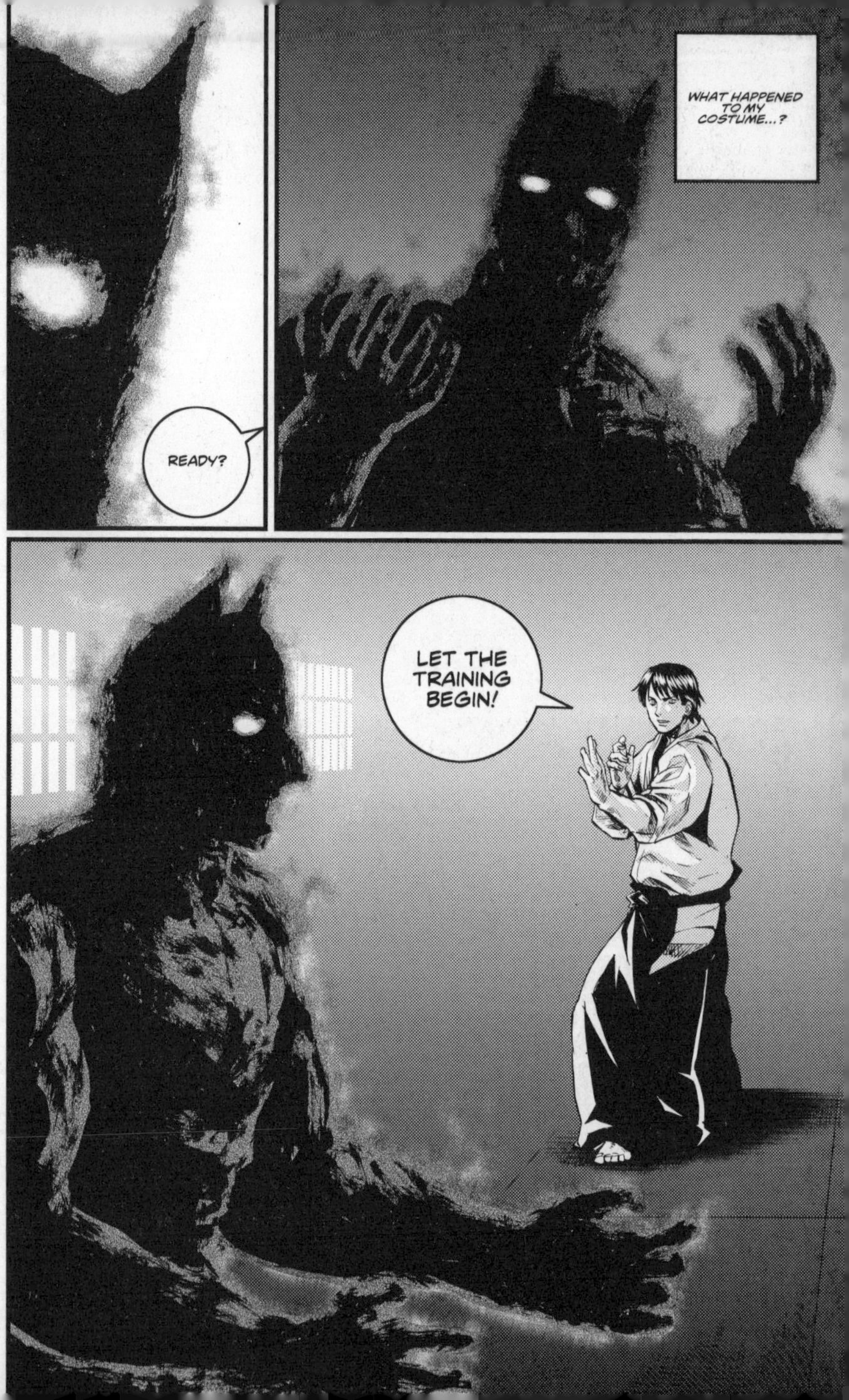

READY?
WHAT HAPPENED TO MY COSTUME...?
LET THE TRAINING BEGIN!

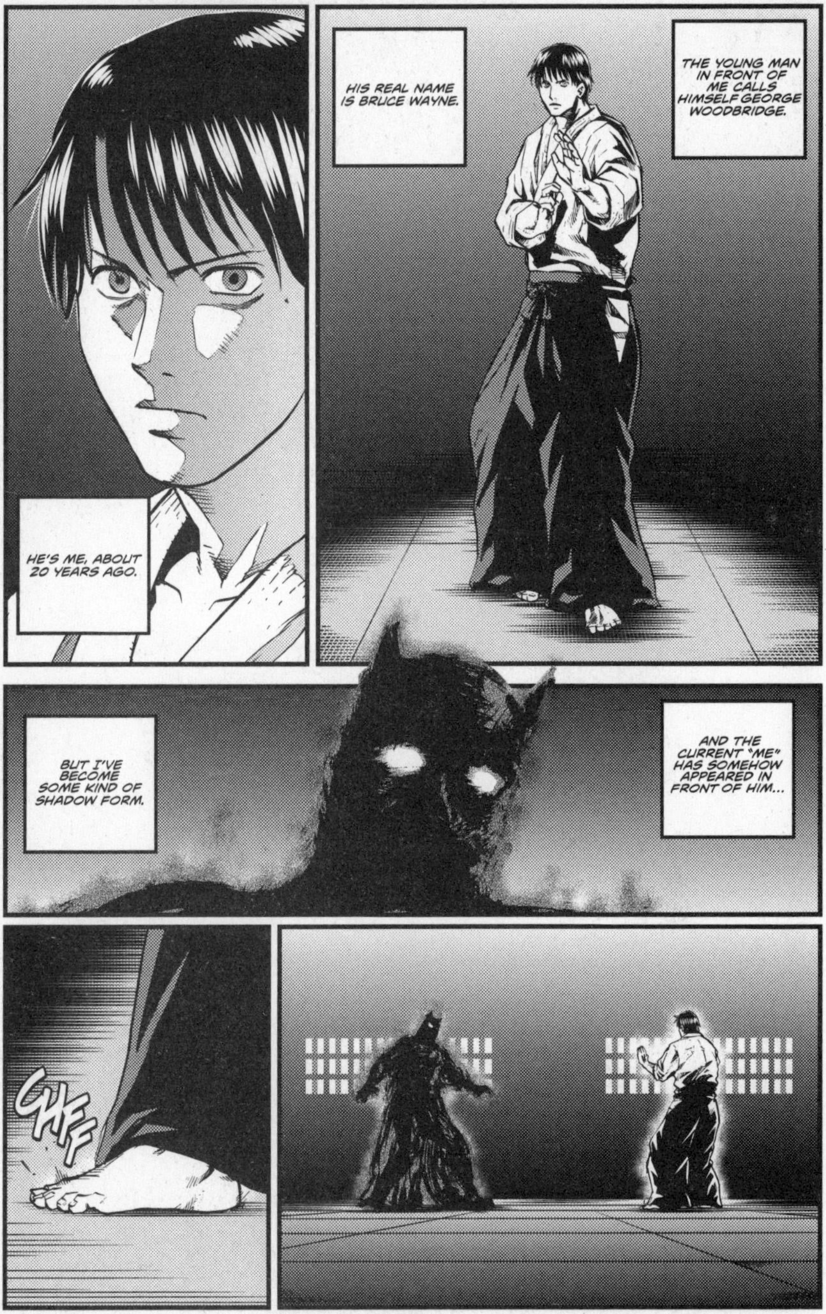
THE YOUNG MAN IN FRONT OF ME CALLS HIMSELF GEORGE WOODBRIDGE.
HIS REAL NAME IS BRUCE WAYNE.
HE'S ME, ABOUT 20 YEARS AGO.
BUT I'VE BECOME SOME KIND OF SHADOW FORM.
AND THE CURRENT "ME" HAS SOMEHOW APPEARED IN FRONT OF HIM...
GYAFF

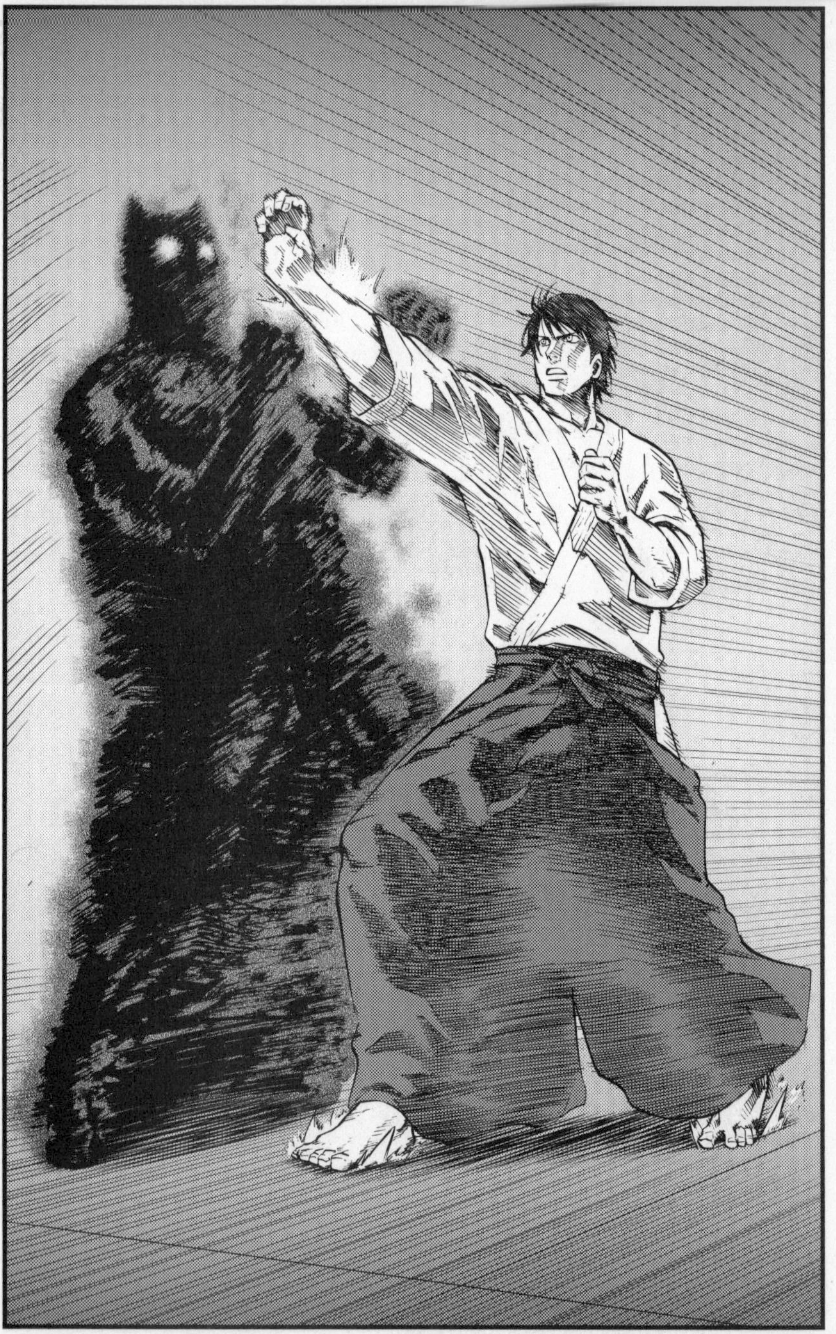

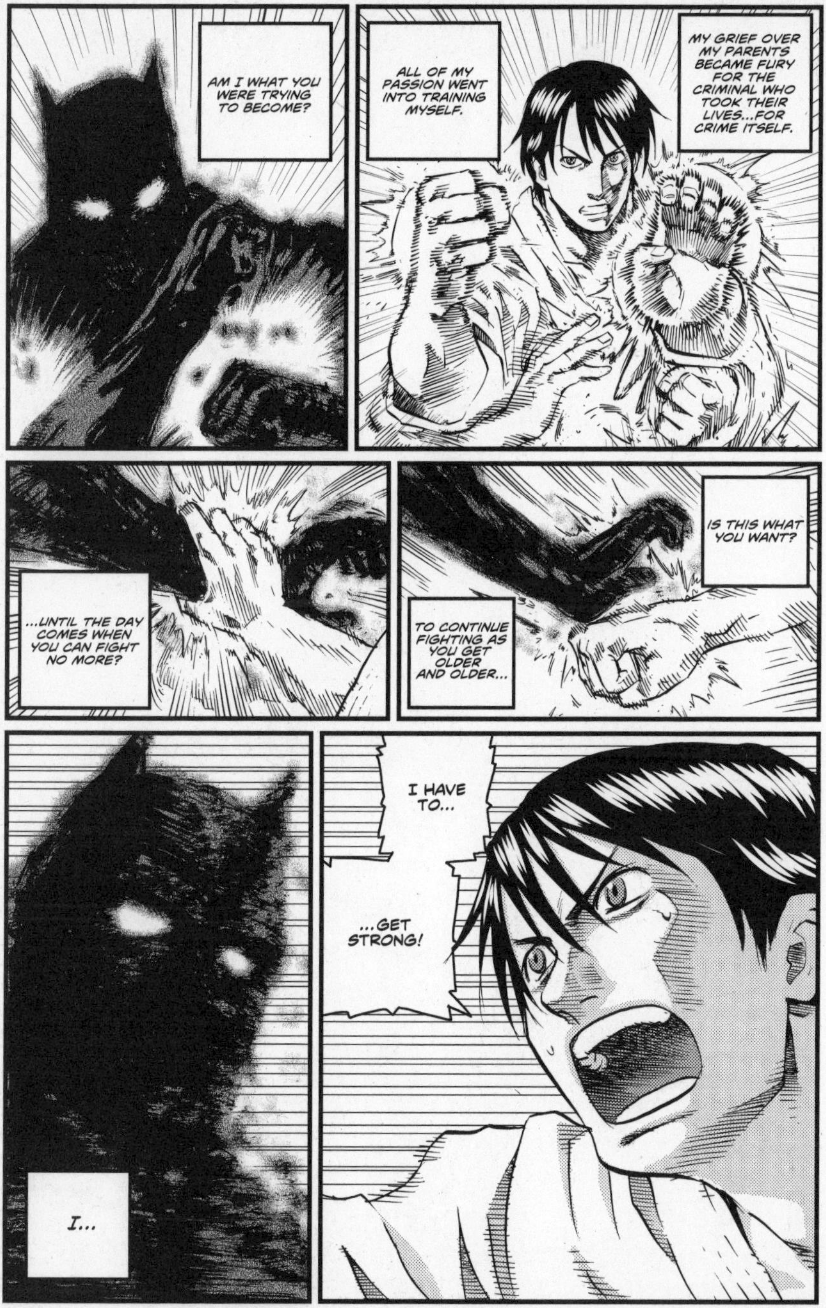
AM I WHAT YOU WERE TRYING TO BECOME?
ALL OF MY PASSION WENT INTO TRAINING MYSELF.
MY GRIEF OVER MY PARENTS BECAME FURY FOR THE CRIMINAL WHO TOOK THEIR LIVES...FOR CRIME ITSELF.
...UNTIL THE DAY COMES WHEN YOU CAN FIGHT NO MORE?
IS THIS WHAT YOU WANT?
TO CONTINUE FIGHTING AS YOU GET OLDER AND OLDER...
I...
I HAVE TO...
...GET STRONG!

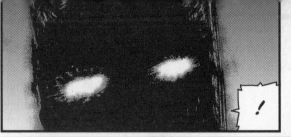

"AND IN YEARS TO COME, EVEN IF THE PAST CATCHES UP TO YOU, LOOK TO THE FUTURE."

!!

KK

RKKK

KRAK

OPEN YOUR EYES, BRUCE!!

HOW DO YOU KNOW THAT NAME?!

!

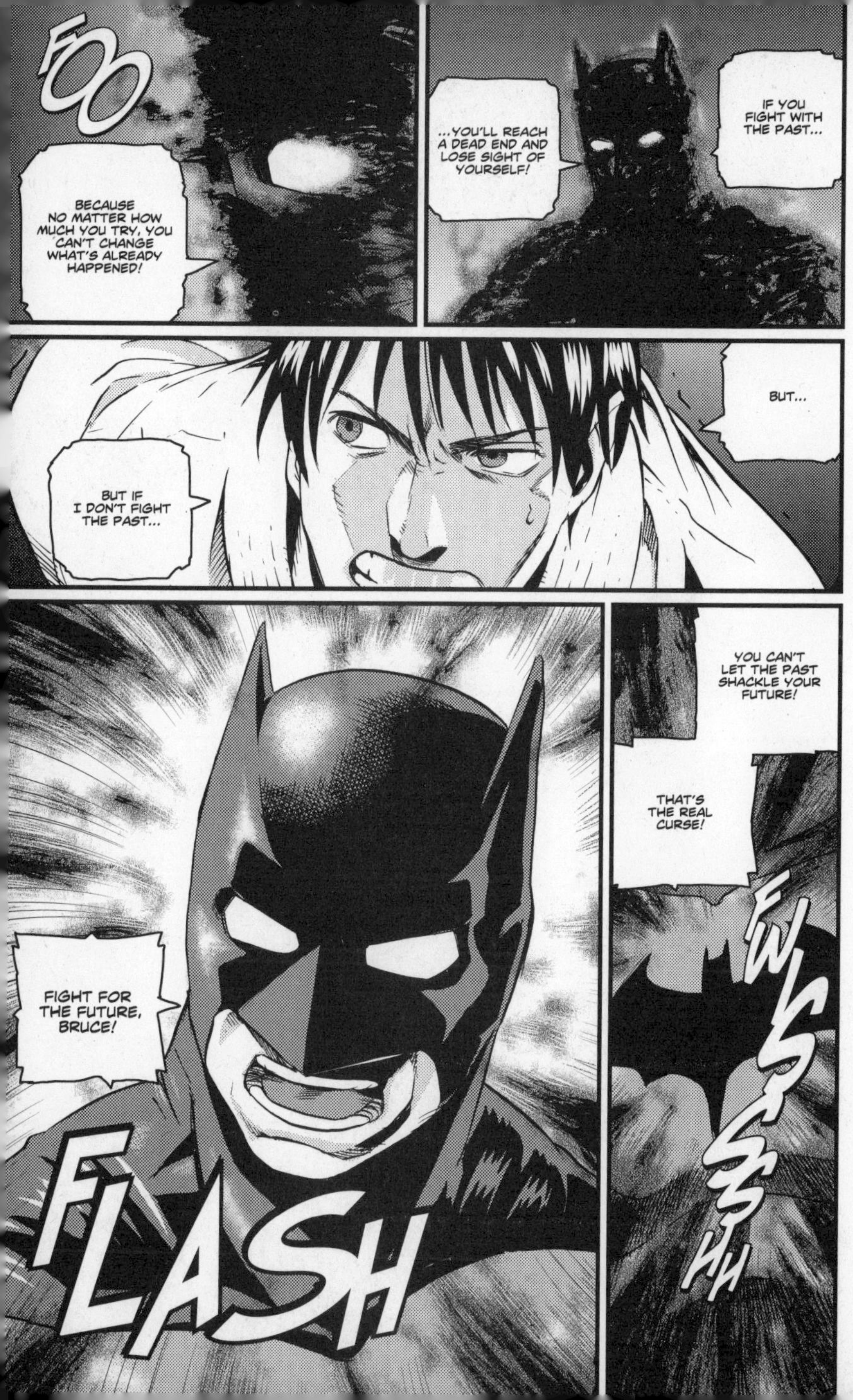
FOO
BECAUSE NO MATTER HOW MUCH YOU TRY, YOU CAN'T CHANGE WHAT'S ALREADY HAPPENED!
...YOU'LL REACH A DEAD END AND LOSE SIGHT OF YOURSELF!
IF YOU FIGHT WITH THE PAST...
BUT IF I DON'T FIGHT THE PAST...
BUT...
FIGHT FOR THE FUTURE, BRUCE!
FLASH
YOU CAN'T LET THE PAST SHACKLE YOUR FUTURE!
THAT'S THE REAL CURSE!
FWSSSHH

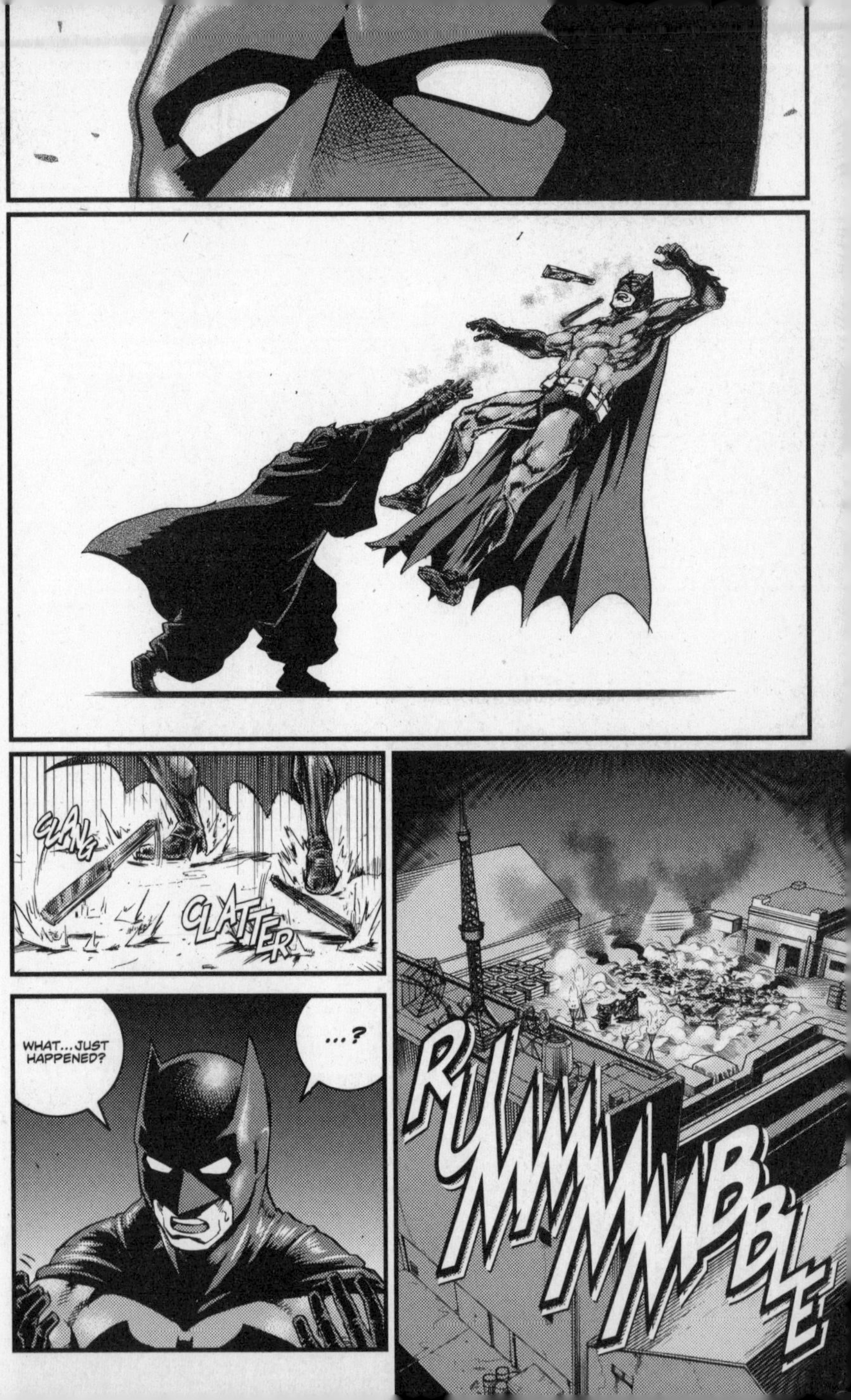
CLANG
CLATTER
WHAT...JUST HAPPENED?
...?
RUMMMMBLE

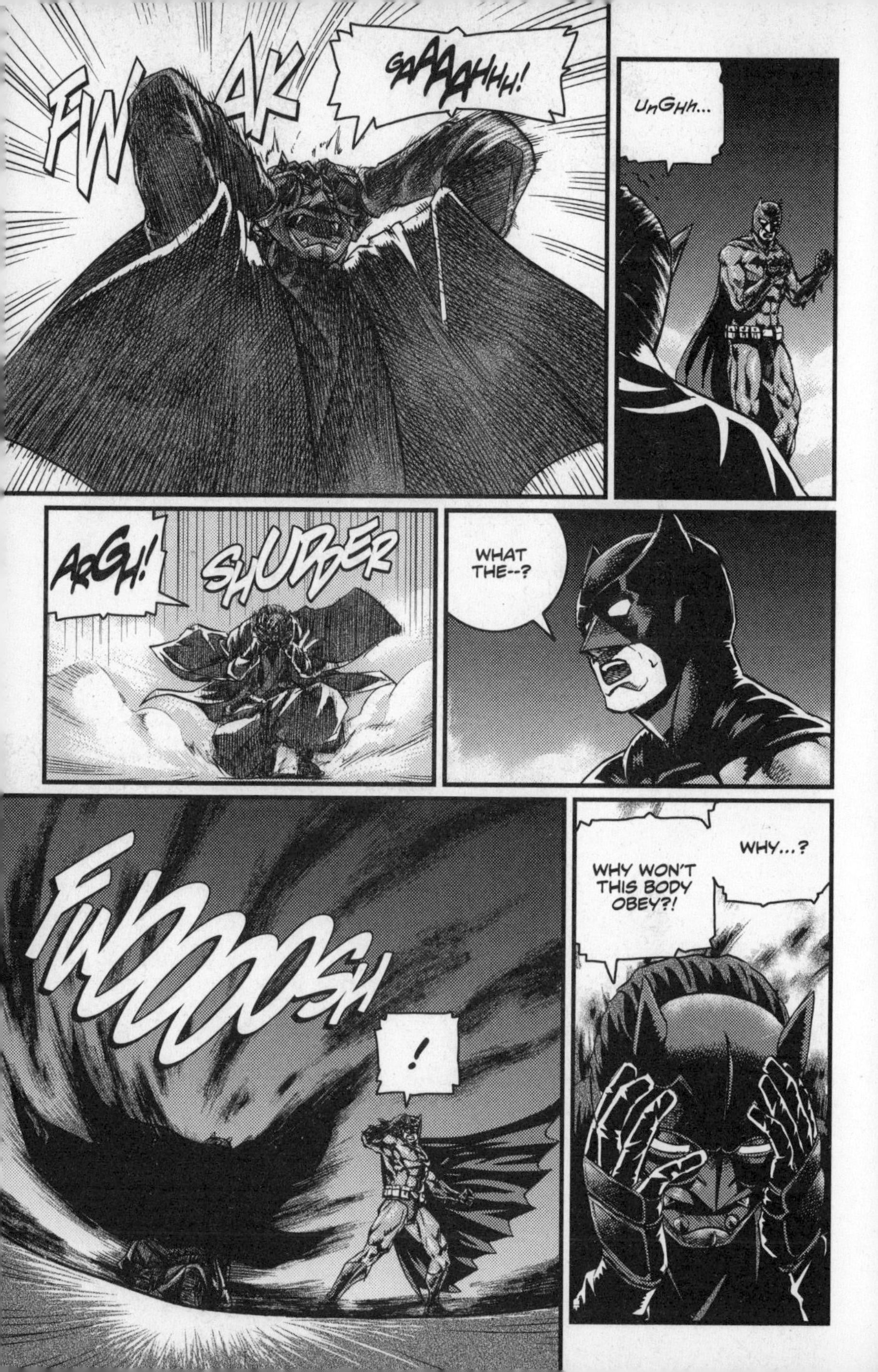
FWAK
GAAAAAHHH!
UnGHh...
ARGH!
SHUDDER
WHAT THE--?
FWOOOOSH
!
WHY...?
WHY WON'T THIS BODY OBEY?!

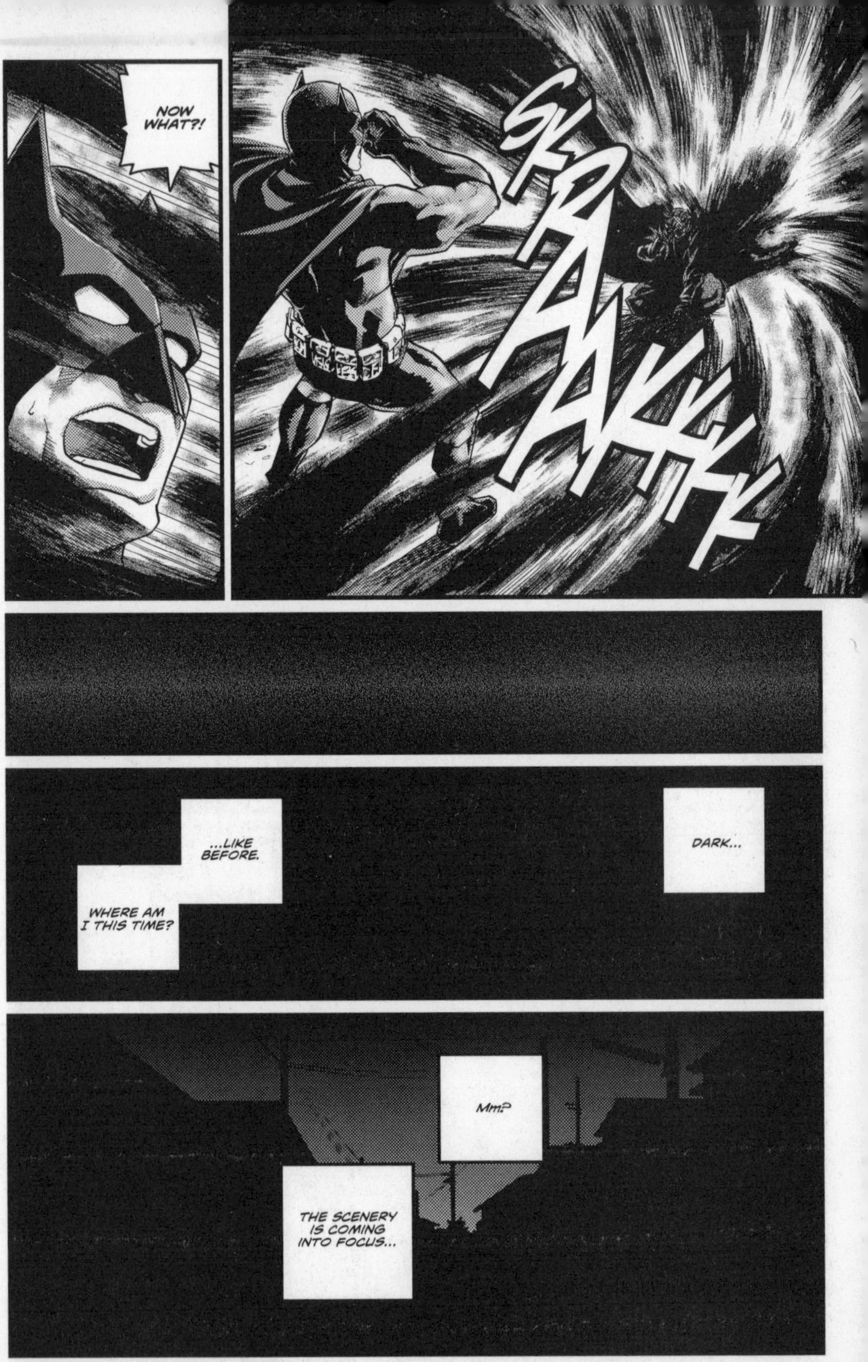

NOW WHAT?!
SKRAKKK
...LIKE BEFORE.
DARK...
WHERE AM I THIS TIME?
Mm?
THE SCENERY IS COMING INTO FOCUS...

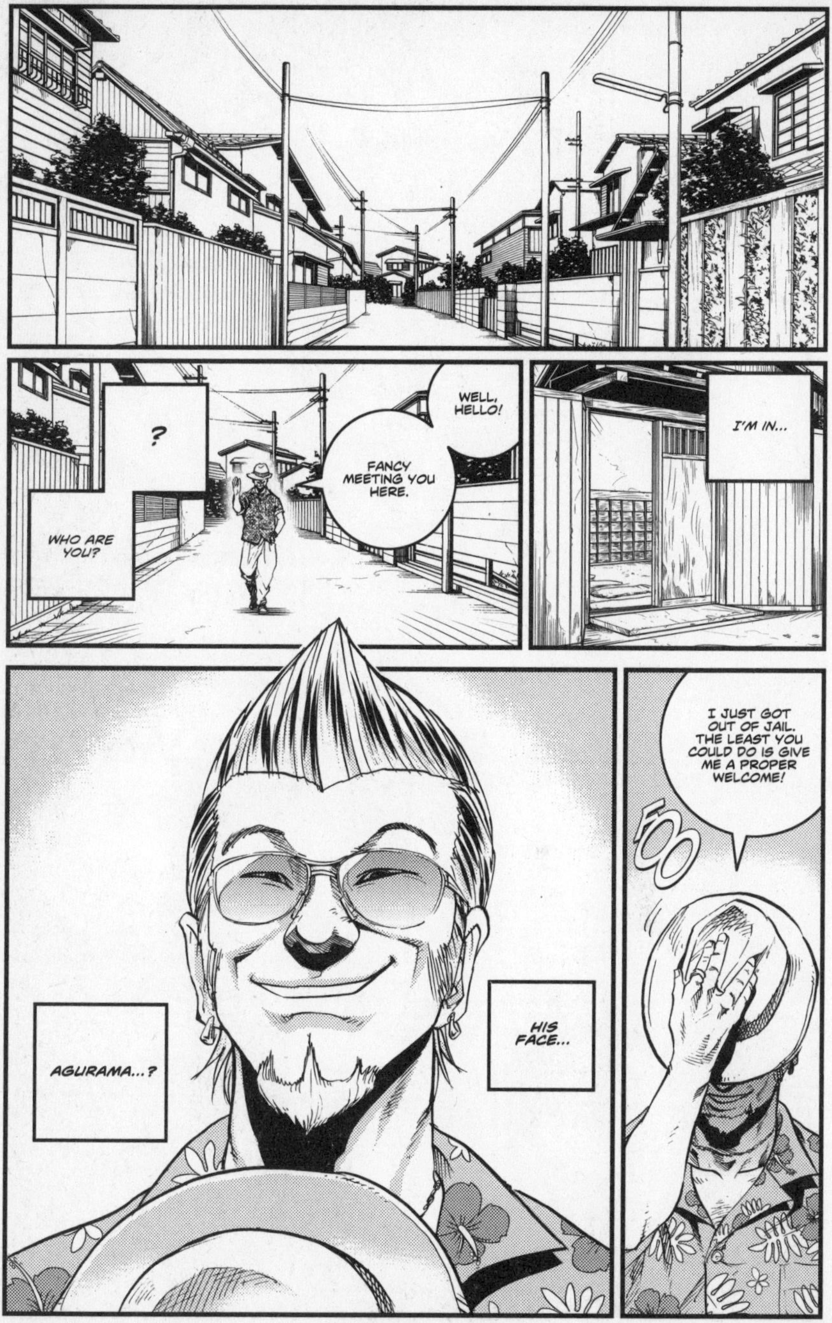

I'M IN...
?
WELL, HELLO!
FANCY MEETING YOU HERE.
WHO ARE YOU?
I JUST GOT OUT OF JAIL. THE LEAST YOU COULD DO IS GIVE ME A PROPER WELCOME!
FOO
HIS FACE...
AGURAMA...?

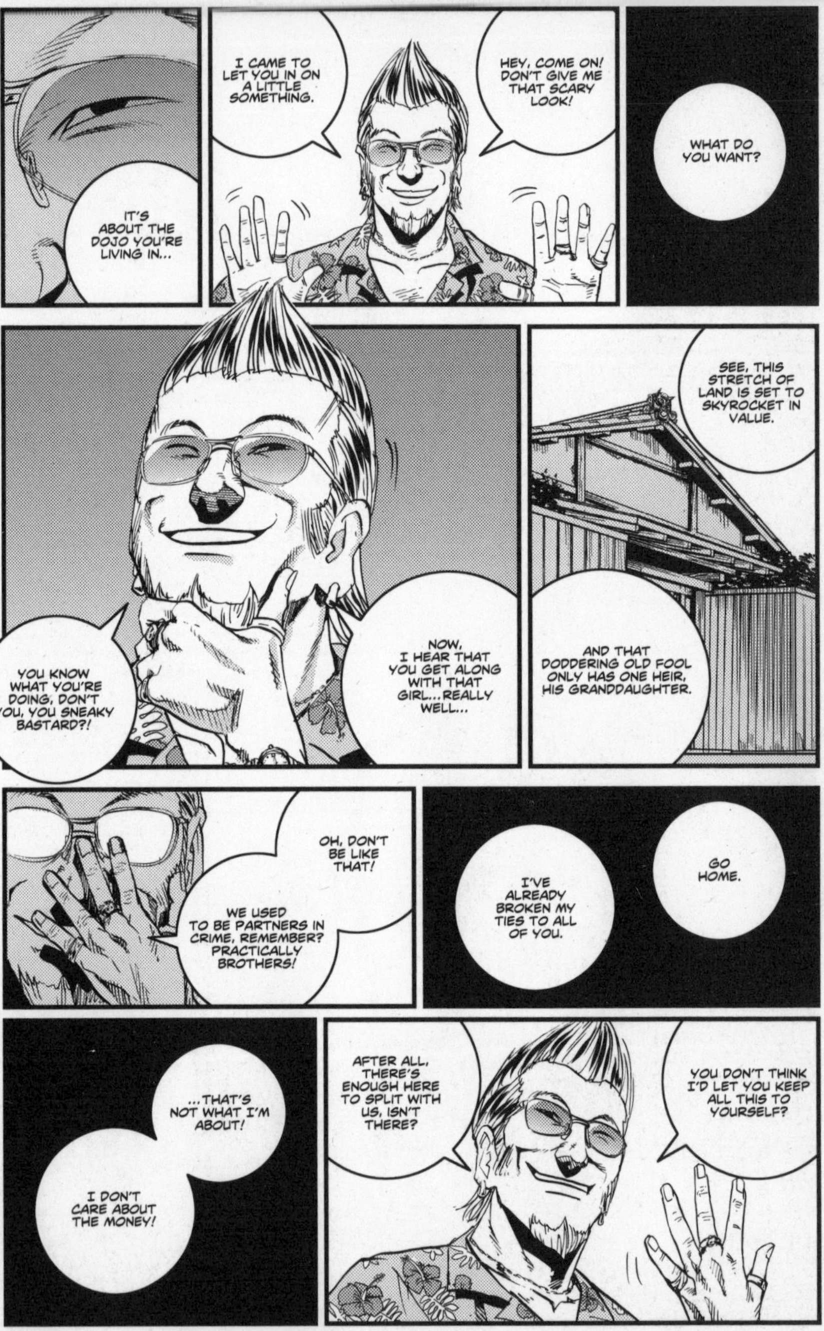
I CAME TO LET YOU IN ON A LITTLE SOMETHING.
HEY, COME ON! DON'T GIVE ME THAT SCARY LOOK!
WHAT DO YOU WANT?
IT'S ABOUT THE DOJO YOU'RE LIVING IN...
SEE, THIS STRETCH OF LAND IS SET TO SKYROCKET IN VALUE.
AND THAT DODDERING OLD FOOL ONLY HAS ONE HEIR, HIS GRANDDAUGHTER.
NOW, I HEAR THAT YOU GET ALONG WITH THAT GIRL... REALLY WELL...
YOU KNOW WHAT YOU'RE DOING, DON'T YOU, YOU SNEAKY BASTARD?!
OH, DON'T BE LIKE THAT!
WE USED TO BE PARTNERS IN CRIME, REMEMBER? PRACTICALLY BROTHERS!
GO HOME.
I'VE ALREADY BROKEN MY TIES TO ALL OF YOU.
YOU DON'T THINK I'D LET YOU KEEP ALL THIS TO YOURSELF?
AFTER ALL, THERE'S ENOUGH HERE TO SPLIT WITH US, ISN'T THERE?
...THAT'S NOT WHAT I'M ABOUT!
I DON'T CARE ABOUT THE MONEY!

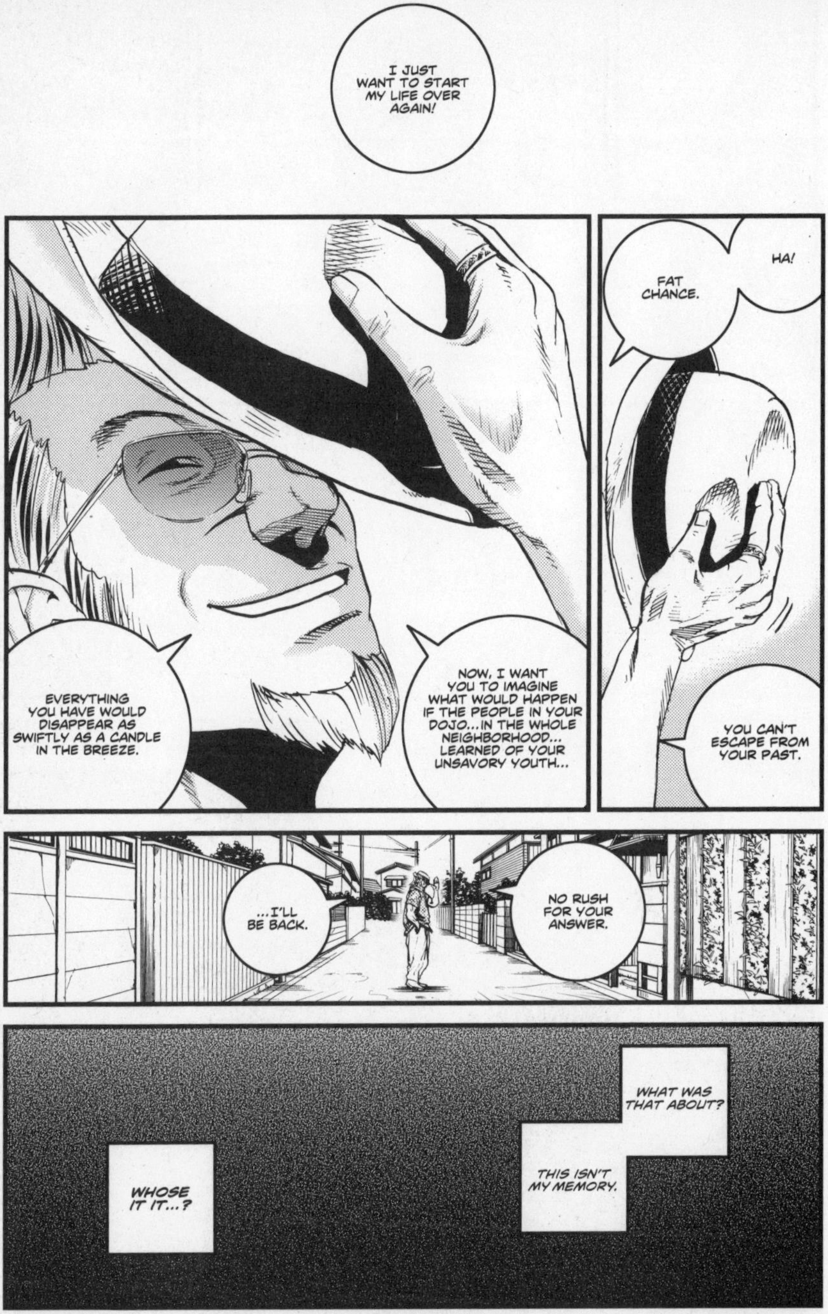
I JUST WANT TO START MY LIFE OVER AGAIN!
NOW, I WANT YOU TO IMAGINE WHAT WOULD HAPPEN IF THE PEOPLE IN YOUR DOJO...IN THE WHOLE NEIGHBORHOOD... LEARNED OF YOUR UNSAVORY YOUTH...
EVERYTHING YOU HAVE WOULD DISAPPEAR AS SWIFTLY AS A CANDLE IN THE BREEZE.
HA!
FAT CHANCE.
YOU CAN'T ESCAPE FROM YOUR PAST.
...I'LL BE BACK.
NO RUSH FOR YOUR ANSWER.
WHAT WAS THAT ABOUT?
THIS ISN'T MY MEMORY.
WHOSE IT IT...?

...HATE.

IS THIS HATE I FEEL?

THEN HATE I WILL.

HATRED WILL GIVE ME STRENGTH.

IT WILL REVIVE THE STRENGTH THAT I HAVE LOST OVER THE YEARS.

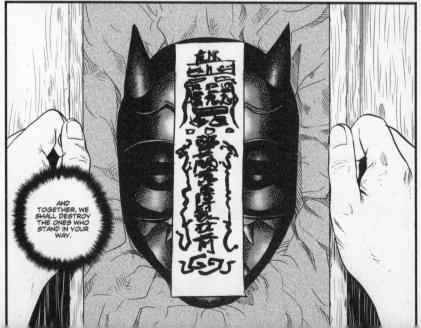

YES. OPEN THE CABINET. BREAK THE SEAL.

IF YOU LEND ME YOUR BODY, I WILL GIVE YOU POWER.

AND TOGETHER, WE SHALL DESTROY THE ONES WHO STAND IN YOUR WAY.

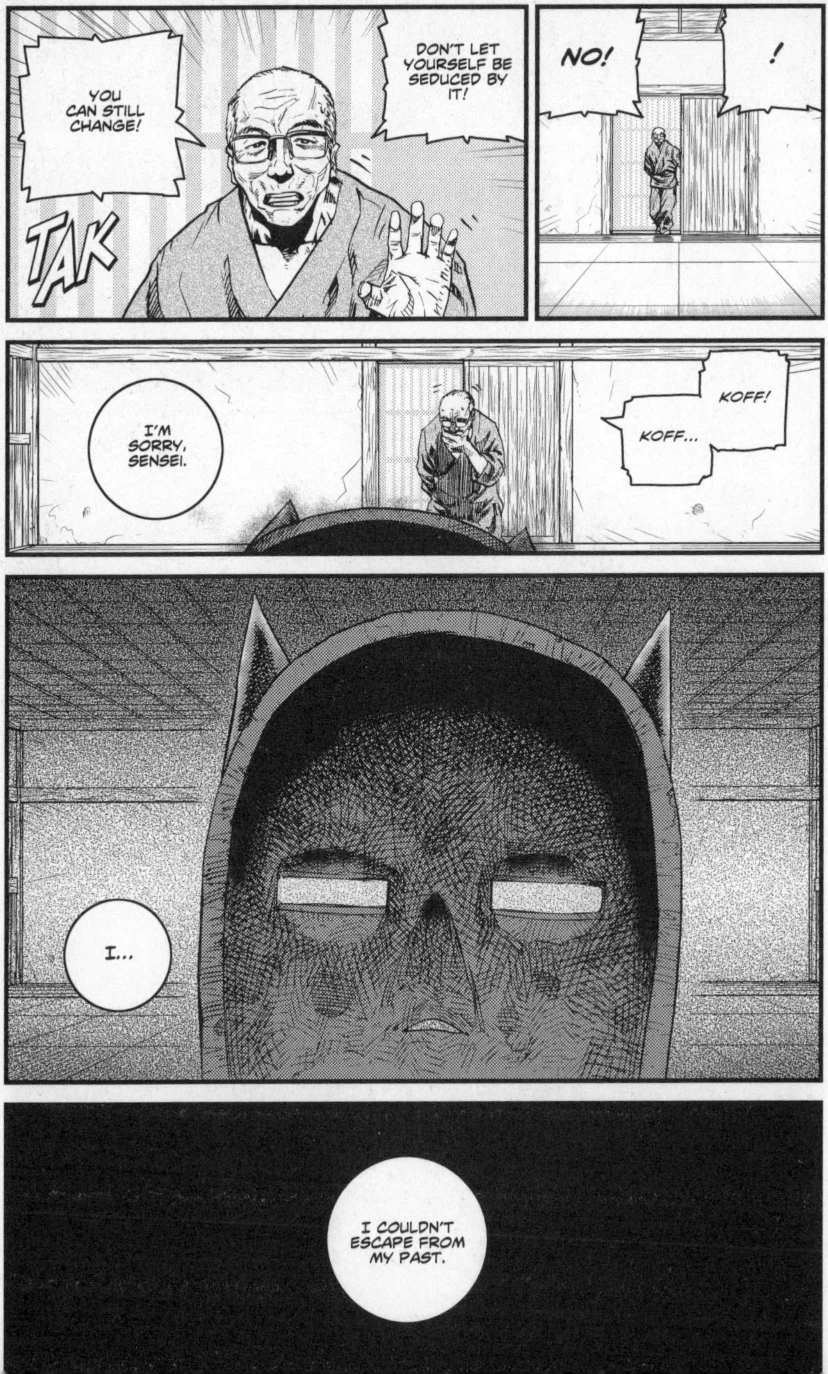
YOU CAN STILL CHANGE!
DON'T LET YOURSELF BE SEDUCED BY IT!
TAK
NO!
!
I'M SORRY, SENSEI.
KOFF!
KOFF...
I...
I COULDN'T ESCAPE FROM MY PAST.

ROARRRRR

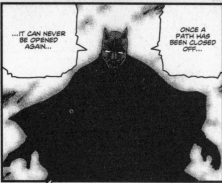

...IT CAN NEVER BE OPENED AGAIN...

ONCE A PATH HAS BEEN CLOSED OFF...

MY GOD...

YOU...

...FOR IT IS BLOCKED BY A WALL THAT CANNOT BE SURMOUNTED FOR ALL ETERNITY.

FWOOOOSH

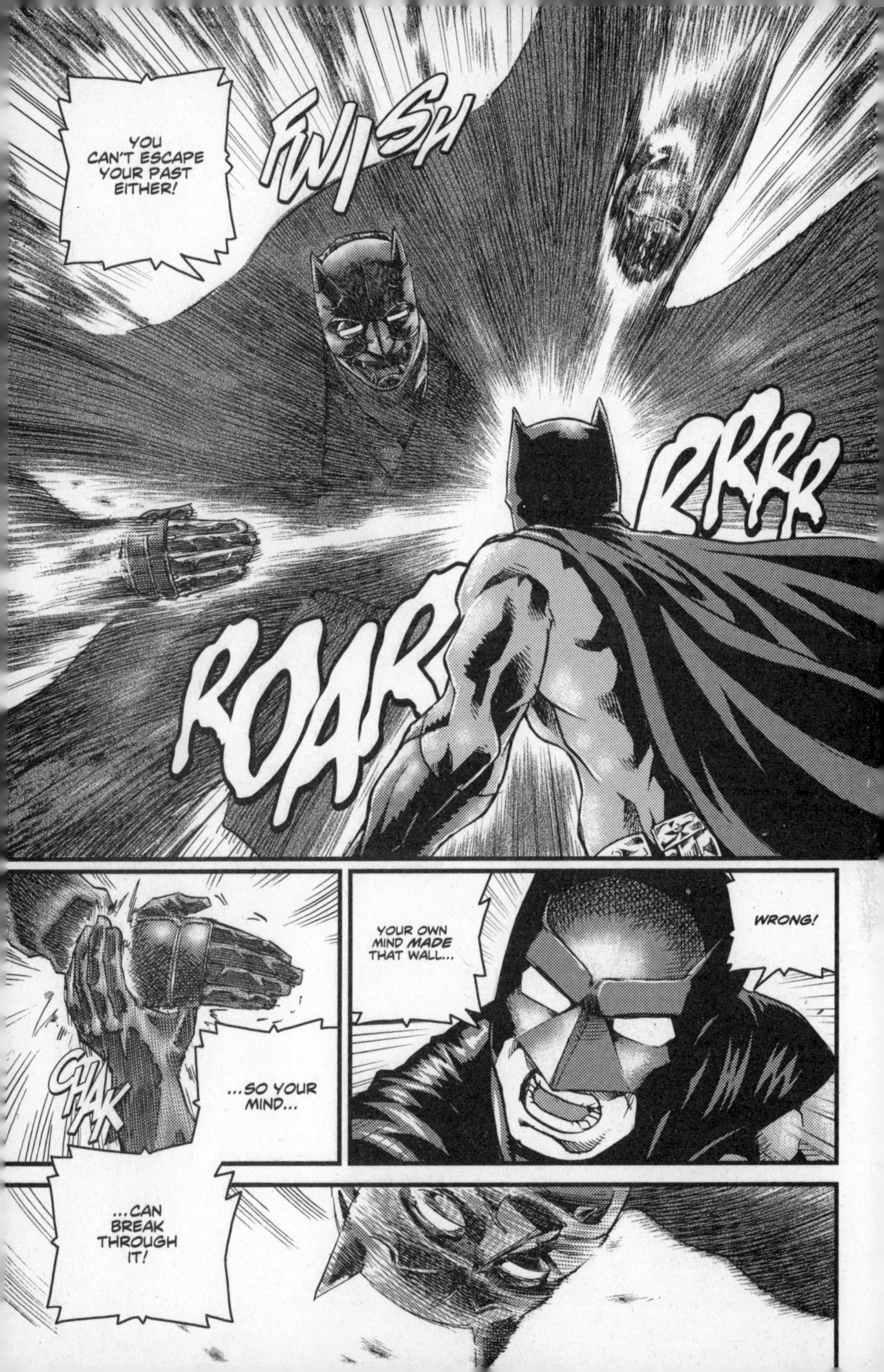
YOU CAN'T ESCAPE YOUR PAST EITHER!
FWISH
RRRR
ROAR
YOUR OWN MIND *MADE* THAT WALL...
WRONG!
CHAK
...SO YOUR MIND...
...CAN BREAK THROUGH IT!

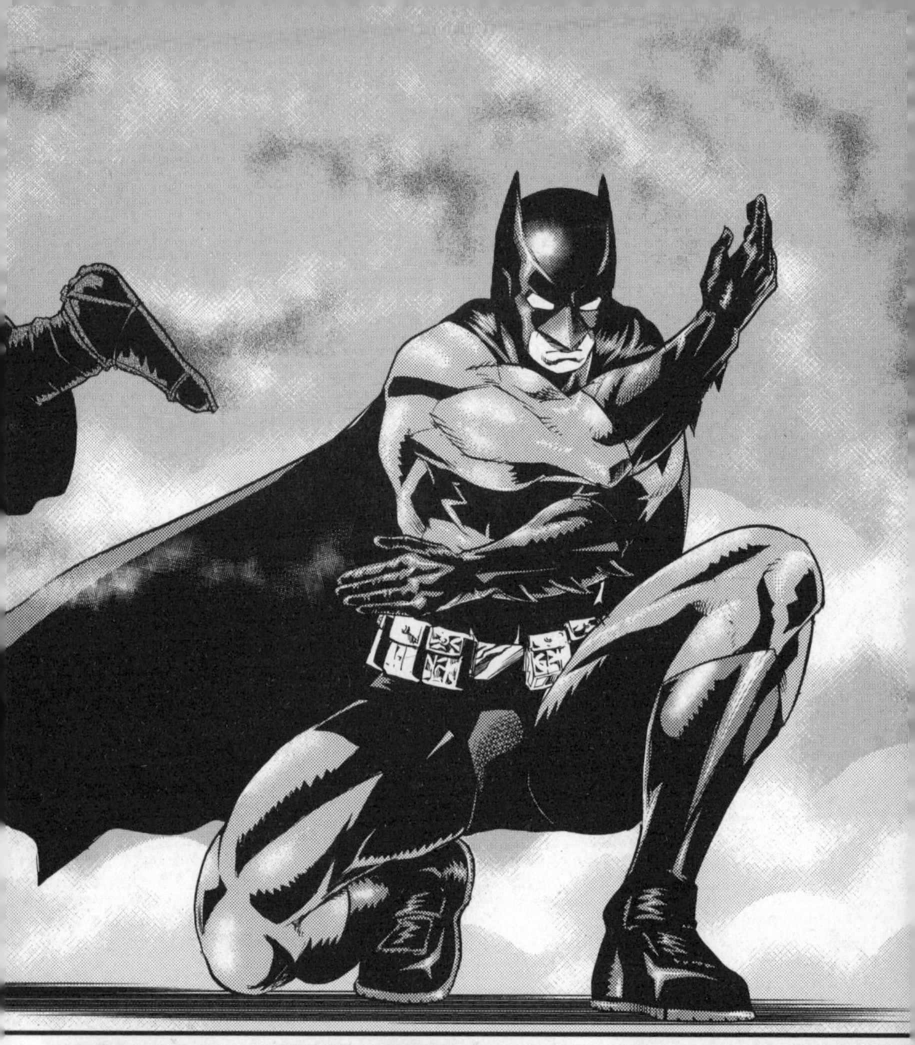
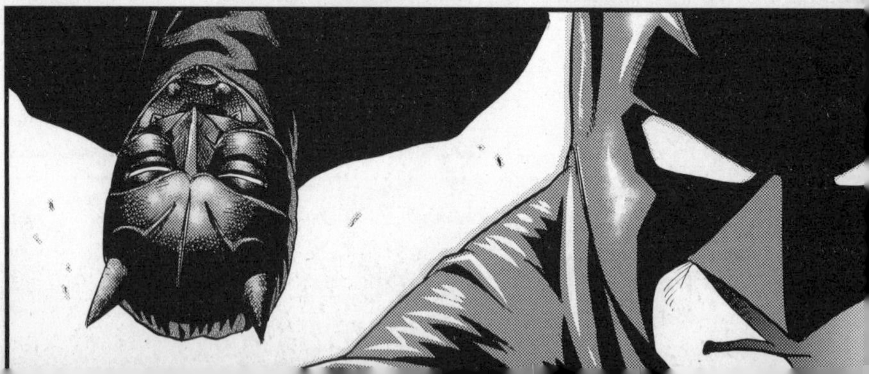

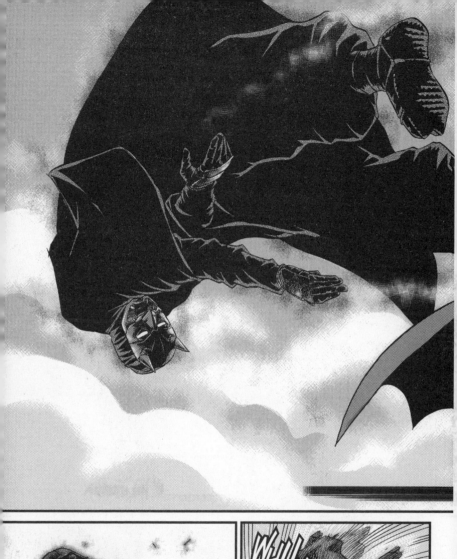

WHUNK

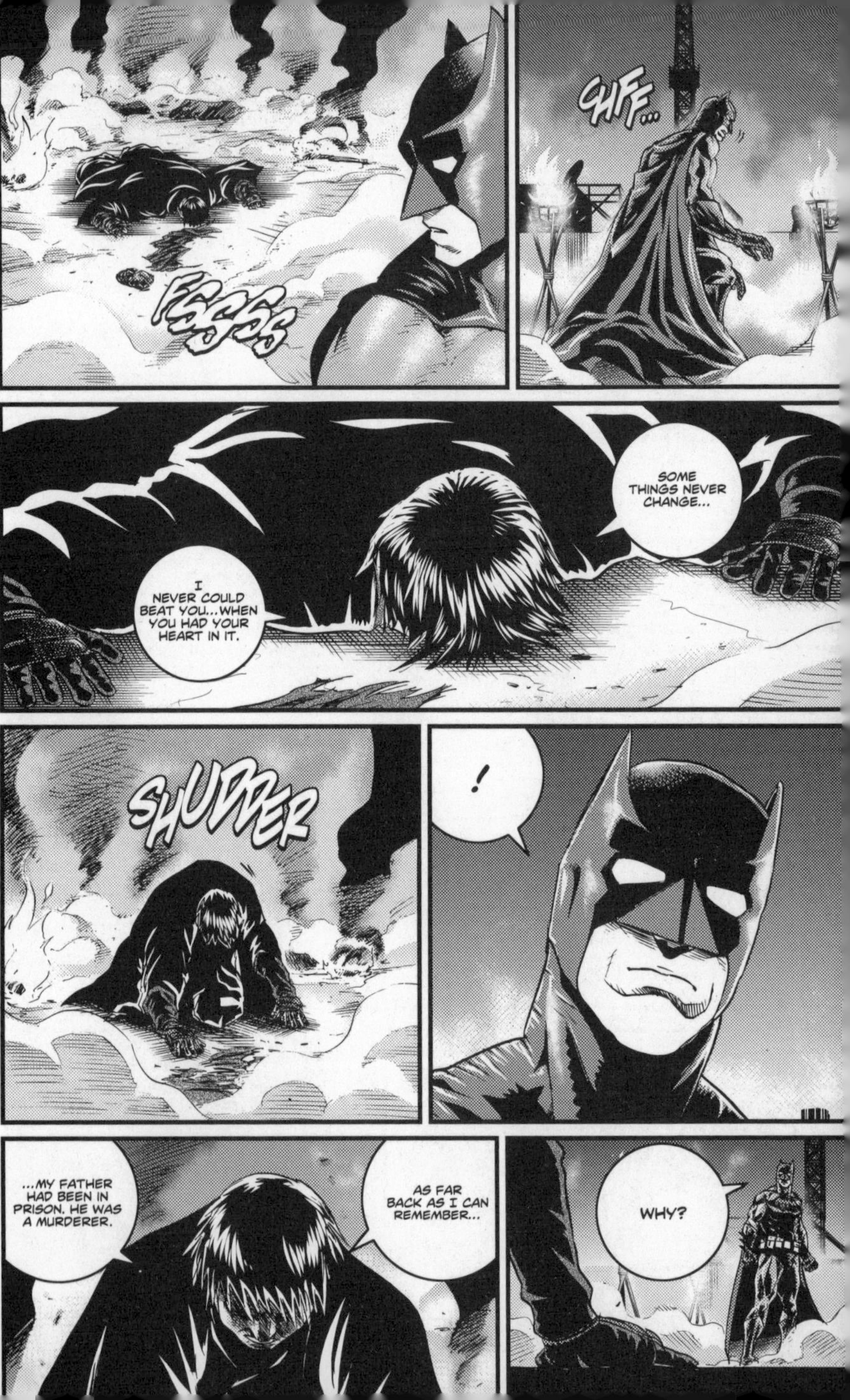
FSSSS
CHFF...
SOME THINGS NEVER CHANGE...
I NEVER COULD BEAT YOU...WHEN YOU HAD YOUR HEART IN IT.
SHUDDER
!
WHY?
AS FAR BACK AS I CAN REMEMBER...
...MY FATHER HAD BEEN IN PRISON. HE WAS A MURDERER.

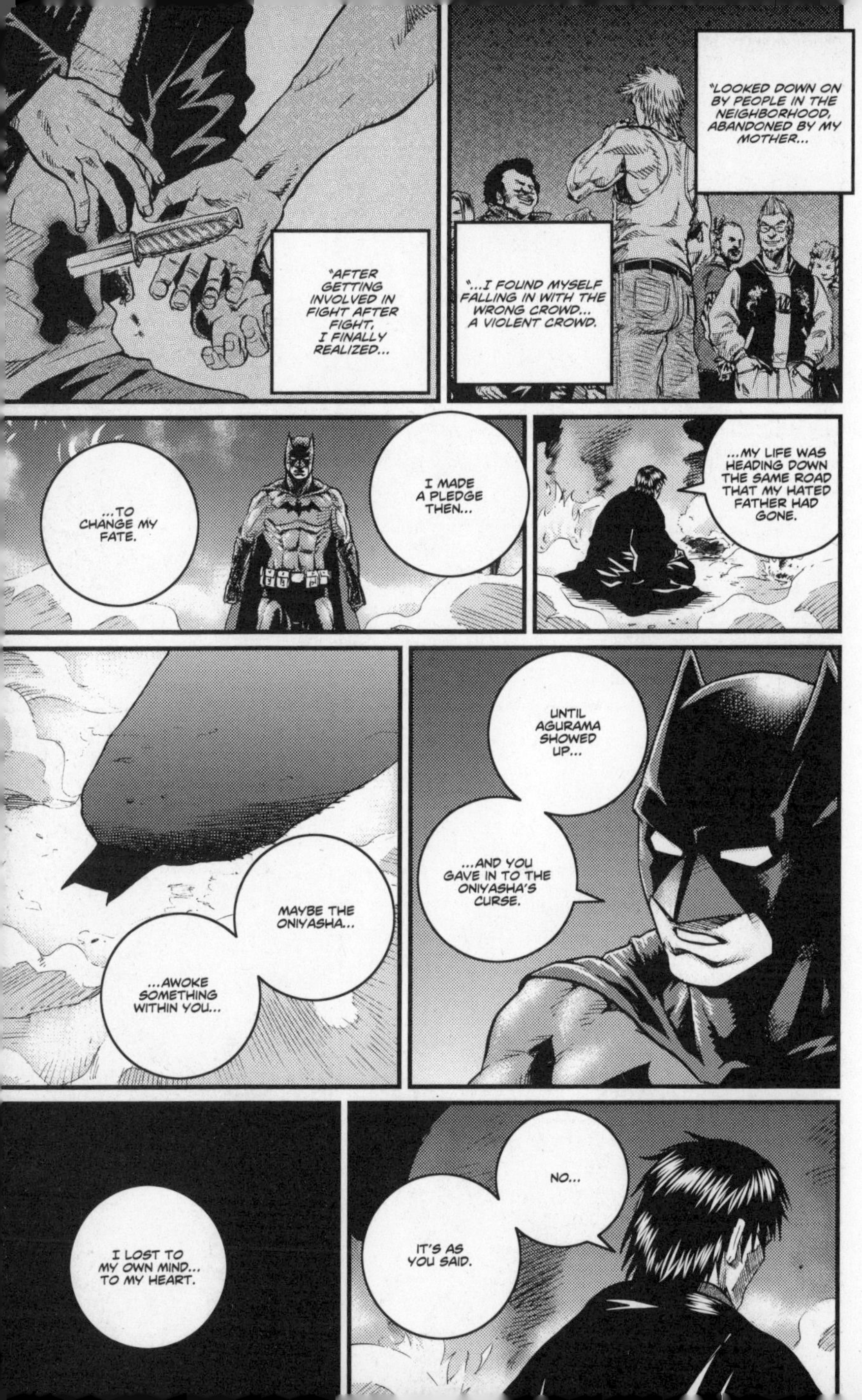
"LOOKED DOWN ON BY PEOPLE IN THE NEIGHBORHOOD, ABANDONED BY MY MOTHER...
"...I FOUND MYSELF FALLING IN WITH THE WRONG CROWD... A VIOLENT CROWD.
"AFTER GETTING INVOLVED IN FIGHT AFTER FIGHT, I FINALLY REALIZED...
...MY LIFE WAS HEADING DOWN THE SAME ROAD THAT MY HATED FATHER HAD GONE.
I MADE A PLEDGE THEN...
...TO CHANGE MY FATE.
UNTIL AGURAMA SHOWED UP...
...AND YOU GAVE IN TO THE ONIYASHA'S CURSE.
MAYBE THE ONIYASHA...
...AWOKE SOMETHING WITHIN YOU...
NO...
IT'S AS YOU SAID.
I LOST TO MY OWN MIND... TO MY HEART.

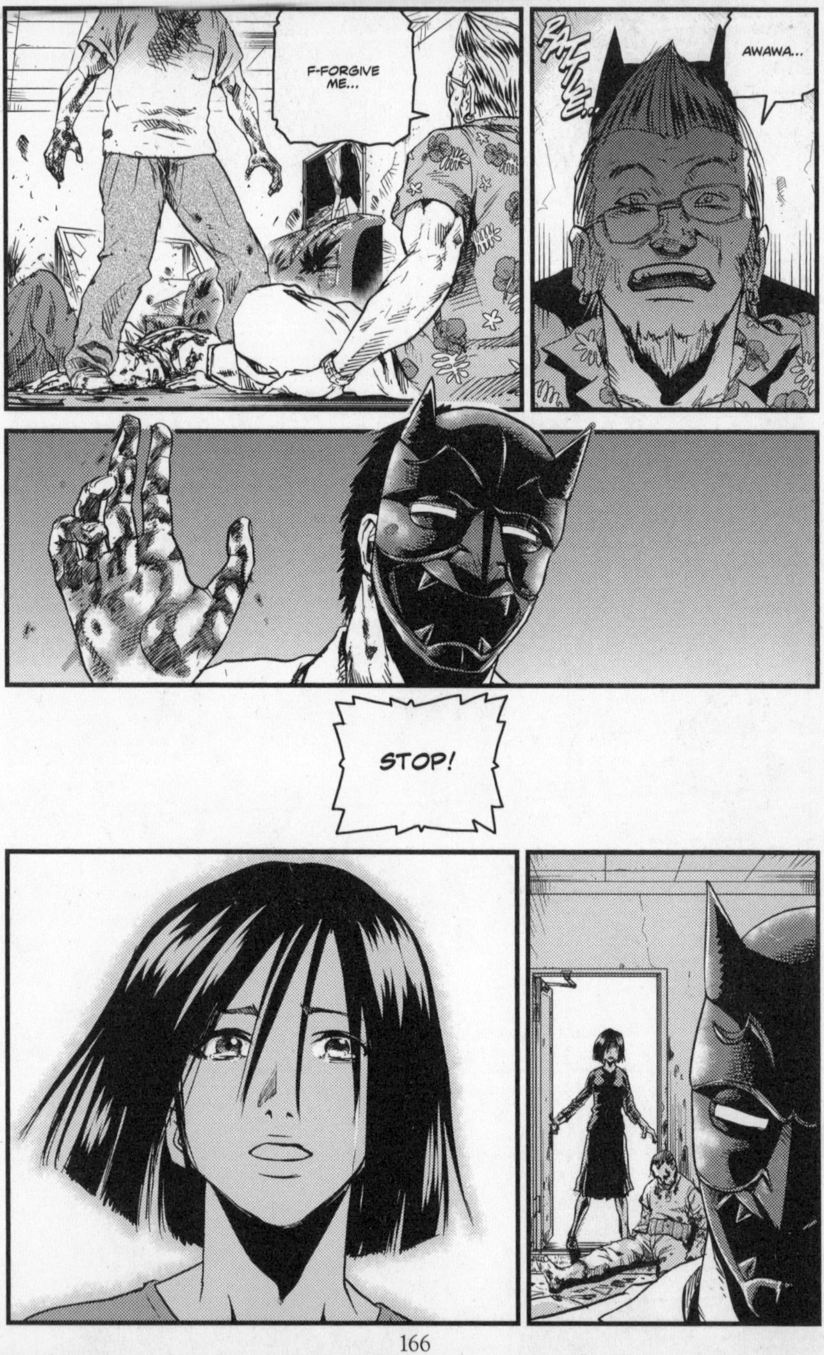
AWAWA...
RATTLE...
F-FORGIVE ME...
STOP!

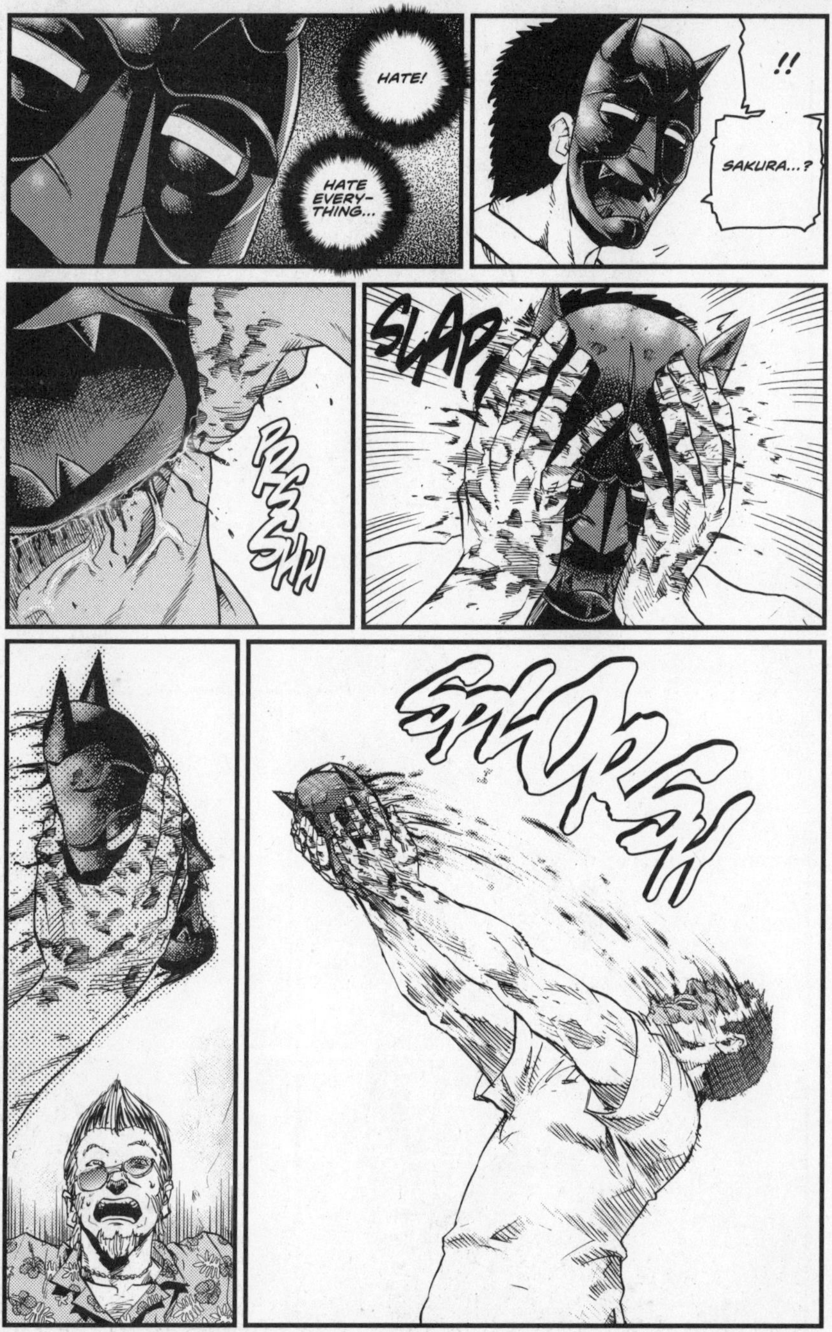

!!
SAKURA...?
HATE!
HATE EVERYTHING...
SLAP
PRSSHH
SPLORSH

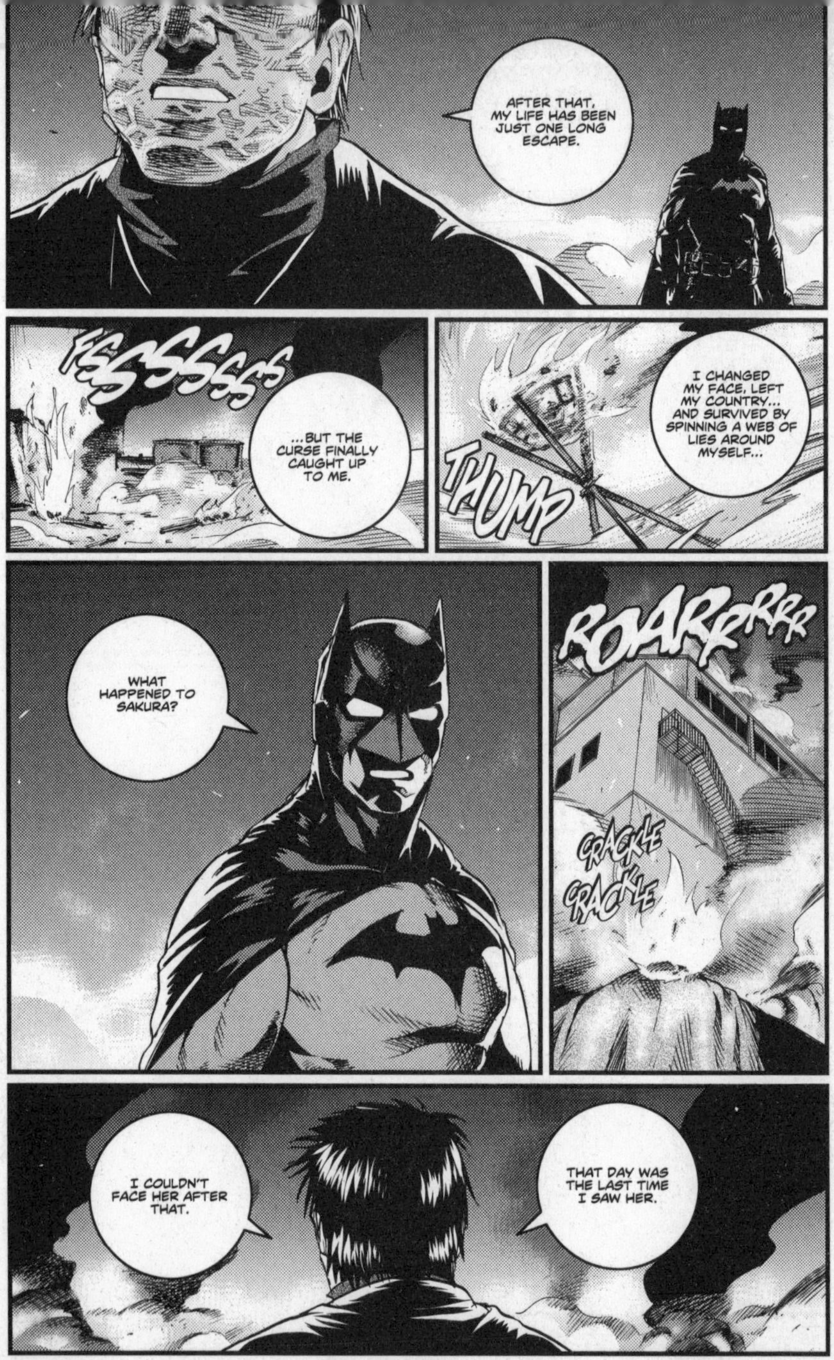
AFTER THAT, MY LIFE HAS BEEN JUST ONE LONG ESCAPE.
FSSSSSSS
...BUT THE CURSE FINALLY CAUGHT UP TO ME.
I CHANGED MY FACE, LEFT MY COUNTRY... AND SURVIVED BY SPINNING A WEB OF LIES AROUND MYSELF...
THUMP
WHAT HAPPENED TO SAKURA?
ROARRRRR
CRACKLE
CRACKLE
I COULDN'T FACE HER AFTER THAT.
THAT DAY WAS THE LAST TIME I SAW HER.

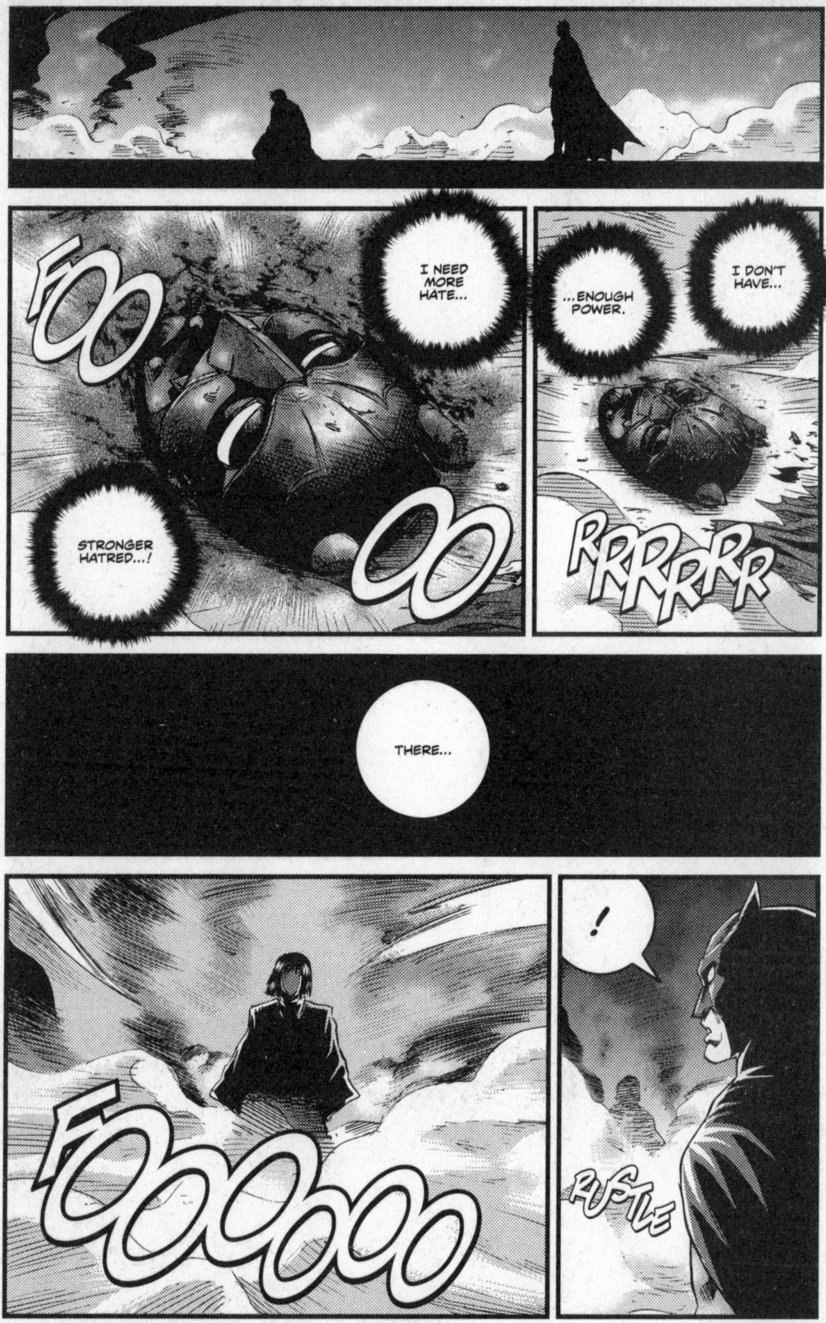
FOO
I NEED MORE HATE...
STRONGER HATRED...!
OO
I DON'T HAVE...
...ENOUGH POWER.
RRRRRRR
THERE...
FOOOOOOO
!
RUSTLE

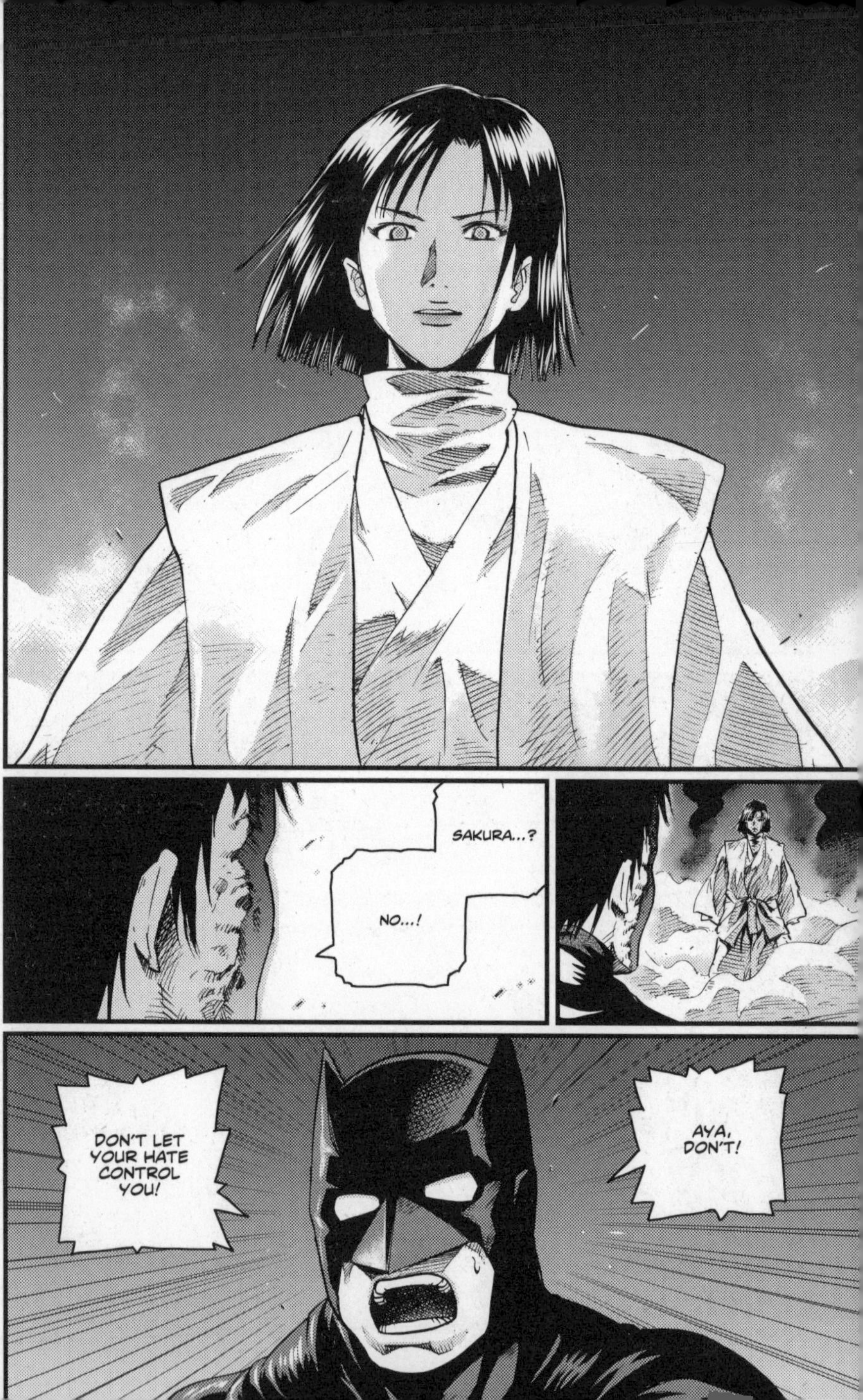
SAKURA...?
NO...!
DON'T LET YOUR HATE CONTROL YOU!
AYA, DON'T!

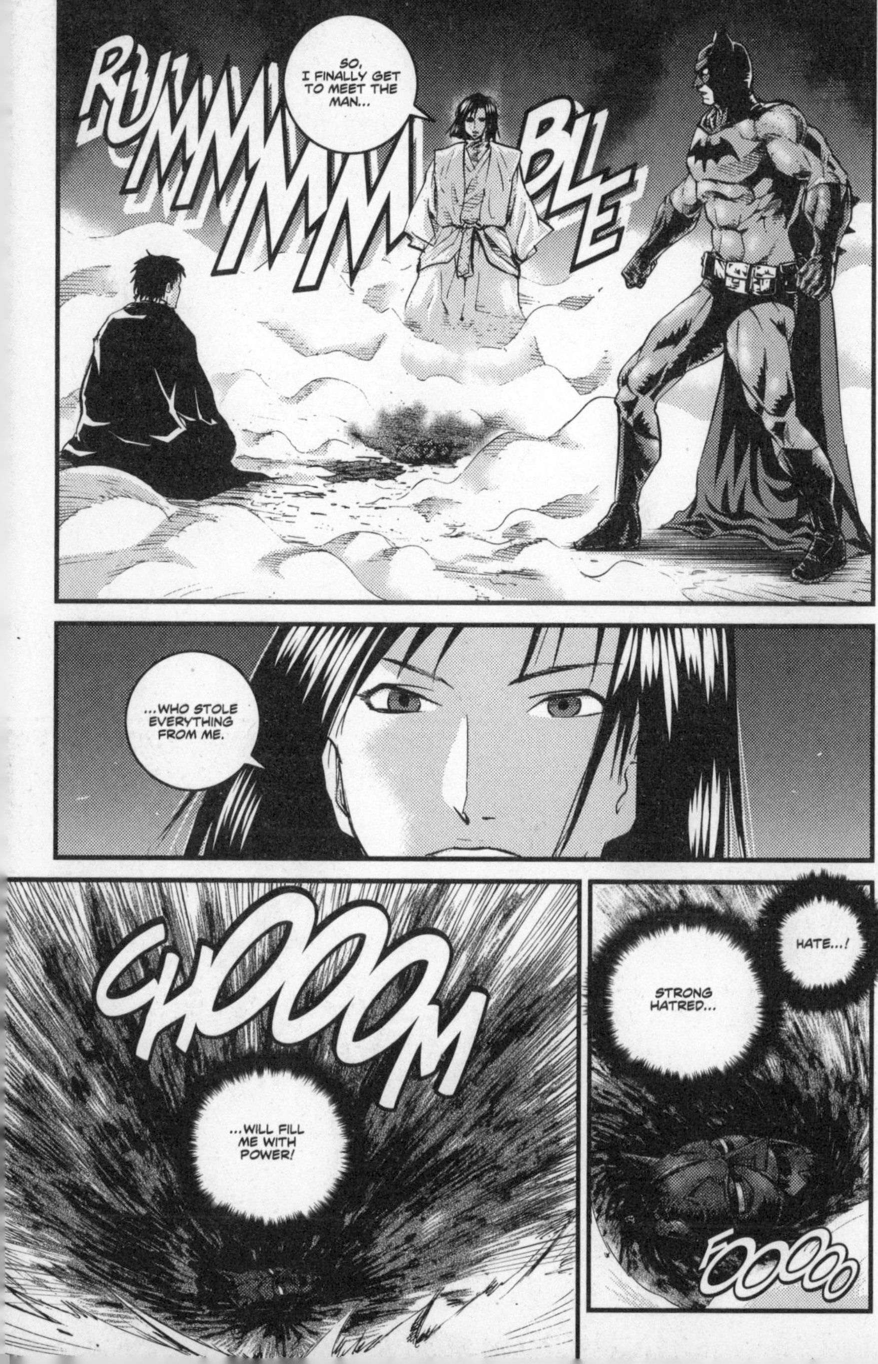
RUMMMMMMBLE
SO, I FINALLY GET TO MEET THE MAN...
...WHO STOLE EVERYTHING FROM ME.
CHOOOOM
...WILL FILL ME WITH POWER!
STRONG HATRED...
HATE...!
FOOOOOO

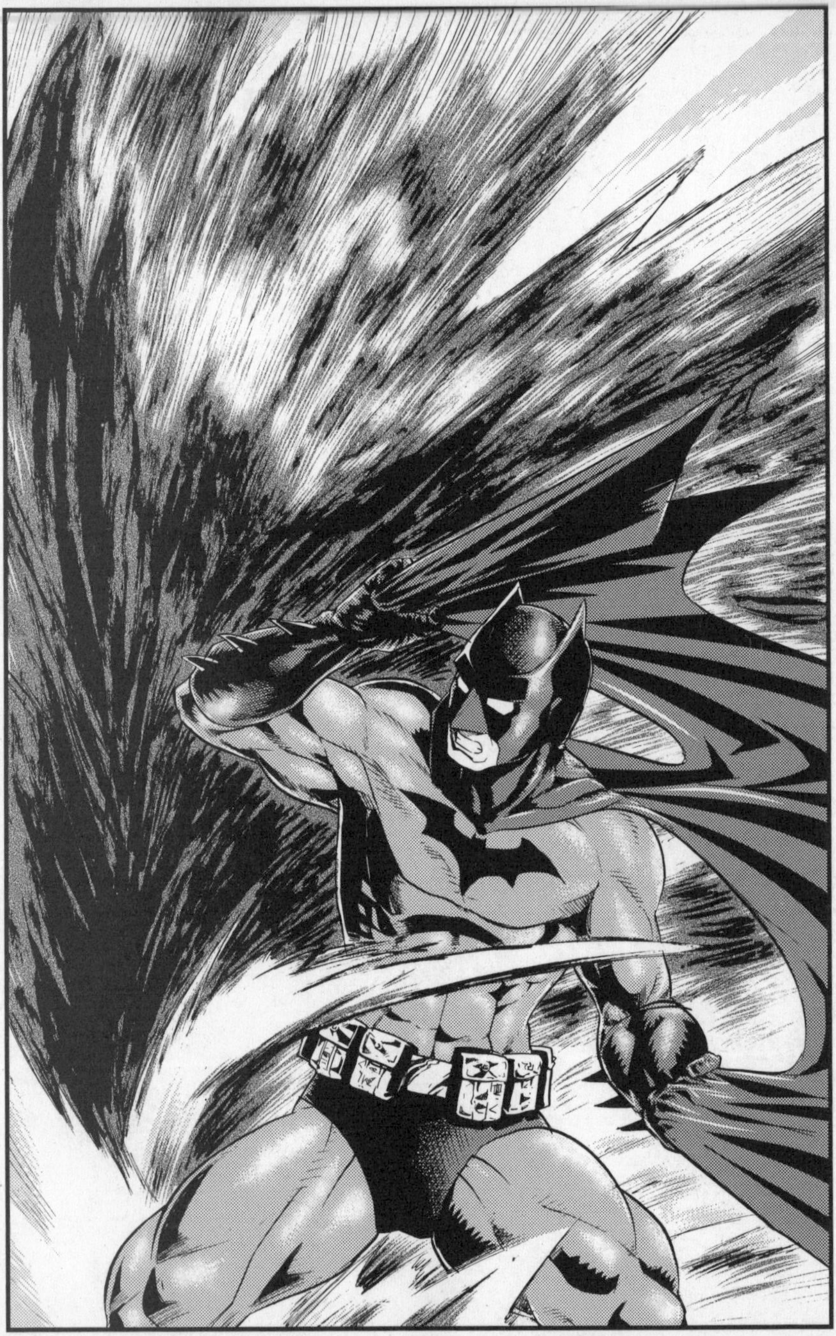

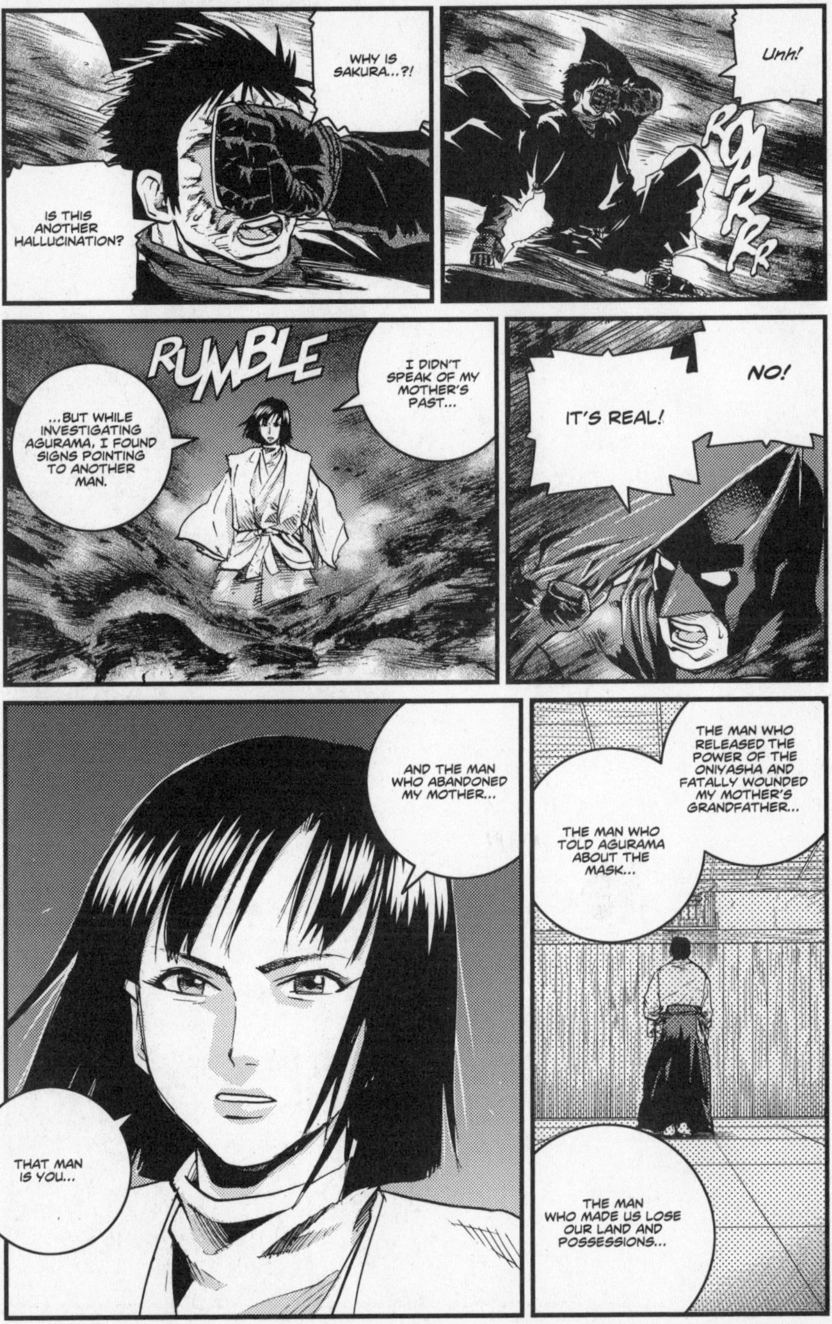
WHY IS SAKURA...?!
IS THIS ANOTHER HALLUCINATION?
Unh!
ROARRRR
RUMBLE
I DIDN'T SPEAK OF MY MOTHER'S PAST...
...BUT WHILE INVESTIGATING AGURAMA, I FOUND SIGNS POINTING TO ANOTHER MAN.
NO!
IT'S REAL!
AND THE MAN WHO ABANDONED MY MOTHER...
THAT MAN IS YOU...
THE MAN WHO RELEASED THE POWER OF THE ONIYASHA AND FATALLY WOUNDED MY MOTHER'S GRANDFATHER...
THE MAN WHO TOLD AGURAMA ABOUT THE MASK...
THE MAN WHO MADE US LOSE OUR LAND AND POSSESSIONS...

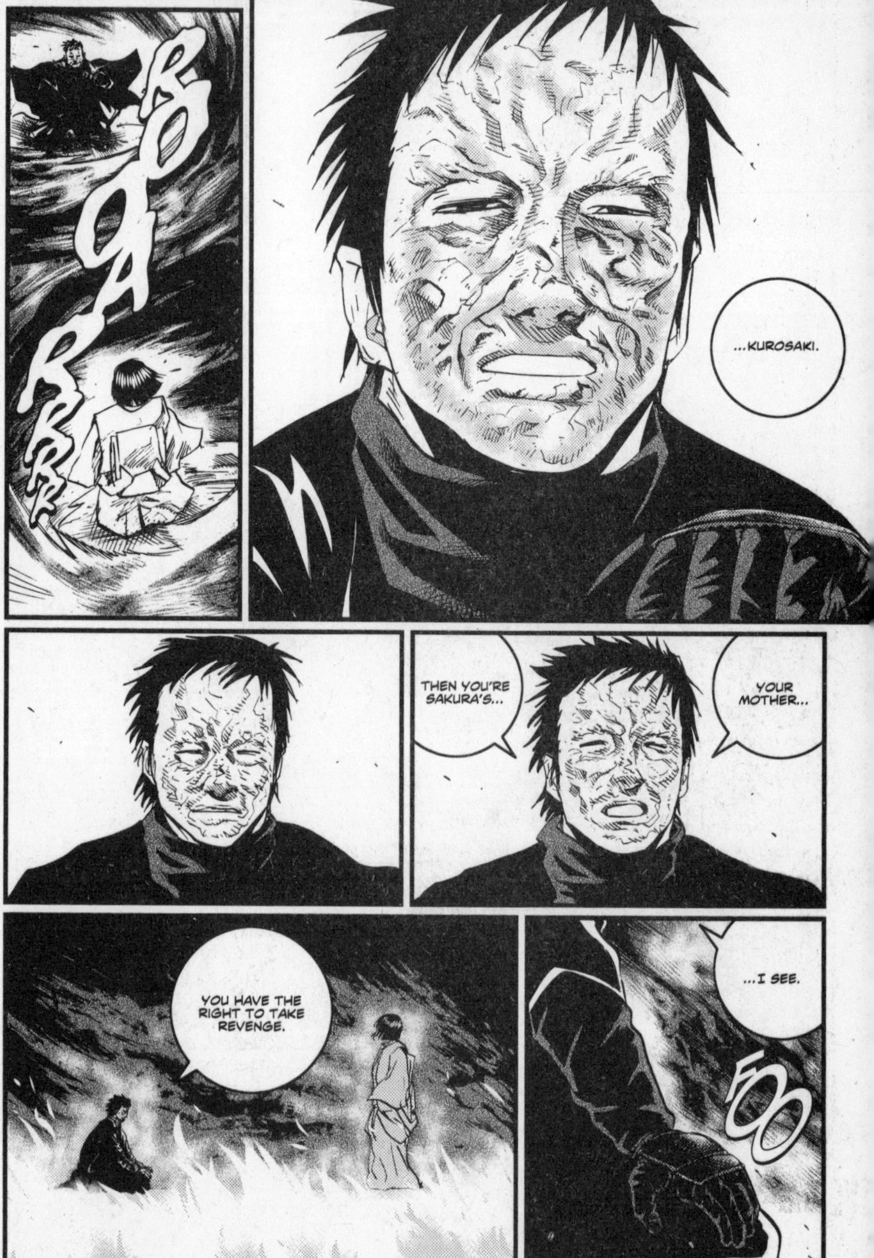
ROOAARRRR
...KUROSAKI.
THEN YOU'RE SAKURA'S...
YOUR MOTHER...
YOU HAVE THE RIGHT TO TAKE REVENGE.
...I SEE.
FOO

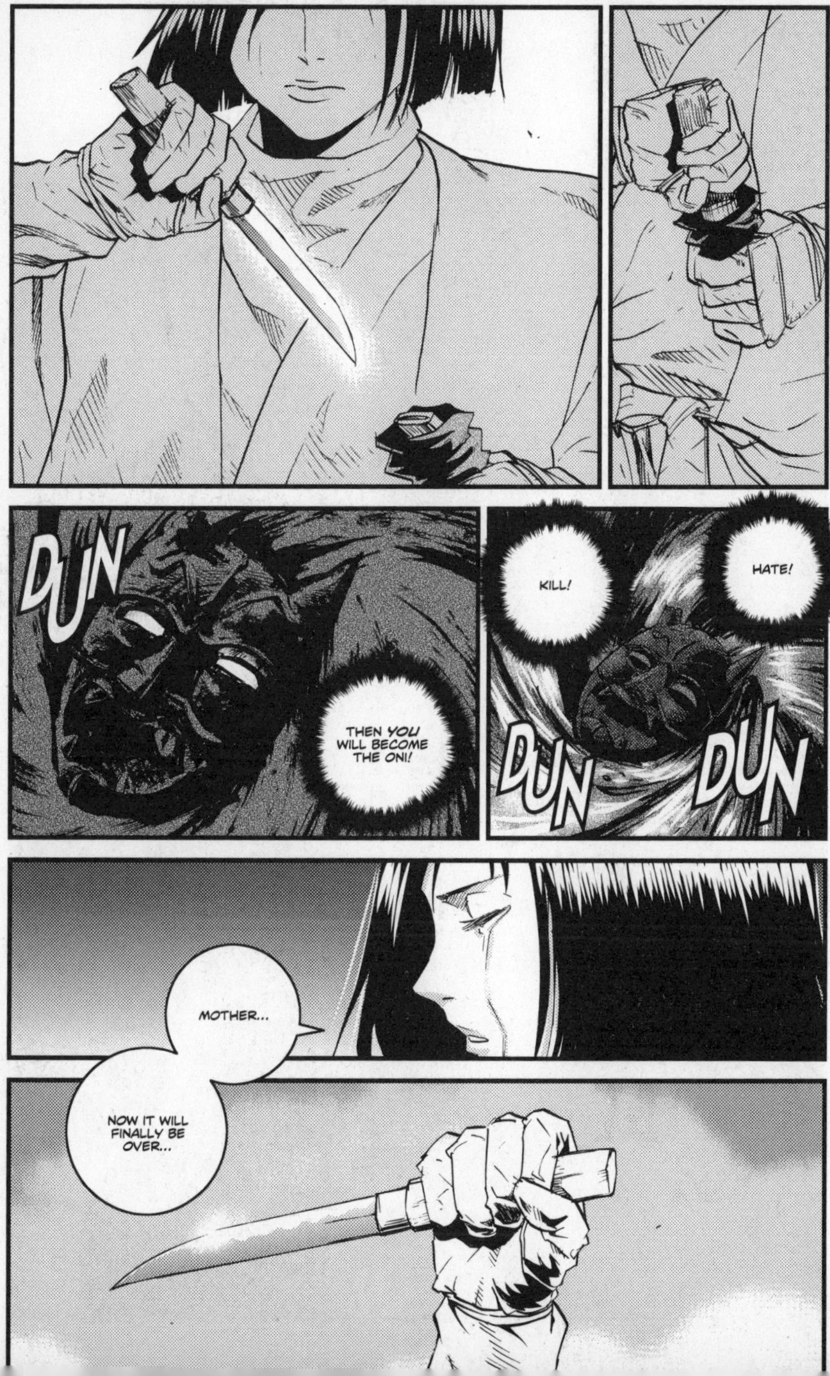
DUN
THEN YOU WILL BECOME THE ONI!
KILL!
HATE!
DUN
DUN
MOTHER...
NOW IT WILL FINALLY BE OVER...

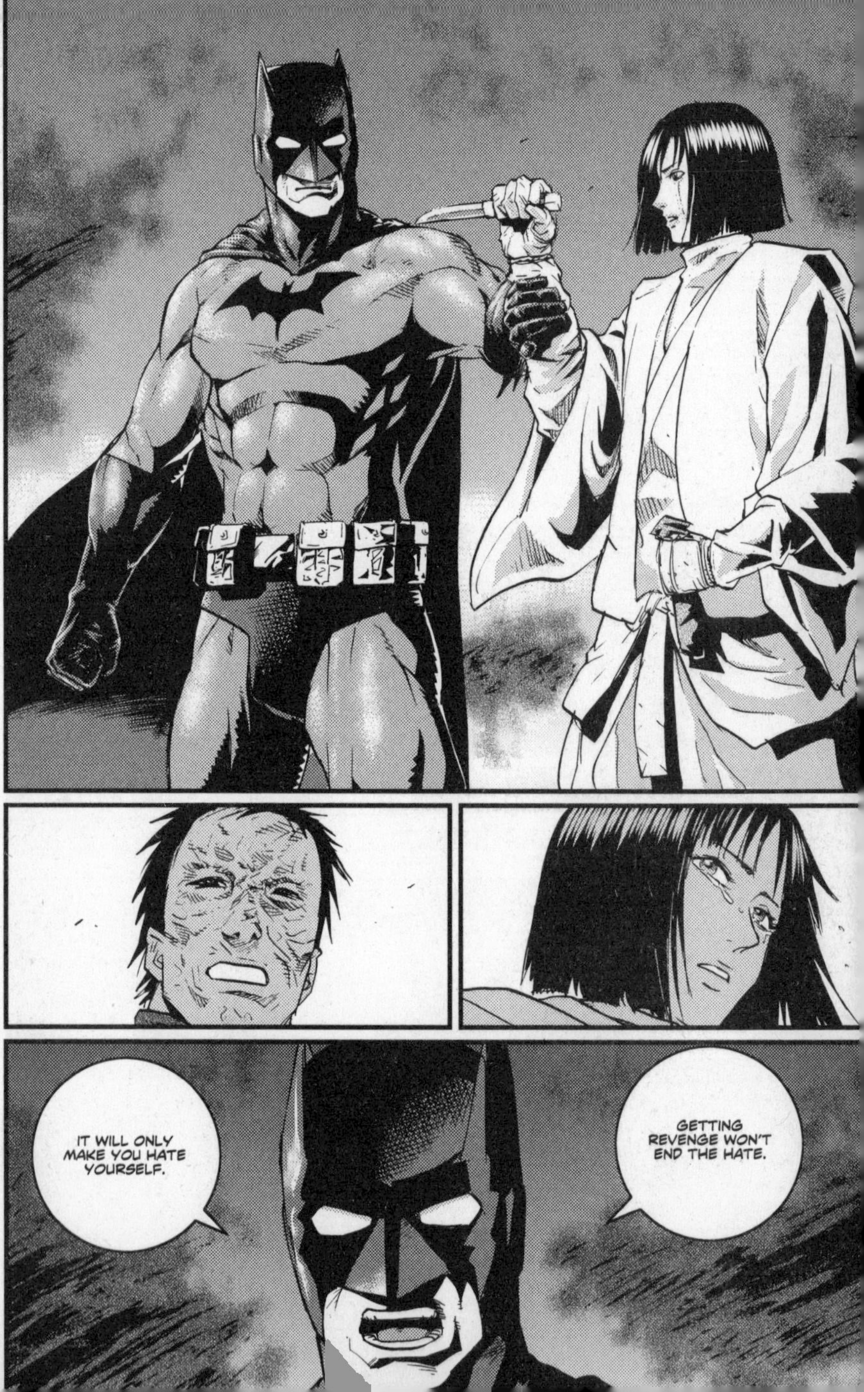
IT WILL ONLY MAKE YOU HATE YOURSELF.
GETTING REVENGE WON'T END THE HATE.

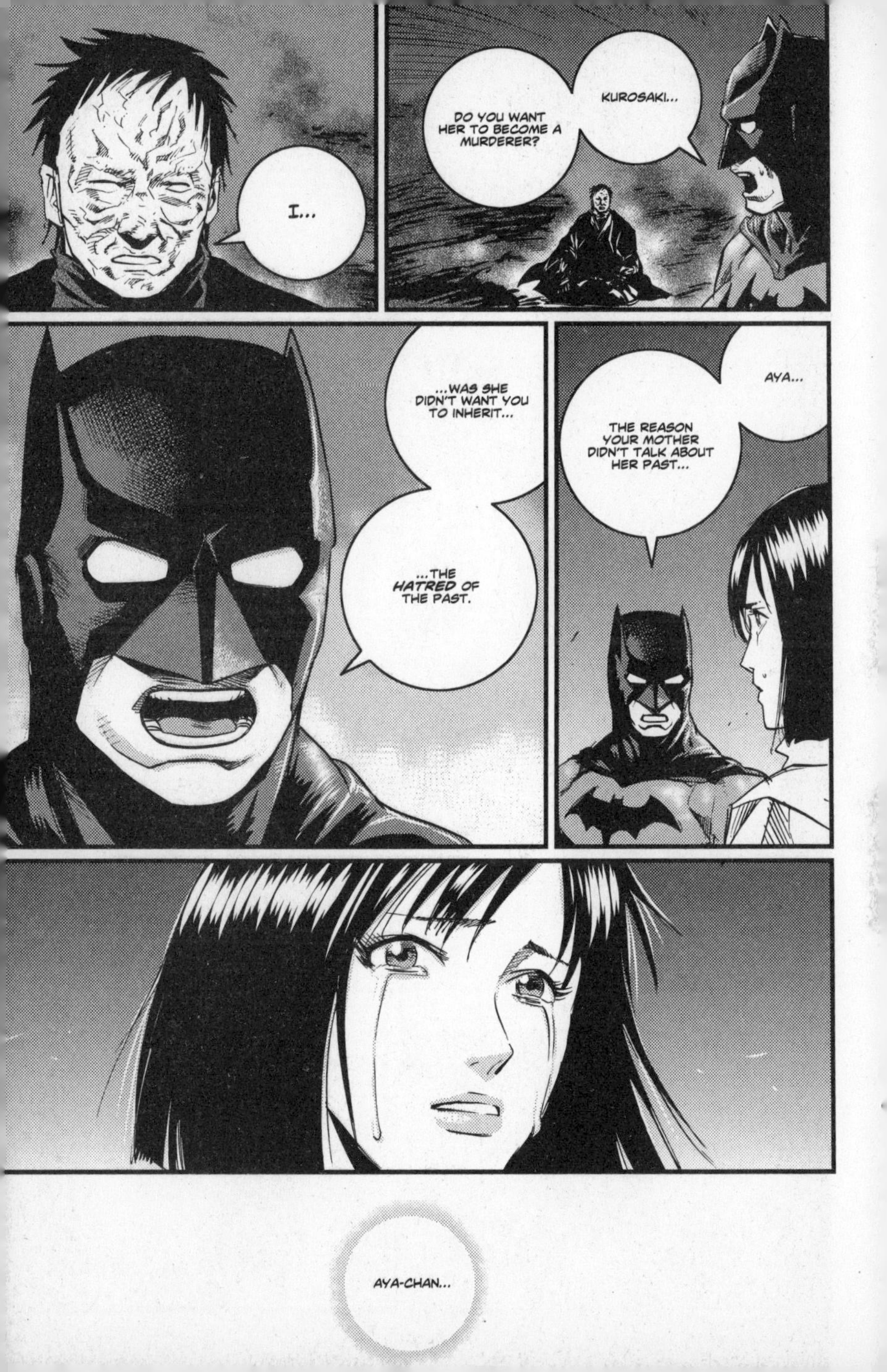
I...
KUROSAKI...
DO YOU WANT HER TO BECOME A MURDERER?
AYA...
THE REASON YOUR MOTHER DIDN'T TALK ABOUT HER PAST...
...WAS SHE DIDN'T WANT YOU TO INHERIT...
...THE HATRED OF THE PAST.
AYA-CHAN...

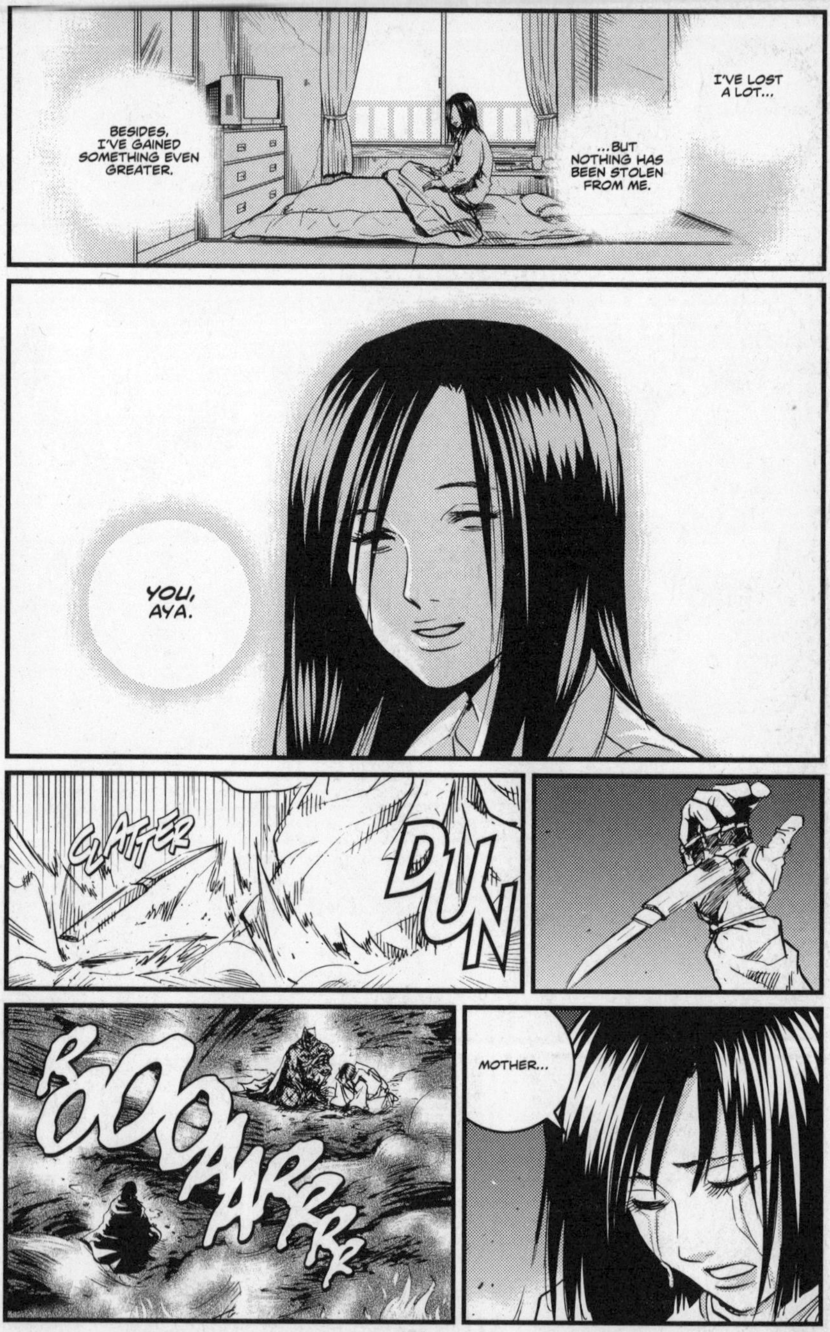
I'VE LOST A LOT...
...BUT NOTHING HAS BEEN STOLEN FROM ME.
BESIDES, I'VE GAINED SOMETHING EVEN GREATER.
YOU, AYA.
CLATTER
DUN
BOOOARRRR
MOTHER...

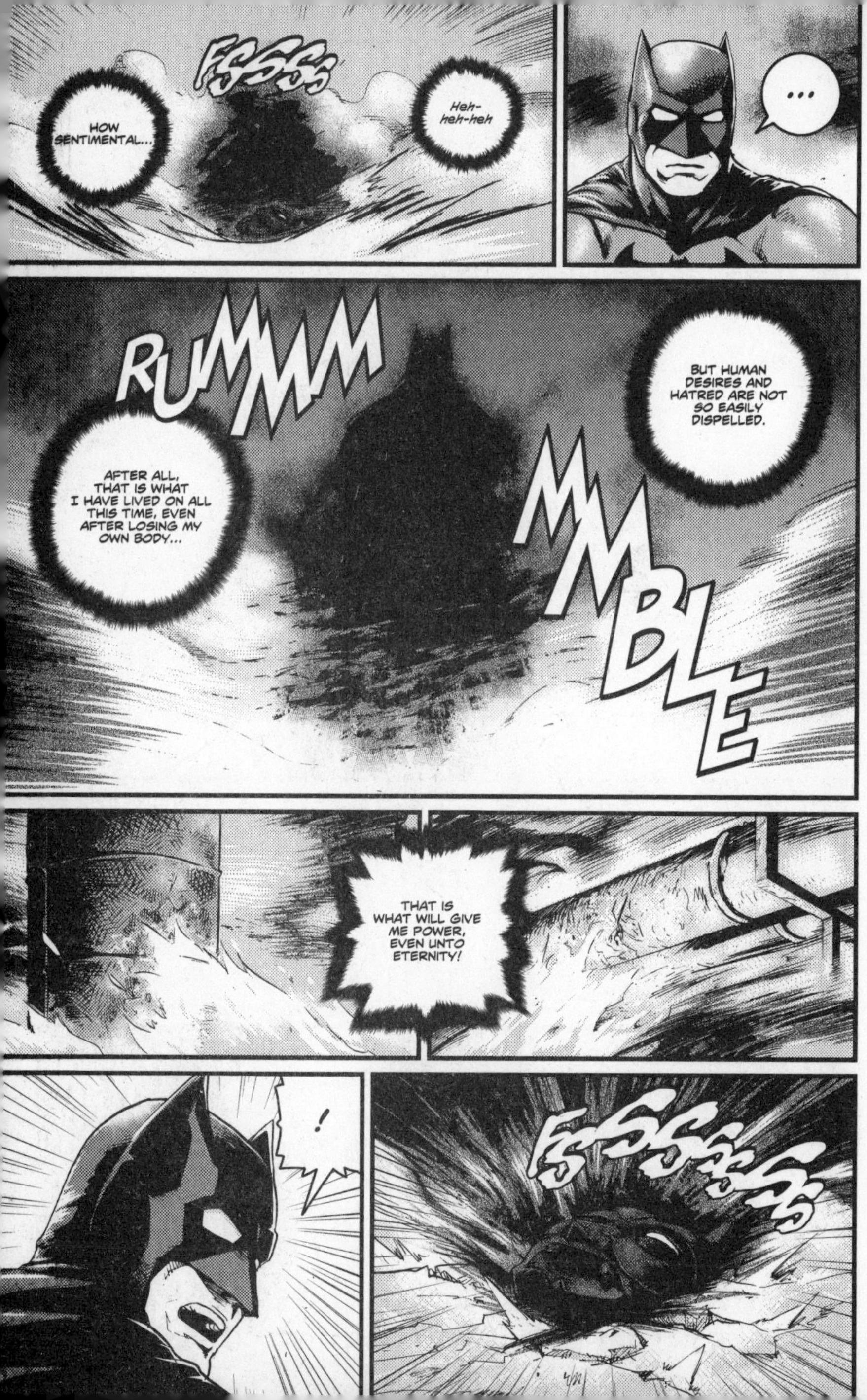
FSSSS
HOW SENTIMENTAL...
Heh-heh-heh
...
RUMMMMMMBLE
BUT HUMAN DESIRES AND HATRED ARE NOT SO EASILY DISPELLED.
AFTER ALL, THAT IS WHAT I HAVE LIVED ON ALL THIS TIME, EVEN AFTER LOSING MY OWN BODY...
THAT IS WHAT WILL GIVE ME POWER, EVEN UNTO ETERNITY!
!
FSSSSSS

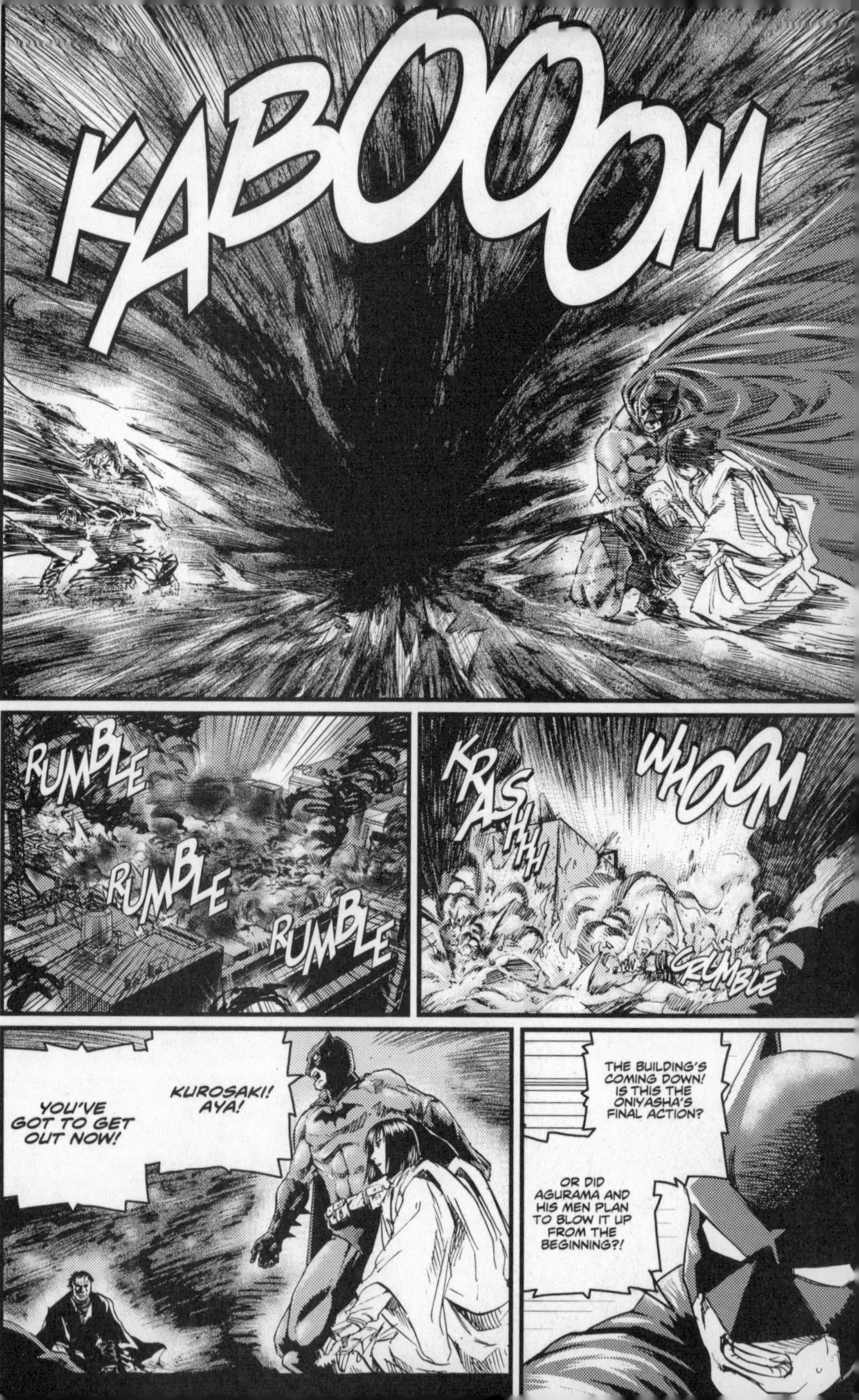
KABOOOM
RUMBLE
RUMBLE
RUMBLE
KRASHHH
WHOOOM
CRUMBLE
KUROSAKI! AYA!
YOU'VE GOT TO GET OUT NOW!
THE BUILDING'S COMING DOWN! IS THIS THE ONIYASHA'S FINAL ACTION?
OR DID AGURAMA AND HIS MEN PLAN TO BLOW IT UP FROM THE BEGINNING?!

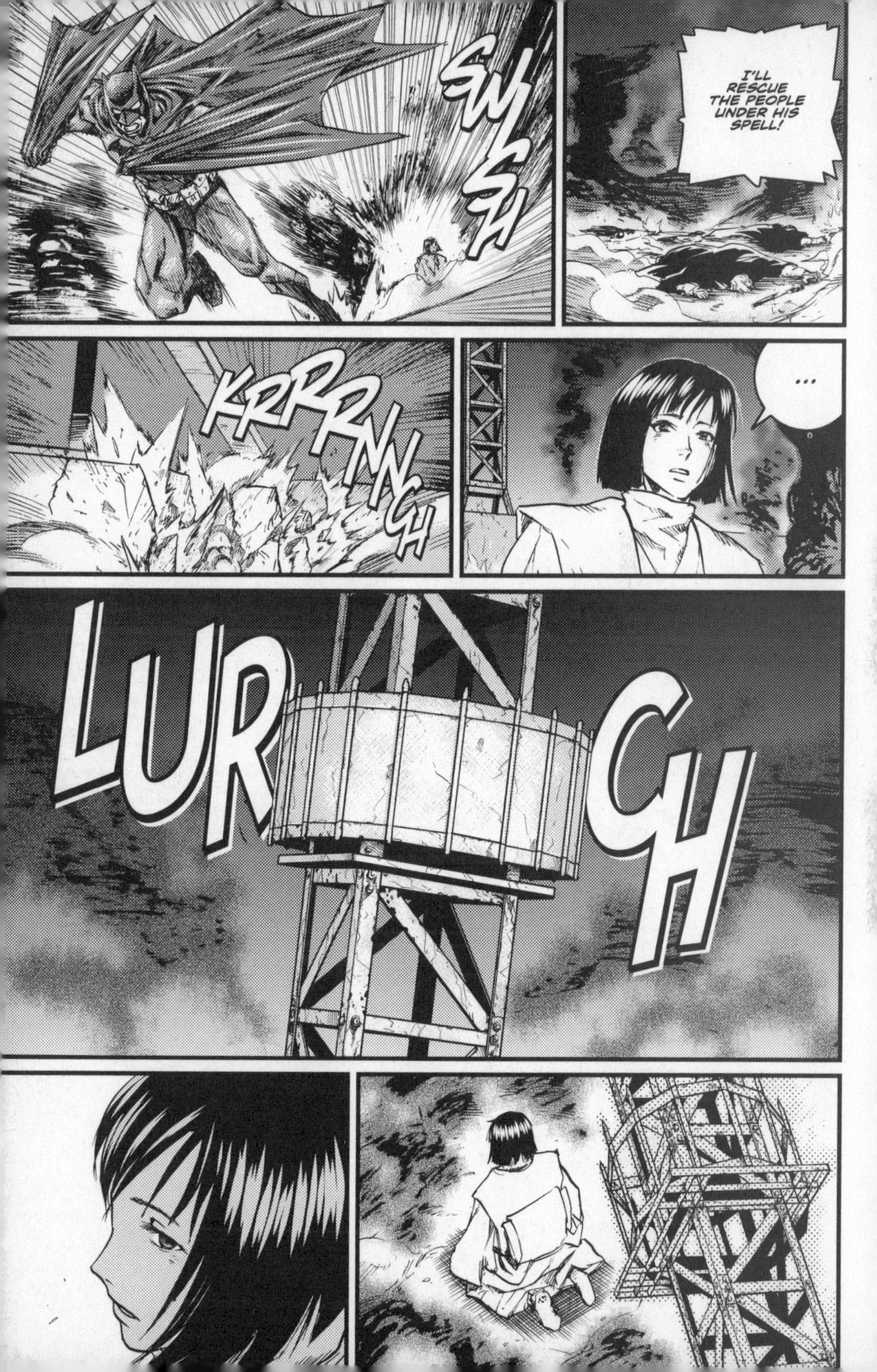
SWISH
I'LL RESCUE THE PEOPLE UNDER HIS SPELL!
KRRRNNNCH
...
LURCH

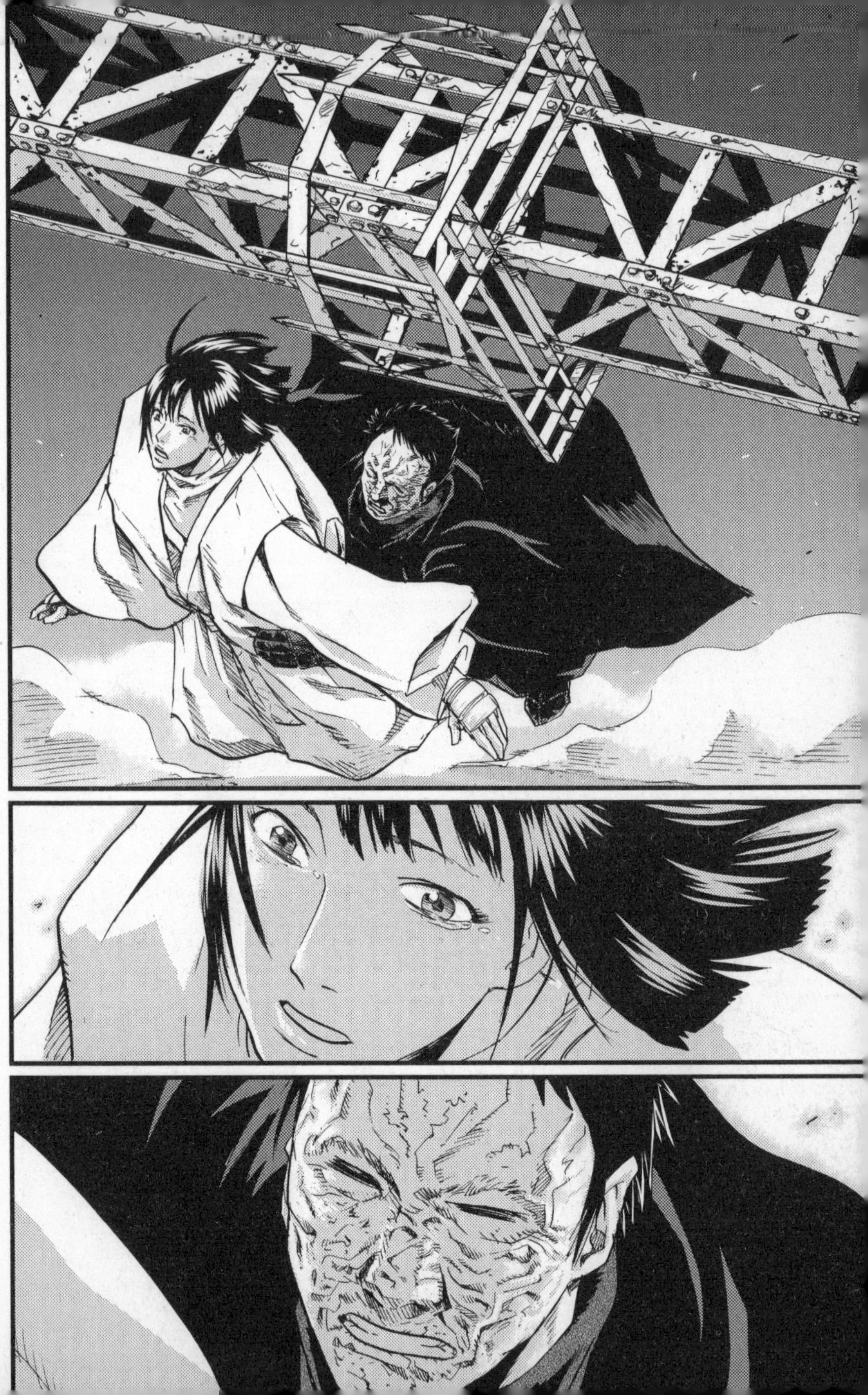

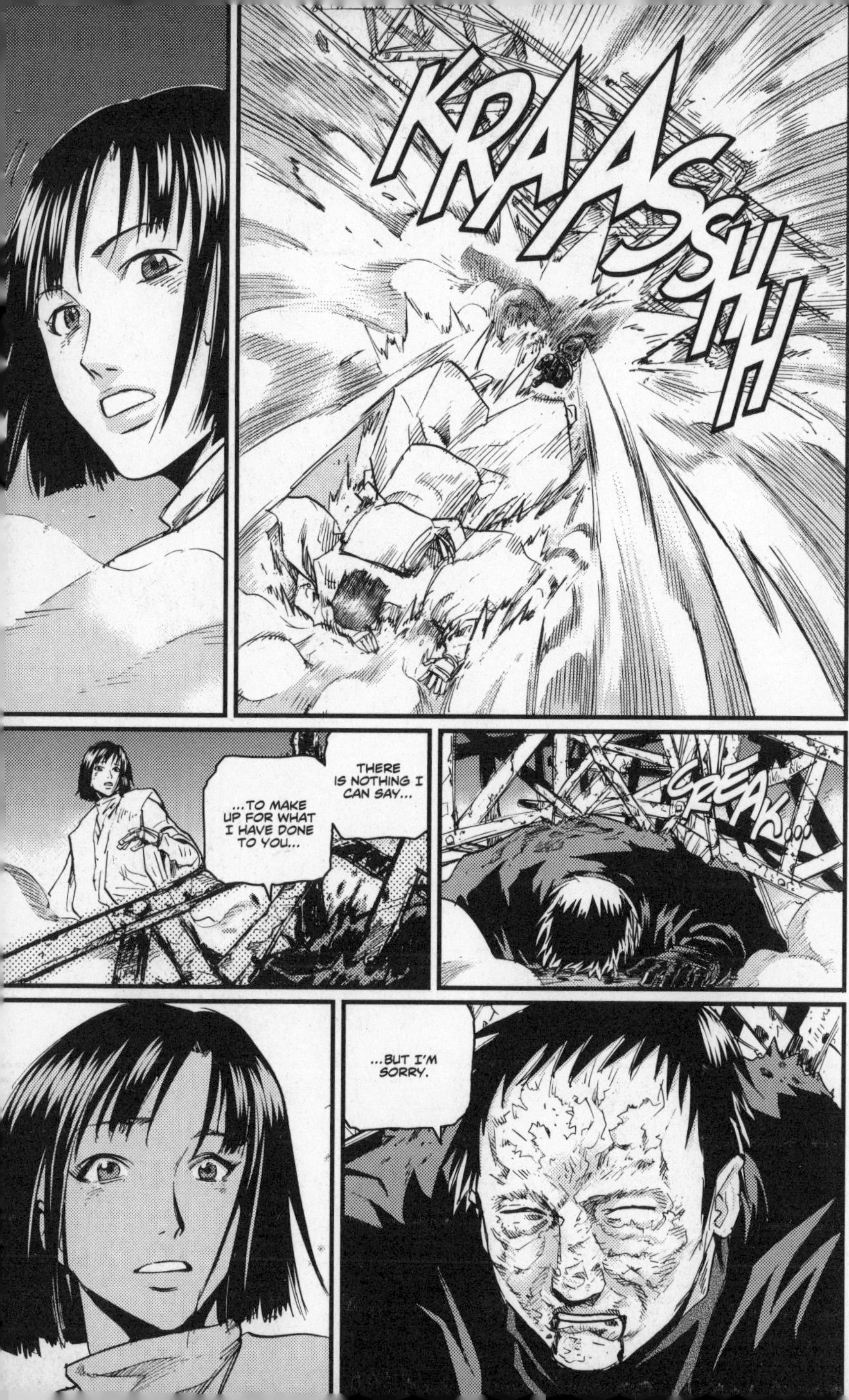
KRAASCHH
THERE IS NOTHING I CAN SAY...
...TO MAKE UP FOR WHAT I HAVE DONE TO YOU...
CREAK...
...BUT I'M SORRY.

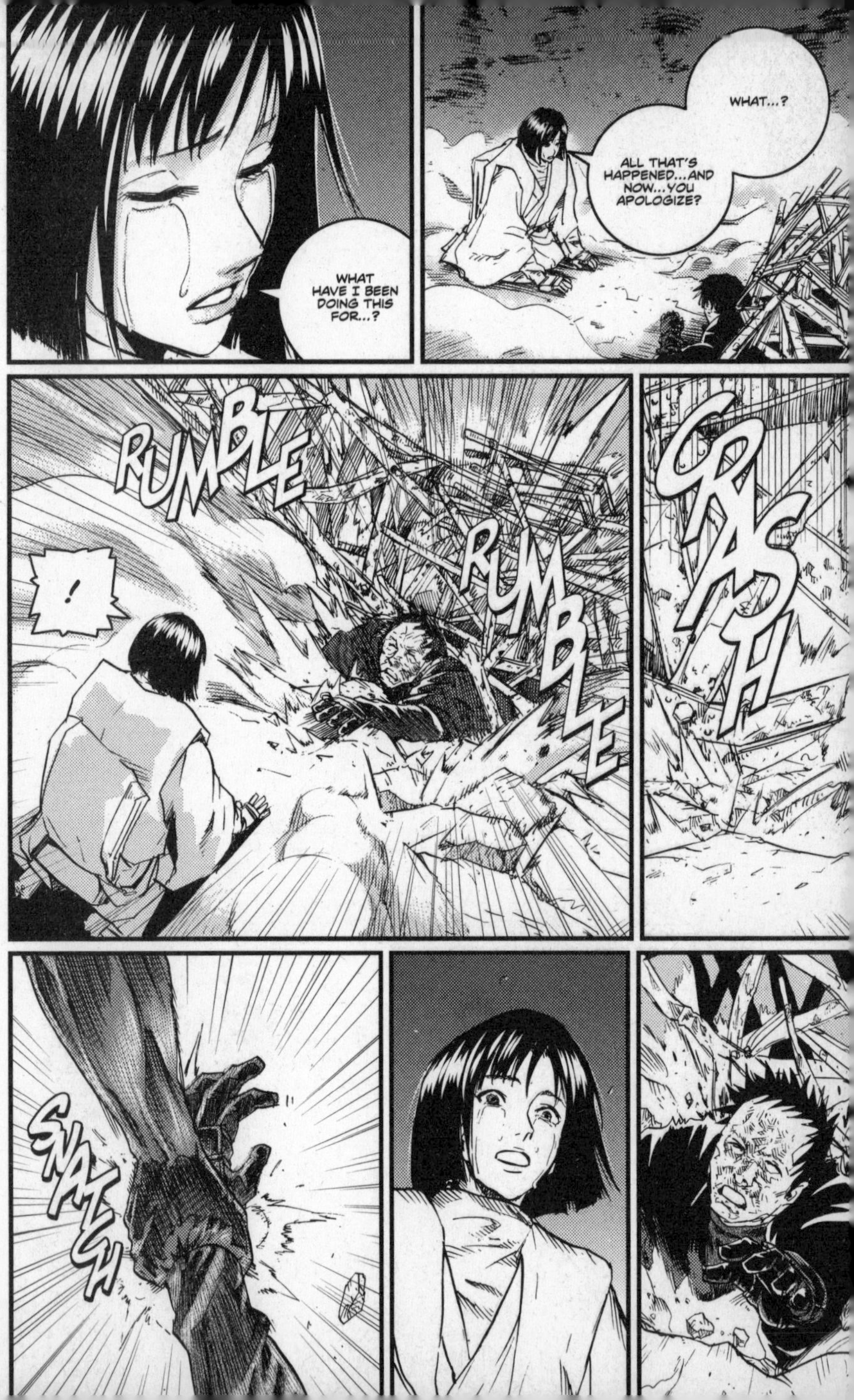

WHAT HAVE I BEEN DOING THIS FOR...?
WHAT...?
ALL THAT'S HAPPENED...AND NOW...YOU APOLOGIZE?
RUMBLE
RUMBLE
!
CRASH
SNATCH

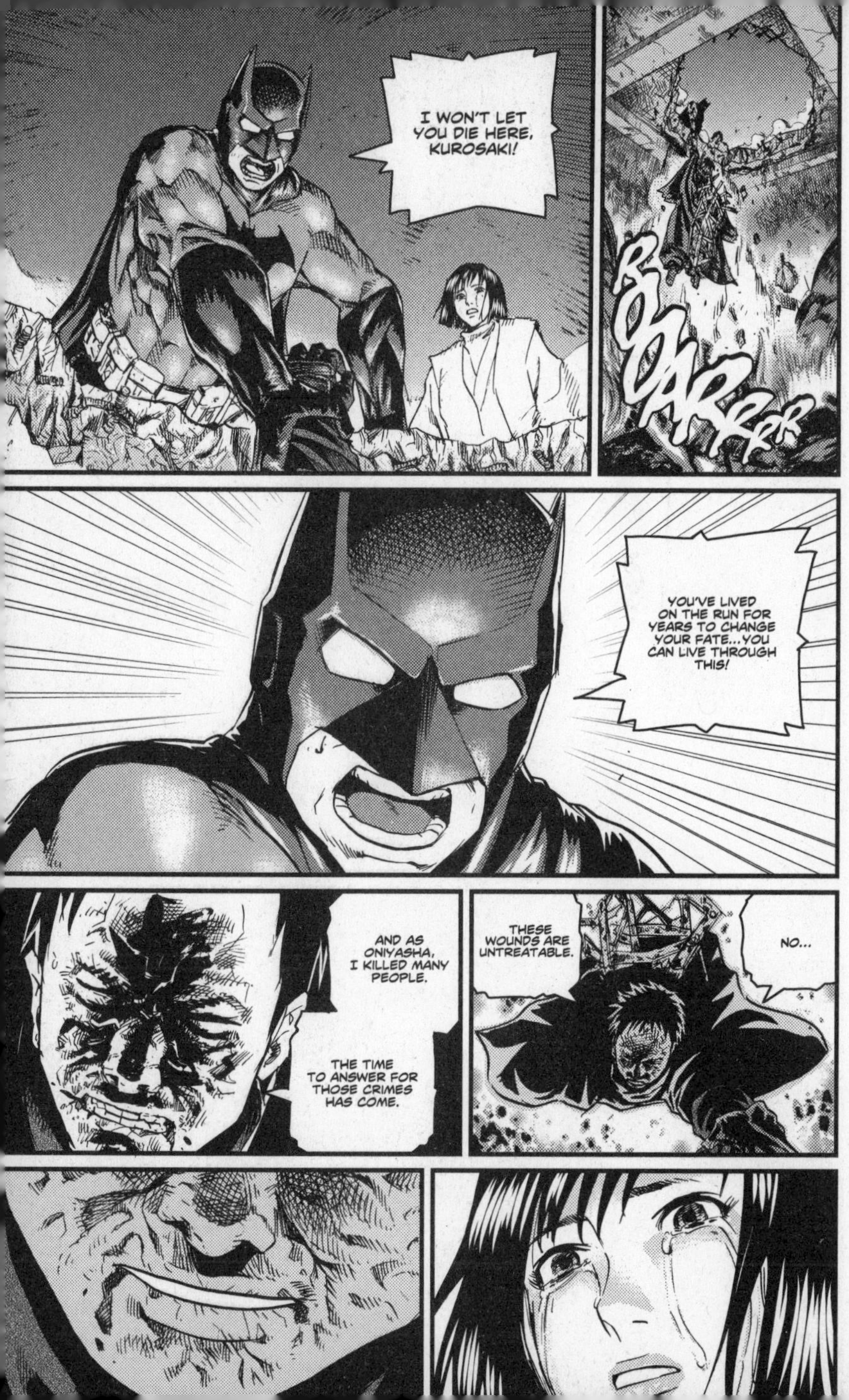
I WON'T LET YOU DIE HERE, KUROSAKI!
BOOARRRR
YOU'VE LIVED ON THE RUN FOR YEARS TO CHANGE YOUR FATE...YOU CAN LIVE THROUGH THIS!
NO...
THESE WOUNDS ARE UNTREATABLE.
AND AS ONIYASHA, I KILLED MANY PEOPLE.
THE TIME TO ANSWER FOR THOSE CRIMES HAS COME.

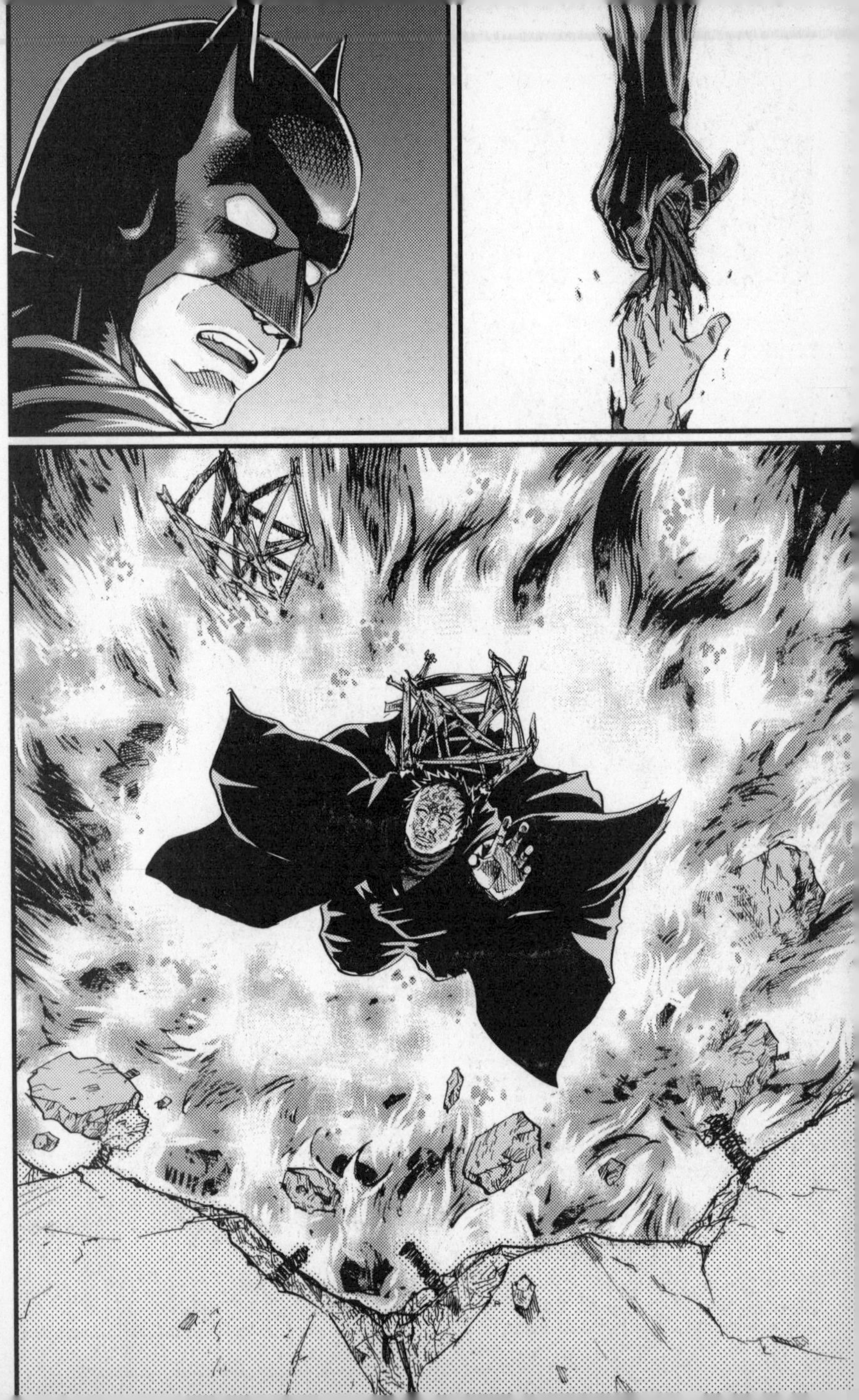

...

HE WAS...

...MY FATHER.

LET'S GO.

IT'S DANGEROUS HERE.

CHFF

FOOOM

AARGH

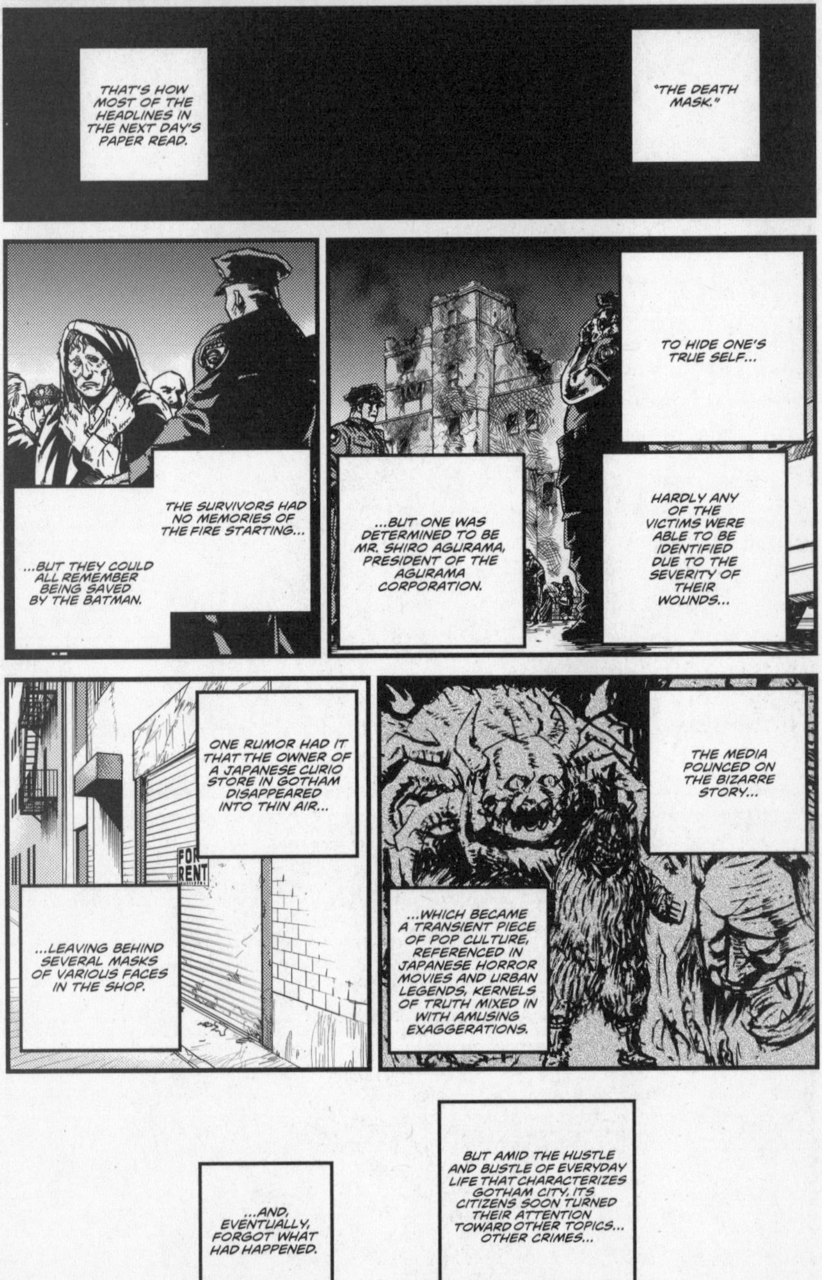

THAT'S HOW MOST OF THE HEADLINES IN THE NEXT DAY'S PAPER READ.
"THE DEATH MASK."
THE SURVIVORS HAD NO MEMORIES OF THE FIRE STARTING...
...BUT THEY COULD ALL REMEMBER BEING SAVED BY THE BATMAN.
TO HIDE ONE'S TRUE SELF...
HARDLY ANY OF THE VICTIMS WERE ABLE TO BE IDENTIFIED DUE TO THE SEVERITY OF THEIR WOUNDS...
...BUT ONE WAS DETERMINED TO BE MR. SHIRO AGURAMA, PRESIDENT OF THE AGURAMA CORPORATION.
ONE RUMOR HAD IT THAT THE OWNER OF A JAPANESE CURIO STORE IN GOTHAM DISAPPEARED INTO THIN AIR...
FOR RENT
...LEAVING BEHIND SEVERAL MASKS OF VARIOUS FACES IN THE SHOP.
THE MEDIA POUNCED ON THE BIZARRE STORY...
...WHICH BECAME A TRANSIENT PIECE OF POP CULTURE, REFERENCED IN JAPANESE HORROR MOVIES AND URBAN LEGENDS, KERNELS OF TRUTH MIXED IN WITH AMUSING EXAGGERATIONS.
BUT AMID THE HUSTLE AND BUSTLE OF EVERYDAY LIFE THAT CHARACTERIZES GOTHAM CITY, ITS CITIZENS SOON TURNED THEIR ATTENTION TOWARD OTHER TOPICS... OTHER CRIMES...
...AND, EVENTUALLY, FORGOT WHAT HAD HAPPENED.

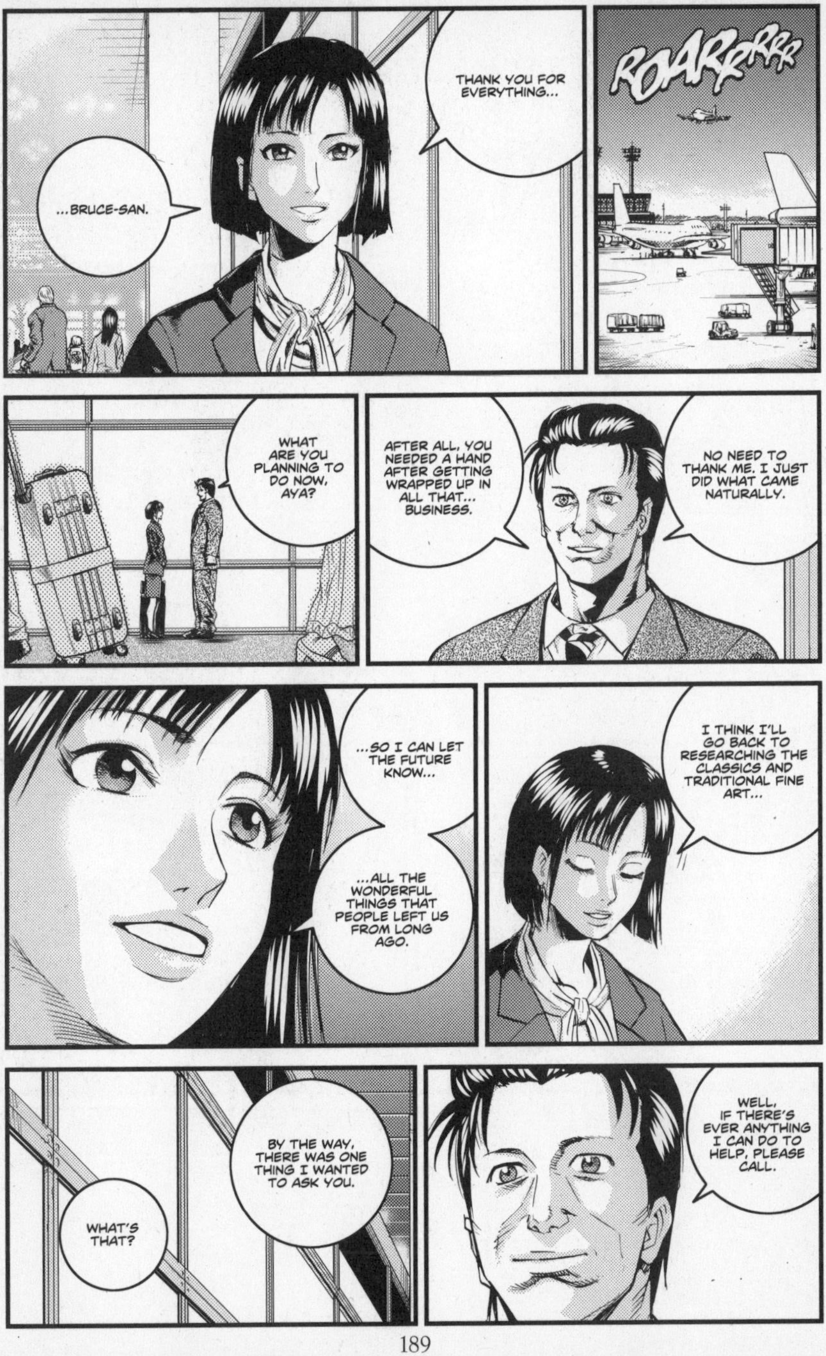
ROARRRRR
THANK YOU FOR EVERYTHING...
...BRUCE-SAN.
NO NEED TO THANK ME. I JUST DID WHAT CAME NATURALLY.
AFTER ALL, YOU NEEDED A HAND AFTER GETTING WRAPPED UP IN ALL THAT... BUSINESS.
WHAT ARE YOU PLANNING TO DO NOW, AYA?
I THINK I'LL GO BACK TO RESEARCHING THE CLASSICS AND TRADITIONAL FINE ART...
...SO I CAN LET THE FUTURE KNOW...
...ALL THE WONDERFUL THINGS THAT PEOPLE LEFT US FROM LONG AGO.
WELL, IF THERE'S EVER ANYTHING I CAN DO TO HELP, PLEASE CALL.
BY THE WAY, THERE WAS ONE THING I WANTED TO ASK YOU.
WHAT'S THAT?

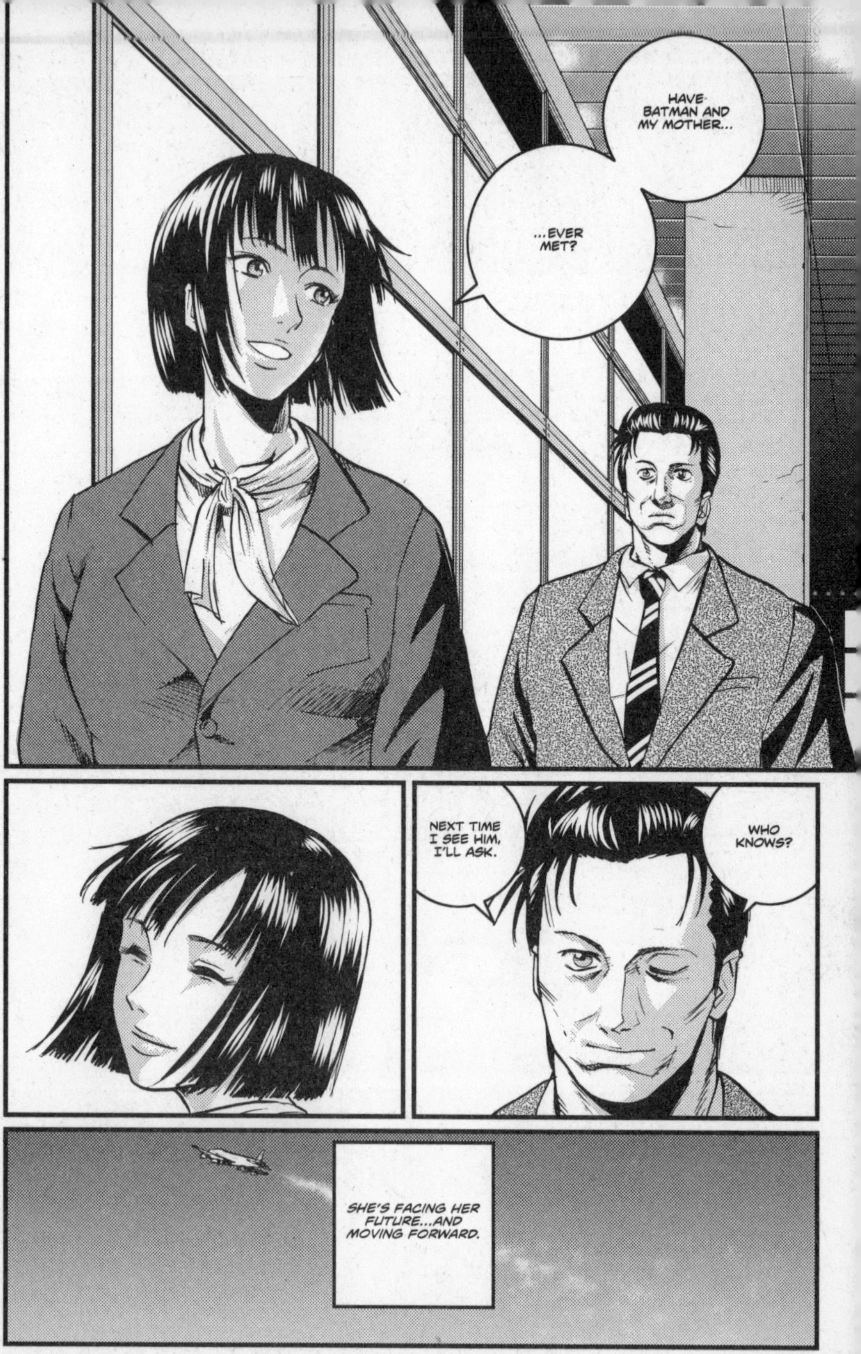
HAVE BATMAN AND MY MOTHER...
...EVER MET?
NEXT TIME I SEE HIM, I'LL ASK.
WHO KNOWS?
SHE'S FACING HER FUTURE...AND MOVING FORWARD.

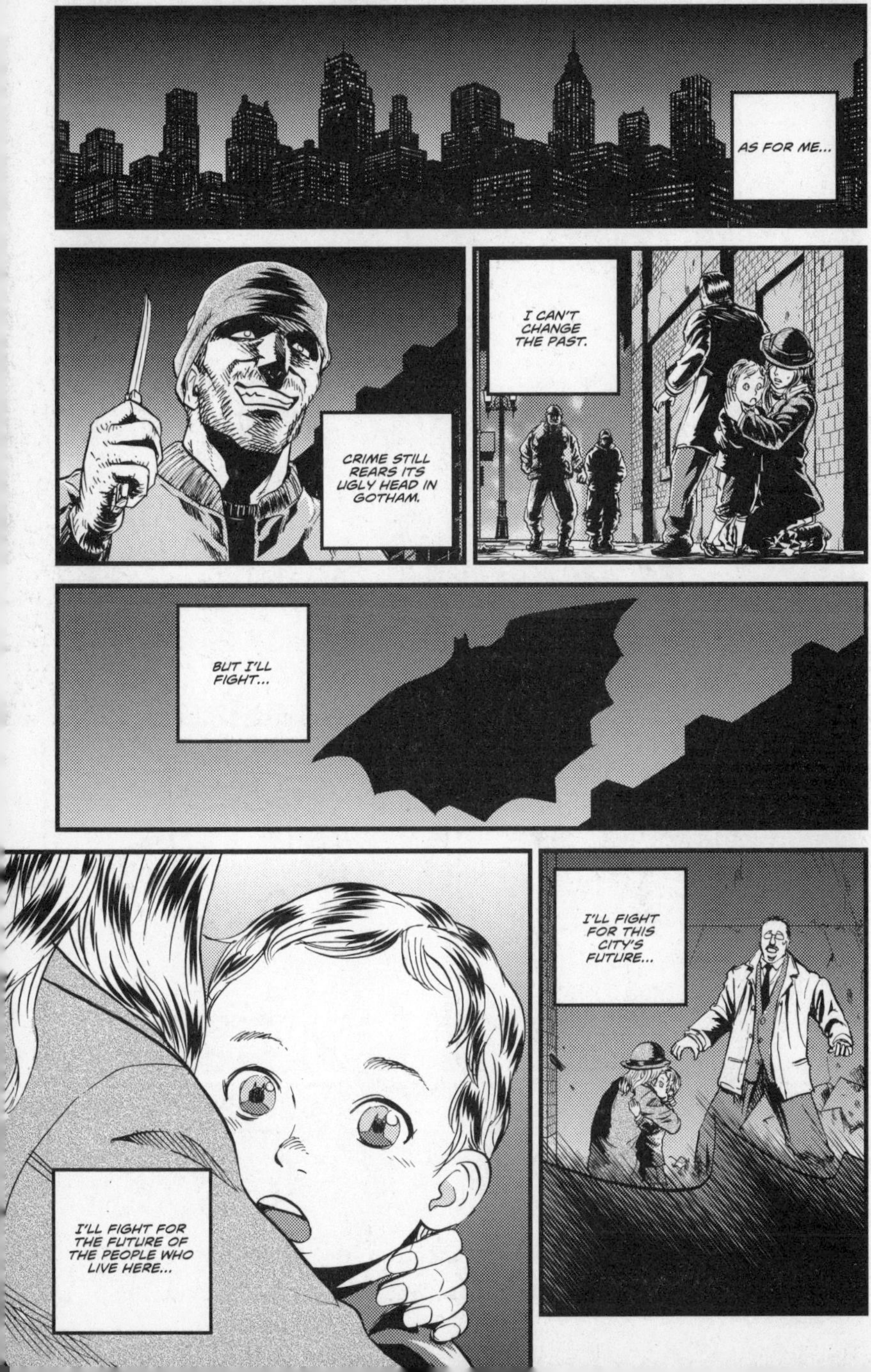
AS FOR ME...
CRIME STILL REARS ITS UGLY HEAD IN GOTHAM.
I CAN'T CHANGE THE PAST.
BUT I'LL FIGHT...
I'LL FIGHT FOR THE FUTURE OF THE PEOPLE WHO LIVE HERE...
I'LL FIGHT FOR THIS CITY'S FUTURE...

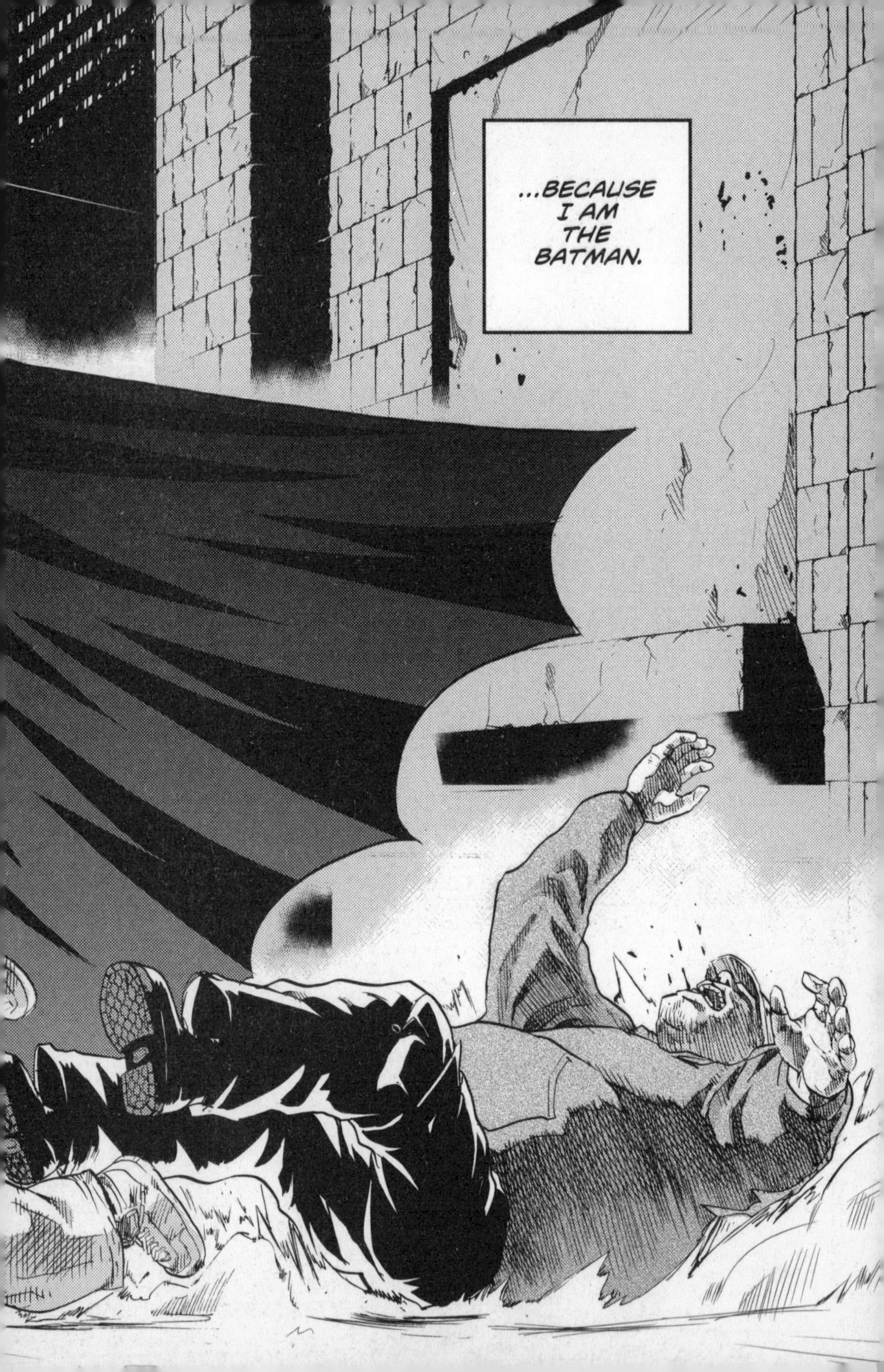
...BECAUSE I AM THE BATMAN.

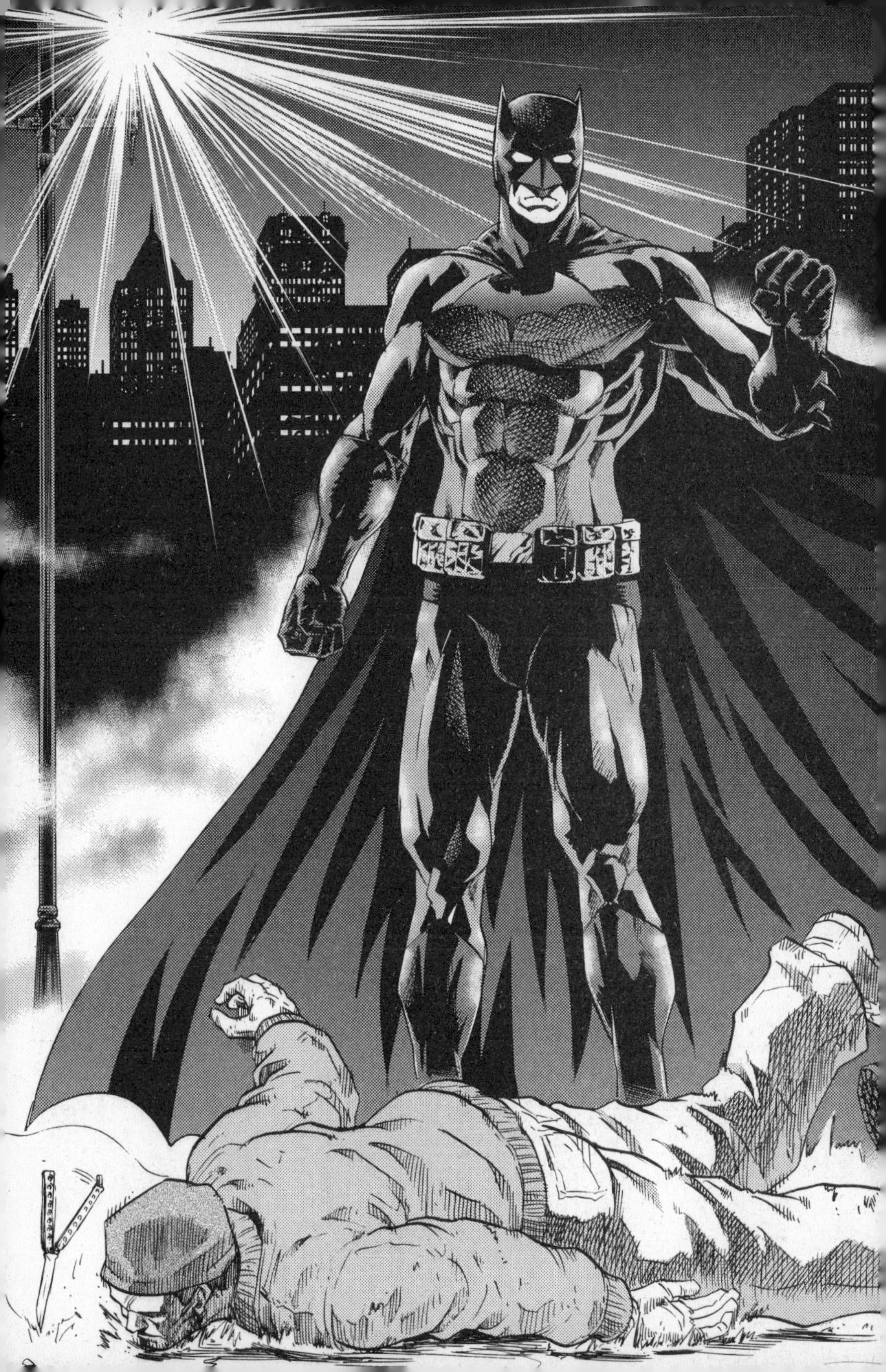

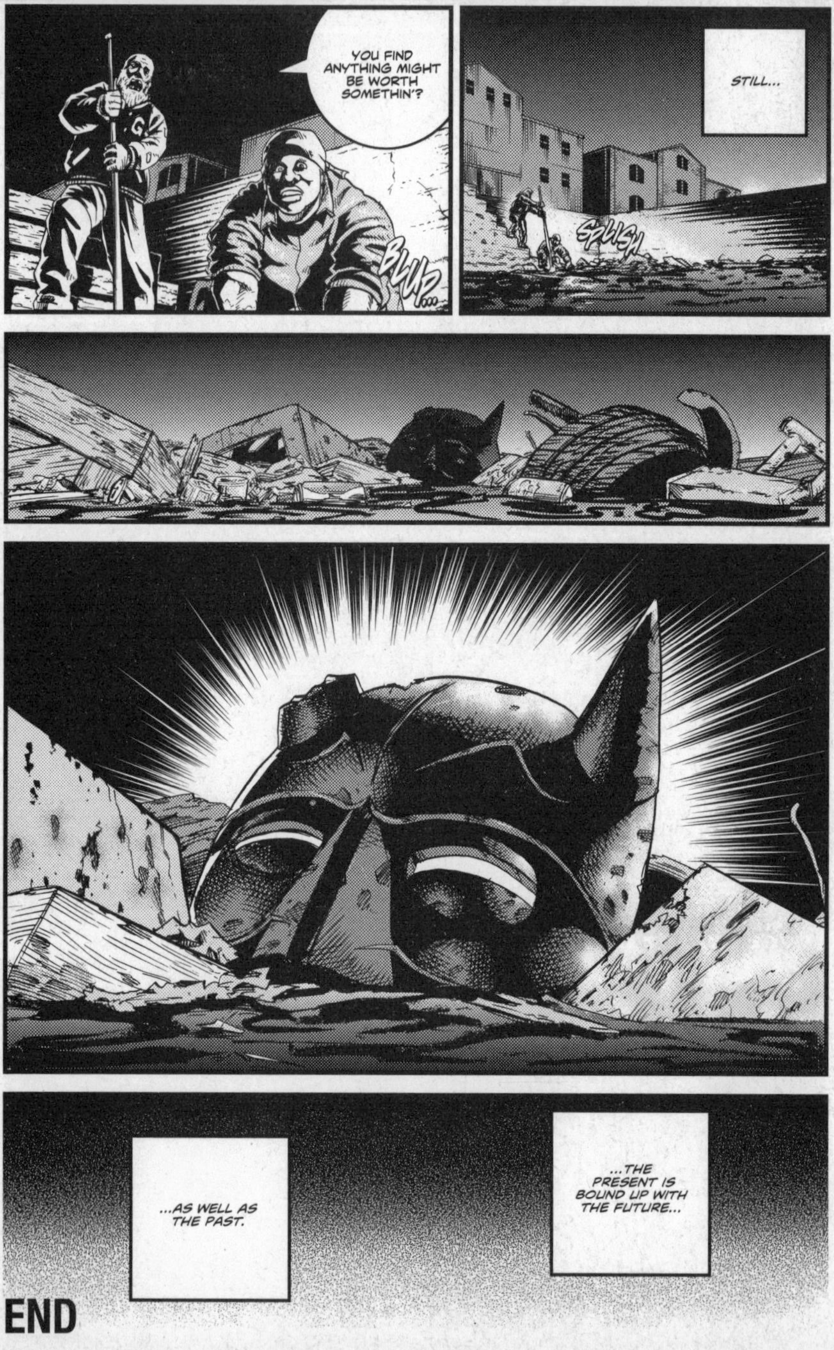
YOU FIND ANYTHING MIGHT BE WORTH SOMETHIN'?
BLUP...
STILL...
SPLISH
...THE PRESENT IS BOUND UP WITH THE FUTURE...
...AS WELL AS THE PAST.

END

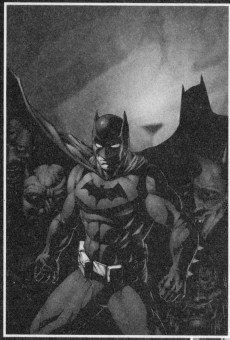

**Cover art for BATMAN:
DEATH MASK #1**

**Cover art for BATMAN:
DEATH MASK #2**

**Cover art for BATMAN:
DEATH MASK #3**

**Cover art for BATMAN:
DEATH MASK #4**

The Dark Knight
in the Land of the Rising Sun:
An interview with Yoshinori Natsume

For this special interview for the collected edition of BATMAN: DEATH MASK, we asked writer and artist Yoshinori Natsume to reflect on the evolution of this project. He shared with us his ideas about Batman, his experience working for an American publication, and his own artistic and creative influences.

Editor Jim Chadwick posed the interview questions, which were translated by CMX Director of manga Asako Suzuki. Answers were translated by series translator Sheldon Drzka.

JC: The origin of Batman has been told many times. Bruce Wayne's youthful excursion to Japan is a relatively recent addition to the story. Did this seem to provide a natural point of entry for you into the Batman mythos?

YN: I was thinking that since this project was being done by a Japanese mangaka—namely me—giving it a Japanese flavor would likely please American readers. We know that Batman is the guardian of Gotham and that in his younger days, Bruce traveled around the world to learn martial arts, detective skills, etc. so it seemed to make the most sense to set the Japanese scenes during his period of training. Also, my image of Batman is of a fully mature, adult hero. I was interested in exploring the period of his life before he became that man.

JC: The visual connection between Batman's cowl and the mask of the Oni struck me as a simple but brilliant touch. Can you tell us how you came up with this idea?

YN: While I really appreciate the praise, I have to admit the answer is a simple one. When I looked at a drawing of Batman's silhouette, those extended "ears" just looked like horns to me. There are a lot of legends about Onis in Japan and though very often they appear in the stories as a symbol of evil, once in a while, it's the opposite. In those tales, they use their power to punish evildoers, thus becoming symbols of righteousness. I thought that concept fit Batman perfectly.

JC: While this story was commissioned for a Western audience, it has now been released in Japan as well. How do you feel about possibly helping to shape the image of Batman in your own country?

YN: I assumed the story would be released in Japan, but came to the conclusion that the most important thing was how the story would be taken by American readers, who know the Batman well, so I focused on writing a story for an American audience. It's beyond my ability alone to awaken Japanese readers to the appeal of the Batman, but I'd be happy if this mini-series got at least some Japanese readers interested in American comics.

JC: Were there any artistic influences that inspired you in coming up with your own version of Batman?

YN: Oh, there are plenty! I used many references for drawing my panels, but when it came to the character, I did a lot of reading of Batman stories from both American and Japanese creators. I've read Batman stories done by Japanese creators such as Katsuhiro Otomo and Kia Asamiya and I returned over and over again to the short manga stories of Yuji Iwahara, which have an atmosphere that's close to American comics. I also love the art of Tetsuo Kamiyama. He's especially great at drawing silhouettes and human musculature. I learned a lot from poring over the most successful Batman comics from the U.S., especially from creators like Jim Lee, Frank Miller, Mike Mignola, etc. Specifically, their use of light and darkness and "stage direction" gave me some pretty clear ideas about the pace at which American readers read comics. But no matter what comics I looked at, all I thought about was how I could bring Batman to life and put my own spin on the character.

JC: What were the easiest and the most difficult things about writing this character?

YN: Once I actually started working on this, it didn't really prove to be any different than working on my previous series, and this was thanks to the gracious people at DC, who let me stick to my usual Japanese manga style and format as much as possible. I suppose the most difficult thing was being certain that each party understood the other side's intentions. Because my English is limited, everything I said or wrote always had to be translated, and since it wasn't direct communication, it made me overly insecure about whether everything I wanted to say was actually getting across.

In Japan, a story is usually serialized first in magazines, so an author gets a lot of feedback from readers while it's still in progress, which is used to make adjustments as needed. But I didn't have that in this case, so I was extremely nervous about whether what I was doing was "good" or not.

JC: Do you feel like there are more things you would like to do with this character?

YN: I'd like to think up some new characters to pit against Batman. While I'd also like to use pre-existing characters, it would be important for me to have the freedom to create within the framework of Batman's world. Also, I think it'd be fun to do an Elseworlds story about a Bat-man who fights the spread of evil in the Edo period of Japanese history.

JC: I have enjoyed the experience of working on this very unique project with you. Thank you very much.

YN: No, thank you! Even if just one person draws the manga, it goes through several hands before it reaches the readers. Only then, when it's read, does the manga begin to have life. I'm very happy that this series has gone on the market, that I've been able to hear the opinions of various readers and that I was given the opportunity to do this project.

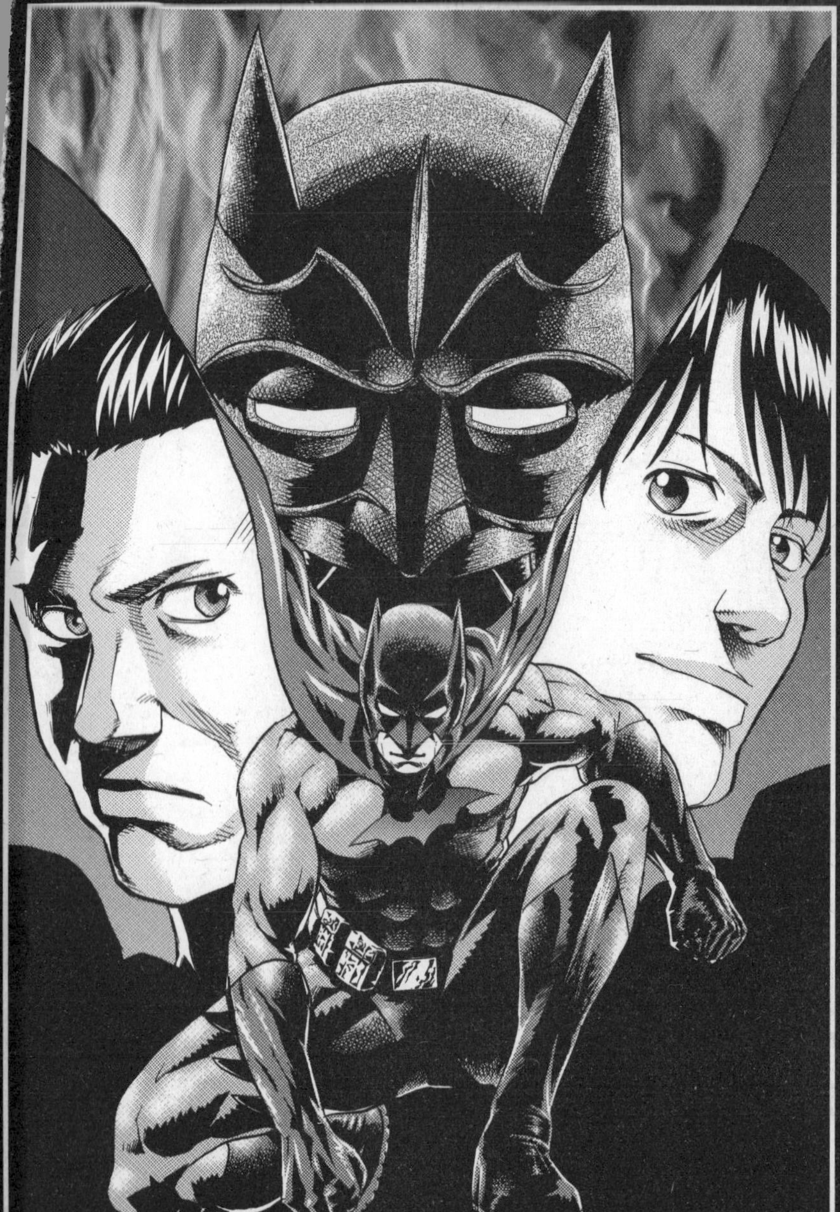

New illustration by Yoshinori Natsume,
specifically commissioned for this collection.